THE FIBERGLASS BOAT HANDBOOK

JACK WILEY

TAB
TAB BOOKS Inc.
Blue Ridge Summit, PA 17214

FIRST EDITION

FIRST PRINTING

Library of Congress Cataloging in Publication Data

Wiley, Jack.
The fiberglass boat handbook.

Includes index.
1. Fiberglass boats. I. Title.
VM321.W527 1987 623.8′207 86-30116
ISBN 0-8306-0499-5
ISBN 0-8306-0399-9 (pbk.)

Questions regarding the content of this book should be addressed to:

Reader Inquiry Branch
Editorial Department
TAB BOOKS Inc.
P.O. Box 40
Blue Ridge Summit, PA 17214

Cover photograph courtesy of Bertram Yacht, P.O. Box 520774, Biscayne Annex, Miami, FL 33152

Contents

Introduction

Fiberglass is a combination of glass fiber reinforcing material and plastic resin. It was first used for boatbuilding on an experimental basis in the 1940s. Since then it has gained acceptance and is chosen today over wood and other boatbuilding materials by pleasure boat manufacturers.

While there are certainly both advantages and disadvantages in using fiberglass, the advantages largely outweigh the disadvantages. Fiberglass does not suffer from dry rot or worms, a common problem with wood; from rust, a common problem with steel; or from electrolysis, common problems with both steel and aluminum boats. Fiberglass boats require relatively little maintenance, certainly less than required by other materials. They are, however, still far from maintenance-free.

This book is primarily about the fiberglass part of boats. Most so-called "fiberglass" boats use a variety of other materials in their construction, such as wood for bulkheads and trim, rigid foam for core and flotation purposes, metal for engines and fittings and fasteners, and fabrics for upholstery. While the whole boat will be treated to some degree, the focus will be on the fiberglass portion.

The vast popularity and acceptance of fiberglass boats have created a real need for a how-to handbook on the subject. There are three main aspects to this book. The first deals with understanding, selecting, purchasing, and owning fiberglass boats. The second part covers caring for, maintaining, equipping, altering, and repairing fiberglass boats. The third aspect is an introduction to finishing out bare hulls and fiberglass kit boats, which are available from a number of manufacturers, and one-off fiberglass boatbuilding methods.

Inflation has heavily hit the boating industry in recent years. The information presented in this book should enable you to get the most fiberglass boat for your money, one that is most closely matched with your needs and budget. While most boats are purchased with fun and enjoyment in mind, they can sometimes be considered a good investment. Many fiberglass boats have appreciated, sometimes greatly, in value over the years. After a number of years, some owners can even sell them for more than they originally paid. Whether or not this trend continues is a matter of speculation.

Once you own a fiberglass boat, you must properly care for it, maintain it, and keep it in a good state of repair. You might also want to improve it by adding extra equipment and making alterations. You have two basic choices: doing the work yourself or having the work done for you. You can also do some of the work yourself and hire out the rest. This book details how to do this work yourself, while at the same time pointing out what skills and equipment are required and what jobs are best left to professional workers.

Some people, though certainly not most, will want to build a fiberglass boat from scratch or finish out a bare fiberglass hull or fiberglass kit boat; these subjects are introduced to show what the possibilities are. For those who have the necessary skill and dedication, these build-it-yourself methods can result in the most boat for the least money. If you do not have this skill and dedication and blindly set out to build a large fiberglass yacht, the results can be disastrous.

Building from scratch is most difficult of all, because it requires extensive fiberglassing—that is, using a liquid resin, adding a catalyst or curing agent, combining this with glass fiber reinforcing material, and coming up with a hard fiberglass reinforced plastic material. This is known as *chemical* boatbuilding and differs considerably from making things out of wood, metal, and other existing materials.

Much easier, but still a large project, is to purchase a fiberglass hull and other moldings from a factory and then finish out the project yourself. While some fiberglassing is usually still required, this is minimal compared to building a fiberglass boat from scratch.

While much of the material in this book comes from my own experience with fiberglass boats and boats of other materials, many other people along the way shared their ideas and techniques with me. It is impossible to acknowledge all the help given for the compilation of this book. To the many people who freely shared their ideas, I would like to extend a sincere thanks.

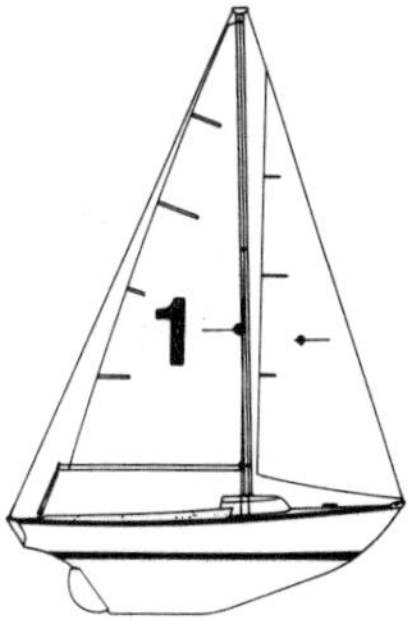

Overview

There is no well-documented history of the first fiberglass boats built. By 1938, glass fibers were being produced for insulation purposes, but a useable polyester resin did not appear until about 1946. Experimental work in plastic boat construction was carried out prior to this, however. A California company called Chemold is reported to have produced molded plastic boat hulls using osnaburg, a coarse, durable cotton, as a reinforcing material and combining this with an acetate resin to form a rigid plastic. The hulls were formed using male molds.

The Wizard Boat Company purchased the tooling from Chemold in about 1946 and soon after this began using polyester resin and glass fiber reinforcing materials to produce boat hulls. These were also formed over a male mold.

In 1947 the Glasspar Company started producing fiberglass boats. Other companies followed, and by 1950 there were a dozen or so companies producing fiberglass boats, some having switched from wood boat production.

In the years following World War II, the word "plastic" had negative connotations. This is probably why the term "fiberglass" came into use.

Most of the early fiberglass boats were small. As contact molding methods using polyester resin and glass fiber reinforcing material were developed and refined, however, larger boats were constructed. At least one 42-foot fiberglass hull had been constructed by 1950.

In a very short period of time, fiberglass made most traditional wood boatbuilding techniques obsolete. When the first fiberglass boats were produced, almost all small pleasure craft being manufactured were wood. Many traditional wood boatbuilders laughed at fiberglass boats, or perhaps that anyone would try such a stupid thing as "chemical boatbuilding." Even today there are those who say that wood is the only "real" boatbuilding material, and fiberglass boats are often referred to as "plastic bleach bottles."

Today, fiberglass has firmly established itself as the most popular material for building pleasure boats. Fiberglass has made quantity boat production possible and, because of this, has made boat ownership possible for millions of additional people. While no exact statistics are available, it is estimated that there are over five million fiberglass pleasure boats in the United States. And more fiberglass boats are being added to this figure as more are being produced than are being destroyed. Fiberglass boats generally have a long life expectancy. Some of the earliest fiberglass boats constructed are still around and in sound, useable condition.

Most present pleasure boat owners have fiberglass boats, and most people who will be buying boats in the near future will purchase fiberglass boats. Perhaps someday a material will be developed to replace fiberglass, but today, at least from a manufacturing point of view, fiberglass is the number one boatbuilding material.

FIBERGLASS

Fiberglass has several meanings. It was first applied to thin glass

Fig. 1-1. The Bayliner 2950 Encounter Sunbridge—a modern fiberglass powerboat. (Courtesy of Bayliner Marine Corporation)

filaments or fibers. It later also meant felt-like mat and woven reinforcing fabrics made from these fibers. It finally came to mean the plastic material that is a two-part structural unit consisting of glass fibers and a resin. In boat construction, polyester resin is normally used. In some cases, a more expensive epoxy resin is used.

For a time, *fiberglass reinforced plastic* (FRP) was used to refer to the cured two-part structural unit of glass fibers and resin. This was perhaps an attempt to prevent confusion. "Fiberglass" referred to the glass fibers. The "plastic" was the cured resin, which was "reinforced" by the glass fibers. This terminology did not catch hold outside the plastics industry in the United States, although it is commonly used in Great Britain today.

A boat that has a fiberglass hull is commonly referred to as a fiberglass boat, regardless of whether deck and cabin structures and other components are constructed of fiberglass or some other material. Most fiberglass boats use many other materials in their construction besides fiberglass. There are usually wood components and trim; metal fittings, rigging, engines, and other mechanical fittings; and a variety of plastics.

It is unclear when a boat becomes a fiberglass boat. Plywood boats that are covered with a sheath of fiberglass are not generally called fiberglass boats. These boats might be called "wood, covered with fiberglass" or "wood, sheathed with fiberglass" or even "wood and fiberglass." Only one side of the plywood is normally covered with fiberglass. But what happens when both sides are covered with fiberglass, and the fiberglass skins are made thicker? At some point this would become fiberglass sandwich core construction and, eventually, become a "fiberglass" boat.

Many early fiberglass boats were essentially wood boats with fiberglass hull shells. The cabin and deck structures were wood, and the hulls were reinforced with wood bulkheads, frames, stringers, and other members. The hull shell material alone was sufficient to justify calling the boat fiberglass.

I have seen a few boats that have been built in reverse: they had wood hulls, but the deck and cabin structures were fiberglass. I'm not certain what the reasons were for this type of construction. If anything were built of fiberglass, it would be the hull. In any case, these boats were referred to as "wood."

In summary, the term "fiberglass" is used to mean any or all of the following: glass fibers, reinforcing materials woven from or otherwise made up of glass fibers, and the material formed from glass fibers combined with polyester or epoxy (and perhaps other types) of resin. The term "fiberglass boat" means a boat that has at least a hull shell constructed of fiberglass.

An additional problem in terminology is encountered when polypropylene, acrylic, polyester, Kevlar, carbon fiber, and other nonfiberglass reinforcing materials are used instead of glass fiber reinforcing material. Is the resulting laminate still fiberglass? So far there doesn't seem to be a definite answer to this question. Most production fiberglass boat manufacturers make limited, if any, use of these reinforcing materials, perhaps because they are more expensive than glass fiber reinforcing materials, which is usually adequate for their purposes. Even in custom boats where nonfiberglass reinforcing material is used, this is often used along with glass fiber reinforcing materials. Perhaps a new name will evolve or that will be applied to laminates and boats laid up completely without glass fiber reinforcing materials.

FIBERGLASS VERSUS OTHER MATERIALS

Fiberglass materials and chemistry had developed to the point where practical applications to boat construction were possible by the end of World War II. Over the years the materials and chemistry, as well as methods and techniques for using them, have improved dramatically. Unless otherwise noted, modern materials, formulations, and methods of handling will be referred to.

Fiberglass was first used as a substitute for other materials. In the case of small boats, it was mainly a substitute for wood.

What was wrong with using wood? Wood has been a traditional material for building boats for centuries. Why would anyone want to change to another material?

It is difficult to find precise answers to these questions. Some people say that there are centuries of proof that wood is an unsuitable material for building boats. In the earliest recorded history, worms, dry rot, methods of fastening separate pieces of wood together to form a boat, and a variety of other problems plagued wood boats. To this day, these problems have not been completely solved. Even cold-molded wood construction, with or without epoxy saturation, has not completely solved these problems. Besides, this method should probably be considered a composite construction, sort of like using the wood to reinforce the epoxy.

Wood boat enthusiasts point out that there are hundreds of wood boats that were built before 1900 that are still afloat. On closer examination, however, it's found that some boats have been replanked, reframed, refastened, and re-about-everything-else over the years to the point where there is nothing really old left.

Those who argue against wood boats point out the large number of wood boats that decay or other otherwise beyond practical repair in a very few years. The wood boat enthusiasts say that wood boats covered with fiberglass dry-rot in a few years or less to the point where they are useless. Therefore fiberglass isn't any good. But it seems to me that the wood—which dry-rotted—was the problem, not the fiberglass.

There are other problems associated with using wood as a primary boatbuilding material. Good boatbuilding woods are scarce and expensive, and the situation is rapidly getting worse.

From a boat manufacturing point of view, wood boats have even less going for them. Wood boatbuilding methods, especially the traditional ones, are too labor intensive and require skilled labor. This makes them hard to mass-produce. Even with modern machinery and automation, production has never approached anything like an automobile assembly line.

The scarcity and resulting high cost of boatbuilding woods has been another factor. The use of less suitable, less expensive woods creates more problems than it solves.

Even with the present world oil prices (polyester resin is an oil product), it is much more expensive to manufacture a wood boat than a comparable fiberglass boat. And while the wood boat might seem to have more value to a wood boat enthusiast, the fiberglass boat is more suitable for the boating marketplace.

Wood boats seem to have a poor reputation. They require constant maintenance. They don't last. They have low resale value. These points can be debated, but there is some truth to them. Wood suffers dry rot and/or worm damage if not properly maintained. And "proper" maintenance can translate to "considerable" maintenance. Repairs are not only expensive, but require specific skills to do the work properly. As one person put it, "I wouldn't advise anyone who isn't an expert on wood boatbuilding to own a wood boat."

I have known several people intent on world cruising who settled on used wood sailboats. They all thought they were saving money. Even though all these boats were surveyed and given clean bills of health, they all turned out to have "a little" dry rot. As this wood was replaced, more and more dry rot was found. Boat surveyors don't give guarantees. To date, none of these people has set off on the long dreamed about world cruising. Two of these owners have the boats up for sale, but they are having a difficult time finding any buyers. It seems that old wood boats are much easier to buy than to sell. I'm sure that there are many people who purchase wood boats who have better success, I just don't happen to know any.

There are those who claim that, compared to fiberglass, wood is natural, warm, friendly, and nice to work with. The remarkable success of a recent magazine on wood boatbuilding shows the considerable interest in wood boats. But perhaps this interest is as much in building and working on them as in using the boats. For these people, wood boats make sense. For the vast majority of people in the United States, however, fiberglass boats are probably more suitable, considering everything.

Steel, aluminum, and ferrocement as boatbuilding materials all have advocates. Each of these materials has advantages and disadvantages as compared to each other and wood and fiberglass. Other than aluminum for small lightweight boats, these materials can't match fiberglass. Steel is becoming more popular for offshore cruising sailboats. Rust and electrolysis can be considerable problems, but with proper precautions and maintenance, these factors can be kept under control. Steel makes a strong boat. Aluminum is popular for one-off racing sailboats. It produces a boat that is light in weight, yet adequate in strength. The main disadvantage is the high cost, approximately three times that of fiberglass when a suitable grade of aluminum is used. Ferrocement has been used mainly for "home-built" boats. While a few ferrocement boats have been produced, this has not caught on. Ferrocement boats have a poor reputation, perhaps because of the many monstrosities turned out—many only partially completed—by backyard builders. This could explain why manufacturers have never shown much interest in building ferrocement boats.

At least for the manufacturer, fiberglass is by far the most accepted primary boatbuilding material. From its beginning as a substitute for wood in boatbuilding, it has come into its own. Fiberglass proved to be such a good substitute that wood was relegated more and more to minor roles. First it was fiberglass hulls finished out mainly with wood, including deck and cabin structures, interiors, and reinforcing members. Next a layer or two of fiberglass reinforcing material was added over the wood on the cabin and deck structures. This usually stopped the leaking problems, but speeded up the formation of dry rot in the wood below.

The next logical step was to make the deck and cabin structure entirely out of fiberglass. The wood was relegated to a core

Fig. 1-2. The Bayliner 68—a high-performance fiberglass motor yacht. (Courtesy of Bayliner Marine Corporation)

or reinforcing material and thick fiberglass was laminated on one or both sides so that the fiberglass itself would provide considerable structural strength.

This trend has continued over the years with wood gradually eliminated from most interiors until it is now used mostly for trim and core purposes. Many recent manufactured fiberglass boats have even eliminated most of the trim wood, using metal and/or plastic materials instead. On one fiberglass boat that I owned, I spent more time maintaining the teak rub rail, the only wood on the exterior of the boat, than I did on the entire rest of the boat with the exception of the engine.

LIFE EXPECTANCY OF FIBERGLASS

Fiberglass boats generally last a long time. Most fiberglass boats built thus far are still functioning. Those that aren't were probably damaged as opposed to worn out.

The long life expectancy of fiberglass boats can be an advantage or disadvantage, depending on your point of view. For the boat owner, it is an advantage. For boat manufacturers, it is a problem. Fiberglass boat owners don't buy a new boat because the old one wears out, but rather because they want a larger boat or perhaps different type of boat. This has created a huge market for used fiberglass boats. A typical production fiberglass boat might have a number of owners during its lifetime.

Without planned obsolescence, fiberglass boat manufacturers keep adding to the number of already existing fiberglass boats. Selling the boats requires increasing the number of boat owners.

In the case of trailerable boats, the number could increase substantially without much problem. For boats kept in the water at docks and marinas, however, space is limited. The construction and development of new dockage space has not kept up with the demand. In some areas, such as Long Beach, California, the waiting list for getting a boat slip is over 10 years. Even the dramatic increase in the cost of renting slips has done little to decrease the demand for them.

It is often difficult to sell nontrailerable boats unless a boat slip can be guaranteed. Unavailability of slips can hurt boat sales, especially those of new boats.

Fiberglass boat manufacturers have not been able to do much about this other than to support the development of new harbors, marinas, and dry storage areas. The fiberglass boat manufacturers who have tried planned obsolescence by making boats that don't last have put themselves out of business by earning bad reputations, even lawsuits, because of the failures of their boats.

Manufacturers who have tried the "new model" concept, similar to that used in the automobile industry, have generally not been very successful. Unlike automobile owners, few fiberglass boat buyers fall for this scheme.

What is the life expectancy of a fiberglass boat? When fiberglass boats were first manufactured, a figure of about 10 years was often given. It was said that at that point the resin would become brittle. Ten years later, when many of the first fiberglass boats were still around and judged to be in sound condition, the 10-year estimate was changed to 20 years. Then when there were a number of 20-year-old boats still in sound condition, the figure was changed to 30 or even 50 years or more or less indefinitely, assuming proper care and maintenance and barring accidents.

Inflation has hit the fiberglass boating industry to an even greater extent than most everything else. The prices of new fiberglass boats are at a record high, which in turn has driven up the prices of used fiberglass boats. As a buyer, then, you can expect to pay a high price for either a new or used fiberglass boat. If the present trend continues, however, the boat will probably increase in value over the years and, if sold, bring in a higher price than was originally paid for it. Because of the large investment involved, anyone contemplating buying a fiberglass boat, or anyone who already owns one, should know as much about fiberglass and fiberglass boats as possible.

FIBERGLASS AS A BOATBUILDING MATERIAL

As a boatbuilding material, fiberglass has both advantages and disadvantages.

Advantages

Fiberglass is inert to most common chemicals, including most fuels and common pollutants, and it does not rot or corrode. Fiberglass holds up well under the severe environmental conditions that most boats are used in. Fiberglass is not susceptible to electrolysis, an important advantage for boats used in salt water. These factors are extremely important, as a person who has owned wood, steel, and fiberglass boats could tell you.

When properly designed and fabricated, fiberglass laminates

Fig. 1-3. The Cape Dory 25 is a modern four-berth fiberglass sailboat. (Courtesy of Cape Dory Yachts)

are strong and lightweight. They have approximately twice the structural strength of wood or steel of the same weight.

Fiberglass can be molded to most any desired shape in one piece that is seamless and essentially leakproof. For reasons that are detailed in later chapters, most fiberglass boats consist of more than one separate molding. There is one molding for the hull, another for the deck and cabin structure, and so on. The hull molding itself is one piece. The fact that fiberglass can be molded into complex shapes allows fiberglass boat designs that are difficult to achieve in wood or metal construction.

By using color-pigmented resin gel coats, colors can be molded in as part of the fiberglass laminate, making painting unnecessary. When properly applied, resin gel coatings provide protective and long-lasting color surfaces.

When properly fabricated, fiberglass laminates are very durable. They will last many years with no significant degradation in laminate properties. Some of the first fiberglass hulls constructed are still in sound condition and might have many more years of useful life. Fiberglass hasn't been around long enough for us to know what the limits are.

Laying up fiberglass laminates is essentially "chemical" construction. This allows making maximum use of the materials (resin and glass fiber reinforcing) needed to make fiberglass. For example, laminate thicknesses can vary in the same molding. The laminate can be thick in areas where strength and stiffness are needed, and thinner and lighter in weight in areas where less strength and stiffness are required. And most of the resin and glass fiber reinforcing material ends up as part of the moldings. Compare this with wood construction where there are usually many scrap pieces that end up as firewood rather than part of the boat. Similar problems exist when using other preformed materials.

Fiberglass laminates, when damaged, are fairly easy to repair. Even major damage can usually be repaired without much difficulty, to the point where it is as strong as or even stronger than it was originally. Methods and techniques for repairing fiberglass boats are detailed in Chapter 12.

The fiberglass part of fiberglass boats requires little maintenance compared to similar wood boats and boats made from most other materials. Fiberglass does require some maintenance, however, if it is to be kept in top condition. I consider the ease of maintaining a fiberglass boat to be one of the most important advantages.

Disadvantages

Fiberglass laminates lack stiffness. They have less stiffness than steel and even aluminum. This means that most fiberglass boat moldings require adding stiffening members. The moldings could be made thicker to the point where they have adequate stiffness, but this would be too expensive and add too much weight for most boatbuilding applications.

As compared to steel, fiberglass has low fatigue and buckling strengths. This can cause problems in areas where stress concentrations are located.

Fiberglass is vulnerable to fire unless special, more expensive, fire-retardant resins are used. It's the resin and not the glass fibers that burn. A laminate constructed using regular resin will support combustion about the same as plywood.

The low abrasion resistance of fiberglass is a disadvantage, or at least a problem. Rub rails made of wood or other materials and other protective devices are used to protect vulnerable areas of fiberglass on boats.

Fiberglass construction is expensive, generally more than wood or steel on a per-pound basis. Fiberglass has other advantages, however, that make it economical for boat construction.

Construction of the cavity or female molds used by most fiberglass boat manufacturers is expensive. This cost can be reduced by using the same mold to make a large number of moldings. It is not unusual for several hundred or more fiberglass boat hulls to be laid up in the same mold.

There are a number of "one-off" fiberglass boat construction methods that do not require expensive female or cavity molds. These methods are more suitable for custom construction where only one or very few boats of the same design will be constructed or for backyard boatbuilding. One-off fiberglass boatbuilding methods are detailed in Chapter 14.

INTRODUCTION TO FIBERGLASSING

Even if you do not intend to do any actual fiberglassing, it's important to have at least a basic understanding of how the process works. This discussion will be limited to polyester resin, which is used for most fiberglass lay-up work in production fiberglass boat manufacturing.

There are two liquid ingredients: *polyester resin*, which is formulated by the manufacturer with the necessary accelerator already mixed in; and *catalyst*, which is methyl-ethyl-ketone (MEK) peroxide.

Only a small amount of catalyst is added to the resin to start the cure at room temperature. The exact amount to be added depends on the amount of resin used, the working or room temperature, and the desired curing time. For example, 2 percent by volume of catalyst would give about 15 minutes working time before the resin started to gel or harden. If the working temperature is higher, less catalyst is required to give the same working time; if the working temperature is lower, more catalyst is required to give the same working time. At the same working temperature, more catalyst will give less working time; less catalyst will give more working time.

Once the catalyst is added, the resin will cure or harden even if the mixture is sealed in a container. You must be ready to use the resin before you add the catalyst.

There are several types of glass fiber reinforcing materials used in fiberglass boat laminates. The most important are mat (a felt-like arrangement), cloth, and woven roving. These materials are detailed in Chapter 4.

In the example here, mat is used. The other reinforcing materials are used in a similar manner.

The catalyzed polyester resin is applied to the mat. This can be done by brush or other means. The mat used must be specially treated, usually by chroming, for use with the resin. The mat is thoroughly saturated with resin. This must be done within the working time, before the resin starts to gel or set up. Once the resin starts to gel, it should no longer be used.

The amount of resin used to saturate the mat must be carefully controlled. Too little resin gives a resin-starved laminate; too much resin gives a resin-rich mixture. A mat laminate is generally about 65 to 75 percent resin by weight and 25 to 35 percent glass fiber mat by weight. Other reinforcing materials, such as fiberglass cloth and woven roving, use different ratios of glass to resin.

After the resin is applied to the mat and smoothed out, the laminate is allowed to harden or cure. This usually happens soon after the resin starts to gel. Then additional layers of mat or other fiberglass reinforcing materials can be laminated to this first layer in a similar manner.

This is basically how fiberglass laminates are laid up in a mold. This form of chemical construction might seem strange if you've never seen it before and are used to working with wood and other preformed materials. Liquids and highly flexible glass fiber reinforcing material form a solid reinforced plastic.

Why not use resin alone without the glass fiber reinforcing material? When this is done, you still get a hard plastic material, but it is very brittle. This would never do for boat hull material.

Glass fibers without the resin are strong in tension, but there is nothing to hold them in position. When the resin is combined with the glass fibers, however, it forms a two-part structural unit that has a high strength-to-weight ratio.

SELECTING A FIBERGLASS BOAT

This book will give you the information necessary to select a fiberglass boat. Before purchasing a boat, you must first decide what type and size of boat is right for you. This might be a rowing boat, a powerboat, a houseboat, a sailboat, or some combination. It might be an open boat, a partially decked boat, or a cabin boat. You must make a realistic appraisal of your requirements, while taking your boating budget into consideration.

Next, you must know something about fiberglass boat design. For any given type and size of boat, a variety of designs are available. Which one is best for you? It's also important to understand

Fig. 1-4. The Hunter 37—a modern fiberglass sailboat. (Courtesy of Hunter Marine)

how designing boats for fiberglass construction differs from designing boats for construction in other materials.

This leads to the construction of manufactured fiberglass boats. There are two major aspects: molding the fiberglass components and the assembly of these and other components into completed boats. An understanding of how fiberglass boats are manufactured can be very helpful for selecting one. All fiberglass boats are not constructed equally.

The purpose of a boat survey is to evaluate the existing condition of new and used fiberglass boats. While most boat buyers hire a professional boat surveyor before finally purchasing a boat, learning the basic techniques and procedures in this book may help you weed out unsatisfactory boats. Even for fiberglass boat experts, hiring a professional boat surveyor may well be worth the price of a "second opinion."

An important advantage of doing your own preliminary surveying is that you can also consider the design and original construction, things that professional surveyors are reluctant to do. They do not like to say whether a certain design or make of boat is good or bad.

There are a number of steps in selecting a fiberglass boat. You must first find boats for sale, then you must evaluate them and determine how much they are worth. Warranties, guarantees, resale value, and sea trials are other considerations. You might buy new or used or from a private party, boat dealer, or boat broker.

Extremely important and often overlooked in the excitement of boat buying are the costs and responsibilities of boat ownership. You must consider not only the purchase price of the boat, but also interest on financing, taxes, registration, insurance, a place to keep the boat, and the costs of maintenance and operation. In short, you must make a realistic estimate of what the total cost of boat ownership will be. There are also certain legal matters and responsibilities to consider.

Most new fiberglass boats are sold as basic boats. To this is added optional extras. Some "basic" boats are so basic they will not function without some of the optional extras. In some cases sails and/or engines are considered to be optional extras. Most boats are shipped by manufacturers to dealers in partially completed form; that is, rigging and setup still needs to be done, masts stepped, and optional extras added. These jobs are called *commissioning* and are done for an extra charge. Some boat buyers save money by doing their own commissioning. Even when used boats are purchased, most owners want to add or change equipment, fittings, and accessories. These jobs are detailed in Chapter 8.

Because fiberglass boats usually represent a large investment, proper care and preventative maintenance are extremely important. This includes cleaning and waxing as well as a variety of other jobs. Most fiberglass boats require antifouling bottom painting about once a year, depending on how and where the boat is used.

DO YOUR OWN FIBERGLASSING

Many people want to make changes in their fiberglass boats. A number of projects for improving interiors and exteriors to make them more suitable to specific needs are detailed in Chapter 11.

While fiberglass is tough and durable, it can be damaged. Minor and even major repairs are within the scope of many do-it-yourselfers, once the basic skills and techniques of fiberglassing are mastered, as detailed in this book. It's often the unfamiliar chemical aspect of fiberglassing that causes people to shy away from doing this work themselves. This is quite different than, say, taking a piece of wood and cutting and shaping it. Once you learn how, however, fiberglassing can be quite predictable.

Many people are reluctant to work with fiberglass because of health and aesthetics. The fiberglassing chemicals are sticky and messy. The reinforcing material can make your skin itch. Sanding causes dust, which can also make your skin itch and is dangerous to breathe. With protective clothing and equipment and proper handling of chemicals and materials, however, it's possible to avoid these problems. Once the basic techniques and safety procedures are learned, fiberglassing can be enjoyable, challenging, and creative.

Here are some reasons why people do fiberglassing work themselves:

- To save money. Fiberglassing boat alterations and repairs can be expensive. When you do your own work, you save money by providing your own labor and by purchasing materials and supplies at the lowest possible prices from discount supply firms.
- To get the work done the way you want it. It is very hard to get quality fiberglassing work done. And if the job is a small one, it's often difficult to find anyone who will bother with it. There are no real standards or qualifications for becoming a "professional" fiberglasser, so it's often difficult to know in advance what type of job will be done on your boat. By doing the work yourself, you

have the opportunity to do it the way you want it done, assuming that you have the necessary skills. You have an important advantage over the professional. You can take enough time to do the job right.

■ For the challenge and satisfaction of doing it yourself. Many people get satisfaction from doing fiberglassing work themselves. They like the challenge of doing a job that requires skill. I know of a number of people who enjoy working on their boats more than they enjoy using them.

FINISHING OUT FIBERGLASS HULLS

For the person who has the necessary talent and dedication, this is an excellent way to get the most boat for the least money. The basic idea is to purchase a bare fiberglass hull from a manufacturer (a number of firms offer these; see Appendix) and then to finish this out yourself. You can use materials that you supply yourself or components and materials supplied by the manufacturer (or some combination of these).

In most cases, even when you start with a fiberglass hull and all the other molded fiberglass components, there's still considerable work to do. For the right person, this can present a challenge. The savings over a comparable factory-finished boat can be considerable. This method of boatbuilding is detailed in Chapter 13.

FIBERGLASS BOATBUILDING FROM SCRATCH

Even more difficult is to build a fiberglass boat from scratch using one of the methods shown in Chapter 14. These one-off fiberglass boat construction methods take considerable skill and dedication if a successful boat is to result. This is an area where I have seen many failures and a few successes. I only recommend fiberglass boatbuilding from scratch to those who have had considerable fiberglassing experience and have a good idea of what they are getting themselves into. Even a person who can easily finish out a bare fiberglass hull might fail here. Most people will at least want to start with professionally drawn plans.

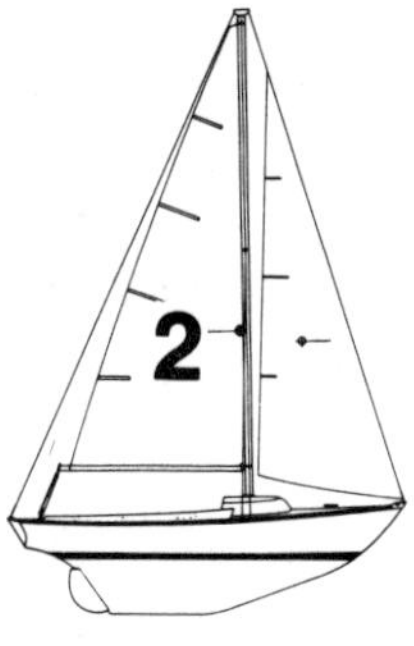

The Right Boat for You

Most all types and sizes of pleasure boats are available in fiberglass. One way to classify boats is by the means of propulsion—oars or paddles, engines, and sails. But even here there are problems because boats can be propelled by more than one means.

This chapter considers three general types of boats: (1) small open boats for rowing and/or outboard power, (2) powerboats, and (3) sailboats. Boats that can go in more than one category, such as motorsailers, will be arbitrarily placed.

SMALL OPEN BOATS

Small open boats include dinghies, canoes, kayaks, and other boats that can be rowed or powered by a small outboard motor. As fiberglass boats go, these boats are all at the low end of the price scale. Boats such as special purpose rowing shells might also fit into this category, but they will not be covered here.

Dinghies

Fiberglass dinghies are available in a variety of shapes and sizes. Some rowing dinghies can be rigged for sailing; others are rowing or sailing dinghies; still others are primarily sailing dinghies. My concern here is with rowing dinghies, regardless of their sailing capabilities, and dinghies that can be powered by small outboards. These boats are sometimes called *tenders*. They are carried on deck or towed by larger boats and used for getting to and from shore when at anchor. They can also be fun boats.

Fiberglass, like wood, is suitable for making boats of any size. Manufactured dinghies are available in lengths of 6 feet or less. Fiberglass allows strong and lightweight construction of these. Materials such as steel and ferrocement are too heavy for making a boat this small.

Dinghies are available in pointed bow and pram designs. Designs and hull shapes vary widely, as do seating arrangements, flotation compartments, location and mounting of oar sockets, and reinforcements of transoms for small outboard motors. For a given size dinghy, weights can also vary.

Dinghies are designed for various purposes. Those to be used for tenders should have protective rails and some type of skids on the bottoms for abrasion protection. There's even a fiberglass dinghy that dismantles into forward and aft sections and stows on boat decks in half the normal space.

Care must be taken in selecting dinghies because there are many poorly designed and/or constructed ones on the market. It's also important not to confuse fiberglass dinghies with those constructed from other plastics. Those of fiberglass are superior in most ways, but also more expensive and perhaps heavier. It has been my experience that most dinghies constructed from other plastics won't hold up under normal use. Many of them are little more than toys.

A fiberglass dinghy should have added flotation material for buoyancy. Then, if it fills with water or capsizes, it will not sink.

Most dinghies are designed for a certain maximum horsepower outboard. Do not try to go beyond what is recommended.

Make certain the dinghy has the capacity to carry intended loads (passengers and whatever else). Also, if you intend to row the dinghy, try the dinghy out. Rowing performance between various designs of dinghies can vary widely, especially in windy conditions where poorly designed dinghies tend to scoot sideways.

Canoes and Kayaks

Both canoes and kayaks are available in various designs and sizes constructed of fiberglass. Canoes are also available in aluminum construction, which might be more suitable for some uses than those made of fiberglass. Both canoes and kayaks come in plastics other than fiberglass. Sailing rigs and outboard motor attachments are available for canoes.

Other Small Open Boats

A number of other boats designed for rowing are also available in fiberglass. These usually take small outboard engines for power. This class of boats is sometimes called *fishing* and *car-top* boats. It is difficult to draw the line between this type of boat and a runabout or powerboat. For purposes here, I'll draw the line at the point where the boat no longer has oar sockets set up for rowing.

Boats in this group have displacement hulls with flat, round, or V-bottom hulls. Designs, sizes, and performance characteristics vary widely. They are suitable for recreational use, rowing for exercise, utility, and fishing.

Fiberglass is ideally suited for this type of boat, but aluminum is a strong competitor. The same size aluminum boat can be lighter in weight and often sells at a lower price. If the boats are to be used in salt water, the advantages would switch to the fiberglass. While there are aluminum alloys suitable for use on salt water boats, they require an expensive grade of aluminum that isn't normally used on small open boats.

Some of these fiberglass boats are light enough to be carried on car and camper top racks. Others are too heavy for this and are more suitable for boat trailers.

The boats are rated for maximum load capacities and maximum outboard horsepower. They have positive flotation by means of compartments filled with flotation foam material.

These fiberglass boats are sometimes molded by pressure molding techniques rather than by contact molding, the common manufacturing technique for larger boats. Pressure molding, unlike contact molding, results in molded surfaces on both sides of the laminate. This means that the boat will have a finished appearance not only on the outside of the hull but also inside.

The seats in these fiberglass boats might be molded fiberglass (often with buoyancy compartments underneath), wood, or other material. They can also have rub rails made of wood, metal, vinyl, or some combination of these.

POWERBOATS

A variety of open and partially decked boats with outboard, inboard/outboard (I/O), and inboard power are available in fiberglass. In this category are runabouts and speedboats. The next main category is power cruisers. They can also be powered by outboard, inboard/outboard, and inboard engines. The third main category is houseboats, which are similar to power cruisers but usually have larger cabins or "houses" and less boating ability.

Before examining each of these categories more closely, powerboat hull types and characteristics will be discussed.

Hull Types and Characteristics

Powerboat hulls can be displacement, semidisplacement, or planing.

Displacement Hulls. A displacement hull is the oldest hull form. Through the full range of speeds that the boat operates at, the weight of the water displaced by the boat is equal to the weight of the boat. This type of hull is easily driven through the water at moderate or even low power. They usually have round bottoms (Fig. 2-1), which can give a comfortable ride even in rough weather conditions. The tendency to pound is less than with flatter bottom shapes, although the round bottom forms do tend to roll under certain conditions. The tendency to roll depends on a number of factors, such as beam, height of cabins and placement of weight above waterline, and draft.

Displacement hulls have a definite limit to the speed at which they can be operated. The limit depends on the waterline length and is called *hull speed*. This will be discussed more fully in Chapter 3. For now note that additional horsepower will not drive the boat significantly beyond hull speed and that this would be a wasteful and inefficient use of the power.

Some displacement hulls have aft bottom sections that are flat-

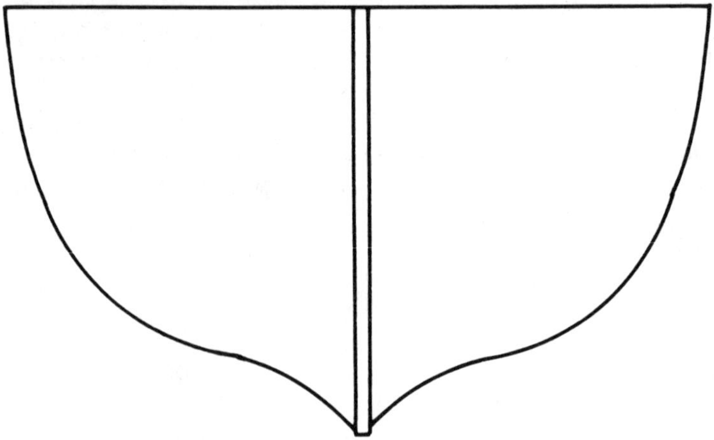

Fig. 2-1. Round bottom displacement hull.

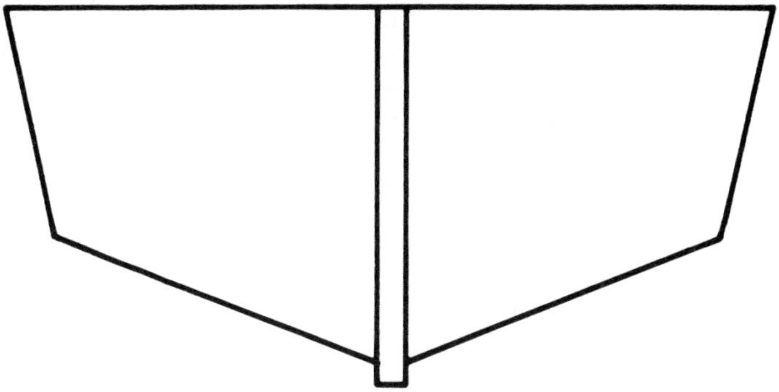

Fig. 2-2. V-bottom hull.

tened. This reduces the rolling tendency and provides more cockpit room.

The compound curves used in the bottoms of most displacement hulls lend themselves well to molded fiberglass construction.

Semidisplacement Hulls. A semidisplacement hull works as a displacement hull at slower speeds and as a planing hull at higher speeds. These hulls have a semi-V hull form with a pronounced V-shape at the bow and a flatter V-shape at the stern.

Planing Hulls. Planing hulls are shaped so that the boats will plane by lifting as they gain speed. This can be achieved by several different hull shapes. One popular shape is the V-bottom (Fig. 2-2). These have a hard chine that extends the full length of the hull. This hull form is popular on runabouts and express cruisers.

Deep V-shaped hulls are another popular planing type. These are used on high-speed boats, especially those used on rough waters. The deep V-shaped hulls have a fairly deep V shape at the transom. It takes considerable horsepower to drive these hulls. The main advantage is that there is less pounding than with a regular V-bottom, which allows higher cruising speeds to be maintained in rough water. Because this type of hull form has a steep angle of deadrise, it sacrifices interior space for accommodations.

Other planing hull forms include the cathedral (Fig. 2-3) and tunnel (Fig. 2-4) forms, as well as variations of these. Because fiberglass can be molded, these complex shapes are possible.

Open and Partially Decked Boats

Open and partially decked boats usually have regular V-bottoms or cathedral hull shapes or some variation of these. They are popular

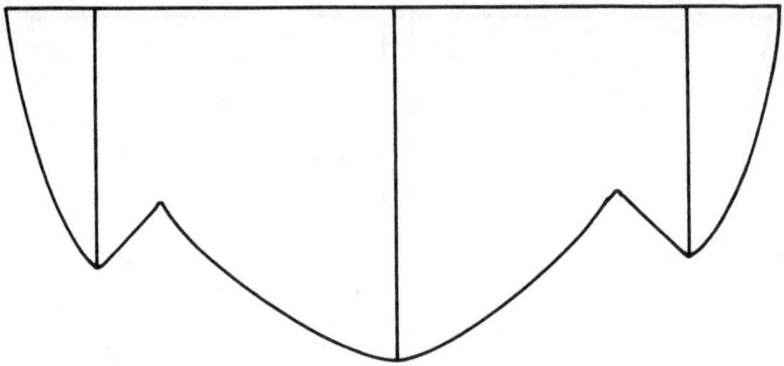

Fig. 2-3. Cathedral hull.

for recreational use, fishing, and waterskiing. These boats are often partially decked with a windshield. Seating arrangements vary.

The boats are powered by outboards or inboard/outboards, also called *stern drives* (Fig. 2-5). A number of years ago, dual outboards were frequently used; but outboards have improved greatly since then, and these days a single outboard engine is common. Outboards are now available with 150 horsepower or more, which makes the dual engine arrangement unnecessary.

A single inboard/outboard is often used instead of an outboard. These have the power and efficiency of an inboard with direct thrust steering like an outboard. The outdrives can be tilted up.

Straight inboards, with shaft and propeller extending from stuffing box through the bottom of the hull, were popular on early speedboats. These often used converted automobile engines. The main disadvantage of this arrangement is that a separate rudder is used

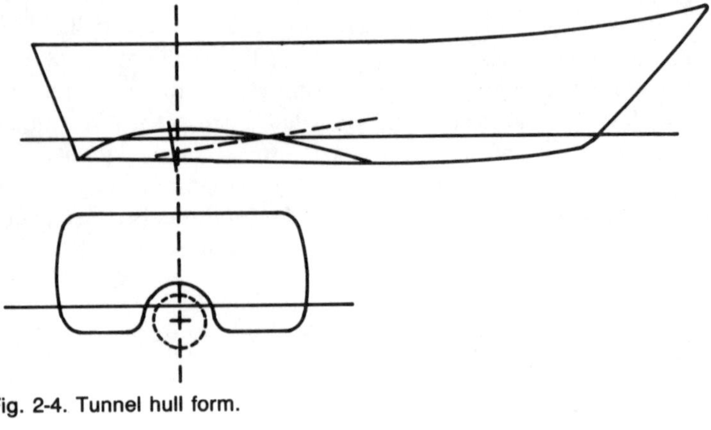

Fig. 2-4. Tunnel hull form.

Fig. 2-5. This Bayliner 2350 Cobra has a racy profile. (Courtesy of Bayliner Marine Corporation)

for steering. This gives much less control than steering by prop thrust. The separate rudder, however, can be steered to a certain extent when the engine quits—if the boat is moving. Straight inboards seem to have all but lost out to outboards and inboard/outboards as far as present-day manufactured fiberglass boats of this type are concerned.

Power Cruisers

Power cruisers have cabins and interior accommodations, and they are usually larger than runabouts (Fig. 2-6). Power is supplied by

Fig. 2-6. Bayliner Saratoga Sunbridge powerboat features a raised helm station and self-bailing cockpit. (Courtesy of Bayliner Marine Corporation)

single or twin outboards, inboard/outboards, and straight inboards. While runabouts and speedboats generally have gasoline engines, diesel inboard/outboards and straight inboards are an option for power cruisers, especially those with displacement hulls.

Power cruisers have round displacement hulls, semidisplacement modified V hulls, regular V hulls, or deep V hulls (Fig. 2-7). Some smaller power cruisers have cathedral hulls. The choice depends on where and how the boat is used.

Power cruisers have various locations for steering stations. Sometimes it's in the forward area of the cockpit or inside the cabin or deckhouse. Some have dual steering stations with one set at a *flying bridge*—a raised platform located above the cabin that gives unobstructed vision for navigation and steering.

Cabin cruisers range in size from 16 or 17 feet to 50 feet or more in length. Accommodations and comfort varies widely and can include sleeping, eating, lounging, and toilet arrangements. Some also have showers, heating systems, and other conveniences.

A 16- or 17-foot power cruiser would typically have limited cabin space, perhaps only room for two V-berths and a toilet. In some cases, a small galley and locker area can also be fitted in.

In larger boats, more elaborate accommodation plans are possible. Longer boats have wider beams and greater headroom, although not much more headroom than 6 1/2 feet. Any more would result in a higher cabin structure that would increase wind resistance and add weight at the top, which is undesirable.

Fig. 2-7. Bayliner 3270 Explorer is a long-range, semidisplacement cruiser with dual steering stations. (Courtesy of Bayliner Marine Corporation)

So that TAB BOOKS Inc. can better fill your reading needs . . .

please take a moment to complete and return this card. We appreciate your comments and suggestions.

1. I am interested in books on the following subjects:

- ☐ automotive
- ☐ aviation
- ☐ business
- ☐ computer, hobby
- ☐ computer, professional
- ☐ electronics, hobby
- ☐ electronics, professional
- ☐ finance
- ☐ how to, do-it-yourself
- ☐ engineering (specify): ____________
- ☐ other (specify) ____________
- ☐ other (specify) ____________

2. I own/use a computer:

- ☐ IBM ____________
- ☐ Apple ____________
- ☐ Commodore ____________
- ☐ Macintosh ____________
- ☐ ATARI ____________
- ☐ AMIGA ____________
- ☐ Other (specify) ____________

3. This card came from TAB book (specify title and/or number):

____

4. I purchase books:

- ☐ from general bookstores
- ☐ from technical bookstores
- ☐ from college bookstores
- ☐ through the mail
- ☐ by telephone
- ☐ by electronic mail
- ☐ other (specify) ____________

Comments ____________

____

____

Name ____________

Company ____________

Address ____________

City ____________

State ____________ Zip ____________

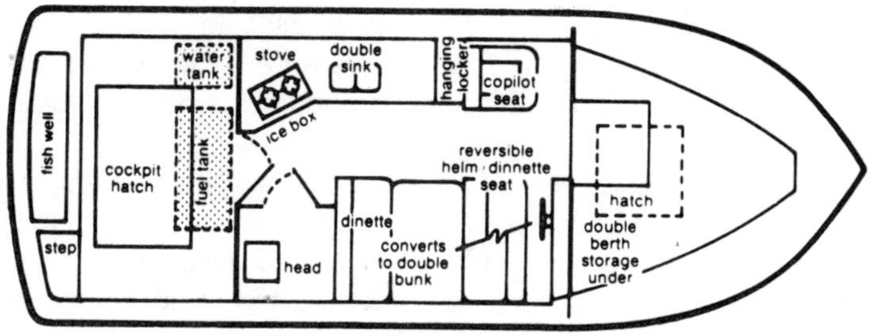

Fig. 2-8. The accommodation plan for the Bayliner 2550 Saratoga Command Bridge cruiser has a 24′9″ centerline length. (Courtesy of Bayliner Marine Corporation)

The accommodations must be designed to fit into the shape of the boat, which is the reason for V-berths. Figure 2-8 shows the accommodation plan for a power cruiser with a 24-foot, 9-inch centerline length. It has a double berth forward, a dinette that converts to a double berth aft, a galley, and a head or toilet compartment. Lockers are located under berths and seating. The galley has a counter with a small sink, storage areas, and a small icebox located under the sink counter. The toilet room is a separate compartment.

Similar accommodations can sometimes be fitted into even smaller power cruisers, provided that the cabin is kept large by having a small cockpit area. Berths have minimum practical sizes, however, as do galley areas, dinettes, toilet compartments, and other areas, so there are limits. To use limited space to best advantage, many areas serve multiple purposes. Dinettes lower to form berths, seats pull out to form wider berths, and so on (Fig. 2-9).

A typical 28-to-30-foot power cruiser might have a similar cabin arrangement, but with more space devoted to each area. For example, the toilet compartment might also have room for a shower. The dinette could seat more people and offer more comfort.

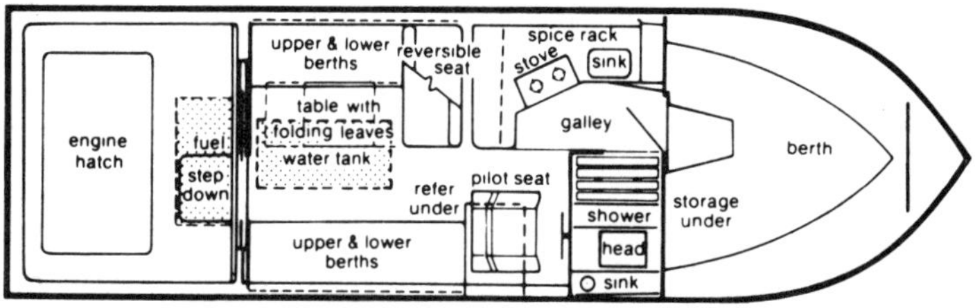

Fig. 2-9. Deck plan for 27-foot Bayliner 2750 Victoria Command Bridge powerboat. (Courtesy of Bayliner Marine Corporation)

Dinette area soles or floors are often raised above the level of the main cabin floor or sole. This allows wider seats in hulls that flare outward and also gives better seating positions for looking out windows.

As the boats get even larger, increased accommodations are possible. Sleeping quarters can be in separated compartments. Raised deck cabins can have inside steering stations that take part of the space as well as room for lounging, sleeping, and dining. Galleys are sometimes located in this area as well.

Power cruisers from about 35 or 40 feet in length frequently have an owner's stateroom. These can be small and simple or larger and more elaborate, perhaps with a double berth with access on three sides.

Sleeping Accommodations. Stock manufactured boats have various numbers and arrangements of berths. These boats are usually advertised as sleeping so many people aboard in the berths, which can be singles or doubles. It often is not practical, however, to sleep this many people, at least not for long periods of time.

If space permits, sleeping quarters should be separated from the main lounging and dining areas. On smaller boats, this usually isn't practical. Converting tables to form berths might look okay on accommodation drawings but often isn't convenient in practice, though it's probably better than not having a berth at all.

Some fiberglass boat manufacturers try to fit as many berths as possible into a certain size boat. A more important consideration for the boat buyer, however, is how comfortable the berths are. They must be long enough, wide enough, and have thick enough cushions to give good sleeping comfort—unless you want to get rid of unwanted guests.

To learn about various arrangements, study accommodation plans found in magazines and advertising materials provided by manufacturers. Berths are usually marked "berth." Until you have considerable experience comparing the actual boats with the accommodation plans, it might be difficult to visualize what they look like. I suggest that when you look at boats in a dealer's showroom and at boat shows, compare the accommodation drawings with the actual boats.

Eating Areas. The dining area consists of a table and seating. The seating should be comfortable, and the table at a convenient height and stable.

The dining area should be conveniently located in relation to the galley, if possible on the same level without intervening steps. Also if possible, the dining area should have a good view for looking out the windows. In smaller boats, dining areas often double as lounging areas.

Galley Areas. Galley areas vary from simple to quite elaborate. This in part depends on the size of the boat and the amount of space that can be devoted to the galley. A basic galley consists of a counter, a small sink, a one- or two-burner cooking stove, storage compartments, a small icebox. Larger boats have larger galley areas—larger sinks, cooking stoves with four or more burners and ovens, and refrigerators and/or iceboxes.

Adequate storage space should be provided. Drawers should have notch locks so that they have to be lifted before they can be opened. For boats to be used in rough waters, sea rails around the galley counters will keep things from sliding off. There should also be adequate space and arrangement for garbage disposal.

Lounging Areas. Most pleasure boats are used for fun and relaxation. Comfortable lounging areas are important. If possible, provide comfortable lounge-type seating—in addition to the seats for the dining table—that are well padded with slanted backs.

Toilet and Bath Facilities. Toilets should be of adequate size so that doors can be easily closed and still leave space to move around. If possible, there should be enough space for changing clothes. This might not be possible on smaller powerboats, but on larger boats it often is. Compromises must be made, of course. In a given space, something larger means something else smaller. Legal types of toilets include those with holding tanks for shore pumpout and approved treatment systems for discharge overboard.

Many larger power cruisers have showers. The least desirable arrangement is the type that sprays water throughout the toilet compartment getting the toilet, vanity counter, and practically everything else wet. This makes a shower possible in boats that do not have enough space for a separate shower stall, which is perhaps better than no shower at all. A separate shower stall with a plastic spray curtain or a door is a more satisfactory arrangement.

Some power cruisers have bathtubs or combination showers and/or bathtubs. These are found only on larger size boats, however.

Inside Steering Stations. Power cruisers sometimes have inside steering stations, especially larger ones, that take up part of the interior space. This should provide good visibility, a comfortable seat, and convenient operation of controls.

Navigation and Communication Areas. Navigation and

communication areas are often arranged as part of the steering stations on smaller boats, but larger boats might have separate areas devoted to these functions. A typical navigation and communication setup would include a navigation table, chart storage area, book rack, depth sounder, radio, and so on. Navigation centers on stock fiberglass boats are frequently inadequate, but these can often be improved by making alterations.

Cockpits. Cockpits vary in design and size. Some are self-bailing so that any water will drain off; others aren't. Some cockpits are deep; others are at deck level.

Many smaller powerboats have the steering station in the forward area of the cockpit. There is a windshield on the aft section of the cabin top. This might be fitted with a folding canvas top or even a fixed top made out of fiberglass or other materials. The top usually extends back over only part of the cockpit area, but in some cases it extends all the way to the stern, or there is a top extension that can be added. The sides of the forward area of the cockpit can be protected by a window, which might or might not open, or side curtains that snap in place. In some cases, canvas attachments are used to make the cockpit area into an enclosed room.

Cockpit soles or floors should have a nonskid surface. If they are of molded fiberglass, the nonskid surface is sometimes molded in.

Flying Bridges. Some power cruisers have flying bridges (Fig. 2-10). These include an alternate steering and control setup. Flying bridges provide unobstructed vision and are popular on boats used for fishing. They often have windshields forward and can be fitted with canvas or even fixed tops. Safety rails are important both for the ladder and along open sides of the flying bridge.

Engine Access and Engine Rooms. Powerboats with inboard/outboard or straight inboard engines should have easy access to engines for maintenance and repair. Larger boats often have engine rooms, sometimes with standing headroom.

The exact arrangement depends in part on the boat size and design. Even in similar boats there can be considerable differences in ease of engine access. This also applies to control cables and other mechanical equipment.

Hatches, Doors, Windows, and Ports. These vary greatly in type, size, and design. They should be neat in appearance, while still being functional. Outside hatches, doors, windows, and ports should not allow water to get below. Opening windows

Fig. 2-10. This 38-foot Bertram Convertible powerboat has a flying bridge. (Courtesy of Bertram Yacht)

and ports can be a special problem. They often leak even when closed.

Good, bad, and indifferent designs will be found on stock manufactured fiberglass power cruisers. Try to make comparison between similar boats by different manufacturers.

Houseboats

Houseboats are similar to power cruisers, but often with larger and boxier shaped cabins. This can result in a loss in boating performance.

Houseboats are designed and constructed for use in protected waters, although some recent designs are similar to power cruisers and have greater seaworthiness. Early houseboats typically had flat bottoms or pontoon hulls. These have largely been replaced by molded fiberglass hulls with contour designs similar to those typically found on power cruisers. This has improved performance, but has also increased the draft somewhat.

Modern houseboats have wider beams than power cruisers of the same length. The cabins are typically rectangular shapes, which give maximum interior space.

Power can be by outboard, inboard/outboard, or straight inboard engine. These are usually gasoline powered, but some inboard/outboard and straight inboard engines are diesel.

Modern houseboats are available with displacement or planing hulls. Most use some form of V or cathedral hull. While a few pontoon types still come in fiberglass, they seem to be losing popularity.

Primary steering stations are usually forward inside the cabin. Some designs also feature flying bridges with a second set of controls. In the California Delta area, these are popular because they allow seeing over the levees. The farms on the other side are usually below water level.

Manufactured fiberglass houseboats range in size from 20 feet or less to lengths up to 60 feet and more. Many have outside patio areas both fore and aft. The cabin tops or roofs often serve as sun decks.

Sleeping Accommodations. Stock manufactured fiberglass houseboats have various sleeping arrangements, though it might not be practical to sleep the maximum number aboard. Some houseboats have hide-a-beds. Space often permits standard size single, double, and even queen- and king-size beds with standard box springs and mattresses.

In larger houseboats, sleeping quarters or bedrooms are often separate rooms from the main lounging and dining areas. On smaller boats, this isn't practical. In this case, dining tables lower to form berths, and sofas and lounging areas often double as berths. The important considerations should be privacy and comfort, not how many berths can be squeezed in. Berths should be large enough with mattresses that give good sleeping comfort.

Eating Areas. Houseboats usually have built-in dining areas, but free-standing tables and chairs are sometimes used. These can be a problem or even dangerous in rough water conditions, however, unless they are clamped or firmly mounted in place.

Dining area should be near the galley and, if possible, on the same level without intervening steps. The dining area should be arranged for a good view. The large windows found on most houseboats are ideal for this purpose.

In smaller houseboats, dining areas often double as lounging and sleeping areas.

Galley Areas. Galley areas vary from small and simple to large and elaborate. A basic galley area in a small houseboat might consist of a counter, a small sink, a two-burner countertop cooking stove, storage compartments, and a small icebox. Medium and larger size houseboats often allow galley areas similar to kitchens found in small efficiency apartments. They can include large sinks, cooking stoves with full-size ovens, full-size refrigerators, and other conveniences, including storage cabinets, drawers, and compartments.

Lounging Areas. Houseboats are designed for fun and relaxation. Comfortable lounging areas are an important part of this. On larger houseboats, lounge-type seating is possible in addition to the seating used for the dining areas. Standard house-type sofas are often used on larger houseboats, often with hide-a-beds.

Toilet and Bath Facilities. While small houseboats might only have room for a small toilet compartment, larger ones have true bathrooms, more like those found in trailerhomes than those aboard typical boats. Legal toilets include those with holding tanks for shore pumpout and approved treatment systems for overboard discharge. Vanity counters with sinks, showers, and even bathtubs are found on many houseboats.

Inside Steering Stations. Most houseboats have inside steering stations located at the forward section of the cabin or "house." They should provide good visibility, convenient operation of steering and other controls, and comfortable seating.

Houseboats seldom have separate navigation and communication areas. Instead, these are usually fitted in as part of the steering stations. Because houseboats are mostly used on protected inland waterways, navigation is fairly simple.

Flying Bridges. Some houseboats have flying bridges, with alternate steering and controls. Flying bridges provide unobstructed vision. They give a choice of inside or outside boat operation. Some flying bridges are equipped with windshields at the forward section. Canvas tops are frequently used. These can attach to the windshield or be the bimini type. Safety rails should be provided for ladders to flying bridges and along any open sides of the flying bridges.

Cockpits and Patio Decks. Cockpit areas are often considered to be patio decks on houseboats. Many houseboats have open deck areas both forward and aft, often with joining walkways along both sides of the cabin or house. In some cases, there are roof extensions from the cabin out over all or part of the patio areas.

The patio floors should have a nonskid surface. If they are of molded fiberglass, the nonskid surface can be molded in. The patio areas and joining walkways should have protective rails for safety of crew and passengers.

Engine Access and Engine Rooms. Houseboats with inboard/outboard or straight inboard power often have engine access hatches on the aft cockpit or patio floors. How to get to the engine varies greatly on manufactured fiberglass boats, however. Some have little more than crawl space around the engine or engines; others have true engine rooms.

Hatches, Doors, Windows, and Ports. These vary greatly in type, size, and design. Because houseboats are designed and constructed for use in protected waterways, they usually have more and larger windows than typical power cruisers, even picture windows.

Hatches, doors, windows, and ports should be designed and constructed so that water does not get inside the cabin or house. Opening windows can be a special problem, because they can allow water in even when closed. Early model houseboats often used trailer house windows. Modern ones have designs and arrangements made especially for houseboats.

Seaworthiness. There is a tremendous range in seaworthiness in the design and construction of manufactured fiberglass houseboats. While barge structures with houses on them have all but disappeared from the fiberglass manufacturing scene, there are still some models available that have very little seaworthiness. These are often intended more as floating houses than boats.

The trend, however, is to increase seaworthiness and performance. In some cases, it is very difficult to draw a line between a houseboat and a power cruiser.

SAILBOATS

A wide range of sailboats are available in fiberglass. These have various shapes, sizes, rigs, and so on.

Masts and Sails

One way to start sorting out the types of sailboats is to begin with the rigs. Most manufactured fiberglass sailboats have sloop rigs with a single mast positioned about a third of the way between the bow and stern. *Marconi* or *jib-headed* sails are generally used. These are triangular-shaped sails. Figure 2-11 shows a typical sloop rig with marconi sails.

Marconi sails have all but replaced *gaff* sails, which have four sides instead of three. Gaff sails had some good features. The mast

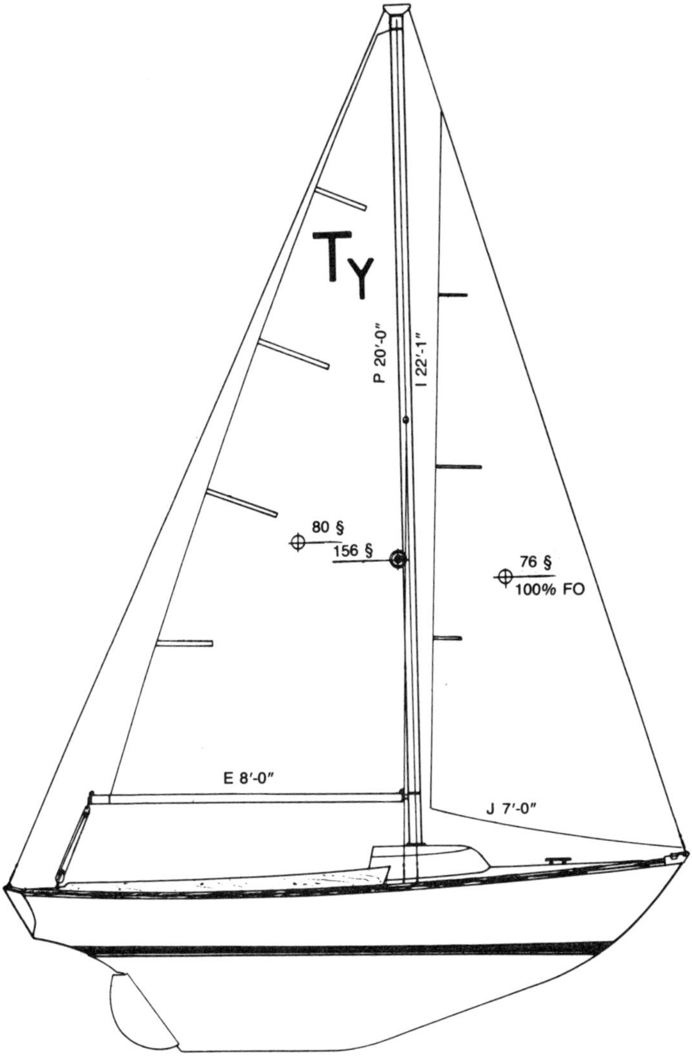

Fig. 2-11. A sloop rig with marconi sails. (Courtesy of Cape Dory Yachts)

could be shorter than for marconi sails. Gaff sails worked well on all points except sailing close to the wind. But they had some disadvantages, too, which offset the advantages and allowed marconi sails to take over. Perhaps the most important factor was that marconi sails give much better performance close to the wind. Another disadvantage of the gaff was that it needed a gaff spar, which was usually heavy, made it difficult to hoist the sail, and could be dangerous.

Another four-sided sail is the *lug* sail. Variations of this are used on a few offshore fiberglass sailboats. These have an unstayed mast and full-length battens. These boats are designed and constructed especially for offshore passage making. The sails can be handled and reefed from the cockpit. Because the lug sail is used on such a small percentage of manufactured fiberglass boats, it will not be considered further here.

Other types of sails include *lateen* and *sprite*. These are sometimes used on dinghies and other small sailboats.

The most common rig, the *sloop*, has already been mentioned. This is a split-rig. Two sails are ordinarily carried, a jib forward and a mainsail aft the mast.

A variation of the sloop that is gaining popularity is the *cutter* rig (Fig. 2-12). This also has a single mast, but it is further aft than on a sloop. Also, the cutter is usually designed to carry two sails, a jib and a staysail, forward of the mast.

A very simple rig found on some manufactured fiberglass boats is the *cat* rig. This has the mast positioned near the bow and uses a single sail with a boom similar to the mainsail on a sloop or cutter. With this rig, there is only one sail to worry about. While the cat rig is most common on small sailboats, manufactured fiberglass boats 30 feet in length and over are available with this rig.

Another rig used on some small boats is the *sliding gunter* rig. Like the cat rig, this setup uses only one sail.

There are also rigs that use two masts. The most common of these are the *ketch* (Fig. 2-13), *yawl*, and *schooner*. On ketches and yawls, the forward mast is the tallest. On the ketch, the aft mast is usually taller than that of a yawl. On the ketch, the aft mast is located forward of the rudder; on the yawl it is after the rudder. In each case, the aft mast is called the *mizzenmast* and the aft sail is the *mizzen*.

The schooner has the mainmast aft, which carries the mainsail. The forward mast, called the *foremast*, carries two foresails

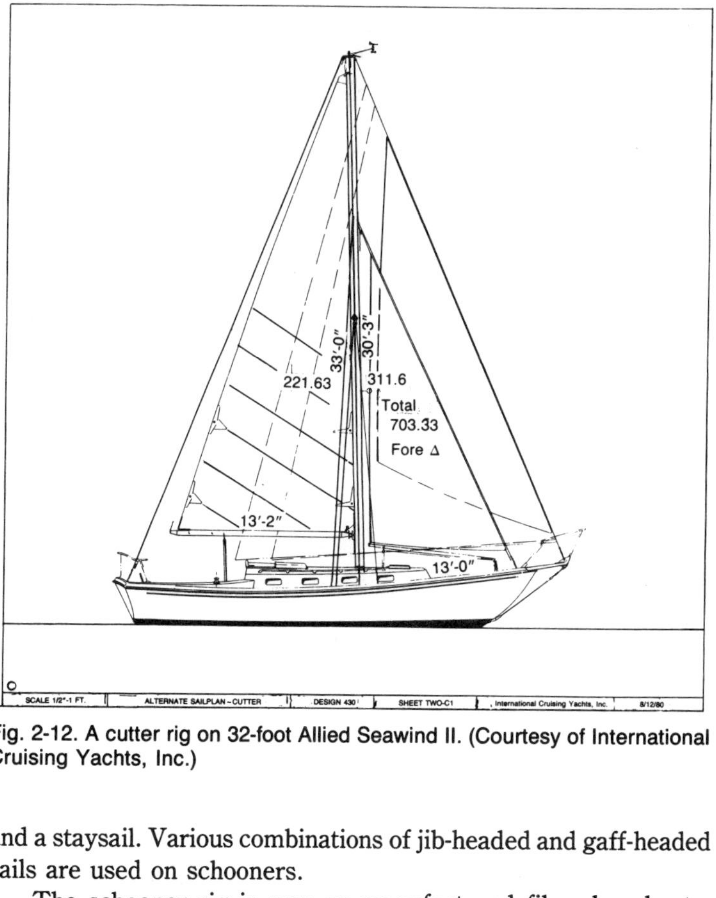

Fig. 2-12. A cutter rig on 32-foot Allied Seawind II. (Courtesy of International Cruising Yachts, Inc.)

and a staysail. Various combinations of jib-headed and gaff-headed sails are used on schooners.

The schooner rig is rare on manufactured fiberglass boats. Ketch and yawl rigs are options on some boats that come standard with sloop or cutter rigs. These rigs are seldom found on boats under 25 feet in length. On larger boats, they reduce the size of any single sail as compared to a sloop or cutter, and they give many more options for sail combinations. Because they require two masts, additional rigging, and more sails, they add considerably to the cost of the boat.

Sailboat Hulls

There are two main types of hulls: displacement and planing.

Displacement Hulls. Most manufactured fiberglass sailboats have displacement hulls. The weight of a displacement boat mov-

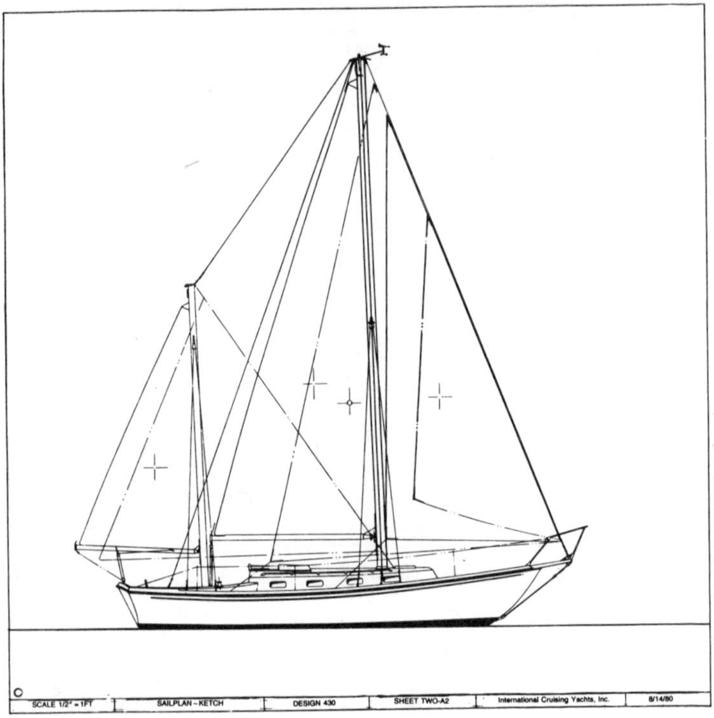

Fig. 2-13. A ketch rig on 32-foot Allied Seawind II. (Courtesy of International Cruising Yachts, Inc.)

ing through the water is equal to the weight of the water displaced. The maximum speed is usually limited by the length of the boat at the waterline. To determine this speed, multiply the square root of the waterline length by 1.34. More details on this are included in Chapter 3.

Planing Hulls. At slow speeds, planing hulls perform as displacement boats. As speed increases, however, a point is reached where the hull raises higher in the water and planes on the surface. Some planing hull sailboats can reach speeds over four times as high as displacement sailboats of the same size.

Planing hulls are specially designed with a minimum wetted surface and nearly flat bottoms on the after section, usually from before midship to the stern.

Planing hulls can lack stability, which makes for tricky sailing. Speed is the main asset.

Full Keel. Full-keel sailboats have long keels with attached rudders, as shown in Fig. 2-14. These keels almost always are ballasted. The ballast is placed at the bottom of the keel. This hull shape is very traditional for heavy-displacement sailing boats.

Full-keel sailboats of heavy and moderate displacement are popular for ocean cruising. The long keel provides outstanding

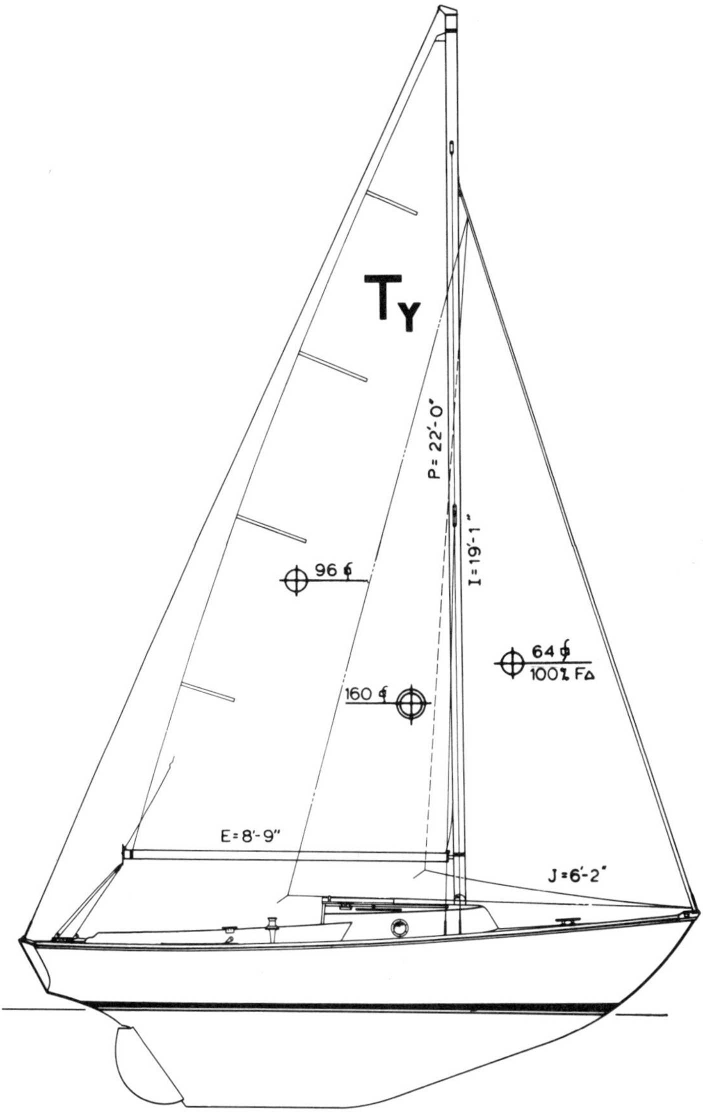

Fig. 2-14. The Cape Dory Typhoon has a full keel with attached rudder. (Courtesy of Cape Dory Yachts)

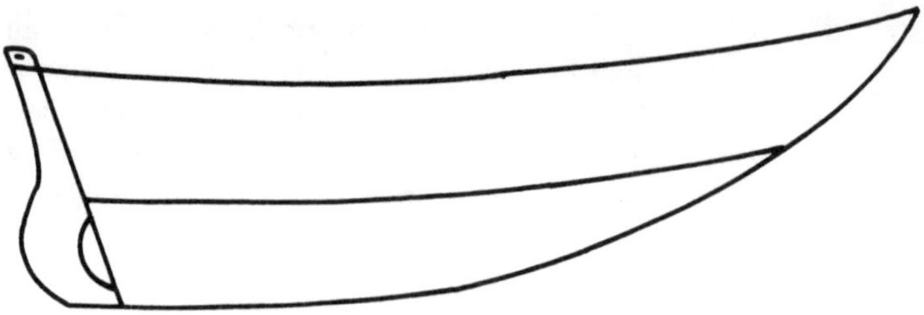

Fig. 2-15. Full keel with full forward section.

tracking or ability to hold a course. They have a smooth motion in rough water and are very seaworthy.

There are actually many possible designs for full keels. Wineglass configurations are typical. The forward edge can be full (Fig. 2-15) or cutaway (Fig. 2-16). The rudder can be after the transom, or more forward with the rudder tube passing through a port to the cockpit. In either case, the rudder is hinged to the aft section of the keel.

Full-keel boats tend to be slow in comparison to those with fin keels (described later in this chapter). Full-keel boats have a proven record for long-distance cruising, however.

Anyone considering world cruising in a small sailboat should realize, however, that some argue that full-keel boats are too slow for long-distance cruising. These people argue in favor of fin keel, spade rudder boats, or even trimarans.

For years I have heard these arguments. I have cruised in both fin keel and full-keel boats. I have seen the condition that people have arrived in from long ocean passages in the two types of boats. In my opinion, from practically every point of view except perhaps for speed, the full-keel boats win out. I've also noticed that while many sailors make one or even two long passages in fin keel boats,

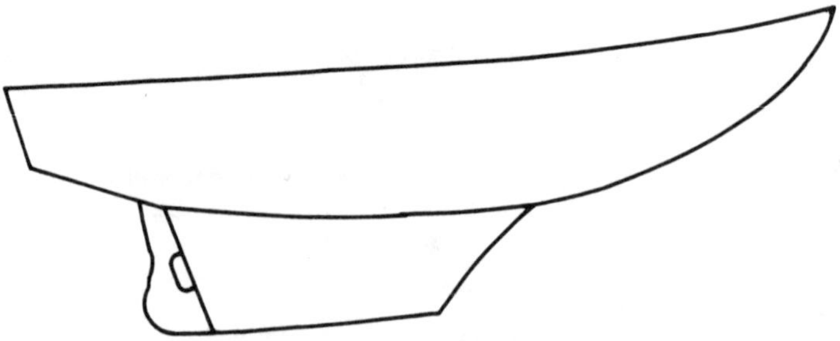

Fig. 2-16. Full keel with cutaway forward section.

those who have made ocean cruising a way of life for periods of years usually do so with full-keel boats.

The fact that the rudder on the full-keel boat is hinged to the aft section of the keel is an important advantage. This type of rudder mounting is much stronger than a spade rudder. Using a skeg with the rudder on a fin keel boat, however, can partially offset this difference.

Some full-keel boats have partial cutouts, such as shown in Fig. 2-17. This can give greater speed while still retaining most of the advantages of the full keel. While this design and variations seemed popular a few years back, the present trend seems to be back to the full keel again for cruising boats.

In recent years, many new designs of full-keel fiberglass boats have come on the market. There is now a wide choice available in practically all sizes. These boats are often advertised as "full-keel" or "full-keel cruising" sailboats.

Some boats with long full keels also have centerboards. With the centerboard up, these boats have shallower draft. This arrangement is not common in manufactured fiberglass boats.

Fin Keel. Fin keel boats can give a lively performance. A fin keel boat with a spade rudder is shown in Fig. 2-18. The rudder shaft usually passes through the hull to the cockpit sole or aft deck by means of a rudder port. This type of rudder is quite vulnerable and subject to damage.

A fin keel with a transom-hinged rudder is shown in Fig. 2-19. The rudders can also have skegs. Fin keel sailboats generally have less wetted surface than full-keel designs.

Centerboards. Some day sailers, small racing sailboats, and trailerable sailboats (Fig. 2-19) have centerboards instead of fixed keels. The centerboard might or might not have added weight. In some cases it is just a metal plate or a smooth piece of wood.

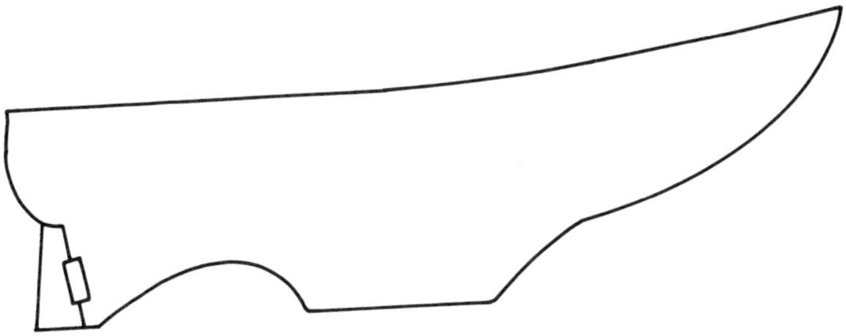

Fig. 2-17. Full keel with partial cutout.

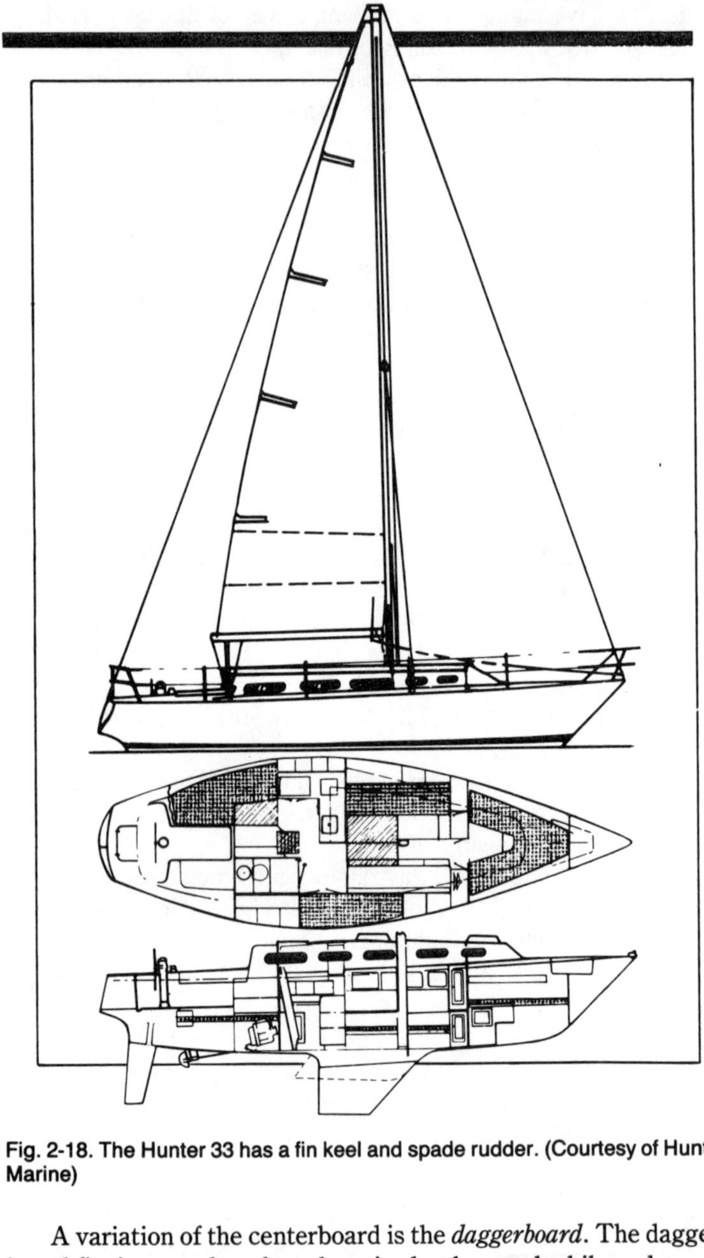

Fig. 2-18. The Hunter 33 has a fin keel and spade rudder. (Courtesy of Hunter Marine)

A variation of the centerboard is the *daggerboard*. The daggerboard fits in a trunk and can be raised or lowered while underway.

Still another arrangement is the *leeboard*, which is mounted on the side of the boat. This is generally not as efficient as a centerboard or daggerboard. It does have the advantage of not requiring a trunk in the center of the boat.

Both displacement and planing hulls are available with centerboards.

Twin and Bilge Keels. Twin and bilge keels have never been very popular in the United States. A number of them are manufactured in fiberglass in England, however. They usually have shallow draft and will stand upright if the tide goes out. I once owned and cruised extensively in one of these boats and found the twin keel arrangement highly satisfactory.

Multihulls. Some catamaran designs are available in fiberglass. There are a number of racing classes of these. Most are small catamarans with fabric trampolines between the two hulls and frames joining the hulls. These boats can be fast and lively.

Large cruising catamarans with cabins are also available in fiberglass. While catamarans have made ocean passages, they are not self-righting, a disadvantage should they capsize. Even small racing catamarans are difficult to right when they capsize.

Trimarans become popular boats for home construction in the 1960s. While trimarans are no longer very popular, some manufactured fiberglass versions are available. Trimarans are extremely fast on some points of sailing. They have made many ocean passages, but they also have the disadvantage of not being self-righting should they capsize.

Interior Accommodations

Many larger fiberglass sailboats have cabins with interior accom-

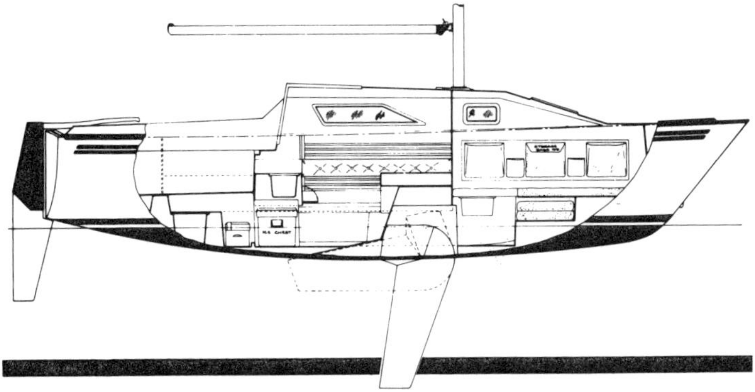

Fig. 2-19. The Hunter 22 has a transom-hinged rudder and a retractable centerboard for easy trailering. (Courtesy of Hunter Marine)

modations (Fig. 2-20). A minimum overnighter might have two V-berths, a portable toilet, and little more. From here, the interior accommodations become more elaborate. Larger boats have more space. Longer boats have wider beams. Some small cabin sailboats have less than standing headroom. Sailboats from about 25 feet in length may have standing headroom, although this depends on the particular design. One popular cruising 20-foot sailboat has 6 feet, 2 inches of headroom; some 25-foot or larger boats have considerably less. Because high cabins reduce performance, the cabins are kept as low as possible. Very large sailboats typically do not exceed 6 1/2 feet of headroom.

The accommodations must be designed to fit into the shape of the boat. This is why V-berths are forward near the bow. Dinettes and galleys are further aft in the main cabin in the widest part of the boat. Quarter berths often extend aft under cockpit seats. Figures 2-21 and 2-22 show accommodation plans for various size sailboats.

Sleeping Accommodations. Manufactured boats are often advertised as sleeping so many people. For example, a 30-foot sailboat might have berths for six people (two V-berths forward, a dinette that converts to a double berth in the main cabin, and two quarter berths further aft. This boat would be advertised as sleeping six. It would not be practical, however, to have this many people sleeping aboard a 30-foot boat, at least not regularly.

When selecting a boat, it is important to examine the quality of the berths in addition to the number of them. The berths should

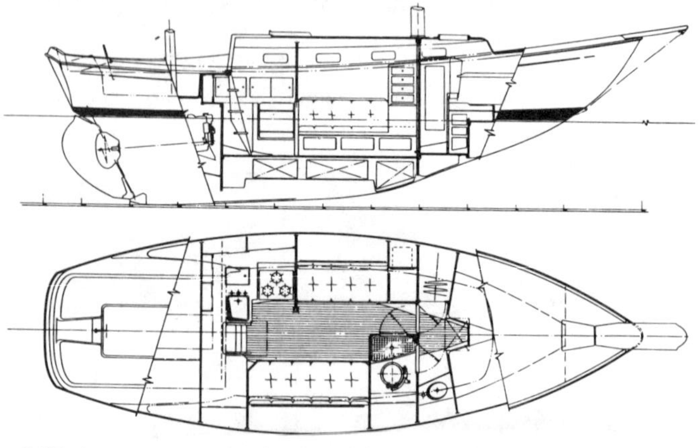

Fig. 2-20. Arrangement plan for the 32-foot Allied Seawind II. (Courtesy of International Cruising Yachts, Inc.)

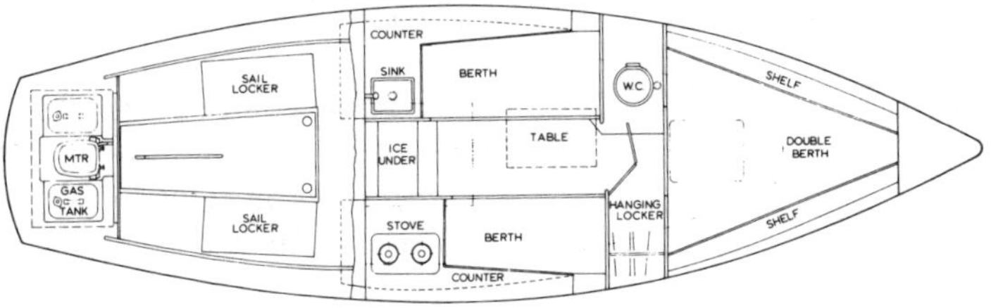

Fig. 2-21. Accommodation plan for the Cape Dory 5. (Courtesy of Cape Dory Yachts)

be long enough and wide enough for the people who will be sleeping in them. They should also have thick, comfortable mattresses. When possible, some of the berths should be separate from lounging and dining areas. Converting tables to berths can be inconvenient.

Eating Areas. The dining area consists of a table and seating. The seating should be comfortable and at the right height for looking out the windows or ports. The table should be stable, at a convenient height, and firmly held in position. In smaller sailboats, the dining areas often double as lounging areas.

Galley Areas. Galley areas vary depending on the size of the boat, design, intended use, and other factors. Most have a counter, sink, storage areas, a cooking stove, and an icebox. The area can range from simple to quite complex. One boat might have a two-burner cooking stove, another a four-burner stove with an oven. Some boats have small refrigerators and/or iceboxes.

Ample storage space is important. Drawers should be self-locking and must be lifted up before they can be opened. Sea rails around the galley counter will keep things from sliding off.

Galleys can be located near the companionways or further forward and to one side of the boat. Some galley areas are L- and U-shaped.

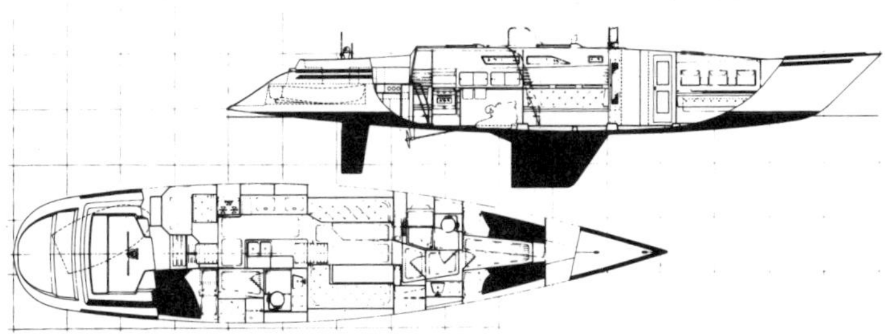

Fig. 2-22. Accommodation plan for the Hunter 54. (Courtesy of Hunter Marine)

Lounging Areas. Comfortable lounging areas are important. On smaller boats, the lounging area is often also used for sleeping and dining. On larger sailboats, this can be a separate area.

Toilet Compartments. Small sailboats might have a toilet located forward between V-berths. Larger boats often have enclosed toilet compartments. If possible, there should be enough space for changing clothes. Toilet compartments often also have small vanity counters and sinks, some even have showers. Legal types of toilets include those with approved treatment systems for discharge overboard and those with holding tanks for shoreside pumping out.

Cockpits. Most manufactured fiberglass sailboats with cabins have cockpits that are self-bailing. The cockpits vary greatly in size. While most have rectangular-shaped wells, some have other shapes. The cockpit seating should be comfortable.

For use on protected waters, the cockpits can be quite large. Cruising sailboats designed for offshore work have comparatively small cockpits. If the cockpit fills with water, there will be less weight, and the smaller volume of water will drain out faster.

Most sailboats have aft cockpits. These often have storage areas under the cockpit seats and sometimes in a compartment at the aft end of the cockpit. These should have lids with gaskets to keep water from getting inside the storage areas.

Some sailboats have center cockpits. This allows an aft cabin. In some cases, there are walkways below between the cabins. This arrangement can greatly increase the interior space. Cockpit soles should have nonskid surfaces.

Some sailboats have tiller steering. Others have wheel steering. There are advantages and disadvantages for each method. The tiller is simple. Wheel steering is more complicated, but many sailors prefer the wheel arrangement. Some tiller steering can be converted to wheel steering by using manufactured components. In others, custom components must be fabricated.

Engines. Many sailboats, especially larger ones, have auxiliary engines. The simplest and most common power for small sailboats is the outboard, which may be mounted in a transom cutout, on a bracket, or in a specially designed well. Steering with the engine is possible in some cases. This greatly increases maneuverability, especially for docking. In other cases, the outboard remains in a fixed position while the steering is done with the rudder.

To keep the prop from coming out of the water when the boat pitches, long shaft outboards are frequently used. To give the necessary power for larger sailboats, special power props are often used.

Larger sailboats usually have inboard power. Both gasoline and diesel engines are used. Gasoline engines cost less, but they have a higher fuel consumption. Diesel engines are more expensive, but they have lower fuel consumption and use diesel fuel. Diesel engines are also safer. Because of the explosion hazard that gasoline presents, many cruising sailboat owners opt for the diesel.

In most cases, the prop shaft passes through the boat hull by means of a stuffing box designed to keep water from leaking in around the shaft. A recent trend is to use special inboard/outdrive units that are designed for sailboats. These are suitable for fin keel boats where there is a reasonably flat area forward of the rudder on the hull bottom. In each case, the engines have gear boxes or other arrangements for providing forward, neutral, and reverse. The steering is done with the boat's rudder.

"Pure" sailboats don't have any auxiliary engine. Boats of this type have made voyages around the world. A recent trend is to use oar power. This seems to be practical for sailboats up to about 25 feet in length.

At the other extreme is the *motorsailer*. Motorsailers usually have good capabilities under engine power alone and some capabilities with sail alone. These can be operated with both engine and sail power at the same time. There are many variations, especially in sailing capabilities. Motorsailers usually have inside steering stations in a deckhouse.

THE RIGHT BOAT FOR YOU

Do you really want to own a boat? The cost and responsibilities of boat ownership are detailed in later chapters. Do you want to spend the necessary money and time involved in boat ownership?

How much will you be using the boat? It might come as a surprise to learn that the average pleasure boat owner in the United States uses the boat less than 12 times a year. When the boat is first purchased, you will probably be using it regularly. But what about in a year or two?

Try to get as much experience in as many types of boats as possible before you buy a boat. Try a friend's boat or rent one. Learn as much as you can, then decide if boating is really for you.

Once a decision is made for boat ownership, decide what type and size of boat meets your needs. Consider how and where you intend to use it and how much money you can afford to spend.

If you are undecided as to whether you want power or sail, and have never tried sailing, take lessons. From this experience alone you can learn whether or not you're a sailboat person. Sailing is slow, quiet, peaceful, and takes a lot of practice and skill. Powerboats are noisy and fast and take little skill to operate, although it can take considerable practice and skill to operate them properly and safely.

Next, consider the particular powerboat or sailboat type, design, and size. This will depend to a large extent on how and where you intend to use the boat. If you are going to use the boat on particular waterways, find out what boats are suitable and what boats other people are using there.

Do you require accommodations? If so, decide on the arrangements that most closely fit your requirements. How often do you intend to stay overnight aboard the boat? This ranges from never to full-time onboard living. Many people are now using boats for their homes. A recommended reference source for those who think they might be interested in this way of life is my book, *Boat Living* (International Marine Publishing Company, Camden, Maine 04843).

Keep in mind that larger boats cost more than smaller ones to buy and to maintain. Slip fees, for example, are usually based on boat length. It is important to make a realistic appraisal of your needs and requirements before buying.

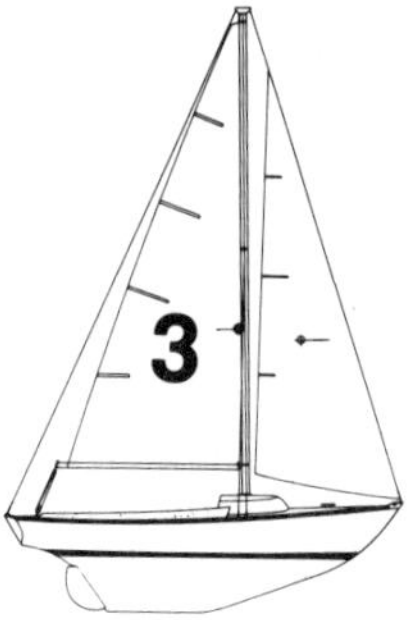

Fiberglass Boat Design

An understanding of the basic principles of fiberglass boat design is important for boat buyers and owners. The actual designing of a fiberglass boat is a long and involved process that requires considerable training and skill. Most fiberglass boats designed by amateurs and actually constructed (fortunately not many) are unsuccessful, if not outright disasters. The few highly successful results that I have seen were designed by "amateurs" in name only. They did not make their livings by designing boats, but most had studied boat designing for years and even taken correspondence courses on the subject.

In spite of this, most people can understand the basic principles of fiberglass boat design. This can be very useful for selecting boats, surveying them, and making repairs and alterations.

FUNDAMENTALS OF BOAT DESIGN

A boat hull must be designed to do many things. It must float or have buoyancy. It must have sufficient stability. The shape must be streamlined for moving through water. The boat must be reasonably light in weight, yet extremely strong. These factors are often contradictory. More of one quality often means less of another. Compromises must be made.

To understand boat design, there must be standard definitions for the parts of the boat and standard ways for expressing dimensions. In addition, boat designers must be able to show a three-dimensional form on paper by means of drawings so that the boat can be constructed.

Buoyancy

The laws of flotation form the basis of boat design. A floating body, such as a boat hull, displaces an amount of water that exactly equals the weight of the body. This law applies to all fluids, including air, but the concern here is with boats floating in water.

With boats, the displacement is the weight or volume of water moved aside. This exactly equals the weight of the body. The displacement of a hull is the weight of the boat and everything aboard it. This is often called *hull weight* or *displacement of the hull,* but it is actually the total weight of the boat and not just that of the hull.

When any object is placed on the surface of water, it will sink to the point where it moves aside or displaces a weight of water equal to itself. An object that has a high density, such as a steel ball, will sink. A block of wood that weighs exactly the same as the steel ball, however, will normally float. The two objects have different densities and thus different volumes. The wood weighs less per cubic measurement than water. Thus, it floats. The steel ball weighs more per cubic measurement than water. It sinks.

How then can a vessel with a steel hull float? The hull is shaped so that it encloses a volume of air from the water. The volume of this air and the weight of the steel used to form the hull weigh less than an equal volume of water.

Fiberglass laminates, like steel, normally weigh more per cubic measurement than water. Density can be expressed in pounds per cubic foot. Mild steel has a density of about 490 pounds per cubic foot. Depending on the particular laminate, fiberglass normally has a density anywhere from about 85 to 125 pounds per cubic foot.

The density of water varies slightly depending on the mineral content. Salt water averages about 64 pounds per cubic foot. Fresh water averages about 62.5 pounds per cubic foot.

This explains why the steel or fiberglass in solid ball or block form sinks, whereas wood normally floats. Sitka spruce, for example, has a density of about 25 pounds per cubic foot, and even white oak, which is considered to be a heavy wood, only has a density of about 42 pounds per cubic foot.

Note that the water is actually displaced or pushed aside. When a boat hull of a certain weight or displacement is placed in a body of water, the water level rises. The water that rose weighs exactly the same as the weight or displacement of the boat.

Most bodies of water that are used for boating are so large that the rise in water level would not be noticed, but the experiment can be carried out with a block of wood placed in a bucket of water. First, fill the bucket exactly full. Place the bucket in an empty pan so that water spilling over from the bucket can be collected. Use a block of wood that weighs about one pound. Place it on the surface of the water in the bucket. The water level should increase and overflow from the bucket into the pan. Weigh the water that spilled over from the full bucket when the block of wood was placed on the surface. The weight of the water should equal the weight of the block. The hull and block of wood are "buoyed" or pushed up by a force exactly equal to the weight of the displaced water.

It is interesting to note that a hull will immerse approximately 3 percent deeper in fresh water than salt water. This is because salt water weighs approximately 3 percent more than fresh water.

Hull Nomenclature

Before continuing with the fundamentals of boat design, hull nomenclature must be discussed.

The following terms refer to directions. *Forward* means toward the front of the hull. *Aft* means toward the rear of the hull. In between is *amidship*. *Abaft* means further aft than something else. *Port* is the left side of the boat when looking forward. *Starboard* is the right side of the boat when looking forward. *Abeam* is off to one side of the boat perpendicular to a fore-and-aft centerline. *Athwartships* means across the boat. *Astern* means behind the boat.

While these terms are relics of an earlier age, they still apply. In addition, more commonly understood "land" terms are used more and more frequently, such as front of boat, back of boat, left side of boat, and right side of boat. Old salts will tell you that correct nautical vocabulary is essential for safety, giving orders, and whatnot, but I think that this is nonsense from a pleasure boating point of view. Nautical language is largely a language of code and exclusion. Many newcomers are having little or no part of it. A kitchen is a kitchen and not a galley; a toilet is a toilet and not a head; and so on.

The *bow* is the forward part of the hull (Fig. 3-1). The *stem* is the forwardmost part of the bow. The *stern* is the after or rear part of the boat. The *transom* is the aftermost part of the stern. The

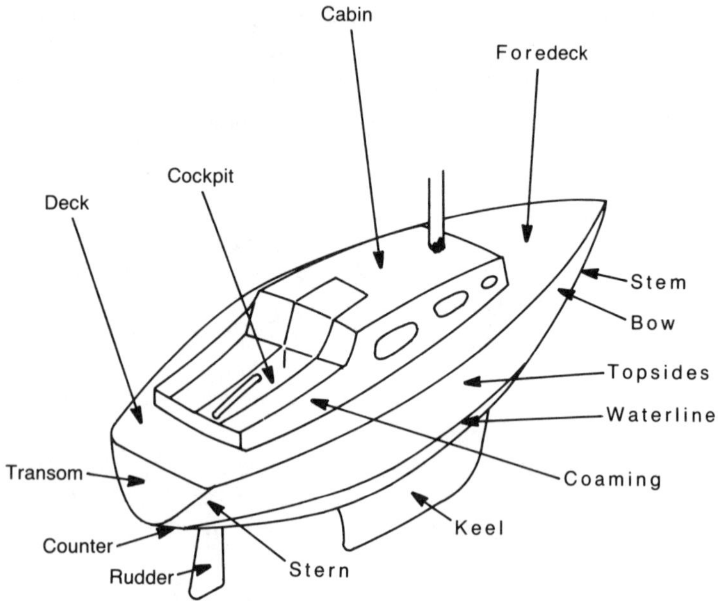

Fig. 3-1. Hull nomenclature.

actual level of the water on a floating hull is called the *waterline.* There is also a *designed waterline,* which is often indicated by a boot top line painted on the hull. Under certain conditions, the actual waterline may vary somewhat from the designed waterline. The designed waterline is also where the designer's calculations say it is going to be. It can be a great embarrassment to the designer if the actual waterline turns out to be considerably different from the designed waterline.

The boat sides from the waterline to the rail are the *topsides.* For powerboats, the *keel* is a main structural member running longitudinally from the stem to the stern along the bottom. For sailboats, the *keel* is a vertical downward extension on the bottom of the hull. The keel is often ballasted and gives stability and lateral resistance. The *forefoot* is the part of the hull between the bow and the keel. The *rudder* extends vertically from the hull and is used for steering the boat. Rudders are usually flat vertical members; there are many shapes, sizes, and methods for mounting them. The *counter* is the part of the boat extending from the waterline to the bottom of the transom.

The *deck* is the platform extending from one side of the boat to the other, often at or near the level of the rail. The *foredeck* is the forward part of the deck. The *cabin house or trunk* is a raised structure that extends up above the deck to give more headroom below. The *cabin* is the enclosed area below. The *cockpit* is a deck well where the tiller or wheel is often located. Cockpits are usually located aft, but sometimes are midship and called *center cockpits.* The *coaming* is a raised area around the cockpit designed to keep water out. Coamings are also raised areas around hatches and other deck openings.

Hull Dimensions

The *length overall (LOA)* is the boat's greatest length, not counting rudders, bowsprits, or other protuberances (Fig. 3-2). The max-

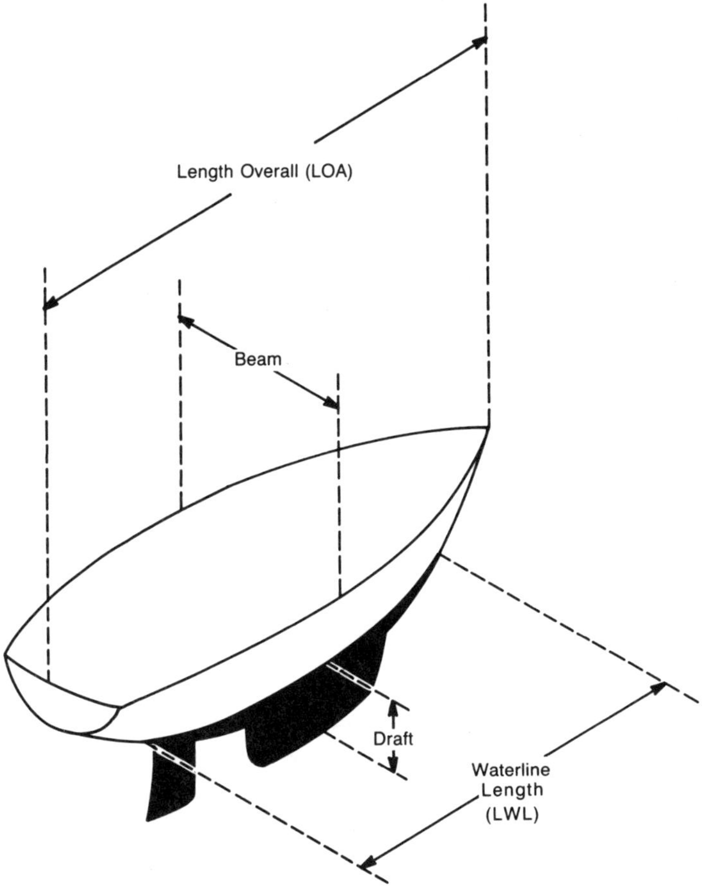

Fig. 3-2. Hull dimensions.

imum breadth of the hull is called the *beam*. The length of the hull at the waterline is called *length of waterline, LWL,* or *waterline length*. The *draft* is the distance from waterline to bottom of keel and is equal to the least depth of water the boat can operate in without "grounding." The draft is the amount of water that the boat draws.

These are dimensions commonly used in boat advertising. There are many others that are used in boat design. These will be detailed as they occur later in this chapter.

Lines Drawing

Early boats were probably natural objects, such as logs. It would be only natural that people would observe that some shapes were better than others. Over the centuries boats changed from natural shapes to constructed shapes. Trial and error gradually led to improved designs. At what point plans drawn on paper or other material were first used remains a matter of conjecture. Before this stage was reached, small models of boats were being carved from wood, and these shapes were transferred to actual constructions of boats. This type of boat designing was much more an art than a science.

Today, most boat designs are first drawn on paper. These are called *lines drawings*. They are essentially two-dimensional representations of three-dimensional objects. These *lines* are topographical maps of solid objects.

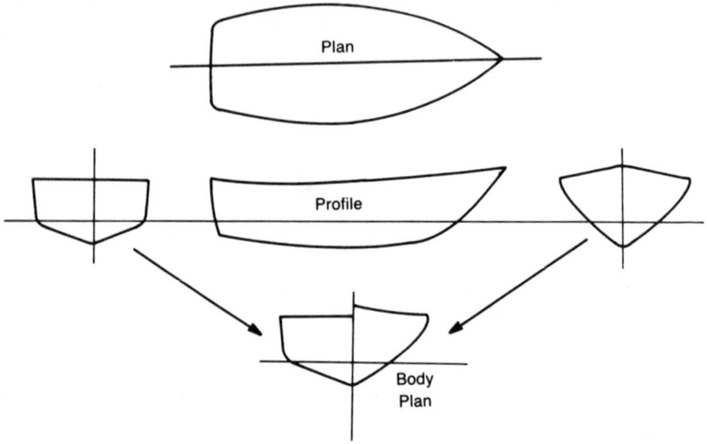

Fig. 3-3. Line drawings showing outlines of three views: profile, plan, and body plan.

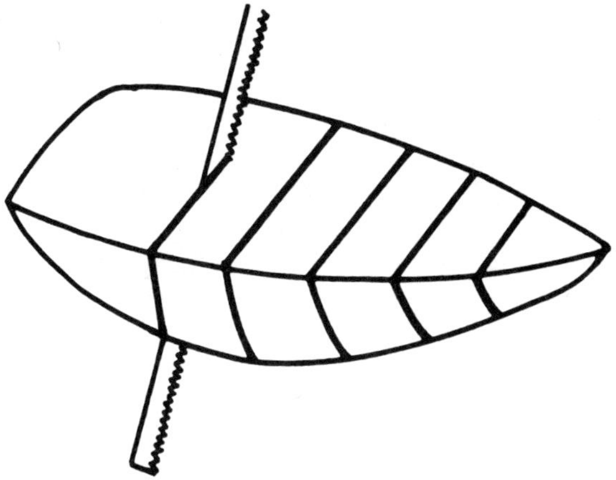

Fig. 3-4. Stations represent athwartship vertical slices.

Three views are usually drawn (Fig. 3-3): a side or *profile* view, also called *sheer* and *elevation* projections; a top or *plan* view, also called *waterlines* and *half-breadth* plans; and a head-on or *body plan,* also called a *section plan.*

The hull shape is defined by three principle sets of lines. All of these appear (sometimes as straight lines and other times as curved lines) in all three views or projections.

Stations (also called *sections*) are athwartship vertical slices or vertical cuts in a transverse plane (Fig. 3-4). Stations appear on profile and plan views as straight lines and on body plan views as curved lines. Stations are placed at regular intervals along the length of the boat.

Waterlines represent horizontal cuts in a longitudinal plane (Fig. 3-5). These are at regular intervals from deck to bottom of keel. The plane on which the boat floats is called the *horizontal waterplane,* and the line on which the boat is designed to float is called the *designed waterline* or *load waterline.* Waterlines appear on profile and body plans as straight lines and on plan views as curved lines.

Buttocks lines represent vertical cuts in a longitudinal plane (Fig. 3-6). These are at regular intervals. They are parallel to the centerline of the boat and perpendicular to the waterlines. Buttocks lines appear as curved lines on profile plans and as straight lines on plan views and body plans.

The following table summarizes how the lines appear on each of the three views.

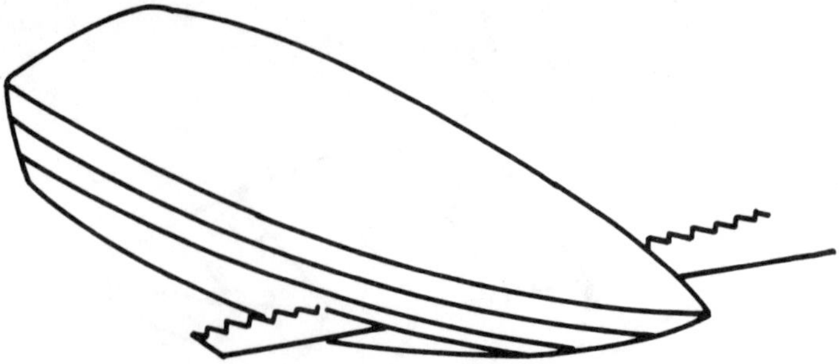

Fig. 3-5. Waterlines represent horizontal slices in a longitudinal plane.

	Profile View	Plan View	Body Plan View
Stations	Straight	Straight	Curved
Waterlines	Straight	Curved	Straight
Buttocks	Curved	Straight	Straight

Each set of lines (stations, waterlines, and buttocks) appears on all three views or drawings (profile, plan, and body plan). On two views, each set of lines appears as straight lines; on the third view each set of lines appears as curved lines.

There is one other important set of lines called *diagonals.* These

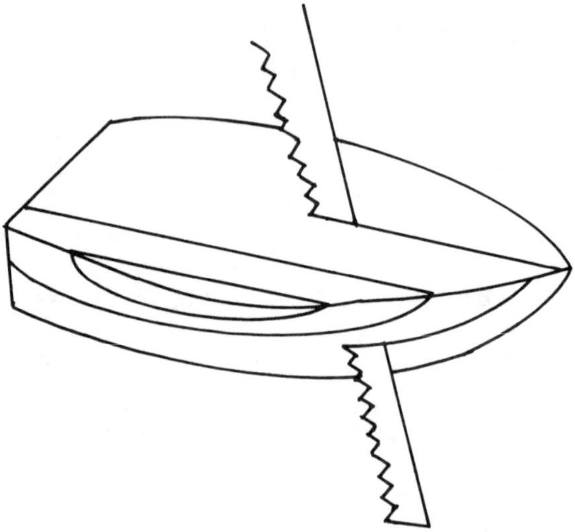

Fig. 3-6. Buttocks lines represent vertical slices in a longitudinal plane.

lines are difficult to understand because they do not represent any shape that can be observed on a hull from any viewpoint. They are drawn in the body plan view at angles that will cross the curved station lines at as close to right angles as possible. These lines are useful for fairing a set of lines. They are a valuable aid for the boat designer, although they won't be much help to a layman in understanding a hull shape.

Displacement

The boat designer must determine the displacement of a boat on the "drawing board." This is done in a roundabout way. The final weight of the vessel (including materials, hardware, engine, and everything carried aboard) is first estimated. This requires complicated calculations. This estimated weight is then used for designing an underwater shape and waterline for the required displacement.

After a first drawing has been made using the estimated weight, various calculations based on cross-sectional areas below the waterline are used to determine (or get a better estimate) of the actual displacement. The process involves using an instrument called a *planimeter* to measure the distance around the perimeter of the station lines on the plan view below the waterline (Fig. 3-7). From this measurement, calculations are made to give the area of irregular

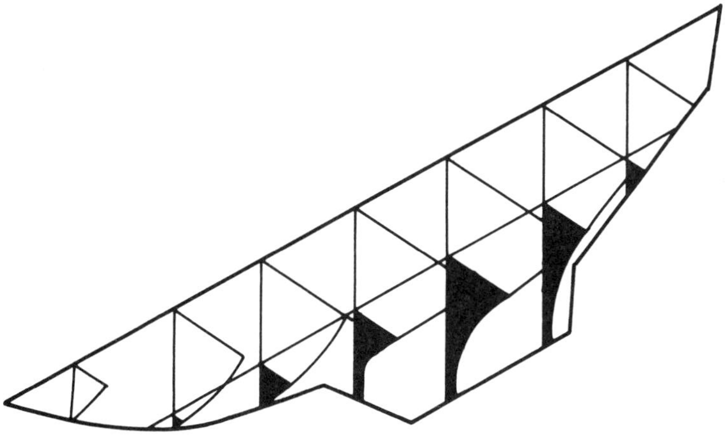

Fig. 3-7. The perimeters of station lines below the waterline are measured and used to calculate the total underwater volume.

shapes, which in turn are used to calculate the total underbody volume. The formula used—*Simpson's Rule*—is fairly involved.

The displacement is then calculated by multiplying the volume by the weight per cubic foot of either fresh or salt water. This figure is compared with the designer's original estimated weight. If the two figures are not close, necessary modifications are made either in the displacement requirements or the drawings.

Basically, you have a planned weight for the boat and a calculated displacement. If the calculated displacement is less than the planned weight, the volume of the underbody must be increased. If the planned weight is less than the calculated displacement, the volume of the underbody must be decreased.

Center of Buoyancy

Buoyancy is an upward force from the pressure of the water that is concentrated at one point on a floating object, Fig. 3-8. This point is the *center of buoyancy (CB).*

With hulls that are symmetrical athwartships, as most boats are, the center of buoyancy is somewhere on the centerline of the boat when the boat is upright (not heeled). This gives one reference plane for determining the center of buoyancy.

Next, the longitudinal location of the center of buoyancy along the centerline is located by various calculations, which are beyond the scope of the discussion here. (The interested reader should consult one of the standard yacht design references.) In a similar manner, the vertical location of the center of buoyancy is located. The center of buoyancy is then located. The transverse center of buoyancy was on a plane vertical to the centerline. The longitudinal location on this plane was then located. Finally, the vertical center of buoyancy was located. This is vertical to the waterline, since the force of buoyancy acts vertically upward.

This gives a more complete picture. In addition to the total volume of the underbody, it is now known how the volume is distributed around a single point.

Center of Gravity

Buoyancy is an upward force. A second major force that acts on a floating boat is *gravity,* which is a downward force. The *center of gravity* is a point on or near the object that is the focus of gravitational force on the object.

The center of gravity is located on drawings in a manner simi-

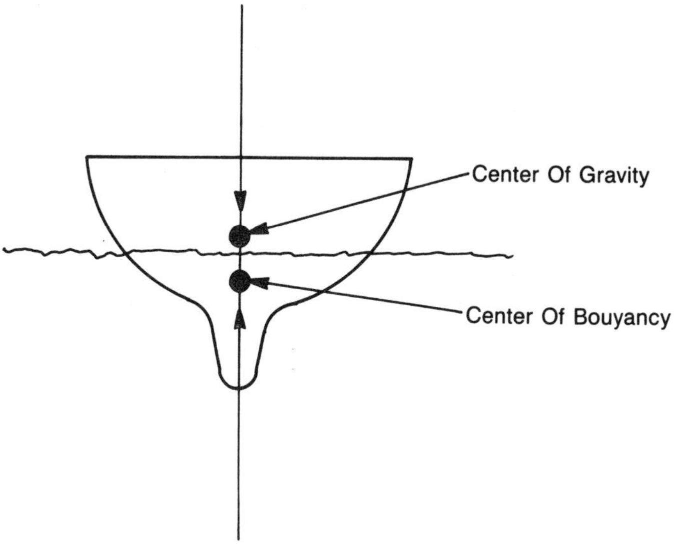

Fig. 3-8. Buoyancy is an upward force; gravity is a downward force.

lar to locating the center of buoyancy, except that this time the concern is with weight rather than volume (see Fig. 3-8). Further, the concern is with all weights on all parts of the boat, rather than just those of the boat's underbody.

The transverse center of gravity is located on a plane vertical to the boat's centerline, provided that all weights are arranged symmetrically (such as a center-mounted engine) or properly counterbalanced. If this is not the case, the completed boat will heel over to one side or the other, as indeed happens with poorly designed boats or boats that have equipment improperly located.

The location of the longitudinal center of gravity is the point along the length of the boat where there is equal weight fore and aft. This is also the balance point.

To locate this point on the drawings, all weights to be used in the construction and carried aboard and their locations must be considered. The calculations used to determine this point are quite involved. The center of gravity is a fulcrum; weights act differently on this point depending on how far away from the point they are. The further away from this point a given weight is placed, the more effect it will have. Thus, not only the weights, but also the reference distances enter into the calculations. This process usually begins with calculations of bare hull weights. This is then extended to include deck and cabin structures, rigging, and other similar factors, even crew weight if this is significant. Next, heavy items such as engines and ballast keels are added to the calculations.

It is important that the longitudinal center of gravity be aligned with the longitudinal center of buoyancy. If the designer sees from the calculations that this is not the case, slight shifting of heavy components on the drawings can be used to give the proper alignment. At this stage of the designing process, some weights will have to be estimated.

Once the longitudinal center of gravity has been located and adjusted so that it is in vertical alignment with the previously determined center of buoyancy, the vertical center of gravity must be determined. The method is similar to that used for determining the longitudinal center of gravity, except that this time the movements are measured vertically.

The vertical center of gravity is in vertical alignment with the previously determined transverse and longitudinal centers of gravity. This gives the single point, which is the center of gravity.

Stability

Stability of a boat is an important consideration. The boat must stay right side up, but beyond this, stability of various boat designs varies greatly. This can affect comfort and performance.

There are three conditions involved in considering stability: stable, unstable, and neutral. These conditions apply both to objects on land and to floating ones. Certain forces, such as gravity, attempt to move a body in an unstable position to a stable one.

As already detailed, two important forces that act on floating boats are buoyancy, which is always upward, and gravity, which is always downward. These are two equal forces acting in opposite directions. In engineering terms, two forces acting in opposite directions form a "couple." A twisting motion or torque results when these two forces are not on the same straight line. If the "couple" or two forces are acting on the same straight line, the result is *static stability* (Fig. 3-9).

This principle can be demonstrated by placing a block of wood flat on the surface of a table. Place your index fingers directly across from each other on opposite sides of the block. Press your fingers toward each other. If your fingers were placed directly opposite each other, the block of wood did not move. The "couple" or two forces acting in opposite directions were on the same straight line. This resulted in a condition of static stability.

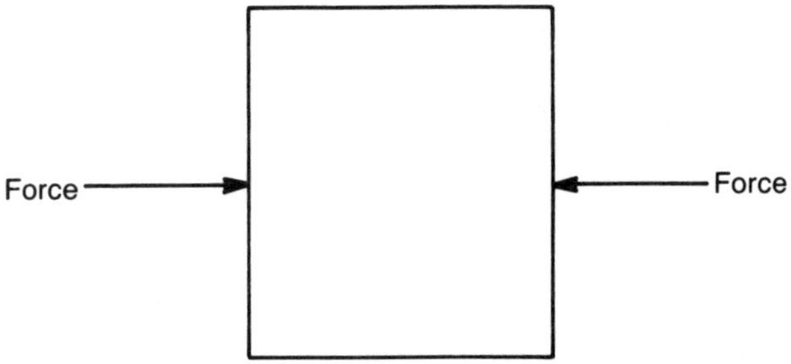

Fig. 3-9. Two forces acting on the same straight line result in static stability.

Next, position your index fingers on opposite sides of the block as was done previously, except this time place them out of alignment (Fig. 3-10). Press your fingers toward points directly across the block. This time the two forces are not on the same straight line. The block turns. This is the resulting twisting motion or torque. You have set up a "couple." The lines of force are parallel to each other but not on the same line.

Repeat the above experiment, except this time have the lines of force further apart. The block of wood should twist more easily this time. The stability of the system is directly related to distance between the lines of force.

This same principle can be applied to the center of buoyancy and center of gravity on a boat. The designer does this at the drawing board. A constant placement for the center of gravity is assumed, at least for heavy displacement boats where a movable crew would have minimum effect. Assume a fixed center of gravity, which is located as already detailed in this chapter. In light displacement vessels, however, a shifting center of gravity is often taken into account in stability calculations.

The center of buoyancy is the point that moves. When wind,

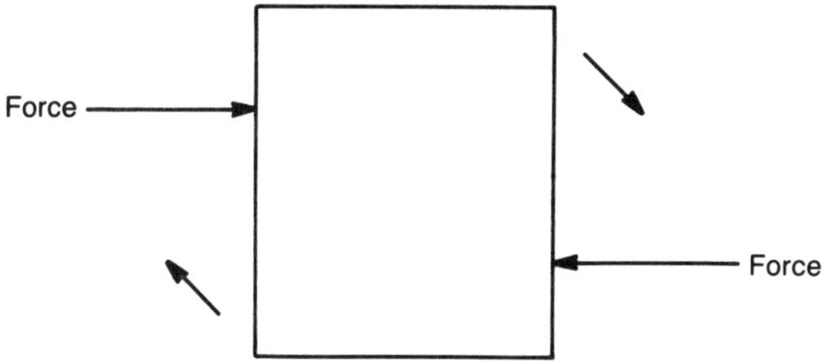

Fig. 3-10. Two forces acting out of alignment result in a twisting motion or torque.

wave, or some other force heels the boat, the center of buoyancy follows the volume shift to the side of greater immersion.

When the boat is upright with no forces causing it to heel, the center of buoyancy and center of gravity are in line and neutralized, as shown in Fig. 3-8. No twisting couple exists.

When the boat is heeled over by some force, the center of buoyancy moves to one side because of the change in shape of the submerged underbody of the hull. The center of gravity does not change because the placement of weight aboard has not been changed. The two forces are not in line. A couple exists. In this case, the torque of the couple tends to right the boat or twist it back to a neutral position (Fig. 3-11).

If the center of gravity were placed high enough, such as by adding a very heavy deck load, a disastrous torque could be set up when the boat heels over. This would cause the boat to capsize (Fig. 3-12). Notice that this time the torque is in the wrong direction.

As the boat heels, the hull shape gives outboard buoyancy. This gives stability that is called *form stability.* Various hull shapes give different amounts of form stability. A narrow hull with slack bilges has low form stability. A broad hull with full bilges has high form stability. Sharp chines, keels, and other similar shapes and protrusions can enhance stability by providing lateral resistance to rolling.

The designer must be concerned with more than one waterline. One of these is the waterline when the boat is static or level. This is called the *static or level waterline.* When the boat is static or level, the up and down forces of buoyancy and gravity are in line and the center of buoyancy, center of gravity, and centerline of the boat are aligned vertically.

For each angle of heel, there is a different waterline. The

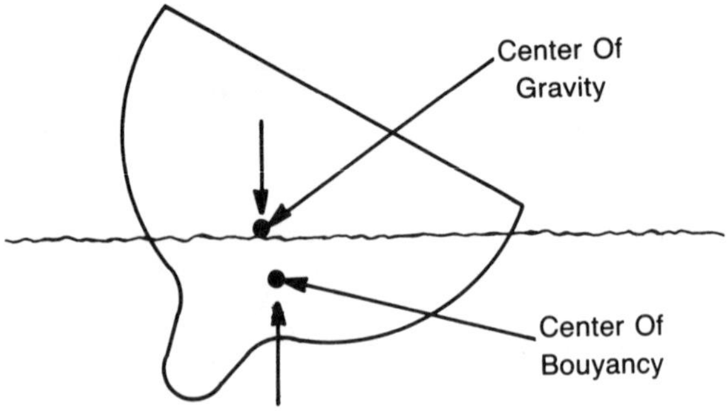

Fig. 3-11. Situation where torque of couple tends to right boat.

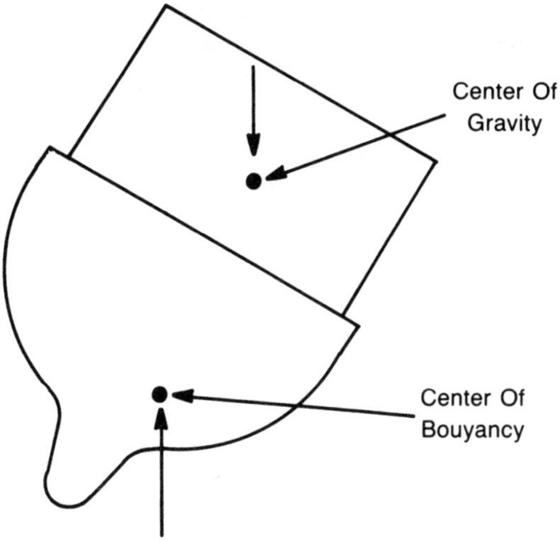

Fig. 3-12. Situation where torque of couple tends to capsize boat.

designer determines the waterlines and centers of buoyancy for a number of heel angles. For each angle of heel, a line is drawn vertical to the heeled waterline in a position so that it passes through the center of gravity. A parallel line is drawn through the center

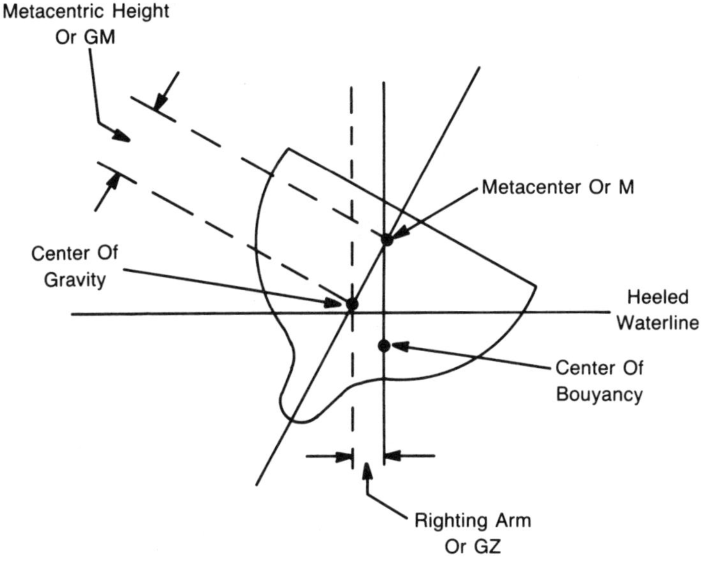

Fig. 3-13. The righting arm or GZ at a given angle of heel.

of buoyancy. The distance between the two lines is the *righting arm or GZ* (Fig. 3-13). The distance that the center of buoyancy moves with a given change in angle of heel is a function of form stability.

The downward force is considered next. This opposes the upward buoyancy force. As the angle of heel changes, so does the relative effectiveness of the couple. The righting force exerted through the righting arm or GZ is equal to the total displacement or weight of the boat in pounds times the length of the righting arm in feet.

The *transverse metacenter or M* is located next at the intersection of the boat's centerline and a vertical line drawn upward from the center of buoyancy at a given angle of heel (Fig. 3-13). The distance between the transverse metacenter point and the center of gravity is called the *metacentric height or GM.*

The metacentric height is an important gauge of the stiffness of the boat. If the metacentric height is relatively large, the boat will be very stiff. If it is relatively small, the boat will be tender. As the metacentric height increases, so does the transverse metacenter. Thus, a tender boat will have a long roll period. A stiff boat will have a short roll period.

As long as the transverse metacenter is above the center of gravity when a boat is heeled, the boat has a positive metacentric height and will right itself. When the transverse metacenter is below the center of gravity, the boat has a negative metacentric height and will capsize from heel. When the transverse metacenter and the center of gravity coincide, the boat has neutral equilibrium. There is no tendency to roll in either direction. Notice that in this case the metacentric height is zero.

Resistance

Another major consideration is hull resistance. While some floating houses are permanently moored, most boats are intended for moving from one place to another. Because various forces resist movement of a boat that is floating on water, a propulsion system must be provided to move the boat. This propulsion system, be it from an engine or sails, must provide enough motive power to overcome resistance to the boat's forward motion. At a constant speed, the power of the boat's propulsion is equal to the resistance to forward motion. The greater the resistance, the greater the power required to move the boat at a given speed.

The greatest resistance acting on a boat results from the water. (Another type of resistance acting on a boat is wind resistance.) There are two main types of water resistance: frictional and residual.

Frictional Resistance. As water passes along the surface of a moving hull, the water molecules close to the hull surface tend to move along with the hull. This causes *skin friction.*

A smooth hull surface has less skin friction than a rough hull surface. Barnacles on a boat's bottom can increase skin friction. Greater skin friction requires more power and fuel consumption to move the boat at a given speed.

The actual process by which water molecules move along with a hull is quite involved. Basically, the molecules closest to the hull skin are induced by adhesion to move along with the hull. By cohesion, these molecules induce neighboring molecules to move along also. As the distance from the hull skin increases, fewer particles move along with the hull skin, and the velocity of the ones that do decreases. There is, then, a zone of water that is moved. This is called the *boundary layer.*

Energy is required to move the boundary layer of water along. With a powerboat, the power is supplied by the engine at the cost of fuel. With a sail, the wind is "free," but moving the boundary layer of water along results in a loss of speed.

As the boundary layer of water moves along the hull from bow to stern, the skin friction becomes less and less. The water is at rest when the bow of the moving boat hull first meets it. The frictional resistance is greatest at this point. As the boat continues to move forward, more and more water is brought along. When this water reaches the stern, some of it is travelling nearly as fast as the boat. The frictional resistance is the least at this point. The greater the distance, the less the frictional resistance. This means that a longer boat has an advantage over a shorter one.

The boat designer tries to keep frictional resistance to a minimum by making the hull smooth and streamlined, keeping wetted surface area to a minimum, avoiding hull projections when possible, and streamlining unavoidable projections.

Residual Resistance. When a powerboat or sailboat moves through the water, it makes undesired waves. The waves cause a residual resistance to increases in hull speed.

Because two things cannot occupy the same space at the same time, the water must be pushed away as the hull moves forward.

It then rushes back to fill the void left by the hull as it moves further forward. This forms waves, which are generated continuously by a moving hull.

There are two kinds of waves: divergent and transverse. *Divergent waves* move diagonally away from the boat and play only a very small part in residual resistance. The familiar bow wave is a divergent wave.

Transverse waves follow alongside the hull and recombine again aft. They are called transverse waves because their crests are at right angles to the centerline of the hull. When the hull is moving slowly, these waves are short and many along the hull. The waves become longer at higher speeds, however, and there are less of them along the length of the hull. This wave lengthening process continues as the hull speed is increased to the point where the wave length is such that the second crest of the bow wave and the first crest of the stern wave coincide. At this point, the wave length equals the waterline length, and the hull is "trapped" between bow and stern wave crests.

In the case of a displacement hull, it would take exponentially more horsepower to drive the boat any faster because any further speed would spread the crests. This puts the boat in a "hole," and considerable horsepower is required to get out.

Displacement hulls are thus, for practical purposes, limited to a certain speed, which is called *hull speed.* The hull speed can be calculated as the square root of the waterline length times 1.34 to give the hull speed in knots.

The underbody shape of displacement hulls, however, is also important because it affects the power required to reach hull speed and even to drive the boat beyond this speed. A slim, lightweight hull of a given waterline length takes less power to reach hull speed than a fuller, heavier boat with the same length of waterline. The boat designer must take all of these factors into consideration when designing a particular boat.

Another type of residual resistance that must be taken into consideration is *eddy-making.* This resistance is created by the water filling the partial vacuum created by the moving boat. Flat sections at the stern and protrusions increase eddy-making.

Basic Plans

So far the focus has been on hull lines and points to consider when designing a particular hull. The three principle sets of lines (stations, waterlines, and buttocks) that appear on three projections (profile, plan, and body plan) define the hull shape so that the hull can be constructed. It is common practice to lay off these lines at full size for the actual construction. This process is called *lofting*.

A model might first be constructed from the designer's hull lines. This will be tank tested. The purpose is to determine if the lines are satisfactory before actually constructing a full-size hull.

Hull lines are only one of a number of basic plans for a boat. Others include construction plan, accommodation plan, sail plan, and so on. A boat designer might make 30 or more sheets of drawings for a single design.

Computer Designing

The computer is used more and more for boat designing. Twenty years ago, boat designers were still using slide rules to make calculations. Then came electronic calculators, which made slide rules obsolete. (I'm saving my old slide rule; it should soon be an antique.) Finally, computers. At first, boat designers used these mainly as calculators. Presently they are used for the actual designing process, even eliminating the traditional "drawing board" method for designing boats.

Who Are Boats Designed For?

The type of plans, number of sheets, and details and instructions vary depending on the intended use of the plans. A boat manufacturer requires one type of plans, an amateur boatbuilder quite another.

Another important factor is the construction material and method to be used. The present trend is to design for a specific construction material (usually fiberglass) and a specific construction method (usually contact molding for fiberglass boats that are to be manufactured). This applies not only to construction plans but to most others as well, including plans for hull lines.

STRUCTURAL DESIGN

The structural design of a boat should accommodate all possible loadings and still maintain its structural integrity. In fiberglass construction, the structural design is complicated because the loads to which a fiberglass boat is subjected are not well defined.

The problem is essentially this. The outside shell of the boat hull is of a predetermined shape. Various loads will be placed on the hull when it is in use. The structural design of the hull (shell thickness, size and placement of supports, and so on) must not break up or lose its shape from these loadings. Because the loadings are not clearly defined, classical engineering analysis is difficult to apply. Instead, the usual process is to measure the load-carrying capabilities of boat hulls that have proven satisfactory in the past and then to apply these to new designs.

Early fiberglass boats were designed conservatively. This required more materials and construction time to make the shell thicker than it really had to be, then use of more and larger supports than were absolutely necessary, and so on. Conservative design was "playing it safe."

Traditional wood boatbuilding with wooden frame and plank construction is based on many years of experience. Successful designs are continued and improved upon. The unsuccessful ones are weeded out. Standard, workable rules for the construction of wooden boats have been formulated.

Fiberglass is a different construction material than wood. The planked wooden hull requires heavy framing and strong fasteners to hold the many separate pieces of wood together and keep them from working and leaking. A fiberglass hull shell is usually one piece with no joints, and fiberglass has different physical properties than wood.

Some of the first fiberglass boats constructed were essentially fiberglass shells with most everything else, including the support framing for the shell, made of wood. This does not take best advantage of fiberglass as a construction material, however. Today, most manufactured fiberglass boats are specially designed for fiberglass construction.

While early fiberglass boats were often conservatively designed and constructed, many manufacturers gradually reduced the shell thicknesses, the number and spacing of supports, and so on. Perhaps this was done to reduce material and labor costs to remain competitive. In any case, these reductions continued until failures began to occur when the boats were in use. Some of these structural failures caused injuries and even loss of human life.

These failures also provided design data. The boats could be examined to determine why the failures had occurred and additional strength was required. The information was then applied to the design and construction of other fiberglass boats. This lead to a compromise between providing a structurally sound boat and keeping the production costs down to a minimum.

Fiberglass boats are designed for intended uses. A boat that is designed for use on protected waters and is structurally sound for this purpose would probably not be suitable for use at sea, nor should it be expected to be. For the boat to be safe and sound at sea, it would have to be "over" built for its intended use. This would not be economically feasible. No boat, regardless of how it is designed or constructed, can be proof against everything.

While a number of countries have had rules and standards for the design and construction of fiberglass boats for some years, until recently the United States was not one of them. The American Bureau of Shipping recently prepared guidelines for scantlings for fiberglass boats as well as for boats of other materials. For information, write to the American Bureau of Shipping, 65 Broadway, New York, NY 10006.

MECHANICAL PROPERTIES OF FIBERGLASS LAMINATES

To this point in this book, strength and other mechanical properties of fiberglass laminates have been considered only in a very general way. To design a structurally sound boat, however, the designer requires specifics on a number of mechanical properties of fiberglass laminates. There is great variability in fiberglass laminates due to factors such as the care and skill used in fabrication, quality of materials, type and arrangement of reinforcing materials, and thickness of laminate. This makes testing fiberglass laminates quite complex. Here are some specific mechanical properties.

Tensile Strength

Tensile strength is the resistance of a material to a force tending to pull it apart. This can be expressed in pounds per square inch (psi). Two types of tensile strength can be measured: yield and ultimate. *Ultimate tensile strength* is the load the material can stand before failure; *yield tensile strength* is the load a material can stand before deforming. Because boat designers use ultimate tensile strength measures for designing hulls, I will use this strength in the discussion here.

Fiberglass laminates have high tensile strength in directions parallel to the layers of the laminate (Fig. 3-14). The tensile strength with loading perpendicular to the layers of the laminate (Fig. 3-15), is usually much less.

In a fiberglass laminate, it's the fiberglass reinforcing mate-

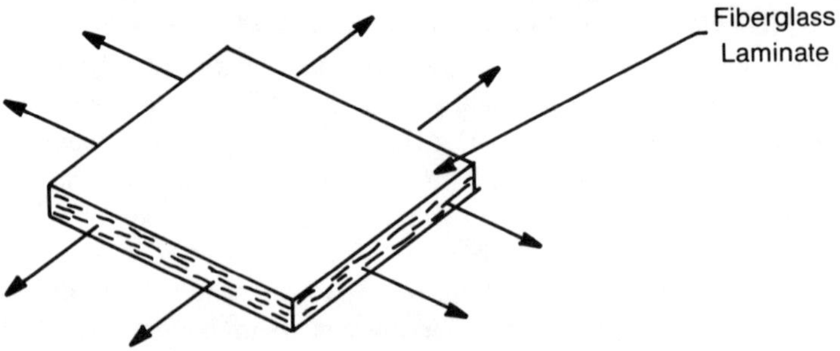

Fig. 3-14. Tensile strength in directions parallel to the layers of the laminate.

rial that provides the strength. The resin provides a means of holding the glass fibers in position. This, in turn, explains why the tensile strength is greater parallel to the layers of the laminate. The tensile strength perpendicular to the layers of the laminate is less because loadings perpendicular to the laminate tend to pull the laminate apart in the relatively weak resin areas. This must be considered when assembling and attaching separate moldings together and when attaching things to moldings. Let's look at ultimate tensile strength of some typical laminates with the loadings parallel to the layers of the laminate.

Three basic types of glass fiber reinforcing material are commonly used in fiberglass laminates: mat, cloth, and woven roving. A single material or any combination of materials can be used for forming the layers of a laminate. Polyester resin is used for production fiberglass boat manufacturing, and the test data included here is for polyester resin laminates. Fiberglass reinforcing materials and laminating and molding methods are detailed in Chapter 4. For now it is important to understand that mat, cloth, and woven roving have different mechanical properties.

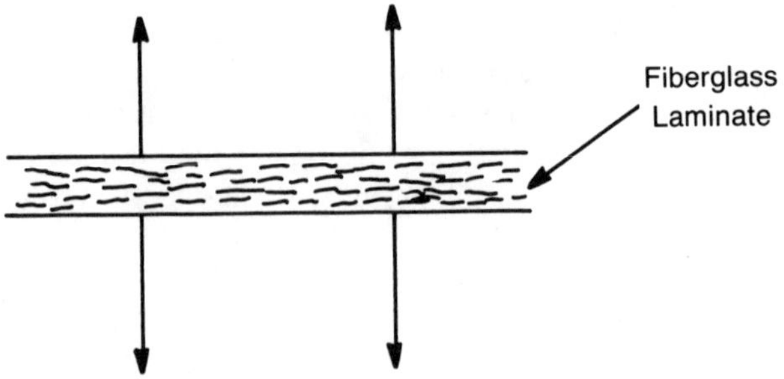

Fig. 3-15. Tensile strength in directions perpendicular to the layers of the laminate.

A typical mat laminate has an ultimate tensile strength of about 12,000 pounds per square inch. This is a little higher than some types of wood (mahogany is about 11,500 psi, sitka spruce is about 10,000 psi) and lower than others (such as white oak, which is about 15,000 psi). These figures for wood are with the grain, however. Typical types of wood used in boat construction often have ultimate tensile strength of less than 1,000 psi across the grain. This is one of the reasons why a wood frame and plank hull requires such heavy framing to hold the planks together.

One type of aluminum alloy used in boat construction has an ultimate tensile strength of 40,000 psi, which is over three times that of a typical mat laminate. Mild steel has an even greater ultimate tensile strength—about 60,000 psi.

It should be noted, however, that each of these materials has a different density. The mat and resin laminate has a density of about 87 lb./ft.^{3}; mahogany about 29 lb./ft.^{3}; sitka spruce about 25 lb./ft.^{3}; white oak about 42 lb./ft.^{3}; aluminum alloy about 166 lb./ft.^{3}; and mild steel about 490 lb./ft.^{3} If you consider ultimate tensile strength divided by the density of the material, you will find that the mat and resin laminate has 138 psi/lb. ft.^{3} Mahogany has 400 psi/lb. ft.^{3}; sitka spruce, 408 psi/lb. ft.^{3}; white oak, 362 psi/lb. ft.^{3}; aluminum alloy, 241 psi/lb. ft.^{3}; and mild steel, 122 psi/lb. ft.^{3} Only mild steel has a lower value than the mat and resin laminate.

Woven roving laminates generally have much higher ultimate tensile strength than do mat laminates. If standard weave woven roving is used, the ultimate tensile strength is usually about 28,000 psi. When unidirectional woven roving is used, it is about 40,000 psi, which is comparable to that of aluminum alloy. The standard woven roving laminate has a density of about 103 lb.ft.^{3}; the unidirectional woven roving, about 122 lb./ft.^{3} The ultimate tensile strength divided by the density for the standard woven roving laminate is about 272 psi/lb. ft.^{3}; for unidirectional woven roving, about 328 psi/lb. ft.^{3} These figures are higher than those for most boat metals (as given in this section), but lower than those for most boat woods.

Cloth and resin laminates have ultimate tensile strength even higher than those of woven roving laminates, often over 40,000 psi.

Mat and woven roving are frequently combined in laminates used in boat construction, usually in alternating layers. The mat fills in the coarse weave pattern of the woven roving and gives better bonding between layers than when woven roving is used alone. The ultimate tensile strength of a typical mat and woven roving (alternating layers) laminate is about 18,000 psi, which is higher than that of a typical mat and resin laminate, but lower than that of a typical woven roving laminate. The density of the mat and woven roving laminate is about 89 $lb.ft.^3$, only slightly greater than that of a typical mat and resin laminate, but considerably less than that of woven roving laminates.

Tensil strength is more closely related to the volume of glass fiber in the laminate than to the type (mat, woven roving, or cloth) of reinforcing material used. Mat laminates have the lowest tensile strength because mat absorbs the most resin when wetted out in the lay-up process. Woven roving uses less resin and thus has a higher tensile strength in a laminate. Even less resin is used with cloth, giving a laminate with the highest tensile strength.

It might appear that the strands of glass running continuously along the length and width of the material gives the higher tensile strength than for mat laminates, which is made up of short strands of glass fiber. Tests indicate, however, that this is not the case. There is little loss of tensile strength until the strands become less than 3/4 inch in length. It's mainly the ratio of glass fibers to resin that makes the difference.

The cloth and woven roving laminates have the greatest tensile strength in the warp and fill directions. (Assuming the same amount of glass fiber in each, the strength would be the same in each of these directions; in unidirectional weaves, it is usually greater in the warp directions.) They have relatively less tensile strength in diagonal and all other directions in the plane of the laminate parallel to the plies. These directions can be varied in a laminate, however, to give the highest tensile strength in the directions where it is most needed.

Mat laminates have the lowest tensile strength because of their high resin content. They have the most uniform tensile strength in the plane of the laminate (parallel to the plies), however, because of the randomness of the glass strands. When the physical properties are essentially the same in all directions, the material is considered to be *isotropic.* Aluminum and steel are typical examples. A mat laminate is considered to be isotropic, at least in directions parallel to the plies. In directions perpendicular to the plies, this might or might not be the case, depending on how the laminate was formed, if the glass fibers are arranged randomly or not, and other factors. When mat laminates are laid up in layers, and one layer is allowed to harden before the next is applied, there will usually be resin-rich areas between plies. In directions perpendicular to the plies, the laminate would no longer be isotropic.

When the physical properties vary with direction, the material is considered to be *orthotropic.* Most fiberglass laminates used in boat construction are orthotropic.

Other Types of Strength

Fiberglass laminates have high *flexural strength* (in some cases more than structural steel), *compression strength,* and *impact strength. Shear strength* varies, depending on the type of reinforcing materials used, the method of lay-up used, and other factors.

Modulus of Elasticity

A main design and construction problem associated with fiberglass laminates is that they are very flexible. A measure of this property is the *modulus of elasticity.* This is a measure of the ability to resist deflections and is usually expressed in psi $\times$ 10^6. A mat and resin laminate has a modulus of elasticity of about 1.0 psi $\times$ 10^6; a standard woven roving laminate about 1.75 psi $\times$ 10^6; a unidirectional woven roving laminate about 2.10 psi $\times$ 10^6; and a mat and woven roving (alternating layers or plies) about 1.30 psi $\times$ 10^6. One type of aluminum alloy used in boat construction has a modulus of elasticity of about 10 psi $\times$ 10^6. This means that fiberglass, depending on the particular laminate, is about five to ten times more flexible than this type of aluminum alloy. Mild steel has a modulus of elasticity of about 30 psi $\times$ 10^6, which means that fiberglass laminates, depending on the particular laminate, are from about 15 to 30 times more flexible than mild steel.

Fiberglass laminates have about the same modulus of elasticity as plywood. The flexibility is similar. Fiberglass laminates are stronger and more costly, however, than plywood of the same thickness. In boat construction, thin laminates are used, then extra support and stiffening are added, because it is normally too expensive to accomplish this by increasing the thickness of the laminates unnecessarily.

The boat designer must consider all these factors in order to make the best use of the materials. Stiffening can be accomplished by extra thickness, shape (a curved panel is stiffer than a flat panel of the same thickness), added supporting members (frames, bulkheads, etc.), and use of sandwich core construction. These methods are detailed in Chapter 4.

Use of Test Data

The boat designer is faced not only with the problem of what the loadings will be on the finished boat, but also what the mechanical properties of the materials used in the construction will be. There is considerable variability in fiberglass laminates due to the type, arrangement, and quality of materials used as well as how and where the laminates were laid up. Samples prepared in a laboratory often vary considerably from those taken from boat moldings in a fiberglass manufacturing plant. The first is often called "lab prepared," the latter "shop prepared."

The designer should use data from shop prepared samples. There are many problems here too. The quality of the laminates can vary considerably, often to the point where using an average measurement can be misleading.

Adding to the problem is the fact that most testing of mechanical properties is destructive testing. Laminates tested are destroyed in the process. As might be expected, fiberglass boat manufacturers are not too eager to sacrifice parts of their boats for this purpose.

Perhaps the best solution is conservative design.

SPECIAL PROBLEMS OF FIBERGLASS BOAT DESIGN

A primary advantage of using fiberglass instead of other construction materials is that fiberglass can be molded to a variety of complex shapes. This can be done relatively easily and economically. Sharp angles and corners are best avoided, however, because these shapes do not mold easily. Still, by and large, fiberglass has given boat designers new creative freedom.

In most cases, fiberglass boat manufacturers use contact molding (Chapter 4), at least for larger boats. The designer must consider this fact. The boat must be practical to mold, and the assembly of separate moldings must be considered. Good planning at the design stage is one of the keys to good fiberglass boats.

I think that it is very important that fiberglass boats be designed for low maintenance. As I look back over the years that fiberglass boats have been manufactured, I see a number of stages. The first fiberglass boats were overbuilt in most regards, but with basic weaknesses, such as use of wood in ways that dry rot would quickly form. Of course, this is an oversimplification. There were good, bad, and indifferent boats. I'm speaking now of trends or directions.

The middle stage, as I think of it, is when the manufacturers tried to reduce the material and labor costs per boat, perhaps to stay competitive. Again, not all manufacturers did this. Unproven hull to deck assembly methods were used. These often parted in use. Many of these boats were "duds." As I look back at fiberglass boats from this period, I realize that enough materials were used to construct a good boat. The problems seem to be in the design and the way the materials were used. These boats were often complicated. What could have been better constructed in one piece was made in two or three. Assembly methods were often poorly thought out. Some methods, such as joining hull and deck moldings together with an aluminum extrusion, and holding the moldings in place with pop rivets, must have simply been quick and easy for the manufacturers.

The final stage, which is still in progress, is better use of materials. There are now more years of experience and more test data to design and build from. Fiberglassing chemicals and materials are improving.

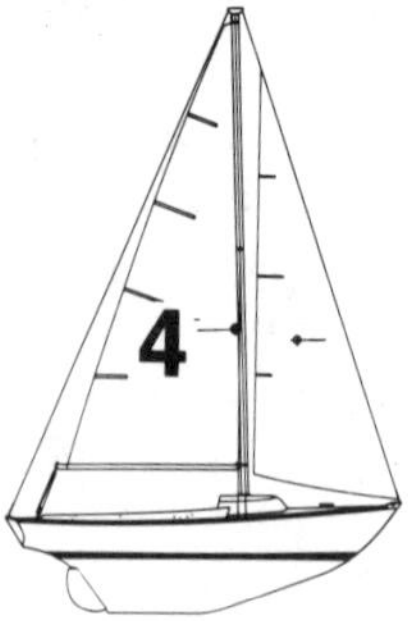

Fiberglass Boat Construction

This chapter discusses how fiberglass boats are manufactured using volume molding methods—that is, where a number of boats are made from the same cavity molds. (One-off construction methods are covered in Chapter 14.) There are two basic aspects to fiberglass boat construction: molding the fiberglass hull and other components and assembling these along with other materials into completed boats.

REINFORCING MATERIALS

Fiberglass originally referred to thin fibers or filaments of glass. While this definition still applies, it has been extended to feltlike mat and woven fabrics made from these fibers and the two-part structural unit consisting of glass fibers combined with resin.

Glass Fiber Reinforcing Materials

Glass fiber is a synthetic dating back to the early 1930s. Molten "E" glass, formed from lime, alumina (aluminum oxide), and borosilicate, is formed into continuous filaments by mechanical attenuation. This is done by pulling the melted glass through small holes in the bottom of an electrical furnace and stretching it into thin fibers. The fibers are formed into yarns, which are in turn formed into glass fiber reinforcing materials by weaving on regular weaving machinery and other means. This material is made suitable for use with plastic resins by adding special finishes, such as chroming, which allow the plastic resins to flow around the glass fibers and minimize trapped air.

Glass fiber reinforcing materials used in boat construction include cloth, mat, woven roving, chopped strands, combination chopped strands and woven roving, and milled fibers.

Glass Fiber Cloth. Glass fiber cloth is probably the most familiar form. Glass fibers are made into threads that are woven into cloth using textile weaving machinery. A plain weave is used for boat construction. Long shaft satin and unidirectional weave patterns are used for some special applications. The long shaft satin weave gives a smoother surface, and the unidirectional weave gives greater reinforcing strength in one direction than the other.

Glass fiber cloth is available in various weights per square yard. Weights from about 4 ounces per square yard to about 20 ounces per square yard are used for boat construction, with 10- or 12-ounce weights used for most applications. These are dry weights before the cloth has been saturated with plastic resin.

When combined with plastic resin to make fiberglass laminates, cloth gives greater strength but less thickness than other types of glass fiber reinforcing materials. A 1-inch thick laminate would take about 40 to 50 layers of 12-ounce-per-square-yard cloth.

Cloth is available in long lengths in various widths up to about 60 inches with salvaged edges to keep it from unravelling. Narrow widths from about 1 inch to 12 inches with salvaged edges are often called cloth *tape*. Because the salvaged edges make the cloth easier to work with, the width is selected for particular applications in boat construction work. At unselvaged ends and where cuts are made, the cloth tends to unravel, requiring special care in handling the dry cloth and applying plastic resin to it.

Cloth works well on reasonably flat surfaces, but is difficult to keep wrinkle-free when used in curved areas. Square corners and other difficult configurations require that cuts be made. Cloth gives a fairly smooth finish when lighter weights are used.

Various reinforcing materials require different amounts of resin. Cloth requires the least, which makes it very strong. It lacks stiffness, though. Because of the limited amount of resin, it is not very waterproof.

On a weight basis, cloth is more expensive than other types of reinforcing material. There are many applications in boat construction, however, where its strength and other special properties make it worth the additional cost.

Both treated and untreated glass fiber cloth are available. Only the kind specially treated (usually by chroming) for resin and fiberglass laminating is normally used in boat construction. Untreated fabric has a dull appearance, whereas the chroming gives the cloth a shiny appearance.

The fiberglass cloth usually has a slip weave that lets the threads slide over each other to some extent. This allows the dry fabric to be shaped to limited compound curves in one piece without cutting it.

Glass Fiber Woven Roving. Woven roving is a thick, cloth-like reinforcing material made from rovings or continuous strands of glass fibers that are grouped together. By weight, woven roving is less expensive than cloth, but more expensive than mat.

Woven roving is available in various weights per square yard, with 24 ounces per square yard (dry weight) commonly used for most boat construction work. Twenty-five layers of 24-ounce-per-square-yard woven roving gives a laminate about an inch of thickness. In actual practice, woven roving is alternated with layers of fiberglass mat to fill in the heavy weave pattern, a combination that give good adhesion, stiffness, and tensile strength.

Woven roving is available in long length in widths up to about 60 inches. The edges are unselvaged, so care must be taken when handling the dry material and saturating it with resin to keep it from coming unravelled.

Woven roving has less strength than cloth, but more strength than mat. Woven roving gives a more rapid buildup of thickness than cloth, a considerable advantage in boat lay-up work, but the heavy weave does not give as smooth a surface as cloth. Another disadvantage is that woven roving is more difficult to wet out (saturate with resin) than either mat or cloth.

More resin is required for woven roving than cloth. A typical woven roving laminate properly laid up is about 55 percent plastic resin and about 45 percent glass fibers. A cloth laminate is about 50 percent resin and 50 percent cloth. Mat requires more resin than either woven roving or cloth, however.

Because woven roving laminates only have a resin percentage slightly greater than cloth laminates, they lack waterproofness. To get around this problem, layers of woven roving are alternated in a laminate with mat, which takes a higher percentage of resin by weight. It's the resin and not the reinforcing material that makes fiberglass laminates highly impervious to water.

Woven roving reinforcing material has a slip weave that allows the rovings to slide over each other to some extent. This allows the dry fabric to be shaped to limited compound curves in one piece without cutting it.

Because of the thick basket weave and heavy weight, woven roving is more difficult to work with than cloth in boat lay-up work. For laying up boat laminates, however, the advantages outweigh the disadvantages. Woven roving is used extensively in boat construction, usually alternated with layers of mat to fill in the heavy weave pattern of the woven roving to prevent a resin-rich laminate, which tends to be brittle. The mat is also used to give a smoother outside surface.

Glass Fiber Mat. Fiberglass mat is made by laying down chopped strands of glass fiber in a random pattern on a flat surface. The strands are held together in a feltlike material by means of a bonding agent.

Mat is available in various square foot (unlike cloth and woven roving which are by the square yard) weights from about 3/4 ounce to 3 ounces. It comes in various widths up to about 60 inches in long lengths. Like cloth and woven roving, it usually comes in rolls.

On a weight basis, mat is the least expensive of the reinforcing materials. This advantage is partially offset because it requires more resin than either cloth or woven roving.

Like the other types of fiberglass reinforcing materials, mat must be treated, such as by chroming, before it can be used with plastic resins in lay-up work.

In a mat laminate, the resin is usually from 25 to 35 percent by weight, and the rest is glass mat. This resin percentage is much lower than in cloth or woven roving laminates. A mat laminate is weaker than either cloth or woven roving because of the higher proportion of resin. The mat forms the stiffest laminate, however.

Because of the random pattern of the glass fibers in mat, its strength is nondirectional, and it has the best inner bonding strength when used in a laminate. For this reason it is used extensively between layers of woven roving in fiberglass boat lay-ups.

The high resin content in a mat laminate makes it highly waterproof. It is much better than cloth or woven roving.

Mat is an easy reinforcing material to lay up; it is easy to saturate with resin. Dry mat is fairly stiff and does not shape easily to compound curves. When wetted out or saturated with resin, however, the resin dissolves the binder holding the glass strands together. The mat can then be easily shaped to compound curves.

Note that the short strands of chopped fibers in mat, about 3/4 inch to 1 1/2 inches, do not necessarily make a mat laminate weaker than one of cloth or woven roving. Tests show that mat laminates are weaker because of the higher resin content and that the length of the glass strands have little effect on the strength.

It takes about 20 layers of 1 1/2-ounce-per-square-foot mat to give a laminate 1 inch thick. The higher resin content, however, gives the mat laminate lower strength and modulus of elasticity than a cloth or woven roving laminate of equal thickness. To have approximately equivalent strength and modulus of elasticity properties, the mat laminate would have to be thicker.

Chopped Glass Fiber Strands. Chopped strands of glass fiber rovings are frequently used in fiberglass boat construction. The strands measure about 1/4 inch to 2 inches in length and must be treated, with croming, for instance, before they can be used with plastic resins.

Chopped strands are added to resin to give a mixture that will form a laminate similar to one of mat, only weaker. This is similar to a mixture sprayed from a "chopper gun," as described later in this chapter.

Combination Chopped Strands and Woven Roving. Chopped strands or mat are combined with woven roving in a single material to speed up lay-up work. This can save considerable time in the build-up of large fiberglass moldings. Instead of laying up a layer of woven roving and then a layer of mat, both can be applied in a single operation.

It comes in various weights per square yard, with 24 ounces per square yard frequently used in boat construction. It's available in various widths up to about 60 inches in long lengths.

Surfacing Mat. Individual glass fibers (rather than whole strands as are used in regular mat) are used to form a special purpose mat that has a thin body and gives a very smooth surface. It's sometimes used in boat construction for surfacing and overlay work. It's available in thicknesses from about 0.01 inch to 0.03 inch and in various widths up to about 60 inches in long lengths.

Milled Fibers. Milled fibers are made from glass strands that are hammer-milled into a fluffy material. They are added to plastic resins to form a putty or filler material. This material has many uses in boat construction work.

Nonfiberglass Reinforcing Materials

A number of nonfiberglass reinforcing materials can be used instead of fiberglass with plastic resins to form a material similar to fiberglass and often still called fiberglass. These materials include Vectra polypropylene, Dynel acrylic, Xynole polyester, DuPont Kevlar 49 Armid, and carbon fiber. These reinforcing materials are more expensive, some considerably more, than fiberglass reinforcing materials and thus are seldom used for production boat construction. Their special properties make them useful, however, in the construction of offshore racing sailboats and other custom boats.

Vectra Polypropylene. Vectra polypropylene is made from an extremely lightweight polypropylene textile fiber. When formed into standard 4.3-ounce-per-square-yard cloth, it has about the same bulk and absorption of plastic resin as 10-ounce fiberglass cloth. The polypropylene laminate gives a higher strength-to-weight ratio than when fiberglass reinforcing material is used. This results in a useful combination of light weight and high tensile strength. Compared to fiberglass, it gives greater abrasion resistance, greater elasticity, and better bonding adhesion to wood. Unlike fiberglass reinforcing materials, the polypropylene is nonallergenic and does not cause skin irritation during sanding and handling.

Disadvantages include higher cost (presently about a dollar more per yard than fiberglass cloth with the same bulk and resin absorption capacity); a tendency to float in wet resin, making it difficult to work with; and a tendency to hold its creases. The high abrasion resistance of laminates laid up with polypropylene makes it difficult to sand.

Polypropylene cloth is available in various widths up to 60 inches with selvaged edges. It has large openings in the weave to allow for easy penetration of resin during lay-up work.

Dynel Acrylic. Dynel acrylic is made from acrylic yarn from Japan that is woven into fabric in the United States. It's available in a 4-ounce-per-square-yard dry weight in a 63-inch width in long lengths. It weighs only about half as much as fiberglass cloth with the same thickness.

Compared to fiberglass, it has greater abrasion resistance, is easier to stretch around sharp corners and curves, and has a higher tensile strength. Unlike fiberglass, it does not cause skin irritation when handled or sanded. The acrylic laminate provides a slick finish when sanded, making it useful as an overlay. A canvaslike nonskid surface is possible by using a minimum of resin in the lay-up.

Dynel acrylic is easy to wet out and provides better adhesion to wood than fiberglass. A main disadvantage is the higher cost. It is presently priced higher than polypropylene cloth.

Xynole Polyester. Xynole polyester is available in a

4.2-ounce-per-square-yard dry weight cloth, which has about the same absorption of resin and bulk as 10-ounce-per-square-yard dry weight fiberglass cloth. The polyester cloth is available in various widths up to 60 inches, including tape form in widths from 1 1/2 to 12 inches.

This material is easy to wet out and useful for overlay work. It wets out rapidly without leaving air bubbles. It conforms well to compound curves and around sharp corners. As compared to fiberglass, it has better laminating adhesion, greater toughness and abrasion resistance, and better weight-to-strength ratio. The polyester does lack stiffness, however, and for this reason is not used alone for laminating in high-stress areas. It is useful, though, as an overlay for a fiberglass laminate. Its main disadvantage is that it is more expensive than fiberglass reinforcing cloth of the same thickness.

Dupont Kevlar Reinforcing Fabric. Kevlar is a synthetic long-chain polymer fiber developed by DuPont in 1972. It's a 5-ounce-per-square-yard reinforcing material that is available in long lengths in 38-inch and 50-inch widths. It has greater tensile and impact strength than when fiberglass reinforcement is used, but it is not as strong in compression or bending.

The main disadvantage is that it is much more expensive than fiberglass reinforcing material. For the added tensile and impact strength, however, it is worth the extra cost for special applications, especially where light weight is important.

Carbon Fiber Reinforcing Material. This material is expensive, so its use is limited to custom boat construction where high strength with minimum weight is called for. For laminating purposes, it is used with epoxy resin, which is more expensive than the polyester resin normally used in production boat construction.

RESINS

There are two main types of plastic resins used in fiberglass lay-up work in boat construction: polyester and epoxy.

Polyester

Polyester resin is used for most of the molding and lay-up work in production fiberglass boat construction. Polyester resin is a *thermosetting* plastic that is set or cured by heat applied chemically from inside the resin (*exothermic heat*) or outside, or by some combination of the two.

To start the chemical reaction that causes internal heat, an *accelerator* (a highly active oxidizing material) and a *catalyst* are added to the liquid polyester resin. This heat is the setting agent. In liquid form, the molecules in polyester resin lay side by side in no set pattern. The addition of heat causes the molecules to link together in chains to form a solid plastic. This hard mass is not softened by the application of heat. This process of changing from a liquid to a solid is called *polymerization.*

The polyester resins used for most boat manufacturing work are manufactured for room temperature cures. These already have the necessary accelerator added to the liquid resin. The commonly used accelerator is *cobalt naphthanate.* To start the cure at room temperature, only a catalyst, usually methyl-ethyl-ketone (MEK) peroxide, is added to the polyester resin that already has the accelerator added to it.

Even without the addition of the catalyst, polyester resin will harden at room temperature. With the catalyst, however, the resin hardens quickly—five minutes to an hour—depending on factors such as how much catalyst is added, room temperature, and humidity. The curing rate is also affected by the thickness of the layer of resin applied. A thin layer does not keep heat inside as well as a thicker layer, causing a thin layer to cure slower than a thick layer.

Polyester resin will cure in time even in sealed containers at room temperature. Because polyester resins have a limited shelf life, always purchase and use fresh resin that has not started to cure in the container.

There are two basic types of polyester resin that are used extensively in boat construction: *laminating resin* (also called lay-up and bonding resin) and *finishing resin* (also called surfacing resin).

The laminating resin is *air-inhibited.* The presence of air does not allow the surface of the resin to fully cure. It remains tacky, a desirable condition when additional layers of fiberglass are to be added to a laminate, such as when molding boat hulls and other components. There is no waxy surface to prevent bonding additional resin layers together properly.

The finishing resin is *nonair-inhibited.* It fully cures in the presence of air. This is desirable for the final layer applied to a fiberglass laminate when a complete cure is desired. Wax or a similar ingredient is added to polyester resin to make it nonair-inhibited. When the catalyzed resin is added to a laminate, the wax rises to the surface, sealing off the air and allowing the resin to fully cure. This surface can then be sanded. The tacky surface that is present when air-inhibited resin is used is gummy and will quickly clog sandpaper.

Air-inhibited laminating polyester resin can be converted to nonair-inhibited resin by adding a special wax that is readily available to the resin before application. Many boat manufacturers use this method so that one type of resin can be purchased for both uses.

Another method of achieving a surface cure when an air-inhibited resin is used is to seal the surface from the air. This happens when the resin is applied against a mold surface or when the surface of a laminate is sealed from the air by covering it with cellophane or by other means so that the air cannot get below.

Finishing resin cures with a waxy surface. To add another layer of laminate to this, the wax should first be removed by sanding or with a solvent such as acetone.

There is also a general-purpose resin that is supposed to work as both a laminating and finishing resin. Most fiberglass experts feel, however, that this type of resin does not do either job well.

Polyester resin is available in various *viscosities*. Higher viscosity resins contain a thixotropic or thickening agent, which results in less dripping and sagging when used on vertical and overhead surfaces.

Special thickening agents and thixotropic powders can be added to regular viscosity polyester resin to give it a higher viscosity. While clay and inert earth weaken the resin, some types actually strengthen the resin.

Polyester resins can also be formulated for various degrees of *flexibility* when cured. These range from quite flexible to very rigid. Most resins used for boat construction are somewhere in between. Highly flexible polyester resin is often used with nonfiberglass reinforcing materials that have greater stretch or elongation than fiberglass reinforcing materials do. When flexible resins are used, a laminate will crack and craze less from impact. More rigid resins give greater stiffness, however, which is desirable for many applications.

When regular polyester resin is used, a laminate will support combustion about the same as plywood. Special polyester resins are available that are more fire retardant. They are also more expensive, but there are areas in boat construction where this extra cost is warranted for the added fire retardancy.

To achieve fire retardancy, a coreactant compound is combined with the liquid resin. This results in a slower curing time for the resin. Adhesion, flexibility, and impact resistance are not usually affected, however. When coreactants are added to resin, a white opacity results and the usual translucency is lost. For most applications this does not matter.

Working Temperatures. Most polyester resins are formulated for a working temperature of about 70 to 75 degrees Fahrenheit. With additional catalyst, this resin can give good results in a temperature range of 60 to 70 degrees Fahrenheit; with less catalyst, satisfactory results can still be achieved in a temperature range of 75 to 90 degrees Fahrenheit. Thus, regular polyester resin is satisfactory for use in a temperature range of 60 to 90 degrees Fahrenheit, with difficulties and working problems increasing near the extremes. For this and other reasons, many boat manufacturers try to keep the molding and lay-up sections of their factories in a temperature range of 70 to 75 degrees Fahrenheit.

Also available are special low-temperature resins that are formulated for a 45-to-60-degree Fahrenheit range. A special accelerator is added to these resins at the factory. They are catalyzed in the same manner as regular polyester resins. The low-temperature resins have an even shorter shelf life in containers than regular resins, usually only about three or four months.

Gel Coat Polyester Resin. Gel coat polyester resin is a specially formulated resin used as a protective color surface on a fiberglass molding (Fig. 4-1). It's available in clear form to which color pigments can be added or with the color already added.

Gel coat resin is usually air-inhibited. It's applied over a mold release agent in a cavity or female mold. The reinforcing material and resin lay-up follows. In the finished molding, the gel coat forms the outside color surface, something like building a house inside a layer of paint. The nonair-inhibited gel coat cures because it is sealed from air against the mold.

In the early days of fiberglass boat construction, gel coatings

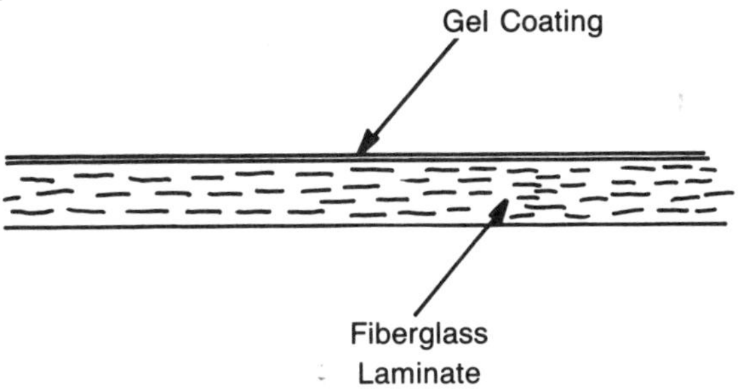

Fig. 4-1. The gel coat is a thin layer of special resin.

were a problem. Cracking, crazing, and uneven color were common. Over the years, the formulations of gel coatings have improved greatly. In addition to giving a color coating, the gel coat must also provide a protective waterproof barrier.

Polyester gel coat resin is catalyzed in a manner similar to regular polyester resin and is sprayed inside the mold over a release agent. The gel coat layer does not have any glass reinforcement, so it must be thin if cracking and crazing are to be prevented.

Other Considerations.

■ Polyester resin is available in various quantities and types of containers. Most manufacturers of fiberglass boats purchase it in 55-gallon drums. Its limited shelf life must be kept in mind, and the resin should be properly stored in a cool place.

■ Use quality brands of resin. Most boat manufacturers do, but a few try to cut costs here, which lowers the quality of the resulting boats in a way that is very difficult for the buyer to see.

■ The amount of catalyst, methyl-ethyl-ketone (MEK) peroxide, must be carefully controlled when added to polyester resin. Special containers with scales on the sides are often used so that the desired amount of catalyst can be added to resin. Manufacturers purchase the catalyst in bulk quantities and then use special squirt applicators that control the outflow.

■ *Styrene* is a coactive thinner that can be used with polyester resins; it is frequently used when spraying is done. Up to 40 percent by volume may be added. Styrene presents safety hazards to workers; special precautions must be taken to use it safely.

■ To suppress bubble formation in polyester resins, *bubble inhibitors* are used. This additive does not affect the curing of the resin.

■ *Polyester putty and filler compounds* are used in production fiberglass boat manufacturing. Some companies used manufactured versions; others mix their own, often by mixing polyester resin and milled glass reinforcing material.

Epoxy

The second main type of plastic resin used in boat construction is epoxy. Like polyester resin, epoxy is a thermosetting plastic that is set or cured by heat applied either chemically from inside the resin (exothermic heat) or from outside, or from a combination of these.

Even though epoxy resin has a number of advantages over polyester resin, its high cost (more than double that of polyester resin) limits its use in production boat construction. Some early production boats were laid up with epoxy resin back when epoxy resin was fairly cheap, and these boats have proven to be outstanding. Today, epoxy resin is only used in production boats in areas where its superior qualities can justify the high cost.

Epoxy resins are formulated in various viscosities from thin liquids to thick pastes. Epoxy resins use a hardener or curing agent that actually enters into the reaction. With polyester resin, only a small amount of catalyst is added. A large proportion of hardener or curing agent (about 30 to 50 percent by weight or volume) is added to the epoxy resin. The volume of the cured epoxy resin will be approximately equal to the combined volume of the epoxy resin and the curing agent or hardener that was added to it. This involves considerable differences in thinking as compared to working with polyester resins. A half gallon of epoxy resin and a half gallon of hardener or curing agent is equivalent to approximately a gallon of polyester resin.

Epoxy resin offers a number of advantages over polyester resin. The epoxy has greater strength and superior adhesion. It bonds well to hardwood, metals, and glass, whereas polyester resin bonds poorly to these surfaces. Epoxy resin has lower shrinkage on curing than polyester resin, an important advantage in some applications. While cured polyester resin has good chemical resistance, epoxy has even better chemical resistance.

Epoxy resin also has a number of disadvantages as compared to polyester resin. One of these, cost, has already been mentioned. This limits the use of epoxy resin in production boat manufacturing to areas where its special properties are required, which means only when polyester resin will not suffice. Epoxy resin is compatible with polyester resin provided that one resin is allowed to fully cure before the other is added. This makes composite construction possible, using epoxy resin only where it is absolutely essential.

Epoxy resin is more difficult to work with than polyester resin. Epoxy resin requires higher temperature and more time for curing. The formulation of some epoxy resins, however, have been improved to the point where they are only slightly less convenient to use than polyester resins. Heat lamps and other flameless heating devices can be used to accelerate the curing of epoxy resins.

Safety. Epoxy resins present greater health hazards to workers than do polyester resins. Cured epoxy resin is considered innocuous physiologically. The problem occurs when the epoxy resins and curing agents or hardeners are in their liquid form. Vapor exposure can cause sensitization, skin irritations, and other problems. Skin contact can lead to dermatitis. Strict health and safety precautions should be observed whenever epoxy resins and curing agents or hardeners are used.

Epoxy resins also have a potential danger of spontaneous combustion. Proper storage is essential.

Mixing. Epoxy resins come in two parts in separate containers. One part is the basic resin. The other part is the curing agent or hardener. Depending on the particular formulation and the type of work being done, the ratio of epoxy resin to curing agent or hardener varies, usually four parts by volume of resin to one part by volume of curing agent up to about a fifty-fifty mix. The exact amount of curing agent or hardener used for a particular formulation also varies depending on desired pot life, working and curing temperatures, and other factors.

Once the two parts are combined in a container, the mixture hardens rapidly. The mixture hardens more rapidly in the container than when spread in a thin layer on a surface because the atmosphere cools the surface, reducing the heat generated in the mixture. Once the epoxy is applied in a thin layer, external heat directed at the surface (a heat lamp for instance) reduces the curing time.

Other Considerations.

■ A special epoxy thinner can be added to reduce viscosity without affecting strength or adhesion factors. Addition of up to 40 percent by volume of the epoxy thinner usually will not affect the amount of hardener to be used or the curing time.

■ A special curing agent is available to use with epoxy resin. It gives greater flexibility to the cured plastic than when a regular curing agent is used.

■ The same color pigments and thixotropic thickening powders used with polyester resins can be used with epoxy resins. A variety of epoxy putty and filler compounds are manufactured. Some boat manufacturers mix their own using regular epoxy resin and milled glass fibers or other ingredients. Epoxy resin putties are formulated for a variety of uses. There is even one that cures underwater for making emergency boat repairs.

■ Using quality epoxy products is extremely important. There are many different formulations on the market, and the handling qualities and properties of the cured resins vary widely. Most boat manufacturers find dependable brands and stick with them.

■ Epoxy resins can be formulated without reinforcing materials for use as paints, sealers, and glues. Epoxy has outstanding bonding and adhesion properties.

SOLVENTS

Acetone is commonly used as a solvent for uncured polyester resin. It is useful for cleaning tools and brushes. It should be used before the resin has set up or hardened. Acetone is also useful for removing the wax layer from a polyester fiberglass laminate if an additional layer is to be added to the laminate. Acetone is not recommended as a thinning agent for polyester resin because it evaporates rather than participates in the cure, which causes shrinkage.

Although many workers in fiberglass molding plants routinely wash their hands with acetone, this is definitely not recommended from a health and safety point of view. A special epoxy solvent is formulated for cleaning uncured epoxy resin from tools, brushes, and so on. This solvent is not recommended for hand cleaning. Special hand cleaning solutions are available for this purpose that are much safer and more pleasant to use.

MOLD RELEASE AGENT

Special paste or liquid release agents are used inside molds so that finished fiberglass moldings can be removed without sticking or bonding to the mold. Wax releasing agents and polyvinyl alcohol (PVA) are frequently used. A variety of formulations are available for specific molding applications.

CORE AND FORMING MATERIALS

A variety of core and forming materials are used in the manufacturing of fiberglass boats. Unlike the molds, become part of the finished boat moldings themselves.

The core and forming materials might or might not add structural strength to a fiberglass laminate. A plywood core in a fiberglass deck not only separates two fiberglass laminates but also adds considerable structural strength—that is, it does much more than just separate the layers of fiberglass (Fig. 4-2). Other core materials, such as plastic foams, may serve merely as nonstructural cores for shaping fiberglass stiffeners, in which case it is the fiberglass stiffener and not the core material itself that adds reinforcement

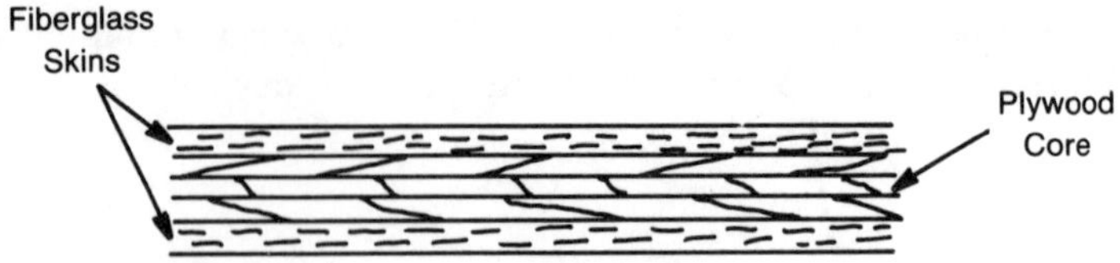

Fig. 4-2. A plywood core used in sandwich construction.

to the fiberglass laminate. Many materials serve both structural and forming functions.

Phenolic Microballoons

Phenolic microballoons are hollow microscopic balloons that can be combined with either polyester or epoxy resin to form a lightweight material that can be trowelled in place. With the cells filled with nitrogen, phenolic microballoons have a density of about 10 pounds per cubic foot. When mixed with resin, a material that will float is formed.

The phenolic microballoons make sanding much easier than if resin (with or without reinforcing material) would be used without adding the microballoons. This is useful when large areas must be shaped or faired by sanding.

Phenolic microballoons have a flourlike consistency and are sold in bulk by weight. They are frequently used in fiberglass boat manufacturing in areas where weight must be kept to a minimum while filling in large spaces. This material is fairly expensive.

Polystyrene Foamed Plastic

Rigid polystyrene foamed plastic is available in precured blocks and sheets of various densities. As a flotation material, polystyrene with a density of about 2 pounds per cubic foot is frequently used. For some applications, polystyrene of 6 to 8 pounds per cubic foot might be used.

The main advantage of polystyrene foamed plastic as compared to polyurethane and polyvinyl chloride (described next) is the lower cost. A main disadvantage is that polystyrene is attacked by polyester resins, so it cannot be used as a forming or core material when liquid (uncured) polyester resins are used. The polystyrene works satisfactorily with the more expensive epoxy resins, however. Polystyrene has less resistance to water, decay, and damage from impact than either polyurethane or polyvinyl chloride rigid plastic foams.

Polyurethane Foamed Plastic

Polyurethane foamed plastic is available in precured blocks and sheets of various densities. It's also available in foam-in-place liquids. This is accomplished by mixing polyol and toluene diisocynate (TDI) together, causing the components to foam and cure into rigid polyurethane plastic foam. It is available in pour-in-place and spray-in-place forms. Proper cure of polyurethane foam is affected by temperature, ratio of components, and other factors.

As compared to polystyrene foam, the polyurethane is usually more resistant to damage from impact, water, and decay. Polyurethane is compatible for use with polyester resins.

Neither polyurethane nor polystyrene, once cured in rigid form, can be shaped to compound surface curvatures, though they can both be shaped mechanically by sawing, filing, rasping, etc. Compartments and cavities of most any shapes and sizes can be filled with foam-in-place polyurethane.

Polyurethane foamed plastic is more expensive than polystyrene. Nevertheless, its compatibility with polyester resins makes it worth the additional cost for most fiberglass boat manufacturing.

Polyurethane rigid plastic foam is sometimes used as a core material in sandwich construction. A layer of the foam is sandwiched between two layers of fiberglass laminations (Fig. 4-3).

Polyvinyl Chloride (PVC) Foamed Plastic

For use as a sandwich core material for boat hulls, decks, and superstructures, polyvinyl chloride (PVC) foamed plastic has a number of advantages over both polystyrene and polyurethane. The PVC foamed plastic is available in a thermoplastic form. It can be formed into compound curvatures by application of heat. Even at room temperature it can be bent in simple curves without cell structures breaking down.

The closed cell structure of polyvinyl chloride foamed plastic does not allow water absorption. It does not become brittle, crum-

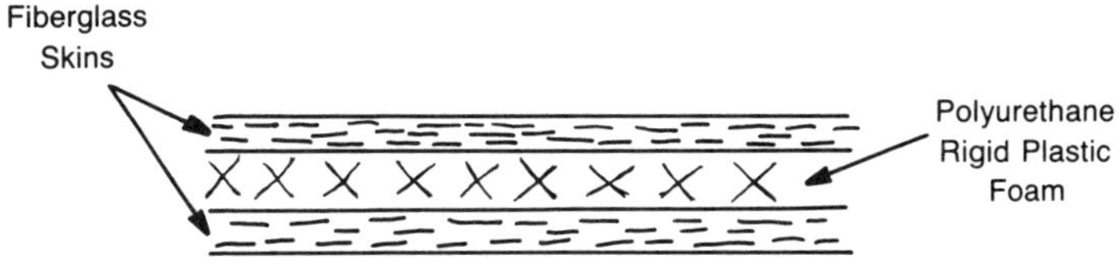

Fig. 4-3. Polyurethane rigid plastic foam used as core material in sandwich construction.

ble, or deteriorate with age, a common problem with polystyrene and, to a lesser degree, with polyurethane foams. The chemical resistance of polyvinyl chloride is better than that of either polystyrene or polyurethane. The main disadvantage of the polyvinyl chloride is that it is more expensive than either polystyrene or polyurethane.

Polyvinyl chloride foamed plastic is available in 1/4-, 3/8-, 1/2-, and 5/8-inch thick sheets, usually 36 inches by 72 inches in size.

Polyvinyl chloride rigid foamed plastic is used as a sandwich core material in some quality manufactured boats. This material has proven ideal for sandwich cores. It is also used in one-off fiberglass boat construction as a planking material that is shaped over a male plug. A fiberglass skin is then laminated over this. The plug is removed and a second fiberglass skin is added to the other side of the foam, which results in a fiberglass laminate of sandwich core construction. One-off fiberglass boat construction is detailed in Chapter 14.

Wood

Wood is frequently used as core and stiffening material in fiberglass boat construction. In early fiberglass boat construction, it was used extensively; today it is used less often. Because of problems and even failures of this material when improperly used in fiberglass construction, its merits are often debated by fiberglassing experts.

The main problem is that fiberglass and wood have very different physical and chemical properties. This becomes apparent when using wood and fiberglass in a composite construction. When the transition from wood to fiberglass boat construction was taking place, plywood boats were often sheathed on the outside only or on both sides with fiberglass. These boats did not last long because the wood almost invariably dry-rotted. Those sheathed on both sides seemed to have the shortest life expectancy. These sheaths were thin layers of fiberglass intended only for waterproofing (which they failed to provide) rather than structural strength. When used as a core and reinforcement for thicker fiberglass laminates, the results seem much better, although there can still be problems if care is not taken.

End-grain balsa blocks fiberglass boat construction (Fig. 4-4). The blocks are about 1/4 to 1/2 inch thick and are held together with a gauzelike backing that allows it to be shaped to complex curvatures in a mold or over a form. The end-grain arrangement

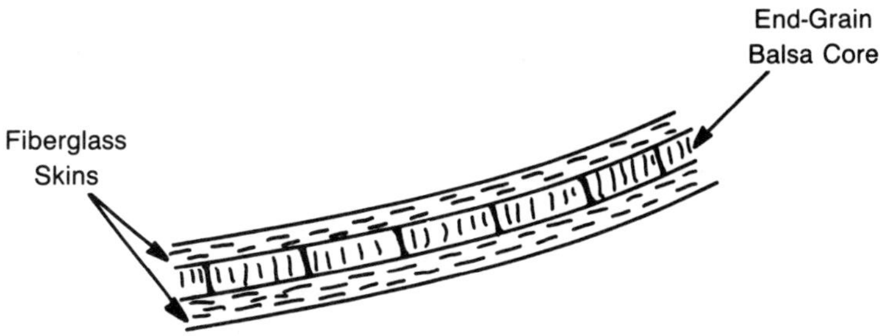

Fig. 4-4. Balsa used as a core material in sandwich construction.

allows the resin to penetrate into the balsa better. The resin also fills in the narrow spaces between blocks, which further seals off the balsa.

Plywood is commonly used as a structural core material and reinforcement for fiberglass laminates, especially for boat transoms and boat decks and superstructures (Fig. 4-5). In many cases both sides of the plywood are sheathed with fiberglass laminates in sandwich form. Unlike foamed plastic cores, the plywood itself adds considerably to the strength and stiffness of the finished composite structure.

In some applications the plywood is bonded to the fiberglass on one side only. My concern here is with plywood used as part of fiberglass laminates. Other uses of plywood, such as for bulkheads and interior structures, are detailed later in this book.

Exterior grades of plywood only should be used, even when the plywood is to be sheathed on both sides. A common problem is in bonding the first layer of fiberglass to the plywood. Because polyester resin does not bond well to wood, epoxy resin is often

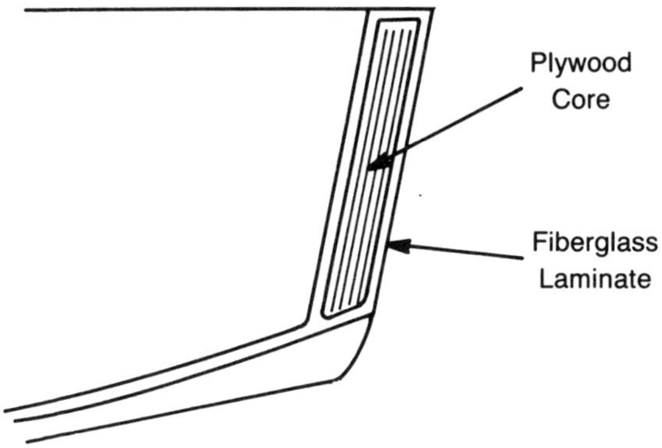

Fig. 4-5. Plywood used as a core material on transom of small boat.

used for this. After the epoxy has fully cured, polyester resin can be used for adding fiberglass layers to the laminate.

The plywood should be sealed over in such a way that the plywood does not become saturated with water. Otherwise, dry rot is likely. A special problem is in drilling holes for fasteners. These should be set in bedding compound in such a way as to prevent water leaking in around the fasteners.

Over the years I've had the opportunity to tear into a number of fiberglass moldings with plywood sandwich cores that had been used long periods of time, often 10 years or more. In some cases there were areas of dry rot, usually around fastener holes. Only in a very few cases did this lead to serious structural problems, especially if substantial fiberglass laminates were used on both sides of the plywood core. Sometimes the plywood was not bonded well to the fiberglass, but only in a few cases did this cause serious problems. Epoxy resin has the advantage of not only giving a better bond, but it also provides a better water barrier to protect the plywood.

Various types of softwood and hardwood cores and reinforcing members are also used in fiberglass boat construction. Wood frames and beams are often added to fiberglass moldings after the moldings are completed.

Bonding wood members to fiberglass, especially hardwoods, can be difficult with polyester resin. For this reason, the more expensive epoxy resin is sometimes used. Substantial fiberglass laminates are required to fully protect the wood from moisture. This keeps swelling and cracking of the wood from damaging the surrounding fiberglass laminate.

The wood is sometimes treated with a wood preservative in an attempt to prevent dry rot. Most wood preservatives make it difficult to adequately bond fiberglass to the wood, although opinions vary on this point. Some fiberglass boat manufacturers do treat the wood with a wood preservative, others don't.

It's important to use only dry, thoroughly seasoned woods. Softwoods bond best. Hardwoods do not bond well with polyester resin; epoxy resin should be used. Select wood for the particular job at hand.

Other Core and Forming Materials

Other core and forming materials include metal and plastics that are compatible with polyester resin or other resins being used. Because polyester resin does not usually bond well to metals, the more expensive epoxy resin is called for. Many plastic materials also present difficult bonding situations. Sometimes even epoxy resin does not bond well. For these and other reasons, metals and plastics are not often used in modern fiberglass boat construction as core and forming materials. There are some exceptions to this, however. Other possible core materials include paper and cardboard, although these are not generally used in boat constructions.

In the early days of fiberglass boat construction, many materials were tried and proved to be unsatisfactory. For example, ferrous metals tend to bleed rust through the surrounding fiberglass. Some materials proved too costly or difficult to bond. In sandwich construction, bonding strength must be considered carefully because it affects the shear strength of the finished composite laminate.

CONTACT MOLDING

Most fiberglass boat hulls, decks, superstructures, and other components are contact-molded. Most production fiberglass boat manufacturers use female or cavity molds rather than one-off male molds or forms (which will be detailed in Chapter 14).

In contact molding, the fiberglass lay-up is in or over a mold without pressure, other than contact pressure, being applied to the side of the laminate that is away from the mold. Basically, the weight of the reinforcing materials and resin holds the mixture against the mold surface until it cures.

Hand Lay-Up and Spray-Up Methods

There are two basic methods of contact molding: *hand lay-up* and *spray-up.* Hand lay-up is, at present, still considered to be the best method. In this method the resin is applied to the mold surface and reinforcing material by brush, rollers, squeegees, and other similar means. The main disadvantage of this method is that it is labor costly. Fiberglass lay-up work is unpleasant work, and it is often difficult to get workers to do this job.

In the spray-up method, the resin and reinforcing material are sprayed on the mold surface with a *chopper gun.* With this device, resin, catalyst, and acetone are supplied under pressure to the nozzle for spraying. The acetone is used for cleaning the nozzle and does not mix with the resin that is sprayed into the mold. There is a special release button for the acetone. The spray gun mixes the catalyst and resin in the desired proportion and sprays it out a nozzle. The second part of the device is the chopper, which chops up fiberglass strands or rovings into short lengths of chopped fibers and combines them with the resin spray at the nozzle of the gun. The result is a spray-up of a material similar to a hand laid-up mat laminate.

The spray-up method results in laminates that are weaker than those laid up by hand with cloth, woven roving, and even mat reinforcing materials. Nevertheless, this device is widely used in fiberglass boat manufacturing, especially for boats that sell in lower price ranges for the particular type and size of boat. Another disadvantage is that the chopper gun equipment and necessary safety equipment for industrial use are quite expensive.

The advantages are that it greatly speeds up molding work. One worker can do the job that requires a number of workers by the hand lay-up method. The cost of the equipment is not prohibitive when these factors are considered.

Some manufacturers use both spray-up and hand lay-up for the same molding. For example, woven roving layers in a laminate can be laid up by hand. The "mat" layers between the layers of woven roving can be sprayed up. This reduces the amount of hand labor considerably and can still result in a molding with adequate strength.

For hand lay-up, spray-up, and combination methods, the gel coat resin is usually sprayed onto the mold surface.

The equipment and tooling for contact molding are much less expensive than that required for pressure molding, as detailed later in this chapter. Large fiberglass structures, such as large boat hulls, can be constructed by contact molding that would be impractical (at the present time) using pressure molding.

Contact molding does have some disadvantages, however. One of these is that the back side of the laminate (side away from the mold surface) is not as smooth and fair as the side against the mold surface because the opposite side of the laminate can't be molded during curing.

Another disadvantage is that contact molding is slower than pressure molding. Contact molding also requires more hand labor and is somewhat less accurate.

Molds

There are two types of molds for contact molding. In one type the smooth and finished side of the laminate goes against the mold surface. This method is used for almost all production fiberglass boat manufacturing. The required molds are expensive, but once the

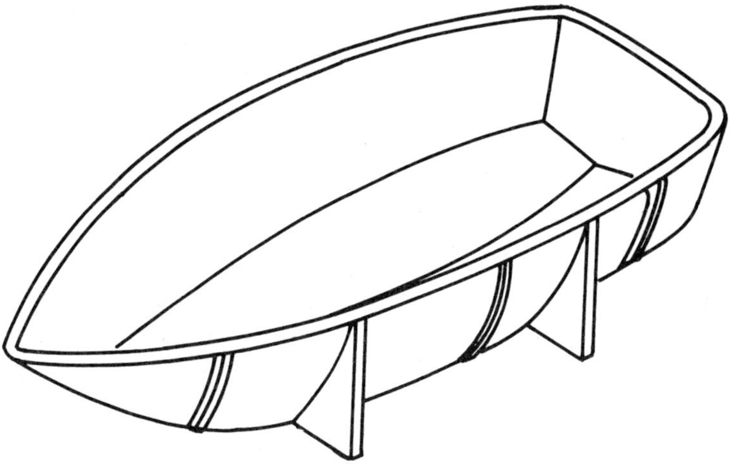

Fig. 4-6. Female or cavity mold for a boat hull.

molds are constructed, the same molds can be used over and over again. Figure 4-6 shows a typical female or cavity mold for a boat hull that uses this type of molding. A typical cockpit mold is shown in Fig. 4-7. Notice that it is shaped like what might be considered a male or plug mold, though there is an important difference. The desired smooth and finished side goes against the mold surface.

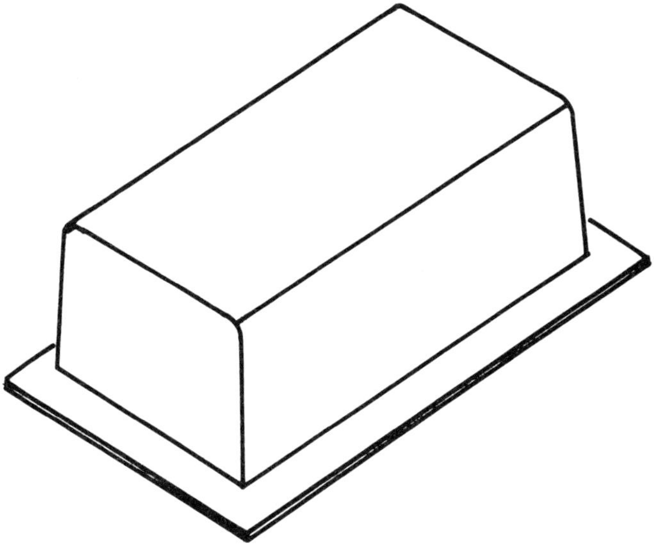

Fig. 4-7. A typical cockpit well mold.

This method eliminates extensive sanding. A smooth finished surface matching that of the mold is on the molding. A color gel coating can even be sprayed into the mold over the release agent before the fiberglass laminate is laid up.

Imagine the problem a manufacturer would face if this were done in reverse. With the boat hull, the desired finished outside would be the rough side away from the mold. It would take considerable sanding to smooth and fair the hull, not to mention the problem of adding a color coating. This is the problem faced in most one-off boatbuilding methods (see Chapter 14). The exchange is basically an expensive female or cavity mold from which many identical moldings can be made or inexpensive molds or forms that require considerable sanding and fairing and usually allow only one boat to be constructed, especially if the form becomes part of the boat. Even if more than one hull can be constructed from the same male mold or plug, each will be slightly different from the sanding and fairing operations.

Sanding and fairing large areas of fiberglass is so expensive and difficult to do well that most fiberglass boat manufacturers go to extremes to avoid it. For example, you want a finished gel coat surface on both the outside and inside of a hull. To accomplish this by contact molding, two separate molds and moldings are used: one for the outside of the hull and a separate liner that fits inside this (Fig. 4-8). The two moldings are then bonded together to form a hull that has smooth gel coat surfaces on both sides.

Most production fiberglass boat manufacturing is accomplished by using female or cavity molds. This means that the desired finished side is formed against the mold surface, regardless of whether the mold surface is shaped like a pan or a plug. A quality female or cavity mold can cost a lot of money to make, but hundreds of fairly accurate duplicates can then be made of moldings from the same mold. In the case of a boat hull, the mold is the form for making the moldings, which are boat hulls.

The moldings must, however, be made one at a time. In a hull mold, one hull molding is laid up, usually over a period of time. A hand lay-up of a large boat hull might take several days to a week or more to lay up. After the lay-up, the molding is allowed to cure and is then removed from the mold. Then the next molding can be started in the mold.

It is not unusual for a hundred or even a thousand moldings of a boat hull or other components to be made from a single mold. There are limits to the useful life of a mold, however. Eventually

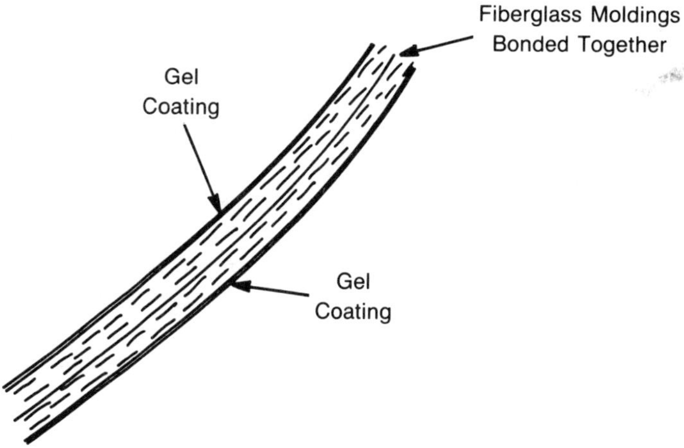

Fig. 4-8. Two separate fiberglass moldings bonded together to give gel coat surfaces on both sides.

they wear out or become damaged and have to be repaired or replaced.

Most manufactured fiberglass boats start with a designer's plans. From the lines and tables of offsets provided by the plan, a mold can be constructed. Most modern designs used by fiberglass boat manufacturers were created especially for fiberglass construction.

This is not the only possibility, however. A mold or series of molds (such as one for hull, another for deck and cabin, and so on) can be taken from an existing boat, regardless of whether it is made of fiberglass, wood, metal, ferrocement, or another material. Problems can arise, however, if a boat designed for construction in one material is not suitable for fiberglass construction. The method can be used if certain design and construction standards can be met.

The general trend today is to design boats especially for construction of a certain material, as detailed in Chapter 3. With fiberglass, this makes the best use of the material, sound structure, and easy molding.

From the design lines, plugs are made in the shape of the finished surfaces desired for the fiberglass moldings. Lips, flanges, overlaps, and other details for the later assembly of separate moldings must be considered at this stage.

Plugs

The plug for a boat hull mold looks just like a boat hull on the outside. This is why an actual existing boat could be used as a plug for making a mold. In fact, when a mold becomes worn or damaged beyond repair, a replacement mold can be made by using a molding that was previously made in the mold as a plug. Fiberglass boat manufacturers often use this method. More than one mold for the same molding can be constructed to speed construction, which is beneficial since storage space at many fiberglass boat manufacturing plants is limited.

Plugs for making molds can be constructed from wood, plaster of paris, concrete, clay, various plastics, or from a combination of materials. The plug must be a duplicate of the desired shape of the molding to be made from the mold. The mold will be taken from the plug. Any lack of fairness or unevenness in the plug will be transferred to the mold and in turn to moldings made in the mold. While some changes can be made in the mold itself, this is extremely difficult and best avoided. Time should be taken to get the plug as exact as possible.

Why not skip the plug and just make the mold? Although extremely difficult, this has been done. You are working with the shape surrounding the desired molding, however, rather than with the shape to be molded. This is difficult to do. In most cases, making a plug first works out best, and most fiberglass boat manufacturers use this method.

Tooling of quality plugs is expensive, but this job must be done properly to get a quality mold. This cost is usually absorbed by the production of many moldings from a single mold.

Making the Mold

The plug is used as a mold for the mold. Molds can be made from a variety of materials, but boat molds are usually made from fiberglass with wood, steel, or other reinforcements. The mold is constructed by laying up a fiberglass laminate over or on the plug. The term "plug" means the shape of the desired finished object that is to be molded. A boat hull looks like the outside of a boat hull. A plug for a cockpit looks like a tub or pan. A plug for a flat surface looks like a flat surface.

Because polyester resin has some shrinkage, epoxy resin is sometimes used to lay up a mold.

The plug is coated with a wax and polished out. A polyvinyl alcohol (PVA) parting agent is sprayed over this. This allows the mold to be removed from the plug when the lay-up is finished and cured.

A tooling gel coat of a color that contrasts sharply with the gel coat colors to be used on moldings is applied next. This is a special, tough coating formulated for use on molds. It is usually sprayed on.

After the tooling gel coat has cured, a layer of fiberglass mat is added. The mat layer is wetted out with resin. This mat layer gives a smooth mold surface. When cloth and especially woven roving are used, the weave patterns often show through.

Additional layers of reinforcing material are laminated to this with resin. Alternating layers of mat and woven roving give a mold that is strong and stiff. Construction must be such that the mold will not flex, sag, or otherwise change shape when a molding is being laid up.

After the mold has been laid up, additional reinforcing is added. This may be from wood, metal, or other materials in the form of ribs, frames, and so on. The reinforcing members often serve additional functions—a base or stand, a frame for wheels to move the mold from one area to another, a frame that allows the mold to be rolled or turned to any desired angle.

An individual mold can be in one piece if there are no undercuts. Even with undercuts, the mold could be removed from the plug by destroying the plug, but this would not solve the problem of later removal of moldings without destroying the mold.

If there are undercuts, the mold can be constructed in two or more pieces, which can be bolted or clamped together for molding work. The mold is then taken apart each time a cured molding must be removed.

Some molds are made in more than one piece to eliminate difficult molding jobs. The individual pieces are then molded separately and bonded or otherwise attached together later. Ideally, a boat would be molded in one piece, including hull, deck, cabin structure, cockpit, etc. This is impractical because the molding layup would have to be done inside a tunnel-shaped mold with closed ends. Usually there are at least two separate moldings for the main boat shell: one for the hull and another for the deck and cabin structures. Sometimes there are three or more separate molds. Adequately attaching separate moldings together can be difficult, however, so the number of separate moldings used for the main boat shell should be kept to a minimum. The assembly of separate moldings must also be taken into account in the tooling for the plugs and in the molds.

A special trouble area has been the molding of hulls in two half sections, which are later bonded together. This method is sometimes used to avoid lay-up work in deep keel areas and other difficult places. Later bonding of the separate moldings together is difficult, though, and a number of boats made in this manner have split apart in use.

Two factors must be taken into account in the design and moldmaking stages: First, molds can be constructed so that they can be taken apart to remove moldings that have undercuts and so on. The second factor is the assembly of separate moldings that will be made from the molds. This assembly is detailed later in this chapter.

When the lay-up of the mold is completed, the resin is allowed to cure. Necessary reinforcements are often added to the back side of the mold before the mold is removed from the plug. Attachment of reinforcements can be made using fiberglass bonding strips and angles and other means. Methods for bonding reinforcements to fiberglass laminates are detailed later in this chapter.

Lay-Up of a Molding

A completed mold is prepared for making the first molding. Fiberglass lay-up work is best done on a level or near-level surface. Inclined and vertical surfaces increase the difficulty. Most difficult, and generally avoided, are overhead surfaces.

In fiberglass boat manufacturing, the mold is angled so that the lay-up work area is as near level or horizontal as possible. Hoists and other special equipment are used to change the angles of boat hull molds and other large molds. Some large hull molds are mounted on large rings or wheels that allow the mold to be rolled to desired working angles.

Before laying up a molding, the mold is thoroughly cleaned. Then wax is applied to the mold surface and buffed out. Next, polyvinyl alcohol (PVA) or other parting agent is sprayed on. This is especially important for the first few laminates. Wax along is sufficient to remove moldings from the mold later on. Improper application of the release agent can make it very difficult to remove a molding from a mold, and could damage the mold and/or molding.

Next, a color gel coating is usually sprayed into the mold. A recent trend is to eliminate the gel coating and then spray paint the molding with two-part polyurethane paint after the molding has been removed from the mold. The reasons for this include the difficulty of applying a gel coat and frequent cracking, crazing, and color fading problems. The gel coating is often damaged in some areas when the molding is removed fro the mold. This necessitates difficult touch-up work. Two-part polyurethane gives a gel coat-like appearance that is often more durable than traditional gel coat applications. The use of gel coating is still the method used by most production fiberglass boat manufacturers, however.

The gel coat is applied to the mold surface and becomes the finished side of the molding. The gel coat is allowed to cure. This is usually an air-inhibited resin so the surface on the side away from the mold will be tacky.

To prevent cracking and crazing, the gel coat must be sprayed on in a very thin, even layer. This is a touchy and difficult area in fiberglass boat manufacturing. A worker who has mastered the "art" of properly applying gel coat is a valued person in most plants.

Fiberglass mat forms the next layer of the laminate. Sometimes a lightweight cloth with a smooth finish is used instead of mat. Some manufacturers use a chopper gun spray-up instead of a hand lay-up of the mat.

The usual method for hand lay-up is to apply a thin layer of resin to the gel coat with a brush or roller. The mat is placed over the wet resin. Additional resin is applied to the mat until it is properly saturated with resin and smoothed out.

The hand lay-up of large moldings is done by a team of workers. To keep seams in reinforcing material to a minimum, the mat often runs the full length of the molding. Depending on the particular application and other factors, either butt or lap joints join separate pieces of mat reinforcing material. This becomes somewhat less crucial as the laminating gets further away from the gel coating.

From this point on, a laminating schedule is followed. Careful control and inventory must be taken so as not to leave out or add extra layers to the laminate or to use the wrong reinforcing material.

The mat layer might be followed by a cloth layer. Sometimes the cloth layer is allowed to harden before the next layer is applied. Other times two or more layers are applied before they have time to cure. After the cloth layer, another layer of mat might be used. For a hull laminate on a large boat, the remainder of the laminate is often alternating layers of woven roving and mat. The total number of layers and weights of reinforcing material used on a particular laminate depends on size and many other factors. The hull for a 30-foot sailboat will usually be at least 1/4 inch thick near deck level and 1/2 inch or more at the keel. This varies considerably with type of boat, size, design, etc.

Considerable care must be taken to produce quality lay-up

work. The proper ratio of resin to reinforcing material, which varies depending on type of reinforcing material used, must be maintained. If too much resin is used in comparison to the glass reinforcing material being saturated, the laminate becomes "resin rich" and brittle.

Instead of using hand lay-up, sometimes the entire laminate is sprayed up with a chopper gun for some small hulls. This method has even been used for large boat hulls, though it has largely proved inadequate. Most manufacturers producing large boat hulls and other moldings entirely by spray-up have gone out of business because of the many failures of these boats. Unfortunately, there are hundreds of existing boats still around with sprayed-up moldings, and a few boats are still manufactured by this method. A number of manufacturers who primarily use the hand lay-up method also use spray-up with a chopper gun for less crucial moldings or combine hand lay-up and spray-up in the same moldings.

A highly skilled operator is required for chopper gun spray-up work. The laminate must be sprayed up to the desired thickness without having a resin-rich or resin-starved mixture. The ratio of chopped glass fiber reinforcing strands and resin is controlled by the operator by adjusting the gun.

The hand lay-up of large moldings presents special problems. Even though the reinforcing materials might run the full length of the moldings, a number of seams still are required. When separate pieces of reinforcing material are joined, they are usually overlapped about 1 to 6 inches. An uneven thickness would result if a number of overlaps were made in one area. To avoid this, the overlaps are spread out, either in set patterns or at random. The patterns of overlaps can also be used to give strength in areas where it is most needed.

Moldings for boat hulls, cabin and deck structures, and other components require laminates of varying thicknesses. With a hull molding, the laminate might be 1/2 inch or more in the keel area and taper to 1/4 inch near deck level. This presents added lay-up difficulties. The high cost of materials makes it necessary to put them where they will do the most good.

The designed lay-up must be followed closely. Just one extra layer of reinforcing material added to a large laminate could add considerably to both the labor and material cost.

If the laminate is to be a sandwich core construction, the core material (balsa, rigid plastic foam, or plywood) is added to the first skin by setting the core material into wet resin. The second fiberglass skin is then laminated in place over the core material. This is done while the molding is still in the mold.

After the laminate has been completed, it is allowed to cure for several days before being removed from the mold. Many fiberglass boat moldings require additional reinforcement, such as bulkheads, beams, stringers, ribs, frames, hat sections, etc. Others require fiberglass liners. These reinforcements are added either before or after a molding is removed from the mold.

Removing the Molding

Fiberglass boat manufacturers want to remove moldings from molds as soon as possible so that other moldings can be started in the same molds. If a molding is removed too soon, however, it can be damaged or ruined.

Moldings are often difficult to remove from molds even though the molds were waxed and a release agent applied before the lay-up. Hoists and other mechanical lifting devices are used for breaking a molding from a mold. A boat hull, for example, might have the plywood bulkheads bonded in place while it is still in the mold. Attachments are then made to the bulkheads, and a hoisting device works the hull molding free of the mold. The sounds of a large boat hull molding breaking free from a mold can be alarming.

After the molding has been removed from the mold, the wax and polyvinyl alcohol or other release agents are cleaned from the gel coat. Perfection is difficult to achieve in contact molding. Most moldings require at least some touch-up work on gel coatings. Some moldings may be rejected for one reason or another, although this is rare. Repairs will be required on some moldings to make them satisfactory. Standards vary. It seems safe to say that some moldings from the same mold come out better than others (Fig. 4-9).

After a molding has been removed from a mold, the mold is then prepared for the next lay-up. It might seem that the time required for molding would hold up fiberglass boat production, and this is sometimes the case. But assembling the moldings into completed boats and added fittings and other components is a more common cause of bottlenecks.

The quality of fiberglass boat moldings depends on the molding method used, original design of the mold and molding, quality of molds and other equipment, quality of materials used, care and skill in fabrication, and many other factors. Fiberglass boat manufacturing is a highly competitive business. Quality costs more money to produce, which means a higher selling price. A lower qual-

Fig. 4-9. Molded fiberglass hull for 42-foot Allied sailboat. (Courtesy of International Cruising Yachts, Inc.)

ity boat produced at a lower cost might result in greater profits, however.

REINFORCING FIBERGLASS LAMINATES

Fiberglass laminates are very flexible, about twenty times more flexible than steel with the same strength and about six times more flexible than aluminum with the same strength. Its flexibility is a major design factor in fiberglass boat moldings.

Fiberglass laminates are springy but not rubbery. They have a flexibility similar to that of plywood, though fiberglass laminates are more costly and stronger than plywood. In most constructions the fiberglass must be thinner than if plywood were used. Because it is too expensive to achieve the necessary stiffness by increasing the thickness of the laminate, some other type of extra support and stiffening is needed.

A variety of methods are used for stiffening fiberglass boat moldings. Some are incorporated in the design and shape of the laminate; others are external additions.

The shape of a molding has important bearings on the resulting stiffness. A curved panel or a panel with corrugations in it has greater stiffness than a flat panel of the same thickness. Corrugations, such as those shown in Fig. 4-10, are frequently used to add stiffness to powerboat hull bottoms. This adds a lot of stiffness

Fig. 4-10. Corrugations add stiffness to a fiberglass panel.

with minimal increase in weight and cost over that of molding a flat panel. The fiberglass lay-up in the mold is more difficult, however.

Hull shapes with simple and compound curves can add considerable stiffness as compared with a similar hull with flat sections. Yet curved moldings are not much more difficult to lay up than flat sections. Fiberglass laminating works well with gradual curves and angles; it is the sharp corners and angles that are difficult to mold. This reverses the situation in plywood boat construction where hard chines and large flat areas are the rule. A fiberglass boat constructed to the same shape would require an extra thick

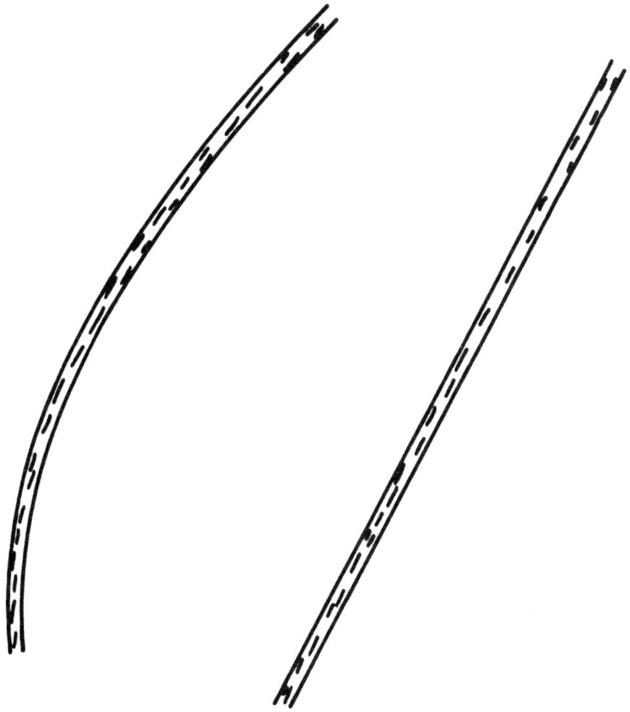

Fig. 4-11. A curved fiberglass panel has greater stiffness than a flat panel of the same thickness.

laminate and/or a large amount of extra stiffening by means of added frames, bulkheads, and so on. Curved sections add stiffness to a fiberglass laminate with minimal increase in weight and cost over that of molding a flat panel (Fig. 4-11).

Increasing the thickness of a fiberglass laminate beyond a certain point is a very costly way to increase stiffness. It also adds an undue amount of extra weight to the laminate. It is often practical to add thickness selectively to certain areas of the laminate, however. Contact molding allows adding additional layers to areas of a laminate where more stiffness is needed.

When adding thickness to a laminate, abrupt changes in thickness should be avoided to prevent a stress concentration at a single point, also known as a *hard spot.* Changes in thickness should be gradual. This can be achieved by progressively adding larger and larger pieces of fiberglass reinforcing material to the laminate (Fig. 4-12). Progressively smaller pieces of reinforcing material could also be added, but this leaves more open edges of reinforcing material, which might tend to delaminate.

A molded-in flange at the edge of a laminate (Fig. 4-13) stiffens the edge of the laminate. This method is frequently used along the edges of hull and deck moldings in areas where the hull and deck will be bonded together.

Sandwich core construction is another way to add stiffness to a molding. In this method, the two fiberglass skins are positioned apart by placing a core material in between. An effective sandwich core construction links the two skins together. When properly designed and constructed, a stiffer laminate is formed than when the two skins are side by side in a single laminate. If a lightweight balsa or rigid plastic foam core material is used, very little weight is added for the considerable gain in stiffness. Sandwich core con-

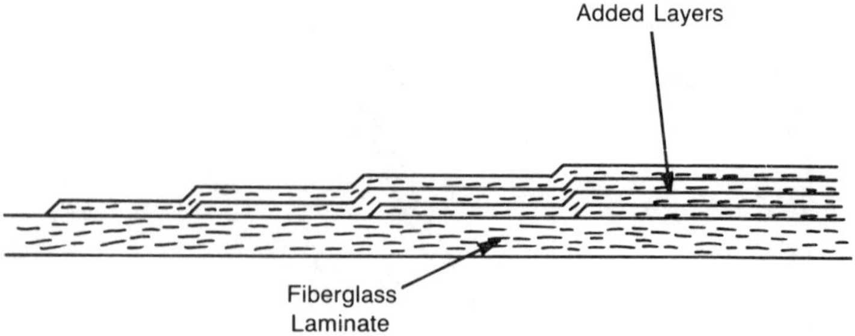

Fig. 4-12. A gradual change in thickness of laminate is achieved by using progressively larger pieces of reinforcing material.

Fig. 4-13. A molded flange at the edge of the laminate stiffens the laminate.

struction also adds insulation and sometimes buoyancy.

To be effective, the core material must provide a certain amount of structural support to hold the two fiberglass skins in position. The entire sandwich should act as a single structural unit. The bonding of the core material to the fiberglass must provide adequate shear strength. The core material itself must also have adequate shear strength.

Sandwich core construction also creates problems for attaching things and using fasteners. These can cause the two fiberglass skins to pull apart from the core or squeeze the two skins toward each other to crush the core material. Methods for solving these problems are detailed later in this chapter.

ADDING STIFFENERS TO FIBERGLASS MOLDINGS

Even after molding in stiffness, additional stiffening might be required for both single-skin and sandwich core moldings.

Plywood Bulkheads

Plywood bulkheads are frequently used in fiberglass boats. These structural members attach not only to hulls, but also to deck and cabin structures and elsewhere. Sometimes the plywood bulkheads are the primary stiffening and strengthening members for the fiberglass moldings.

Plywood bulkheads are commonly attached to the fiberglass moldings with fiberglass bonding strips. These strips, usually 12 inches wide, form an angle between the bulkhead and the fiberglass molding with half the width attached to the plywood and the other half to the fiberglass laminate. This fiberglass reinforcing material is bonded in position with resin.

High stress areas or hard spots might form in the fiberglass in the area where the plywood bulkhead meets the fiberglass molding. This is caused by the slight expansion and contraction of the fiberglass laminate with temperature changes, while there is almost no expansion and contraction of the heavy plywood. The twisting and working of the boat molding when the boat is in use causes further stress. To prevent this, a space is left or a polyurethane rigid plastic foam padding is used between the plywood and the fiberglass molding. The plywood bulkhead is cut short, about 1/4 to 3/8 inch, and the padding is placed in the gap. The padding is shaped to give a more gradual angle for the fiberglass bonding strips.

To gradually taper the fiberglass angle strips into the fiberglass molding, progressively wider strips of reinforcing material are used (Fig. 4-14). This avoids an abrupt change in thickness and spreads the load over a wider area of the molding to which the bulkhead is being attached.

Major bulkheads are bonded in place on both sides. Minor bulkheads and other similar plywood attachments, such as the top of

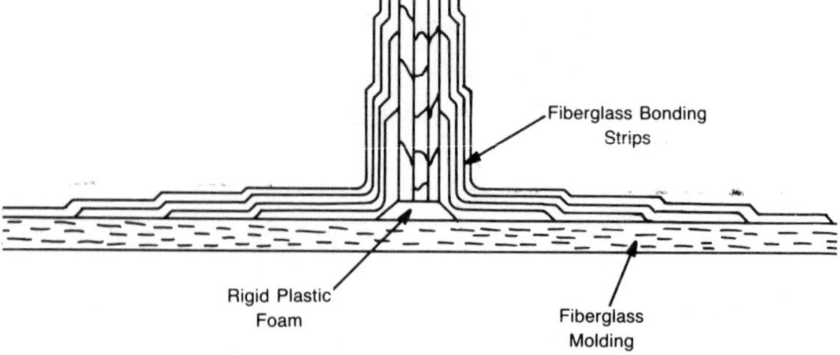

Fig. 4-14. Method for bonding plywood bulkhead to fiberglass molding.

berths and counters, might be bonded on one or both sides, depending on the particular situation.

This method of attaching plywood bulkheads to fiberglass hulls, though still in common use, seems to be losing favor. The recent trend is for fiberglass boat manufacturers to use molded liners, as detailed later in this chapter. The liners are bonded to the shell moldings, and plywood bulkheads, if used, are bolted to the fiberglass liners. For the manufacturer, bonding plywood bulkheads to hull and other moldings present difficult finishing problems, such as sanding or covering up the fiberglass bonding strips on the plywood bulkheads.

Molded Fiberglass Stiffeners

Molded fiberglass stiffeners are frequently used to stiffen boat hull moldings and other components. The stiffener is laid up in a mold. After it has cured and been removed from the mold, it is bonded in place to the hull or other molding either before or after the molding is removed from the mold.

Molded fiberglass stiffeners come in various designs, sizes, and shapes. When properly designed and constructed, they can be very effective, adding considerable stiffness without undue increase in weight. They also serve additional purposes, such as adding strength to the molding, serving as a mounting base for an engine or other equipment, and providing a means for attaching seats, bulkheads, and other items.

Molded fiberglass stiffeners are bonded in place. One way to accomplish this is to set the stiffener in place in a wetted-out layer of fiberglass reinforcing material. The stiffener could also be mechanically fastened in place, but this is not ordinarily done in fiberglass boat construction. For a boat hull, it would mean drilling holes through the hull for bolts or other fasteners, something that is best not done.

The stiffeners are designed and bonded in place in such a way that the original molding being stiffened retains its designed shape. The contact areas between the molding being stiffened and the molded stiffener is large and abrupt changes in thickness of laminate should be avoided. In areas of contact, the stiffener tapers to the molding being stiffened (Fig. 4-15). Hard spots are avoided as the molding, especially a hull molding, works during use. If high stress areas are present, the laminate could fail.

Hollow spaces between molded stiffeners and moldings that

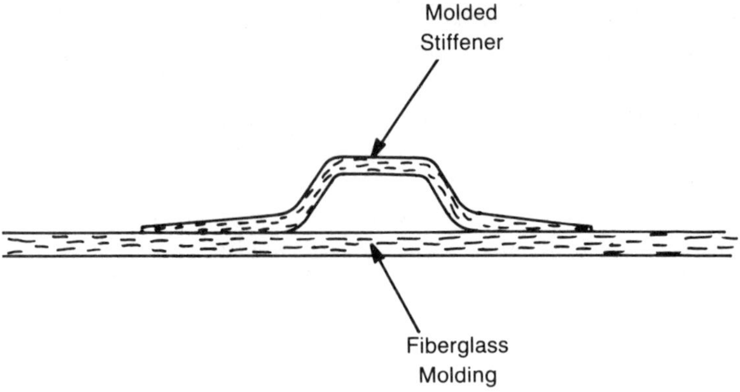

Fig. 4-15. Molded stiffener tapers to molding being reinforced.

are being stiffened are filled with rigid plastic foam. This can give positive flotation to some boats.

Stiffeners Laminated in Place Over Core Materials

Stiffeners can also be laminated in place over the core materials. In some cases, the core material adds strength; in other cases it is used merely as a male mold or form for laminating the fiberglass stiffener in place.

The molded fiberglass stiffeners described in this chapter have a molded, finished side that is usually gel coated. Molding stiffeners in place is akin to one-off boat construction. The desired finished side is away from the mold or form and does not have a molded appearance. This may or may not be important, depending on where the stiffener is used.

A variety of core materials can be used, but most fiberglass boat manufacturers stick to wood and rigid plastic foam. The stiffener can be added to the molding to be stiffened either before or after it has been removed from the mold.

Figure 4-16 shows a typical hat-section stiffener. This stiffener is half round, but shapes such as rectangular and triangular can be used. The stiffeners can also form web and other patterns.

Stiffeners are designed to give maximum stiffening and support while keeping weight addition to a minimum. The manufacturer also strives to be cost, material, and labor efficient.

Special care must be taken when using heavy beams of wood as cores for stiffeners because wood has different physical properties than fiberglass. First the area of the fiberglass laminate where the stiffener is to be added must be stiffened with extra layers of fiberglass laminated to the original laminate.

A typical procedure for adding a stiffener is to first shape the core material, be it wood, rigid plastic foam, or some other material. The core material is then bonded in position by setting it down in reinforcing material wetted out with resin, by epoxy gluing it in place, or by merely setting it in position.

The stiffener is next laminated in place with strips of fiberglass reinforcing material. The particular lay-up depends on the stiffener. It might be three or four layers of 1 1/2-ounce-per-square-foot mat for a small stiffener in a noncrucial area. Heavy wood beams would probably include fiberglass cloth and/or woven roving in the laminate.

Progressively wider strips of fiberglass reinforcing material are used. The narrowest strip goes on first. Catalyzed resin is first applied to the core material and areas of the fiberglass molding where the strip will be bonded. The reinforcing material is then set in place. Additional resin is applied until the reinforcing material is properly saturated. The material is smoothed out and any air bubbles are worked out.

The next wider strip of reinforcing material is then applied, either before or after the first layer has set up. An experienced fiberglass worker can properly apply three or more layers before the resin of the first layer hardens.

This procedure continues until all layers of reinforcing material needed for the particular stiffener have been applied. By applying progressively wider layers of reinforcing material, the laminate tapers to the molding being stiffened. Only the edges of the top layer are exposed. Edges of reinforcing material are most subject to delaminating, so these should be kept to a minimum.

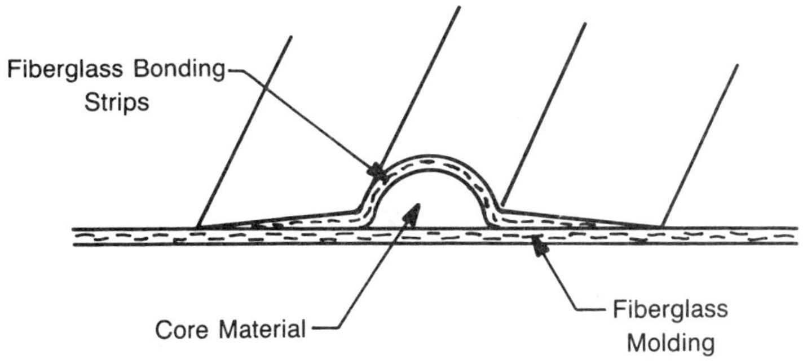

Fig. 4-16. Hat-section stiffener is molded in place over a core material.

This method gives better bonding to the molding being stiffened than molding the stiffeners first and then bonding them to the molding being stiffened. The main disadvantage of molding the stiffeners in place is the unfinished appearance. To sand these and give a finish similar to that of a molded gel coat surface is a long and involved job, one that most fiberglass boat manufacturers go out of their way to avoid.

Laminating Stiffeners in Place with Removable Forms and Molds

This method for laminating stiffeners in place allows the forms or molds to be used over and over again. A typical angle mold or form (Fig. 4-17) attaches to the molding to be stiffened by clamps, props, or other means. A release agent is applied to the contact surface of the fiberglass angle mold or form so that it can be removed after the lay-up of the stiffener is completed. The angle stiffener is then laid up using strips of fiberglass reinforcing material, which are wetted out with catalyzed resin. The reinforcing materials used and the number of layers depends on the particular stiffener. In most cases, progressively wider and wider pieces of reinforcing material are used to form a taper into the laminate being stiffened. After the angle stiffener has been allowed to cure, the angle mold or form is removed.

Sometimes a second angle is molded against the first angle to form an upside down "T" section (Fig. 4-18). Before the second angle is laid up, all wax is first removed from the contact area of the first angle section.

A stiffener with two angles shaped like a "Z" can be laminated in place using a removable mold in a similar manner (Fig. 4-19). Other shapes are also possible.

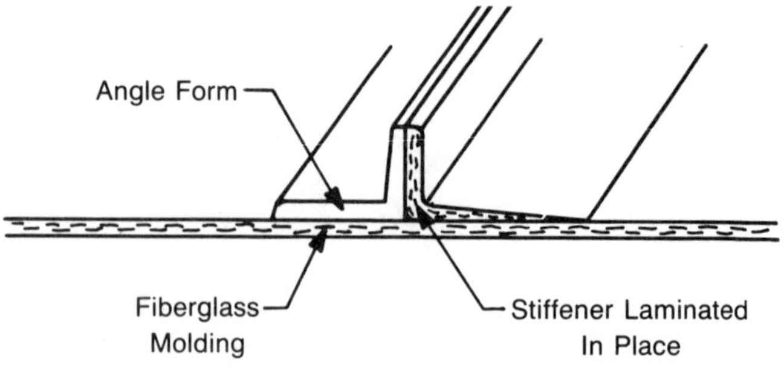

Fig. 4-17. Angle form used to laminate stiffener in place.

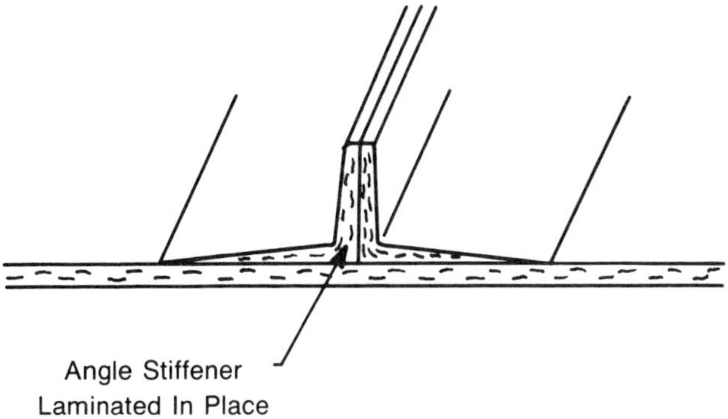

Fig. 4-18. A second angle stiffener is laminated in place using the first stiffener as a form.

Adding Braces, Frames, Knees, and Ribs

A variety of other stiffeners and reinforcing members can also be used. Corner braces or knees can reinforce the transom areas of fiberglass dinghies, as shown in Fig. 4-20. Frames and ribs of various shapes and sizes are possible. These are often made of wood and bonded to fiberglass moldings with fiberglass bonding strips. These members must be well designed and constructed if they are to effectively stiffen, strengthen, and support fiberglass moldings without creating high stress areas that could deform or damage the fiberglass laminate. Appearance may or may not be important, depending on how and where the member is to be added.

When using braces, frames, knees, ribs, and other similar members made from wood or metal, the different physical properties of the materials should be considered.

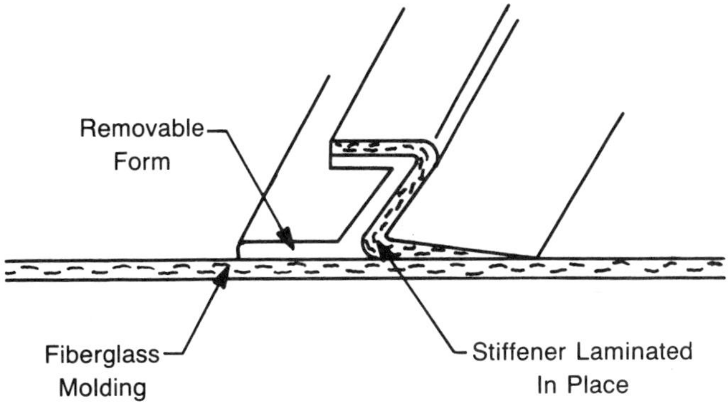

Fig. 4-19. A double-angle stiffener is laminated in place.

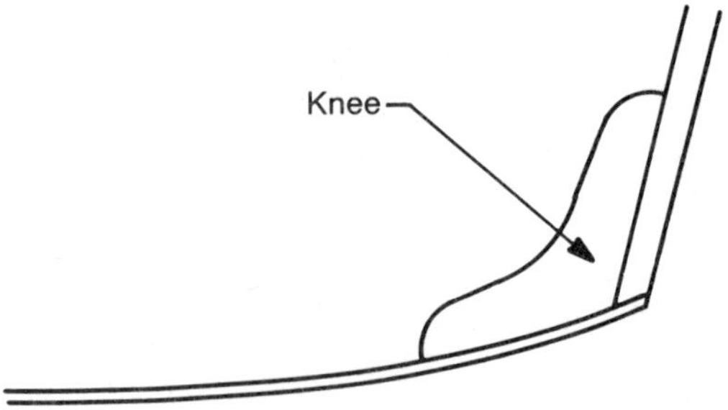

Fig. 4-20. Knee used to reinforce a transom on a dinghy.

Molded Fiberglass Liners

Most fiberglass boat manufacturers try to avoid the stiffening methods previously described—except for the molded fiberglass stiffeners—especially if they show in the finished product. A lot of hand labor is required, and unless considerable care is taken, they can leave much to be desired in the way of appearance. To get around these problems, many manufacturers make extensive use of molded fiberglass liners.

Molded fiberglass liners are essentially molded fiberglass stiffeners but are designed to serve additional purposes. They can give a good appearance; provide a means for attaching things; serve as interior furnishings, such as galley counters, berths, and shower stalls; and so on.

The main problem faced by most manufacturers is that the contact molding method normally used gives only one molded finished side to each molding. This is the side that was in contact with the mold surface.

The basic idea of molded fiberglass liners is to place them rough side to rough side with the moldings that they go with. The result is a single laminate (provided that they are well-bonded together) with finished molded surfaces and color gel coatings on both sides.

The molded liners do not necessarily make a matched contact, however. The molded liners used in fiberglass boats often make contact only in certain areas. The spaces may then be filled with rigid plastic foam for flotation purposes, left hollow, form storage areas, or be used in some other way.

Two popular types of liners in fiberglass boat construction are hull liners and cabin (head) liners. Other partial liners can include an engine mounting and pan liner, a head and shower compartment liner, a galley counter and sink arrangement, etc. The typical liner is designed not only to stiffen shell moldings, but also to support, reinforce, and form functional parts of the boat. They also provide a means for attaching bulkheads and other items.

A typical hull liner forms most of the interior components, gives a neat finished appearance, and provides a convenient means for attaching wood trim. The amount of labor required to hand lay-up the molded fiberglass liner is minimal compared to the hand labor that would be required to construct a similar interior from wood components by traditional methods.

The manufacturer must design and construct an expensive mold for each liner required, but once constructed, the cost of the mold can be amortized by molding hundreds of units in the same mold. And total construction time per boat is usually reduced considerably.

One common complaint about liners in typical manufactured boats is that the interiors look like the inside of iceboxes. Unless large areas are covered up with upholstery, wood, or other materials, this seems to be a valid criticism. Also, fiberglass alone does not provide very good insulation, and condensation is likely to be a problem. Using a rigid plastic core material between the fiberglass laminates helps.

After liners have been molded and allowed to cure, they are then ready for bonding to the main shell moldings. Various methods are used. A typical one is to set the liners into a resin-saturated layer of mat reinforcing material. Though polyester resin is used, epoxy resin gives a better bond. Another possibility is to use mechanical fasteners to hold the liners in place, usually in combination with fiberglass bonding. This method is only used where fasteners would go anyway, such as at hull to deck joints. The liners are sometimes tied in with the same through-bolt fasteners.

There are a number of problems associated with liners. They can make it more difficult to repair damage to the outside fiberglass shell. Should there be damage, it might be necessary to cut out part of the liner to make the repair. Liners make it difficult to examine the back side of moldings that are covered up. Some liners have hollow spaces that water can get inside. This problem can be corrected by providing a way for all hollow compartments to drain to the bilge or be pumped out. It is difficult to find leaks though, because the water might drip out long distances from where it is leaking in.

REINFORCING MOLDINGS TO SUPPORT HEAVY LOADS

This is a somewhat different problem than stiffeners. A boat deck and cabin top must support people walking (and jumping) on it. Chain plates and other attachments must support heavy loads. A boat hull molding must support the weight of a heavy engine. Loads are not only downward but can be in any direction or combination of directions. A cleat can stress a boat deck in a number of directions, depending on the angle of pull of an attached rope.

Fiberglass moldings must be reinforced to support the heavy loads. The main principle is to spread the load over a wide area of the fiberglass laminate. Stiffening reduces distortion when heavy loads are supported or applied, and this is part of reinforcing moldings to support heavy loads. A boat deck, for example, can be reinforced by thickening the laminate, using core construction, adding frames or other reinforcing members, or by some combination of these.

Engine mountings (Fig. 4-21) pose special problems. The fiberglass molding is usually thickened in the laminate in the area where the engine bed is to go. The engine mounts or bed is constructed in such a way that the engine weight and torque (the propeller turning in the water one direction twists the engine and boat hull in the opposite direction) are spread over a wide area of the hull. The bed frames often attach to major structural members, such as bulkheads and stringers.

The engine mounting must withstand the vibrations from the engine when it is running. If the mounting is inadequate, fiberglass bonds might delaminate, cracking might occur in heavy stress areas, or bulkheads might work loose. Engine mounting platforms and beds are often part of hull liners.

In the case of transom mounted outboards, the transoms must be well reinforced. Thick plywood cores with fiberglass sandwich construction are frequently used (Fig. 4-22).

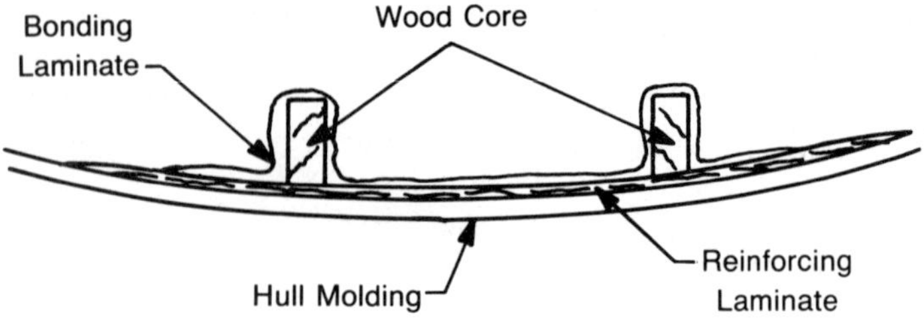

Fig. 4-21. Engine mounts bonded to a hull molding.

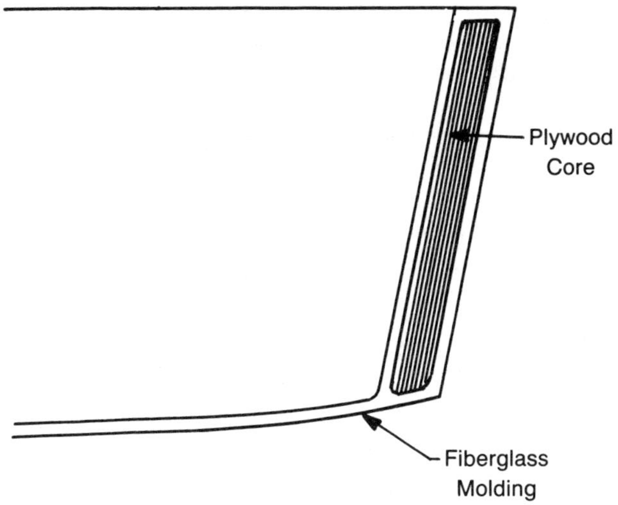

Fig. 4-22. Transom reinforced with thick plywood core for mounting of outboard.

SUPPORTING FIBERGLASS MOLDINGS

Another problem faced by fiberglass boat manufacturers is supporting moldings. Moldings must be well supported when they are moved and stored. This is especially a problem with moldings just removed from a mold. While the polyester resin is in a hard state, the actual cure continues for a long time. Moldings just taken from a mold are subject to distortions if a heavy load is placed on one part of the molding. Such distortions could be permanent.

Boat hulls and other moldings must be supported so that they retain their designed shape. Special care must be taken before stiffening and reinforcing members are added. Cradles and support stands should be designed and constructed so that the support load is spread over large areas of the moldings being supported.

FROM MOLDINGS TO FINISHED BOATS

The fiberglass moldings are only part of most finished boats. The moldings must be joined together and other components and fittings added.

Assembling Moldings

From the beginning of fiberglass boat construction, joining separate moldings together has been a major problem. Ideally, the complete boat shell (hull and cabin and deck structures) should be molded in one piece. Small open boats can be, but present contact-molding techniques do not make it practical to do this on boats with cabins and decks. A mold could be constructed that would allow this, consisting of separate pieces that are clamped or bolted together for molding and taken apart for removal of the molding from the mold. This boat would probably be structurally superior to one molded in sections that are then assembled together by bonding and/or mechanical fasteners. Perhaps future pressure-molding techniques will allow not only this, but two finished color coated sides as well. Today, however, most manufacturers must join separate moldings together to form completed boats.

A typical manufactured fiberglass boat has a hull molding, a separate cabin/deck/cockpit molding, and perhaps inner linings. Hatches, doors, rudders, and other items might also be fiberglass moldings, but these are attachments that present different assembly problems. They will be discussed later in this chapter. The concern now is joining two or more separate moldings to be approximately the same as if they had been molded as a single unit. These joinings are not normally intended to be taken apart again.

The hulls themselves are sometimes molded in halves. These sections are then joined together with fiberglass bonding strips across a butt joint (Fig. 4-23). This is no simple matter, and a number of hulls constructed in this way have split apart or otherwise failed. While the bonding strips can form a laminate strength equal to or greater than the moldings being joined, the bonding strength

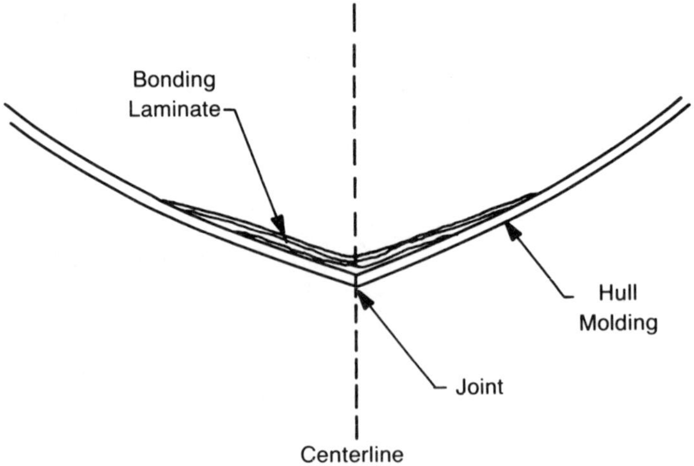

Fig. 4-23. Using bonding laminate to join hull sections together.

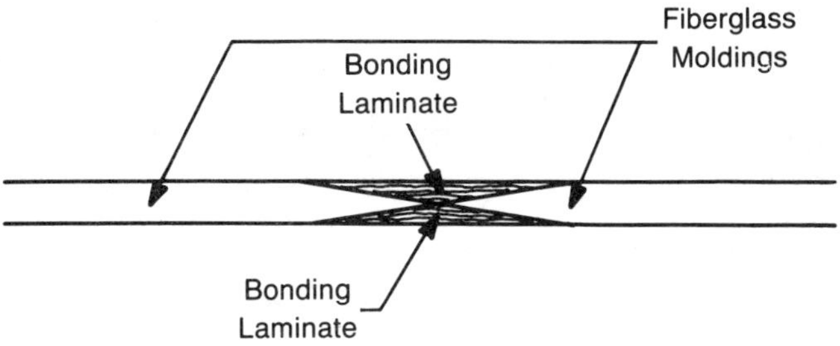

Fig. 4-24. Butt joint with moldings tapered to point.

between the moldings and the bonding strips seldom approaches this. The situation is somewhat improved if the bonding strips are added to both the inside and outside of the hull moldings, but this then presents a difficult sanding and finishing situation on the outside of the hull moldings.

It's little wonder that most fiberglass boat manufacturers are now molding hulls in one piece. I only know of a few manufacturers who are still molding hulls in halves. Ironically, some of them advertise that the hulls are molded in halves; that the halves method allows the workers to do better lay-up work and that the bonding laminate is actually stronger than the hull molding. In my opinion, this doesn't speak very well for their hull moldings.

Fiberglass boat moldings are joined together by bonding or mechanical fasteners or a combination of these two methods.

Bonding. Two moldings can be joined together with either butt or lap joints. A butt joint has limited contact area between the two moldings. Lap joints have greater contact area.

In manufactured fiberglass boat construction, butt joints are avoided because of the main problem with split half hull molding. If butt joints are used, the bonding is done with fiberglass bonding strips. To be effective, these should be on both sides of the moldings. Because the contact area between the fiberglass moldings is so small, epoxy gluing is ineffective. In fact, the edges of the moldings can taper to a point where they join. This allows the bonding strips to build up to a level with the original moldings (Fig. 4-24). Otherwise, the bonding strips have to extend outward (Fig. 4-25). Sometimes the moldings are tapered to one side, and the fiberglass bonding strips are laid up to a flush level on one side and extend outward on the other (Fig. 4-26). Progressively wider bonding strips cover up the edges of the fiberglass reinforcing material on all but the top layer. This arrangement reduces possible delaminating or

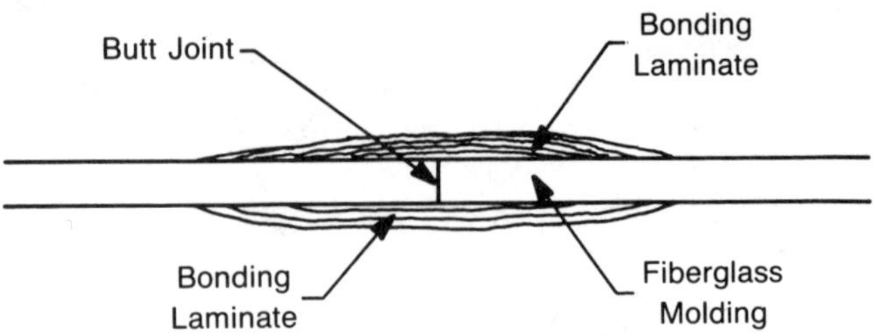

Fig. 4-25. Bonding strips extend outward from an untapered butt joint.

"peeling." To be effective, the bonding strips must extend outward on each side of the butt joint for some distance. For light laminates, this is often several inches or more. For heavy laminates, a foot or more in each direction is not uncommon.

Angle butt joints (Fig. 4-27) and "T" butt joints (Fig. 4-28) are other possibilities.

From a structural point of view, butt joints leave much to be desired, especially if moderate or heavy stresses will be placed on them. Also, these joints are difficult to sand and finish in areas where appearance is important. Again it's the problem of laying the fiberglass up over something instead of forming the desired finished surface against a mold.

In some early fiberglass boats, little thought was given to the assembly of separate moldings. Butt joints were fairly common, as were failures of these joints. Manufacturers and designers searched for better methods.

Lap joints offer a number of advantages over butt joints. The larger contact surface allows more effective direct bonding using epoxy glue or other means. Fiberglass bonding strips are more effective, especially if they can be applied to only one side. Lap joints can be more easily reinforced using mechanical fasteners. Moldings or rails made from metal, wood, or other materials are often

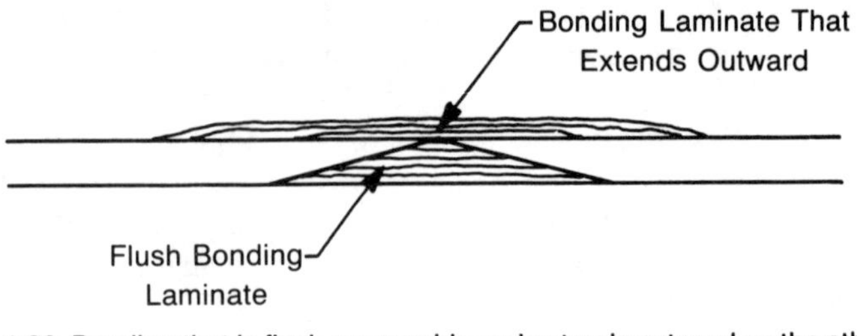

Fig. 4-26. Bonding that is flush on one side and extends outward on the other.

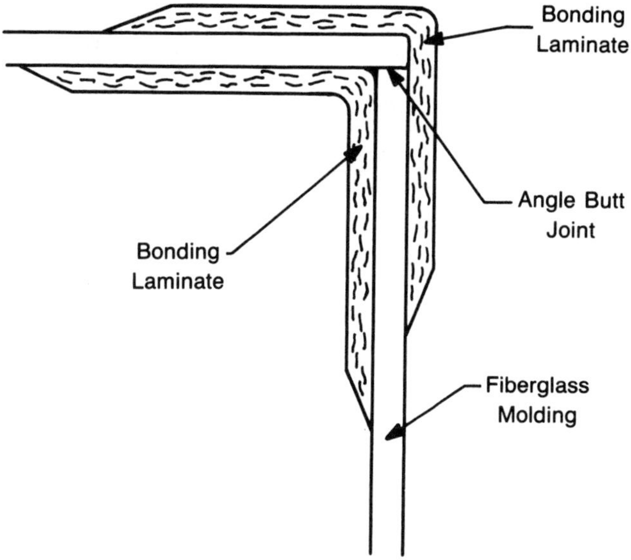

Fig. 4-27. Angle butt joint.

used to cover up the lap joint on the finished side. Hull-to-deck joints can be formed with a lap joint, bonding, mechanical fasteners with a rail on the finished side of the moldings, and fiberglass bonding strips (Fig. 4-29).

Lap joints are specially designed so that the primary loads placed on the joints put them in compression (Fig. 4-30) rather than tension (Fig. 31). Compression pushes the joint together; tension pulls it apart.

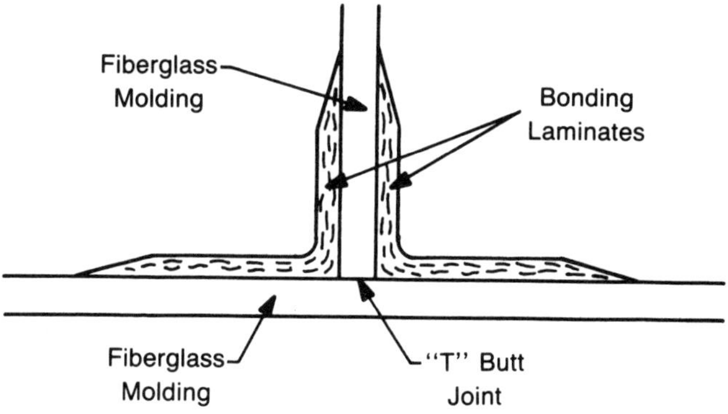

Fig. 4-28. T-butt joint.

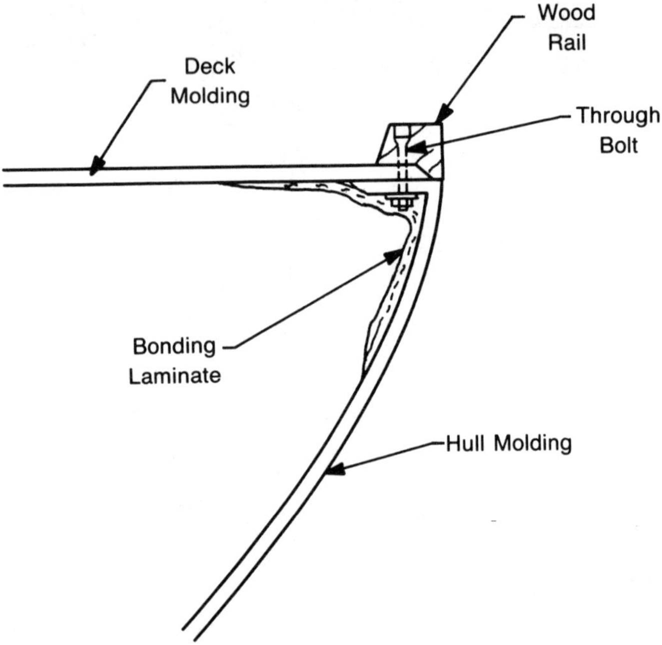

Fig. 4-29. Hull-to-deck joint with rail, mechanical fasteners, and bonding.

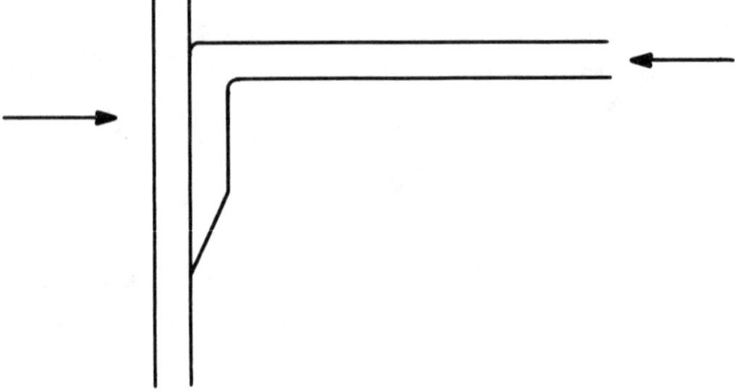

Fig. 4-30. Primary loads place this type of lap joint in compression, which pushes the joint together.

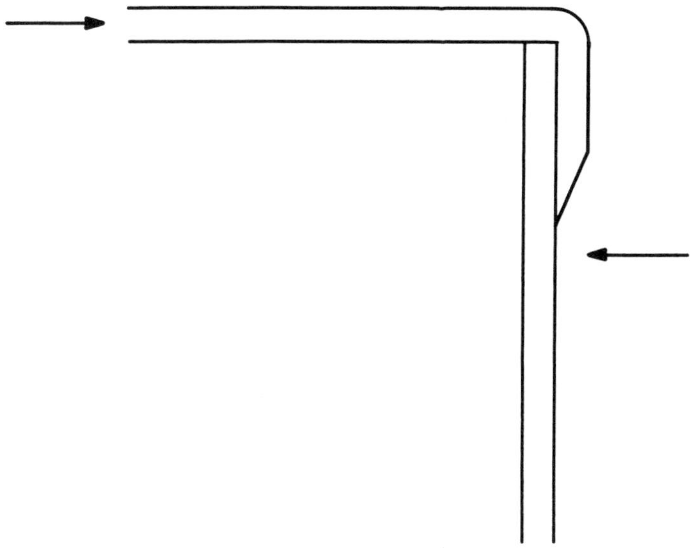

Fig. 4-31. Primary loads place this type of lap joint in tension, which pulls the joint apart.

Joining moldings of sandwich core construction with either butt or lap joints presents special problems. To solve them, during the molding lay-up work the sandwich moldings are tapered into a single skin in areas where moldings are to be joined, then lap joints are used. This method makes standard lap joints possible and also conceals and protects the core material. A typical hull-to-deck joint with sandwich core moldings in shown in Fig. 4-32.

Joining Moldings with Mechanical Fasteners. Moldings can be attached together with bolts, rivets, and other mechanical fasteners. The fasteners are passed through holes that go through both moldings at lap joints, which may also be bonded together as described previously.

Mechanical fasteners must be properly spaced for maximum strength. This depends on the required strength of the joint, the thickness of the laminates, and the type of fasteners used. Through bolts or rivets are most often used in fiberglass boat construction. These must be spaced at least a certain distance from the edge of the moldings. Metal plates, washers, etc., are used with the fasteners to spread the load over a larger area. Screws are unsatisfactory for boat construction.

Sometimes a joint of this type is arranged so that it can be taken apart again. A cockpit well is an example. This may be mechanically fastened in place, yet arranged so that it can be removed for taking out the engine should this ever be necessary. In other cases, the joints are permanent, and the joints are both bonded and mechanically fastened together.

Mechanical fasteners are often used with a rail of wood, metal, or other material. This forms a backing for the fasteners and spreads the load over a wider area of the moldings. Boat hull-to-deck attachment is accomplished with a lap joint, bonding between contact areas, through fasteners that pass through a rail before going through the two moldings, large backing washers, and fiberglass bonding strips on the inside.

This method for attaching hull and deck moldings has proven highly satisfactory. Because the rail covers up the lap joint on the finished side of the boat, little or no sanding is required. Considerable time and labor are required, however, to make this joint. Manufacturers have tried other methods that are faster and less expensive, but none have proved as satisfactory.

Using a Common Member to Join Two Moldings. An early attempt to use this method for a hull-to-deck joint attached the two moldings to a common wood member using bolts or other mechanical fasteners (Fig. 4-33). This method was not satisfactory, however. A similar joint was formed using a metal angle piece and through bolting the moldings to this (Fig. 4-34). This also proved unsatisfactory.

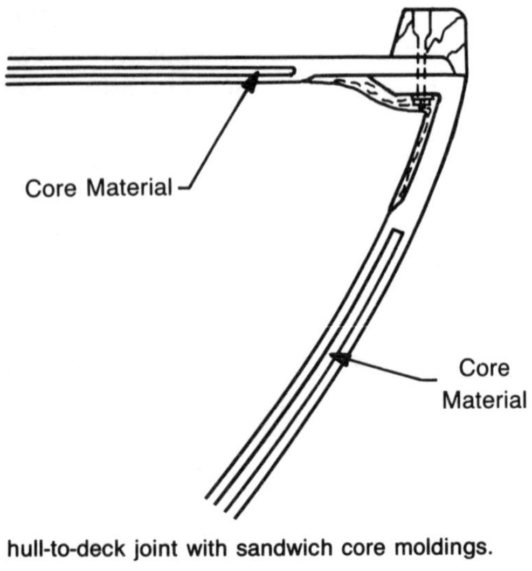

Fig. 4-32. A hull-to-deck joint with sandwich core moldings.

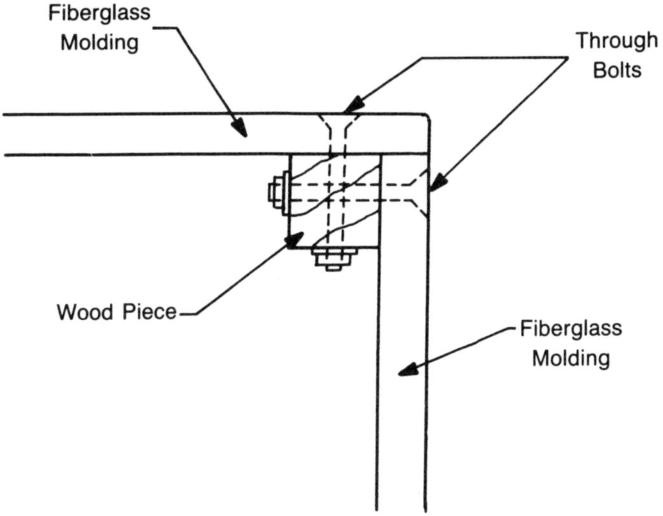

Fig. 4-33. Joining two fiberglass moldings by attaching them to a common wood member using through bolts.

About 10 or 15 years ago, an "H-shaped" aluminum extrusion for joining hulls and decks was introduced. Figure 4-35 shows a typical assembly. The edges of the moldings are set in slots and do not make direct contact. A section of aluminum separates them.

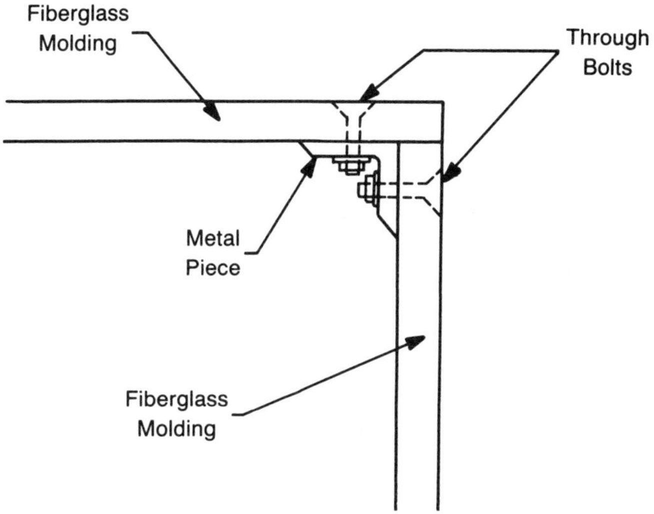

Fig. 4-34. Joining two fiberglass moldings by attaching them to a common metal member using through bolts.

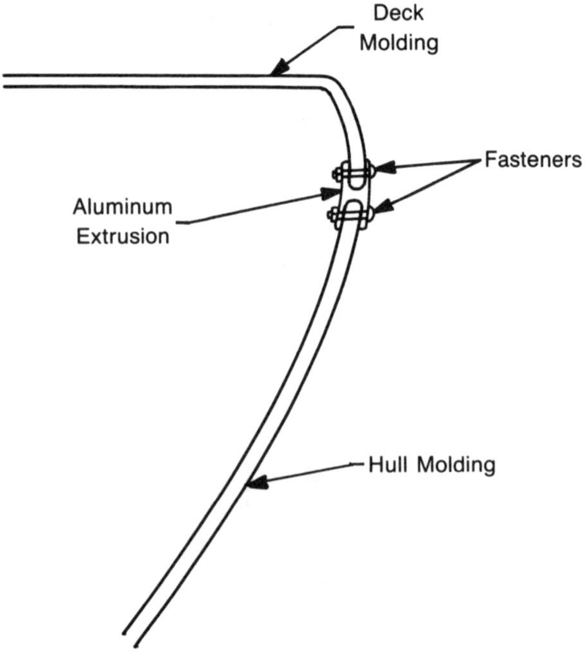

Fig. 4-35. Using aluminum extrusion for joining hull and deck moldings.

The two moldings are set in the slots with bedding compound and then are mechanically fastened in place using rivets or other mechanical fasteners.

Some manufacturers aggressively claim that this method is superior to the one previously described. The method cut costs for the manufacturer—it was inexpensive and fast—but it had the bad habit of failing when the boats were used. Some manufacturers lost all of the increased profits in lawsuits. The method gained such a bad reputation that it is difficult to sell boats with this type of joint. Most manufacturers who tried this method have gone back to the proven method. There are many boats on the used market, however, that have this type of joint. It is something to look out for.

Over the years, I have seen attempts to reinforce this inadequate method of joining boat moldings. So far, I haven't seen any practical modification that will accomplish this.

In actual fiberglass boat assembly, interior components, and other items—including engines—can be installed before the hull-to-deck joining is done. In other cases, these components are installed after the hull-to-deck assembly.

Attachments to Fiberglass Moldings

In assembling most fiberglass boats, attachments must be made to fiberglass moldings. For example, bulkheads, interior woodwork, fittings, and hardware need to be attached. Commonly used methods include gluing, bonding with fiberglass, and mechanically fastening, or combinations of these methods.

Gluing. Epoxy glue is sometimes used for attaching things to fiberglass moldings. Unless used with another means of fastening, however, gluing is only suitable for things that will have light loadings placed on them. One example might be attaching a small piece of wood to a fiberglass molding. A curtain rod bracket might then be attached to the block of wood by means of wood screws.

Similar to gluing is setting the attachment into a wet layer of fiberglassing material placed between the fiberglass molding and the attachment. This method can work reasonably well for attaching soft woods. Using epoxy resin instead of polyester for wetting out the reinforcing material sometimes makes it possible to satisfactorily attach other materials to fiberglass moldings.

Various soft materials, such as rubber gaskets, weatherstripping, and upholstery fabrics, can be attached to fiberglass by gluing, though there can be problems. I haven't yet seen, for example, a satisfactory method for gluing nonskid treads to fiberglass moldings. It seems only a matter of time, and sometimes not much of that, before the edges start peeling upward. Regardless, gluing alone is used for some attachments by many fiberglass boat manufacturers, even if it is a source of frustration to boat buyers to have things come unglued and a poor advertisement for the particular boat.

Bonding with Fiberglass. Attaching bulkheads and stiffeners in place by bonding with fiberglass has already been detailed. This is also a primary method for attaching wood and other materials to fiberglass. This method might be compared to welding in metal construction. Strong attachments are possible without making holes in the fiberglass moldings for bolts and other fasteners. In some cases it's practical to supplement bonding with fiberglass with mechanical fastenings. Also, wood can be fiberglass-bonded to a fiberglass molding. Items can then be attached to the wood with screws or other mechanical fasteners. With this method, holes through the fiberglass molding for fasteners are unnecessary.

Wood and fiberglass interior components are commonly attached to fiberglass moldings by fiberglass bonding without the use of mechanical fasteners. For example, the top sections of plywood for berths can be attached to the hull molding by laminating progressively wider fiberglass bonding strips in place (Fig. 4-36). Depending on the particular attachment, this can be on one or both sides.

Fiberglass boats with interiors mainly of wood components make extensive use of fiberglass bonding. The method is slow and requires skilled labor, however. To get around some of this, many manufacturers are now using molded interior fiberglass liners. Liners must be bonded or otherwise attached, but this is fast work compared to extensive fiberglass bonding of wood components.

Mechanical Fastenings. This is comparable to riveting and bolting in metal work. Use of mechanical fastenings is extremely important in the assembly of most fiberglass boats.

Through-hull fittings for drains and other purposes are installed in fiberglass moldings. Typical installation begins by drilling the appropriate size hole through the molding in the desired location. A backing block of wood is then fitted. Bedding compound is applied to the fitting and around the hole, and the fitting is passed through the hole in the fiberglass molding and then the one in the wood. The holes are drilled to a close tolerance and the through-hull fitting threaded through. The nut is then threaded on and tightened down to hold the through-hull fitting in place. Figure 4-37 shows a typical installation.

Hinges, latches, and similar fittings are attached to fiberglass moldings using through bolts. In order to spread the load over a

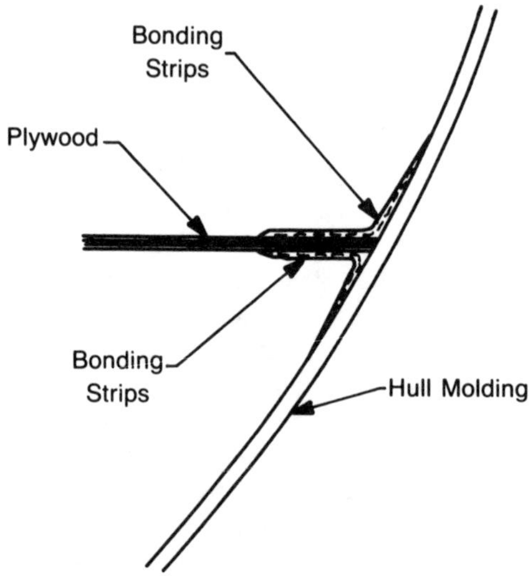

Fig. 4-36. Plywood bonded to fiberglass hull molding using bonding strips.

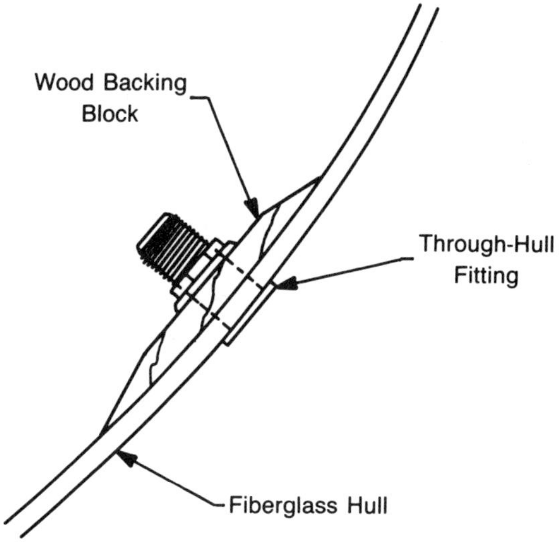

Fig. 4-37. Through-hull fitting.

wider area, large backing washers, plates, or blocks are used. Sometimes the fiberglass moldings require reinforcing by laminating additional layers of fiberglass in place or other means.

In some cases, the loads placed on fasteners will be in compression. In other cases the loads will be in tension with the fasteners. The latter situation requires large backing washers, plates, or blocks.

A typical cleat installation to a fiberglass boat deck is shown in Fig. 4-38. A hardwood backing block is shaped so that the edges taper to the fiberglass molding. The cleat is through-bolted in place using bedding compound and large backing washers, lock washers, and nuts.

A sailboat chain plate might be through-bolted to a reinforced area of a hull molding. In addition, hardwood backing blocks and large backing washers are commonly used. An alternate attachment favored by some fiberglass boat builders is to run the chain plate through a slot in the fiberglass molding and to bolt it to an interior, usually plywood, bulkhead. A deck plate is bedded in place over the chain plate on deck and through-bolted to the fiberglass molding to prevent leaking. It has been my experience, however, that leaking is common when this method is used.

Some boats have chain plates attached externally. While this method provides strong and simple attachment, many manufacturers don't like it because of the appearance. Thus, most manufac-

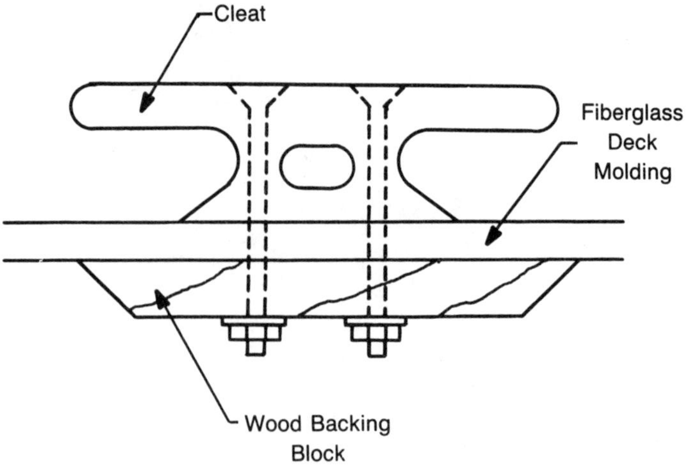

Fig. 4-38. Cleat installation to fiberglass deck molding.

tured fiberglass boats now have chain plates attached internally that pass through slots in the fiberglass moldings.

While chain plates are typically bolted to fiberglass moldings or plywood bulkheads, they can also be fiberglass bonded in place. This method is not often used, however.

Sandwich moldings with cores of balsa, rigid plastic foam, and other "soft" materials present special problems for mechanical fastenings. A compression load on a fastener, such as by tightening the fastener, forces the moldings together and compresses the core material. To prevent this, a section of core material can be removed and fiberglassed in, or a section of the core can be replaced with wood or an insert of some other suitable material. Some manufacturers install these substitutes in areas where mechanical fasteners are required during molding; sometimes they are added later. The purpose of the inserts is to take the compression from the fastener.

Logistics

Methods for assembling fiberglass moldings into completed boats have been explained. Because there are many workers in the typical fiberglass boat manufacturing plant, and a number of boats are under construction at any given time, logistics is important.

Some of the larger fiberglass boat manufacturers use a system resembling an assembly line, but many do not, even though they still construct a number of boats at a given time. The boats stay in one place during assembly, and the workers move about to the various required jobs. Parts of boats are sometimes subassembled. For example, the interior woodwork might first be assembled before being installed in the boat hull molding. Exterior hardware and fittings, including ports and windows, might be installed on deck and cabin molding before the deck is mated with the hull.

Considerable assembly work is often done on hull moldings before the cabins and decks are added. Ballast is added on boats requiring this. Engines are installed; bulkheads and interior components are added; rudders are assembled to the hull molding; and so on. To what extent this is done depends on the particular boat, but access to work areas is often better before the hulls and decks have been mated than afterwards.

There are many other jobs required before the boats are completed: wiring and plumbing must be installed, hatches and windows added, upholstery installed, and cushions made.

Many boats are not completely fitted out and rigged by the manufacturers. For sailboats, the spars are mounted in cradles for shipping. The remainder of the assembly is called *commissioning* and is done at the dealer level. Sometimes the boat buyer does his or her own commissioning (see Chapter 8).

Because many boats have hundreds of separate fittings and components, logistics become very important. Just keeping an inventory of materials, supplies, equipment, fittings, hardware, etc., on hand is a large order. Some fiberglass boat manufacturers have departments or sections for doing canvas and upholstery work, sailmaking, and constructing spars and rigging. Other manufacturers contract some or all of this work out.

QUALITY OF FIBERGLASS BOAT CONSTRUCTION

Most fiberglass boat manufacturers are in business to make a profit. The amount of profit that a particular company makes is not necessarily directly related to the quality of the boats produced. In some cases, a lower quality boat that can be sold for a lower price will result in a higher profit for the manufacturer.

To a person unfamiliar with fiberglass boats, they might look like they are constructed to more or less the same standards. But on closer examination, this is found to be far from true. Fiberglass boats are not all created equally. The quality of manufactured boats depends mains on soundness of design, quality of materials used in the construction, and care and skill used in the fabrication.

Soundness of Design

To construct a quality fiberglass boat, the manufacturer must first have a sound design. This requires the services of competent boat designers. Some large boat manufacturing companies employ their own boat designers, others hire this work out.

Compared with other manufacturing businesses, fiberglass boat manufacturing can be a fairly inexpensive one to get started. Many new companies start with poor designs, however, possibly because they can't afford the services of competent designers or because they don't know any better. Unless they switch to better designs, these companies usually don't stay in business for long. At the opposite extreme, I know of a company that was started on very little money. About the only thing that it had going for it was an outstanding and proven design. The company is a success.

Design means more than just the shape of the boat or how it looks. It also means function or how the boat works and how the boat is constructed, including materials used, lay-up of laminates, assembly, etc. Part of the construction might be left up to the manufacturer.

Quality of Materials

Because some of the materials used in fiberglass boat construction are more or less hidden from view on the finished boats, some manufacturers are tempted to use cheaper materials to lower production costs. This is especially true of materials that are used on inner layers of fiberglass laminates.

As a rule, fiberglass boats are designed and engineered so that they have sufficient strength. To this is added a safety margin. Using lower quality construction materials than are called for in the design reduces the safety margin, sometimes to a dangerous level.

A number of manufacturers who have built their reputations on quality fiberglass boats have gradually lowered the quality of materials used over the years in an attempt to keep price increases to a minimum. The cost of most materials used in fiberglass boat construction is now at a record high. This is partially offset by the fact that some of the materials have been improved to the point where less are required.

Fiberglass boat manufacturing is a highly competitive business. The companies might consider it in their own best interests to lower the quality of materials used. At present, there are no accepted standards for materials. Other companies stick to high-quality construction materials. Probably most manufacturers use materials of some intermediate quality. Cheap and poorly formulated materials are often difficult to work with. What is saved in the purchase of the materials is lost in production difficulties and added labor required.

Care and Skill in Fabrication

A third main factor in determining the quality of manufactured fiberglass boats is the care and skill used in their fabrication. At the present time, both the materials and labor are expensive. It is difficult to find skilled fiberglass workers. Improved industrial health and safety standards for workers have increased the cost of using this labor because the working environment must meet certain standards and expensive health and safety equipment must be used.

Even when skilled craftsmen can be hired, they are often not allowed enough time to do each job right. The trend in fiberglass boat manufacturing has been to reduce the need for highly skilled labor by eliminating difficult jobs and finding easier or simpler ways of doing other tasks. For example, using molded liners greatly reduces the amount of skilled labor required.

Reputation of Manufacturer

The reputation of the manufacturer is an important clue to quality. Poor quality of construction shows up in time. Boat owners talk, and from this, manufacturers gain a reputation for quality construction or lack of it.

Talking to owners of particular boats will often reveal considerable information regarding the quality of construction. Some boating magazines even have an information exchange on manufactured boats. This can be quite different from the manufacturer's advertising. It is interesting to note that boat owners report construction failures in the very things that manufacturers boast about in their advertisements.

Visiting Manufacturing Plants

Another clue to quality of boats produced by a particular manufacturer is a visit to the plant. Most manufacturers will show you the facilities, and some offer tours. Their purpose is to sell boats, and they will try to show you what they want you to see. You can often see beyond this once you know what to look for. And you can ask questions.

Boat Specifications

Most manufacturers provide information and specifications on request. This is often part of the advertising literature. Specifics on the laminates used in the lay-ups, the hull-to-deck joining method, and other construction features can be helpful in attempting to determine the quality of construction. If the information you seek is not included in their literature, request additional information.

Judging Construction of Existing Boats

Judging the construction quality of existing boats presents somewhat different problems, regardless of whether the boat is new or used. Evaluating construction quality is not exactly the same thing as surveying a boat, which focuses on the condition the boat is in (see Chapter 5).

The problem here is to judge or evaluate how an existing boat, whether new or used, *was* constructed. In most cases, this evaluation must be done by nondestructive means. You won't, for example, be able to cut holes in the moldings to see how thick they are or examine the interior of the laminate. You won't be able to pound on the hull with a sledgehammer to see how strong the molding is. The evaluation must be made by eye and by very simple tests.

General Appearance. While general appearance is not necessarily related to quality of construction, it is certainly a clue. Fiberglass boat manufacturers strive for a neat and finished appearance. It must look manufactured and not homemade, which is different from the desirable custom, handcrafted appearance.

Some manufactured fiberglass boats look finished, others don't. If a manufacturer takes the trouble to give a boat a neat and finished appearance, it's an indication that the same care was taken "underneath" where you can't see.

Quality of Moldings. Damage and deterioration of fiberglass moldings is one sign that the moldings were of poor quality. You can damage almost any fiberglass molding by some means, so this must be taken into account. As a general rule, poor-quality moldings are more easily damaged and deteriorate more rapidly than high-quality ones. Evaluating the condition of moldings is part of surveying a fiberglass boat (see Chapter 5).

The quality of moldings depends on the materials used and the construction. While it is often difficult to judge the quality of materials used in a molding by examining an existing molding, the workmanship that went into the construction is more easily visible once you know what to look for.

Does the thickness of the moldings appear adequate? Does the lay-up appear neat and clean on the "rough" side that was away from the mold? Are there any voids, wrinkles, or signs of delaminations? Are there any signs that too little resin was used (resin dryness) or that too much resin was used (resin richness)? Are there any scraps of wood, pieces of paper or string, dirt, or other foreign inclusions in the laminate? This can be an indication that the molding area of the manufacturing plant was not kept clean, and that the molding was contaminated with materials that could reduce the quality of the molding.

Type and Size of Boat. When evaluating construction, the type, size, and intended use of the boat must be considered. Much of my early experience was with offshore ocean-cruising sailing boats. These must be constructed to the highest standards. When I first came to the California Delta, I was dismayed at the way most fiberglass houseboats were constructed. Most of them didn't meet any of my standards for an offshore vessel. Now I have come to accept this. They generally don't have to, because they are intended only for protected waters. In fact, now when I see an offshore ocean-sailing boat on a lazy stretch of the Delta, it almost looks like too much boat.

Hull-to-Deck Joints. A sound hull-to-deck joint indicates quality construction. Any manufacturer who uses a method that has proven unsatisfactory, probably fudges elsewhere in the construction.

Quality of Hardware, Fittings, Rigging and Other Visible Items and Attachments. Cheap and inadequate fittings, rigging, rub rails, and other items are a good indication of poor construction. If a manufacturer cuts corners on items that are clearly visible, one can only imagine what he did in areas not so easily seen. If fittings and rigging look too dinky or small for the boat size, they probably are.

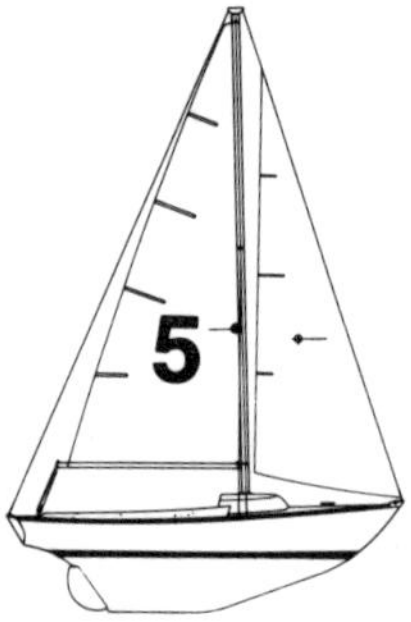

Surveying Fiberglass Boats

The primary purpose of a boat survey is to evaluate the existing condition of a boat, whether new or used. In general, this does not take into consideration the design and original construction, but it will be included here as part of your survey.

I believe that it is valuable to do your own preliminary surveying. This lets you weed out the hopeless boats. When you find a boat that looks promising, you can then hire a professional boat surveyor. If you are going to finance and/or insure a fiberglass boat, especially a used one, you will probably need this service anyway. In any case, the cost of a professional boat survey is small in relation to the cost of most fiberglass boats, and it's well worth the price, even if it's just for a second opinion. I know a boatbuilder who has sailed around the world, but before buying a boat, he still uses the services of a professional boat surveyor.

This chapter is divided into two main parts: doing your own survey and hiring the services of a professional boat surveyor.

DOING YOUR OWN FIBERGLASS BOAT SURVEY

There is considerable survey work that you can do before hiring the professional surveyor. Even if you already own a fiberglass boat, this survey will be valuable for determining what maintenance and repair work needs to be done. Surveying really boils down to something simple—*how to look at boats*. You need to know where to look, what to look for, and what the implications are.

One reason for doing this is to determine the present condition of a boat. This applies not only to used boats, but also to new ones. What repairs are needed?

A second reason is to determine the value of the boat. Is the boat worth the asking price? What should the boat sell for?

A third reason is to evaluate the original design and construction of the boat. How is it in general and how does it compare to similar boats?

Basic Procedures

When you first look at a boat, you see the surface appearance. This "first impression," while it has some value, is only a starting point. Perhaps this first impression is a good one, like love on first sight. If it is a bad one, then perhaps this alone is reason enough to reject buying the boat. I suggest that you give the boat a closer inspection, however. The more boats you can inspect, the more experience you will gain in making comparisons. You will get some good ideas as to what to do and what not to do. If your first impression is a good one, you will want to thoroughly examine the merchandise to see if it lives up to your first impression.

In Chapter 3, destructive testing was mentioned as one way to test the mechanical properties of fiberglass laminates. The fiberglass laminates were destroyed, or at least ruined, in the process. You will most likely be limited to visual inspection and very simple nondestructive testing in evaluating a boat, however. Even professional boat surveyors are similarly restricted, although in some cases they might have instruments for nondestructive testing that you don't have. In rare instances, they can take sample plugs from the fiberglass moldings for lab analysis. The holes in the fiberglass laminates would have to be filled back in, however, so this type of testing is only done in extreme cases.

You can stand on the deck of a boat to see how much it "gives." You can even jump up and down on it somewhat. But hit it with a sledgehammer—no.

Where do you start? You could start anywhere and look at every square inch of the boat, inside and out—but this method generally leads nowhere. There is a lot of boat that you can't see. Tanks are in the way, upholstery and liners cover areas, and so on. It is better to concentrate on small areas of the boat, thoroughly examining one area at a time, then moving on to another area.

Another good method is to trace out entire systems. Trace the fresh water system from tank vents and filler pipes to the water tank and through hoses or pipes to the various parts of the boat to pumps and spouts and so on.

You will need a reference. This is why it is important to examine and survey as many boats as possible. In this way you will have a basis of comparison. Examine every boat you possibly can to whatever degree you can. Other people need not even know you are doing this. Boat shows are excellent places for examining boats, although I don't recommend on-the-spot boat buying at boat shows. You will often have an open invitation to examine boats that are for sale, whether new or used. You can examine boats that belong to friends, although if your comments aren't complimentary, it is generally best to keep them to yourself. And ask questions. Most boat owners like to talk about their boats, and often you can learn the bad points as well as the good ones.

A boat survey evaluates the existing condition of the boat, not its performance. Its performance is sometimes related to its condition—a powerboat probably won't perform at all if the engine won't run—but equally important is the design and construction of the boat. A sea trial, as detailed in Chapter 6, won't mean much unless you have had experience operating and sailing many different boats yourself.

Where to Do Surveys

Some survey work can be done with a boat in the water. A more thorough survey requires the boat out of the water on a cradle, boat trailer, or some other support system. I like to examine a boat both in the water and out, the order is not crucial. If the boat is operational, check it in the water and with a sea trial. If the boat is a fixer upper and obviously not seaworthy at present, you might want to purchase it out of the water as-is if you are certain you know what you are getting into.

Inspecting Fiberglass Laminates

Before going on to specific areas of a boat, inspect the fiberglass laminates. Because you can only see the two sides of a laminate in a fiberglass boat, and sometimes one side is even hidden from view, determining the quality of the laminate can be quite difficult. To add to the difficulty, one side of the laminate is usually covered with a color gel coat and the other side painted. Or a fiberglass linear is used, which essentially gives you a single laminate with a color gel coat on both sides.

The fiberglass boat manufacturer (assuming you are surveying a manufactured boat) made the fiberglass moldings for the boat. The manufacturer used fiberglass reinforcing materials, resins, etc., that were in turn manufactured by other companies, but assuming that quality materials were used, the manufacturer was largely responsible for the quality of the fiberglass moldings.

This is quite different from steel or aluminum boat construction, where the manufacturer uses preformed metal of the correct specifications without internal flaws. Preformed wood is similarly used for wood boat construction, although the manufacturer inspects each piece of wood for natural flaws and defects. These materials are fastened together to form boat hulls and other components, quite unlike forming components in molds from liquid resins and glass fiber reinforcing materials.

One clue to quality is the thickness of the laminate. It is difficult to know how thick the laminate should be, however. If you can get the designer's laminate specifications, you can measure the thickness and determine if the laminates were actually constructed to these specifications. It should be noted, though, that the laminate could be the designed thickness, while still not meeting the designer's specifications for reinforcing materials, etc. The required laminate thickness also depends on the spacing and arrangement of stiffening and supporting members, although a certain minimum thickness is required to give the necessary resistance to impact.

You will not be able to tell much about the thickness of a laminate by measuring the thickness of visible edges because these edges are not usually representative. The edges of a hole or other opening that has been drilled or cut through the laminate is often a useful barometer.

With hull laminate, you might be able to remove one or more through-hull fittings. Most people who have boats for sale, however, will not permit this unless they are extremely anxious to sell and the sale hinges on this.

If you are able to remove through-hull fittings, you can measure the thickness of the laminate in these areas easily. If extra layers have been added to the laminate as reinforcement for the fitting, take this into account also. Often you will be able to tell where the original laminate ends and the added layers begin.

If you can remove through-hull fittings from the same area on opposite sides of the hull, you can compare the laminate thicknesses. If they are in different areas, however, the varying thicknesses might be part of the planned design. It is common practice to use varying thicknesses of laminate in a hull. The hull is thinnest at the sheer and progressively thicker to the waterline, hull bottom, and keel area.

In other areas of the boat, such as deck and cabin structures, you can often determine laminate thickness by removing a fitting, through bolt, or other attachment. Calipers can measure laminate thickness back away from hatch or other openings. These laminates often have plywood or other core materials in sandwich form, so you will actually be measuring the combined thickness of the two fiberglass skins and the core material. And again, it is extremely difficult to know how thick the laminates should be. Fiberglass laminates used in deck and cabin structures, like those of hulls, often have various laminate thickness in the same molding. So while it is possible to measure laminate thickness, it is difficult to know what the measurements mean, except perhaps when you find a boat that has much thinner or even thicker laminates than a similar boat of the same type and size.

There are other ways to measure laminate thickness that you probably won't be able to use. One is with ultrasonic test equipment. This equipment is expensive. Most boat surveyors don't even have it.

Another method is to cut out a plug. This is done in the area where a fitting is to be installed so it will not be necessary to fill in the hole. This can give you the thickness of the laminate, as well as a sample to take to a laboratory for a burn test to determine the glass-to-resin ratio. Again, this is usually beyond the scope of doing your own survey work. Even most professional boat surveyors won't go to this extreme.

A clue to a low-quality laminate are *delaminations*. This means that the plies have separated. For some reason, such as stress, overloading, improper lay-up, or water saturation, the bond between plies has failed or never existed.

You can test for delaminations by using a small metal hammer or similar metal object. Tap the laminate lightly. A sound laminate gives a sharp, hard sound. A tap over a delamination gives a dull thud. In decks and other laminates with sandwich cores, excessive flexing and/or cracking sounds when you walk on the laminate is an indication of delaminations. The problem is often failure of the bond between fiberglass skins and the core material.

Still another clue to a low-quality laminate is the presence of *air bubbles* in the laminate. To check for these in laminates without cores, use a strong lamp. Shine this on one side of the laminate while you look at the opposite side of the laminate. It usually works best to have the lamp on the gel coat side. Air bubbles will show up as spots that are clearly different from the surrounding area of the laminate. A few small air bubbles here and there are not much cause of concern, but large air bubbles and concentrations of small ones can be. These indicate careless lay-up work and may require repair (see Chapter 12).

In areas where the laminate makes sharp angles or corners, it is more difficult to lay up a laminate. This is a likely area for air bubbles and voids. These often lead to gel coat *cracking*, which can be seen by visual inspection. A few of these are not much concern because repairs are fairly easy (see Chapter 12). If they are extensive, however, repairs could be difficult. This indicates a poor-quality original lay-up of the laminate.

Surveying Exteriors

The exterior of the boat is a good starting place for making a complete inspection. To examine all areas, the boat must be out of the water. In clear water, the underwater areas are sometimes inspected with the boat in the water by using diving gear. While this is probably better than nothing, it is a poor substitute for an out-of-the-water examination. Examination should include all fiberglass parts as well as other materials that are typically used in fiberglass boats and engines and mechanical systems.

Start with the hull. Standing some distance away, look at the surface. Because gel coating deteriorates with age—a process that can be slowed down by proper maintenance (see Chapter 9)—the smoothness and gloss of the gel coat will reflect this. Any dullness, especially in a fairly new boat, probably indicates careless construction and/or poor maintenance. If the original gel coating has been painted over, try to find out why this was done. Perhaps the owner just wanted to change the color; more likely the old gel coating had deteriorated to an unsightly state, or extensive repairs were made and it was easier to paint the boat than to touch up the gel coating.

From a distance, professionally applied two-part polyurethane paint finish is very difficult to distinguish from gel coating. Up close you can tell by examining around rails and other attachments for overspray, because masking cannot usually be done exactly. If the paint color is different from the original gel coating, this original color often shows through on nicks and scratches in the paint. Amateur-applied paint finishes are easy to detect by brush marks, runs, uneven color, and so on.

Next, with the boat in sunlight, stand forward of the bow and sight down the hull. There should be a smooth curve from bow to stern without any uneven areas. Bumps that stick outward, assuming they weren't the result of an improperly shaped mold, are caused by bulkheads and other framing and support members that are fitted too tightly against the fiberglass hull molding before being bonded in place. These create hard spots—areas of high stress concentration.

Check especially in major bulkhead areas. If deformities exist here, the problem could be serious. It could have been prevented by properly installing the bulkheads in the first place. This is accomplished by leaving a space between the bulkhead and the hull laminate before bonding the bulkhead in place with strips of fiberglass reinforcing material. Or the hull laminate could have been padded with layers of mat in the contact area of the bulkhead. Or a rigid plastic foam pad could have been used between the bulkhead and the hull molding. Slight deformations might be acceptable, but check carefully to make certain that this has not caused fracturing or other damage to the hull laminate.

If you can see areas of the hull that are dished in, the cause is usually from having too thin a laminate and/or stiffening and supporting hull members spaced too far apart. Heavy loadings then cause the concave areas. These loadings could still be present. A chain plate might be attached to an inadequately reinforced area of the hull molding. In time, even when the loading is removed from the chain plate, the deformation might remain. A similar condition can result from boat trailer rollers that do not spread the load over a wide enough area of the boat hull. These deformations can become "permanent" in time, even when the boat is removed from the trailer and in the water. The same thing can happen from placing the hull on cradles and other supports. The problem can be especially severe when the hull molding is first removed from the mold and has not had time to fully cure.

Ease or difficulty of repair depends on many factors. If the laminate returns to the designed shape when the loading is removed, repair can be made by adding additional thickness to the laminate in the area and/or adding reinforcing members. If the laminate does not return to the designed shape when the loading is removed, the dished in area has, in a sense, been molded into the laminate. Repairs can be difficult (see Chapter 12).

Next, stand some distance forward or aft of the boat and sight along the sheerline at the level of the hull and deck joint. Any unevenness or bumps indicate that the hull and deck do not fit together properly, are separating in some areas, or have been damaged. These areas should be noted and checked more closely later.

The entire exterior gel coat surface should be examined. There might be scratches, nicks, or gouges that should be examined carefully. Repairs are fairly easy if these defects are in the gel coating only. If they extend past the gel coating into the laminate, they are more serious and difficult to repair.

Scratches, nicks, and gouges on the bottom of the keel indicate that the boat has been grounded. Examine these carefully. On powerboats without ballast, beaching can often cause wear on unprotected fiberglass. On sailboats with internal ballast keels, fracturing of the outside fiberglass laminate can be serious. This can allow water to enter between the inside of the fiberglass laminate and the ballast material. If the ballast material is not well bonded and sealed over, the water can leak inside the boat. Even less serious damage can cause water to penetrate the laminate, which can cause delaminations. These defects should be repaired, as detailed in Chapter 12.

The gel coating should also be examined for hairline cracks and crazing. These will be most common in areas of sharp corners and angles. The usual cause here was improper application of gel coat resin—it was sprayed on in too thick a layer. The surface cracks and crazing will also appear in areas of applied stress.

If the cracking and crazing is only in the gel coating, they do not cause a serious structural problem. They do give an unsightly appearance, however, and repairs can be difficult.

If the cracks extend through the gel coating into the laminate, the problem can be serious. If applied loads cause the laminate to repeatedly flex, a condition called *oil canning*, the laminate will eventually crack all the way through. This is especially likely in poorly designed powerboat hulls and in relatively flat areas of the hull that pound into the waves. Check these areas carefully.

All exterior metal parts, including through-hull fittings, propellers, shafts, rudders, and similar items, should be examined for signs of corrosion, such as pitted areas in the metal. As pitting continues, the thickness of the metal will be reduced. The causes of corrosion are quite complicated. It depends on the types of metals used, their locations in relation to each other, whether or not sacrificial zinks are used, and other factors. Corrosion is much greater in salt water than fresh water. Corrosion can still take place in fresh water, especially in marina areas with shore power and where battery chargers are used.

If corrosion is present, try to make a realistic decision of what metal parts need to be replaced. While minor pitted areas may not mean replacing parts, further corrosion must be prevented. Otherwise, it will only be a matter of time before the part fails.

There should not be excessive flexibility in hull, cockpit, deck, cabin, or other fiberglass laminates. One way to test for this is to use a rubber mallet. Tap the fiberglass laminate. You will be able to see and feel any movement. It takes some experience, however, before you can tell what is excessive. Compare it to similar boats of other makes.

If the boat is placed on a cradle, the pods should support the weight of the boat without excess flexing of the hull laminate. Be sure the weight of the boat is supported by the craddle pods and not just by the keel, however.

While repairs can sometimes be made to remove excess flexibility by adding stiffeners or supporting members, this work can be difficult, especially if the hull has an interior liner. With an interior liner, the problem might be that the liner has separated from the hull molding.

Decks, cabin tops, cockpits, and other walking areas can be checked for excessive flexibility by walking on them. You will feel any flexibility. If the laminate has a plywood core, you can hear cracking noises if there is excessive flexibility and/or the fiberglass skins have come unbonded from the plywood core. Another cause of excessive flexibility is a rotted plywood core. If this is the case, repairs can be extremely difficult and quite expensive. The problem often gets started by water leaking in around fasteners that pass through the laminate.

Be sure to write down all of your findings. Based on the survey, you might want to reject the boat completely and not purchase it. Or you might want to determine what repairs are required and go ahead with the purchase anyway, perhaps lowering the asking price in the process. If you already own the boat, you will want to know what repairs are required.

Special consideration needs to be given to hulls that are molded in two halves and then joined along the centerline with fiberglass bonding strips. You can recognize this type of construction by shining sunlight or artificial light through the laminate. The centerline joint can then be seen.

The bonding strips are often placed across the joint on the inside of the hull only. The crack on the outside of the hull is merely filled with resin putty. The putty often cracks and/or falls out. If this is the case on a boat you are inspecting, note this and then inspect the joint and bonding strips on the inside of the hull.

A number of these types of hulls have failed. The manufacturers who use this method do so because the lay-up is easier because it does not require working in a narrow deep keel area or from a scaffold. Fortunately, this method is now used less and less.

While this type of construction might not be a reason to reject a boat, provided you find no signs the joint is failing, it certainly is cause for concern. If I knew of just one hull by the same manufacturer that had split apart in use along this seamline, I would not purchase the boat, especially if any offshore boating is intended.

Examine the underwater area of the hull. Usually this is painted with antifouling paint, which needs to be applied about once a year on a fiberglass hull (see Chapter 9). The condition of the antifouling paint will vary with such factors as length of time since it was applied, type and quality of paint used, surface preparation, and so on. If the old paint is in good condition with no peeling or chipping, the surface preparation was probably good. This should make it easier to apply new antifouling paint when required, because there is probably a good bonding surface under the old paint, making it unnecessary to remove it before applying the new paint.

If the old bottom paint is chipped and peeling, it must all be removed and the fiberglass surface prepared for the new paint. This is in the range of routine maintenance, however, and not of great concern in surveying the boat.

Blisters that form on the bottoms of fiberglass boats are another story. The cause of these is not fully established. Basically, a gas or water bubble forms under the gel coating or between plies of the fiberglass laminate. These sometimes grow in size over a period of time. The usual repair is to open up the blisters and fill them with epoxy putty, as detailed in Chapter 12.

If the boat has a fiberglass rudder, as most fiberglass sailboats do, this should be examined carefully. Rudders are molded in two halves, then bonded together. The center section is filled with a core material, but sometimes it is left hollow. If water has gotten inside, this should be drained out. The hollow area should then be filled in with foam, a mixture of resin and microballoons, or other suitable material. This is a common problem with hollow areas in fiberglass boat structures that cannot be easily drained. Water almost invariably gets inside.

Next, examine all external fittings and attachments. This includes cleats, windows and ports, stanchions and lifelines, bow rails, taffrails, chokes, etc. Does the fitting look adequate? Is it firmly attached? Has it caused damage to the surrounding fiberglass laminate in the area of attachment?

Examine the hatches and doors. If these are fiberglass, examine them in the same manner as other fiberglass laminates. Also examine hinges, slides, latches, and other hardware. These should be attached with through bolts. Screws tapped into holes in the fiberglass laminates indicate poor construction. These have little holding power.

Masts and Rigging

Any meaningful survey of spars and rigging requires extensive knowledge and experience with sailing and sailboats. The chain plates must be attached to the hull, deck, or cabin structures so that they can withstand heavy loadings. Check fiberglass laminates in attachment areas for signs of stress cracks and other damage.

The mast can be stepped on the keel, on deck, or on the cabin top. The deck and cabin top arrangements often have a mast hinge for easier stepping of the mast. A main concern with the deck and cabin top arrangements is that they are adequately reinforced to withstand the loadings, which can be considerable. Indications of trouble include a sunken area in deck or cabin laminate in the area of mast, cracks in the gel coat in the area of the mast step or hinge, and delamination of fiberglass skins from core materials in the area of the mast step or hinge.

Evaluate the condition of the mast, boom, and other spars. Inspect all standing and running rigging. Check all sails thoroughly, hoisting them if conditions permit this. Check all blocks for possible wear or damage. Check travellers and their attachment to the boat, which should be with through bolting.

Surveying Interiors

The exterior and interior surveying cannot be completely separated. Something you see on the exterior will require inspection on the inside, and vice versa. Sometimes you will have to go back and forth.

I usually begin with the forepeak area. The visibility of the rough side of the laminate varies greatly from boat to boat. It might be partly or completely covered up with a fiberglass liner, paneling, upholstery, or some other material, or it might be exposed or even painted. In some cases, the rough side of the laminate can be seen inside the chain locker and/or inside the storage compartments under the berths.

Regardless, examine as much of the laminate as you can. This is like checking a gel coat surface, except this time the cracks or other damage or defects will be in the clear resin or paint surface.

Look at the overall quality of the laminate. Partially dry glass fibers, unraveled strands of reinforcing material, and air bubbles indicate sloppy lay-up work. I like to see woven roving, or at least cloth, as the last layer of laminate. Least desirable is a matlike laminate that was sprayed up with a chopper gun, although a hand lay-up of mat over woven roving is okay. Look especially in out of the way areas, such as inside chain lockers and under berths. Inspect all berths, liners, upholstery, woodwork, and other items in the forward area.

Check that all deck fittings are properly through-bolted with backing plates or blocks. Inspect for leaking, which usually leaves rust streaks on the fiberglass. With sailboats, be sure the chain plate for the headstay is through-bolted and has a backing plate or block.

Next check the hull-to-deck joint, starting at the bow area inside the hull and working along one side to the stern. Quality fiberglass boats have a lap joint that is through-bolted then fiberglassed over with strips of fiberglass. Check the bonding of the fiberglass strips. Look for water stains or other signs of leaking. After checking the hull-to-deck joint on one side, continue around the transom and along the other side back to the starting point at the bow.

The hull-to-deck joint is a frequent source of trouble because hull twisting places heavy loadings on it. A well-designed hull-to-deck joint of good quality effectively combines the two laminates into a single unit. If you find signs of actual separation, the problem can be serious and repair extremely difficult.

The hull-to-deck joint might or might not be in line with the rub rail on the exterior of the hull. Regardless, the area opposite the rub rail attachment should be examined inside the hull. Damage is sometimes caused in this area by the boat banging against pilings or other boats or obstacles.

When surveying sailboats, also check the attachment of chain plates. Look for any signs of overstressing of the laminates to which they are attached. If fasteners are loose, there might be leakage. Look for rust and water stains.

Check all remaining deck fittings to see if they are properly through-bolted with backing plates or blocks. Any fitting that has heavy loadings is a possible source of problems.

Next, check all bulkheads, berth bottoms, countertops, and other items that are bonded to the shell laminates with fiberglass bonding strips. Check the bonds to make certain they are secure.

The quality of woodwork varies greatly in manufactured fiberglass boats. Lower quality boats use plastic laminates to cover the edge grain of bulkheads, whereas higher quality boats use wood trim and wood veneers. Wood pieces should be fastened together with screws and/or bolts, not with nails or staples that tend to work loose. Wood attachments to cabin soles should be bolted in place.

Thoroughly check the bilge and other areas below the waterline. In boats with ballast, check this over carefully. If the ballast is internal, make certain that it is well sealed over with fiberglass and has not been leaking. If the ballast is external, check the keel bolts for signs of rust and leakage. Before this can be done, however, any water in the bilge must be drained away.

Check rudder and propeller shaft stuffing boxes. Check the attachment to the hull for possible cracks and leaks.

Inspections of Systems

I find it helpful to check systems out as a unit.

Icebox. The icebox should have insulation on all sides and at the bottom and top, including the door or lid. Check the drain system. Iceboxes that drain into the bilge can give a bad odor to the interior of the boat. A better arrangement is an overboard drain system, which usually requires a pump. The drain should have a water trap to insulate the inside of the icebox from outside heat.

Water Tanks and Systems. Examine the water tanks. Inspect for leakage and contaminated water. Check all water pipes and hoses, pumps, and faucets. Note any required repairs. Determine if any tanks or other parts of the system require replacement and how difficult it is to do. In some cases, access to the water tank is limited. A removable inspection plate allows you to examine the interior of the tank and clean the inside conveniently. Ease of tank removal varies. It could simply be a matter of unbolting mounting brackets. The tank could also be bonded in place with fiberglass or even placed under a fiberglass liner; this will make removal more difficult. In some cases, the fiberglass hull laminate or a fiberglass liner forms the water tank. These usually have removable top sections.

Two basic types of pumping systems are used: hand (or foot) pumps and electric pressure pumps. Check to see that they operate properly.

Some fresh water systems have water heaters. Most hot water heaters operate at dockside with shore electrical power. Some have heat exchangers to use with the engine when away from shore power.

Leaks in various parts of the piping systems can be a special problem. Check out these systems with water running through the piping.

Sinks and Drain Systems. Sinks and drain systems are simple arrangements. If the through-hull drain fittings are near or below the waterline, they should be fitted with seacocks. Brass gate valves of the type commonly sold at hardware stores are unsuitable. If these are used on a manufactured boat, it indicates that the manufacturing was skimpy, which could result in the sinking of the boat. I've twice had gate valves of this type fall apart as I was opening them, and water then leaked in. Fortunately, the pressure is low this near the waterline and I easily plugged the flow, but what would have happened if they had broken when I wasn't around? Because they were ballast sailboats without positive flotation, they would have sunk.

Stoves. Galley cooking stoves vary considerably. Fuels used included alcohol, kerosene, diesel, and liquified petroleum (LP) gas. The latter is the most dangerous because it is heavier than air and explosive. The gas bottle for these should be located in gastight compartments or in the open on deck. When located in gastight compartments, they should be separate from the rest of the boat. The bottom of the compartment should be overboard vented. There should be shut-off valves at the gas bottles and between the stove and the companionway exit.

Check how the stove is mounted. The stove should either be firmly attached to the galley counter or attached to the gimbals, which are in turn firmly attached to the galley counter.

Engines. Unless you are a highly trained and experienced mechanic, you will probably need assistance here. The engine should be checked thoroughly to determine the condition and if it operates properly. This applies also to gearboxes, exhaust and cooling systems, stuffing boxes, and electrical systems.

The fuel systems require special consideration. Fill pipes for gas tanks should be grounded to the tank and to the grounding system. The tanks should be in properly ventilated compartments and vented to the outside. Gas presents more danger than diesel fuel because it is heavier than air and highly explosive.

The steering system and engine controls should be followed

out and checked for any damage, wear, or improper installation.

Electrical System. Check for proper installation of battery, wiring, and circuit breakers for running lights, interior lights, and other electrical hookups. Electrical systems vary greatly in manufactured boats. Many owners add extra equipment. Sometimes this is done properly, other times it is a mess.

Anchoring Systems. These vary greatly. Some have only an anchor and line. Others have chain lockers, rope or chain deck pipes, hand or power windlasses, anchor rollers, etc. It takes considerable experience to know what is adequate for a particular boat. This depends in part on how and where the boat is to be used.

Other Equipment

Many boats also have other equipment, such as cabin heaters, canvas tops, covers, and other canvas work, toilets, holding tanks, bilge pumps, fire extinguishers, trim tabs, davits, and shore power hookups. Check all these. Specialized knowledge might be required for evaluating some of this equipment, and you might want to seek outside help. This is especially true of electronic equipment such as marine radios, depth sounders, etc.

PROFESSIONAL SURVEYS AND SURVEYORS

Insurance companies frequently require a satisfactory survey by an approved professional boat surveyor before they insure a boat, especially a used one. The same applies to banks and other loan institutions. They want a survey to decide how much money to loan on a particular boat.

Selection of a boat surveyor must be done carefully. The surveyor should have extensive knowledge and experience with many boats. Many good surveyors are also experienced boatbuilders or designers. It is extremely difficult to determine competency of any one surveyor, however, because there are presently no qualification standards or licensing requirements.

Most insurance companies and banks and loan institutions have a list of surveyors that are acceptable to them. To insure with them or borrow money, you must use one of these surveyors. Before making a selection, check their qualifications and reputations. In most boating areas of the United States, there are one or more boat surveyors who are considered to be outstanding. Yacht brokers, boat dealers, and boatyards sometimes make recommendations.

Because you must pay for the survey, you will want to hire the best surveyor available. In return, the surveyor should work with your interests in mind. One of the main complaints I hear against surveyors is that they are actually working for the brokers, banks, loan institutions, and insurance companies, even though you pay for the survey. There is probably some truth to this.

Hire a surveyor who will thoroughly search the boat for defects, needed repairs, and trouble spots. A good surveyor can accurately appraise the boat's present condition and value.

It is common practice for surveyors to give a written report. A typical survey sheet includes such information as the name of the vessel, type of vessel, official number, purpose of survey, intended service, waters to be navigated, date and location of survey, surveyed on dry dock or afloat, and other information.

This is followed by sections for the hull, propulsion machinery, auxiliary power plant, fuel and water tanks, deck and special equipment, fire hazards and protection, sea connections and through-hull fittings, and estimates of market and replacement values.

Next comes a general statement space. For one survey, the general statement said, "Survey indicates vessel is basically in sound condition with exceptions noted." These were then listed.

Finally, there is space for a concluding statement. For one boat survey, this said, "Unless otherwise stated, survey was made without making removal to expose parts normally concealed, taking borings to check laminates, testing for tightness or trying the machinery. This survey is based upon facts presented and discovered, based on my opinion, without warranty either specified or implied." The signature of the surveyor followed. Forms used by various surveyors vary considerably.

The surveyor will want to know the purpose of the survey; that is, if it is primarily for obtaining insurance or a loan, for determining the condition of the boat and its value so that you can decide if you want to buy it, or for a combination of reasons. Before hiring a surveyor, you should have a frank discussion with him as to exactly what you want. The surveyor should in turn tell you if he can provide this. He should also tell you what his fee will be.

Some surveyors specialize, such as fiberglass boats only, sailboats only, or powerboats only. Some will not survey engines and other mechanical equipment. No one person can be an expert in everything, so it's important that you know any limitations.

Finally, it should be repeated that a survey is not a guarantee. It is an opinion and, hopefully, an expert one.

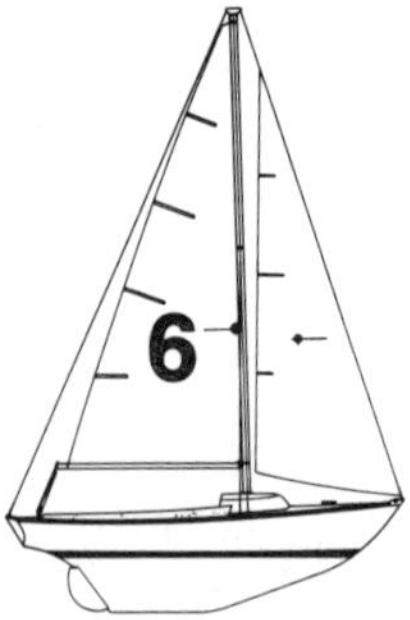

Buying Fiberglass Boats

The material covered so far is basic to buying a fiberglass boat. There are so many types, sizes, and prices for fiberglass boats, both new and used, that you must have some starting point. By now, you probably have a certain type and size of boat in mind, narrowing the field considerably. This must be matched with the price you can afford or are willing to pay. In many cases, this will mean buying a smaller size of boat or buying used instead of new.

In this chapter, new boats and used boats are discussed separately. When you start your search, however, you will probably want to look at everything that is available—both new and used—in the size range you have in mind. I suggest that whenever it is convenient to do so, look at whatever else is for sale. You can learn a lot about boats in this way.

NEW

New boats are sold in various ways. Dealers offer one or more makes of fiberglass boats. Brokers who sell used boats sometimes handle new boats too. Some new boats are available direct from the manufacturers. These sources are listed in phone books. They also advertise in newspapers and boating magazines.

A good starting place is a boat show. While these vary from quite small, such as a few dealers displaying boats at a mall, to the very large ones staged in major cities, they can all be helpful. A word of advice: Look, examine the boats, ask questions, gather up brochures—but don't buy. There are often boat show discounts that seem irresistible, but when you first start looking, almost all boats might look irresistible.

There might be exceptions to the don't buy rule. If you have already done all your homework and legwork and know exactly which boat you want to buy, then perhaps the boat show discount might be the way to go. Boats on display at boat shows do suffer some minor damage and wear because hundreds of people paw through them, trying to pull them apart, etc. If you do purchase here, make certain that the purchase is pending a survey and/or inspection to your satisfaction after the boat show and also a satisfactory sea trial. Make certain that you have the option to reject the boat and get all of your deposit back.

The point is, don't let the glitter and bright lights of a boat show carry you away. It's easier to buy a boat than to sell one. If you purchase a boat that turns out to be unsuitable to your needs, you might have to take a loss to resell it.

Boat shows give you a chance to look at and compare boats put out by different manufacturers. As you narrow your choice down to fewer and fewer boats, you will want to make more detailed comparisons. In a certain price range, you might have a choice of two boats that fit your needs. One is larger and plainer, the other is slightly smaller but better appointed. By going from one boat to the other, you might be able to decide which means more to you.

Before you buy, its a good idea to see the boats again at the dealer's showroom. This gives you more time to think about your choice. The salesman should now be able to spend more time with you. Although policies vary, you might be able to get an in-the-water performance demonstration in the boat you are interested in. The dealer will probably want to be sure you are a serious prospect, however. Some people are just after free boat rides.

I believe that it is worthwhile to visit the manufacturing plant before you buy, or even before you make a final decision about what boat you intend to buy. The cost of this will vary depending on where you live in relation to the manufacturing plant. Sometimes the manufacturer will deduct the cost of the airfare from the price of the boat should you decide to buy. Don't let this factor influence your judgement, however.

Some of the larger manufacturing plants have regular tours for visitors. Most show you around and answer your questions on an individual basis, at least if they think you are a serious prospect. Most try to show you only what they want you to see, but if you know what to look for, you can see more than this. If the advertised specifications say that the moldings are hand laid up and you see moldings being sprayed up with a chopper gun, you might pretend that you don't know anything about fiberglass molding and ask what that man is doing over there.

Some of the largest fiberglass boat manufacturers put out some of the worst boats, some of the smallest ones the best boats. There is no general rule.

Some manufacturers will sell boats to you directly; others sell only through dealers. This sometimes depends on whether there is a dealer in the area where you live. If you purchase direct from the factory, there could be problems getting the boat transported to your area and getting the boat commissioned, unless you can take care of these things yourself (see Chapter 8). If the boat is trailerable and you purchase it with a trailer, you could tow it home. This still leaves the commissioning problem, however, that is ordinarily handled by the boat dealer. You could also have the boat commissioned and launched near the factory so that you can power or sail the boat back to home port, conditions and your boating experience permitting.

While some fiberglass boat manufacturers market their boats only through dealerships, others don't have dealerships and sell only factory direct. This might be less convenient to buy a boat, but it can mean a much lower price. Dealerships add considerably to the price of each boat sold.

Regardless of where you buy a new boat, the boats that you are shown might be for display only. In other cases, these boats are for sale. Sometimes dealers and brokers use a new boat as a demonstrator for a period of time, then sell the boat as a new boat or at a reduced price because the boat was a demonstrator. A boat could also be *the* demonstrator until someone buys it. Some boats are sold as "new" even though they have been used to give in-the-water demonstrations or as displays at boat shows or in showrooms.

If the boats are mainly for display, the dealer will order one for you or a similar one with your choice of color, equipment, etc. Be sure to ask how long it will take for delivery.

Making the Purchase

Once you have found the boat you want and have agreed on a price, you must sign a contract or sales agreement. If you are ordering a boat rather than taking one that is in stock, you must decide on specifics, such as color, upholstery fabrics, equipment, engine, sails, etc. A deposit of 10 or 15 percent of the purchase price is usually required at this point. The balance is due when the boat is delivered, but this should be clearly stated in the contract or sales agreement. It's also a good idea to have the option of cancelling the agreement and getting your deposit back if the boat is not delivered by a certain date.

If you are purchasing a boat that is in stock, there are a number of ways that this might be handled. You can pay the money and take the boat. You might pay a deposit (the amount will vary) to hold the boat for you pending satisfactory financing or whatever. It should be clearly spelled out in the contract or sales agreement that your deposit will be refunded if you are unable to get satisfactory financing. If the boat requires fitting out or commissioning before it is ready for you, you could either pay the full price or a deposit with the balance due when you take the boat.

Financing can be a problem. Sometimes the dealer offers financing or arranges this for you. You can often get lower interest rates, however, if you arrange your own financing through a credit union that you belong to or elsewhere.

Some dealers accept a boat as a trade-in, although they often won't give you as much as you could get by selling it yourself or having a broker sell it for you. Other dealers will not accept trade-ins. This is especially true with larger, higher priced boats. If you do trade a boat in, you only have to pay sales tax on the difference between the amount you are given on the trade-in and the price of the new boat, rather than on the full purchase price. This saves you the trouble and inconvenience of finding a buyer for your old boat.

Warranties and Guarantees

Warranties and guarantees on new boats vary. Make certain that these are clearly spelled out in writing. You will want to know who will take care of any problems that develop. Can the dealer take care of them? Or is the manufacturer responsible? If it is a small trailerable boat and you have a trailer for it, you might not mind bringing the boat in to the dealer for work. But if it is a large boat that is kept in the water, will they come to the boat? Or could the work be done at a boatyard? This should all be spelled out in the warranties and guarantees. Try to get all of these matters settled to your satisfaction before you pay any money. After payment is made, you will lose most of your bargaining power.

The value of warranties and guarantees often depend on the

dealer where you buy the boat. Some have good reputations, which they want to keep. They honor their (or the manufacturer's) warranties and guarantees in a prompt and courteous manner. Other dealers make things as difficult and inconvenient as possible. This is why it is so important to check the reputation of the dealer before you buy.

Read all warranties over carefully before you buy. If it is a limited warranty, make certain you understand what is and what isn't covered. If it is a full warranty, all items covered should be promptly repaired or replaced. There should not be any charge to the buyer with a full warranty.

New Versus Used

There are a number of advantages to buying a new boat rather than a used one. You can get a guarantee or warranty, which is seldom available with used boats. You can get the latest model or be one of the first to get a certain design that has just been introduced on the market. This might also mean that all the bugs have not yet been worked out.

Introducing new boats is costly for manufacturers, especially for larger boats. Many boats are thus kept in production for long periods of time. One manufacturer might make improvements over the years, another might start to skimp. I know of some boats that started out as fairly high quality; then over the years, declined. In several cases, this was the result of change of ownership or management of the manufacturing company.

There is one important advantage to a boat model that has been in production for many years. You know the reputation of the boat and also know what the resale value is likely to be. Talk to owners of the particular boat. Check boating advertisements to find out what used boats of the particular model sell for.

Another advantage of buying new is that you can get the boat in the color you want, equipped the way you want it, with the upholstery fabrics you chose, etc. There are limitations, especially if you don't want to wait for a special order boat but rather purchase a display boat or boat that is in stock.

There is something to be said about having it brand new: you can do the care and maintenance properly. If you like to make changes and alterations however, you might be more hesitant to do this on a new boat than on a used one. Also, every little nick and scratch in the gel coat can be more heartbreaking than with a used boat that already has a few nicks and scratches.

When you purchase a new boat, you won't have to contend with modifications and additions that previous owners almost invariably, it seems, make. Most of the used boats I've purchased, seem to have a maze of holes drilled through deck and cabin moldings and elsewhere that must be filled in. You won't have this problem with a new boat, though you will have to make certain that added equipment is installed properly. Some of this work can be done by the dealer. The quality of workmanship can vary greatly here. While some dealers have highly experienced workers do these jobs, others don't.

There are also a number of disadvantages to buying new. You will probably pay a higher price than for a similar used boat. The new boat is sold as a basic boat and many items, including essential ones, are sold as optional extras. This can be costly. Used boats, however, often already have this extra equipment. Some items can be put off to a later time when you can better afford them, but others are essential to the operation and safety of the boat and must be purchased when you buy the boat or at least before you use the boat.

While you normally think of boat surveys as being only for used boats, they can be useful for new boats too, especially for larger and more expensive ones. Some new boats are actually in poor or unsound condition. Required fiberglass bonding strips, for example, might have been omitted in the construction because of poor inspection, quality control, or some other reason. Or the boat might have been damaged during shipping, loading or unloading, or at some other time.

At the very least, you should conduct your own thorough inspection of the boat before you take delivery. Have all defects and problems taken care of before you complete the purchase transaction. Many boat dealers attempt to put you off on this, saying that they will take care of it later. But remember, after you have completed the purchase, you have lost much of your control over the situation. It is extremely important to avoid situations that involve legal action; this can be expensive and time consuming.

There is always some risk involved when you purchase a new boat. It might not live up to your expectations. It might be defective. You might have unexpected problems. By learning as much as possible about fiberglass boats and doing comparative shopping before you buy, however, you can greatly reduce the risks involved.

New Boat Prices

It is quite difficult to know what a particular model of a certain make of fiberglass boat should cost. There are now a number of boat buyer's guides that are published, usually annually, but these seem to include less and less price information, perhaps because the manufacturers are refusing to release this information to the publishers of these guides. A more complete source is the *New Boat Directory*. It's published by BUC International Corporation, 2455 East Sunrise Boulevard, Fort Lauderdale, Florida 33304, and is issued annually. This publication is expensive, however. Some libraries have copies, or boat dealers and brokers might let you look at their copies.

Manufacturers who sell factory direct usually do so only when they don't have dealerships representing them, at least not in the area where you live. Buying direct from a manufacturer might result in a lower price, although this depends on many factors. While you can expect to save some money because there won't be a dealer markup—usually about 20 to 30 percent—you save only part of this. Without dealerships, the manufacturer has to spend more money for advertising and handling the sales at the factory, which is a sort of dealership in itself. Unless you take delivery at the factory, you also have to pay shipping costs. Some manufacturers might have their own delivery trucks and can give you rates that are lower than standard boat hauling firms charge.

Another factor is that manufacturers who sell factory direct are usually low volume producers. This can mean higher boat prices than those of a manufacturer with a higher production volume and hundreds of dealerships selling the boats.

In most cases, especially with smaller sizes and lower priced boats, you will be purchasing from or through a dealer. The markups over the wholesale prices—or what the dealer pays the manufacturer for the boat and the selling price—varies, but is usually in the range of 20 to 30 percent. Sometimes the retail or selling prices are firmly set by the manufacturer. Sometimes the dealers are allowed to set their own prices. If you can go to more than one dealer that handles a particular boat, you can compare prices. If the prices are exactly the same, they are set by the manufacturer. If they vary, they are set by the dealers. This does not necessarily mean that the dealer offering the lowest price is the best deal for you. You also need to consider the dealer's reputation, service department, and location.

Try to get as much price information as possible before you go to a dealer. This can help you find out approximately what his markup is. Talk to other people who have bought boats recently from the same dealer. They can often tell you what they paid for their boats. They are also a source of additional information about the particular dealer and the boat.

Other Considerations

You must make certain that the boat meets all safety requirements and that it has the required safety equipment aboard.

In many states, you must pay sales tax. This is paid to the dealer when you purchase the boat, or you are billed for this tax later or will pay it when you register the boat in your name.

In most cases, you either have to register the boat in the state in which you are a resident or document the boat with the federal government. Documentation is handled at the Coast Guard district headquarters in the district you live in. The process for documentation of a new boat is fairly simple; it can be quite complicated for a used boat. Most boat dealers will help you with the paperwork and details.

If you register your boat, you must have registration numbers on the bow area of your boat. If you have documentation, you don't. Instead, you get a number that is permanently affixed inside the boat, often by carving the numbers into a main wood beam.

You still must pay state sales tax if you document, but there are a number of advantages. Documentation gives a proof of ownership that is more acceptable than registration, especially in other countries. And because the Coast Guard maintains a record of documented boats, there is a record that you have clear title. This is an advantage if you sell the boat. The buyer can easily check to see that you have clear title. Anyone financing the boat would prefer that the vessel be documented.

Not all boats qualify for documentation. The boat must have 500 cubic feet of internal space. A formula is used to determine this. It's based on the overall length of the boat, the greatest beam, and depth from deck to top of ballast. This measurement is not the weight or displacement of the boat, but rather the internal volume of "air space."

For documentation, you need a Master Carpenter's Certificate. This is a form filled out by the builder of the boat. When you purchase the boat from a dealer, you should get the Master Carpenter's Certificate for the boat and two identical bills of sale, which should be on special Coast Guard forms. You then take these to the Coast Guard district headquarters in the district where you live. There you fill out a form designating the name for the boat and another form swearing that you are a citizen of the United States. You are assigned a permanent number, which stays with the boat no matter how many times it changes owners. There is always the option of discontinuing the documentation and going back to regular registration.

You should get insurance coverage that will be in effect as soon as you buy the boat. Insurance coverage and premiums vary, so check with a number of insurance companies and comparison shop before you buy. You can insure a new boat without a boat survey. Homeowner's insurance policies sometimes cover small boats. Check to see if yours does before taking out additional insurance.

For trailerable boats, you might want to purchase a boat trailer along with the boat as a single package, even include the trailer in the financing. You must register the boat trailer separately from the boat. Registration fees vary from state to state. You must also pay sales tax on the trailer. This will be paid to the dealer that you buy the boat from or when you register the trailer in your name or at some later time.

In addition to the cost of the boat, interest on any financing, sales tax, fee for registration or documentation, and other costs at the time of purchase, there is also on-going costs and responsibilities of boat ownership (see Chapter 7). These should be considered before you buy a boat.

USED

The main reason for buying used instead of new is financial. A used boat usually sells for less than the same model new. However, many used boats now sell for higher prices than the owners paid for them new because the value of the dollar has gone down due to inflation.

Whether or not the used boat is a better buy depends on many factors. It's possible to get a better buy in a used boat, but there are also more risks involved. What type of investment it is depends on the particular boat and how much you pay for it.

Used boats are sold in various ways. You can buy directly from a private party. You can buy through a broker. Some boat dealers also sell used boats. Often, these are trade-ins.

Used fiberglass boats are frequently advertised in newspaper classified ads and in boating publications. You can tell immediately which are by private parties and which are by brokers and dealers. The latter usually gives the name of the firm in the ad.

Banks and other loan institutions sometimes sell used boats that they have repossessed. These are sometimes sold for a stated price or are offered on a bid basis. The rules and procedures vary on this, but usually the bids are sealed and must be in before a certain date. A deposit is sometimes required. This is refunded unless yours is the highest bid. If yours is the highest bid and you decide not to go ahead with the purchase, you lose your deposit, although again this varies. In most cases, the bank or other loan institution has the right to reject any and all bids if they so desire.

Purchasing a used boat by this method requires fast action. You must evaluate and decide if and how much you want to bid by a certain date. To do this effectively, you must have a thorough understanding of fiberglass boats and their value. In general, a bid should be lower than the actual used market value for the particular boat. It's better to miss out than to pay too much, even though it might not seem so at the time in the excitement of boat buying.

I do not recommend the bid method for a newcomer to boating, unless you have access to competent advice from a boat knowledgeable relative or friend. Otherwise, there are just too many possible problems and pitfalls. At the very least, do not bid until you have looked at many used boats offered for sale by private parties and brokers.

Boatyards, waterfronts, and marinas are good places to look for used boats for sale. These boats often display "For Sale" signs. They could be in the water, on boat trailers, or in dry storage.

Spend a minimum of several months looking at used boats before you even think of actually buying one. At first, you might see a boat that looks like a good deal, then you'll see another that looks even better. If you purchase the first boat, you're stuck with it. You might be able to sell the first boat and then purchase the second, but this a time-consuming process. If you want to sell it quickly, you might have to take a loss on it. By the time you sold the first boat, the second one could be sold already. The second boat might not be a good choice either, because you'll certainly find even better buys later. The point is that the odds are extremely small that you will find the best buy in the type and size of boat you want the first time out. After looking at hundreds of used boats, you will be in a better position to recognize a good buy when it comes your way.

In my many years of looking at used boats for sale, I saw very few boats that were outstanding bargains, at least that still seemed so in light of further experience. By this I mean boats that sold for thousands less than their market value at the time. It's better to pay a little more to get a boat that's just right for you than to get a "bargain" that's not quite right.

If you buy a boat from the owner, there is no set procedure. You pay the money, the registration is signed over to you, and you take the boat. You might pay a deposit to hold the boat for you for a certain length of time. If you decide not to go ahead with the purchase, the deposit might be refunded to you. It all depends on what the arrangements have been made and what written agreement you have. In some cases, the deposit will hold the boat for you pending your ability to get financing or a satisfactory survey and/or sea trial. It's important to have this arrangement clearly stated in a written agreement, especially in terms of refunding your deposit if you don't go through with the purchase.

Possible problems and difficulties become greater as the price of the boat increases. This is why boats with higher values are typically sold through boat brokers.

There are many things to look out for when purchasing a used fiberglass boat from a private party. First establish if you are dealing with a boat owner who simply wants to sell the boat because he wants to move up to a larger boat, get out of boating, or has some other standard reason. You must establish that the person legally owns the boat without any liens on it. You must clear title to the vessel in most cases. If the seller still owes money on financing to a bank or other loan institution, this must be paid off to clear the title on the boat. The seller might need to use part of the money you are paying to pay off the balance of the boat loan. How all this is handled should be clearly stated in a written agreement. Especially avoid getting caught in a situation where you have paid for the boat and then find you do not have clear title to it.

Some people buy rundown, damaged, or sunk boats. These are then fixed up and put on the market as used boats. Some people do this as a regular business, even though the boats are often sold as though from a private party.

There are other people who simply buy a used boat at a very low price, then resell it for a higher price. This often amounts to a business run with little overhead and without a business license. Sometimes, these verge on being ripoffs.

And then there are individuals and rings that sell stolen boats. A few unfortunate people have thought they had bought a boat, only to find it was stolen property. Watch out especially for people who want quick cash deals and for boats priced far below market value.

Some people are embarrassed to check a boat's registration.

You shouldn't be. The only people who should really care are those who don't have valid title. In most states, there is a state agency that checks boat registrations and titles.

In most cases, used boats that are put up for sale are legitimate offers. Most people sell used boats because they want to get out of boating. They found that they didn't get enough use out of the boat, it proved to be too expensive, or they want to move up to a larger or different type boat. In only a few cases are boats pawned off by private parties with poorly repaired damaged areas and other cover-ups. You must still look out for these things, but they are rare.

Boats are often advertised as "excellent condition," or "good condition," or "needs tender loving care," or "handyman special." I am often surprised when I actually see these boats. Some labelled "excellent condition" are really "handyman specials." Some "handyman specials" are basically sound boats needing only a good clean-up job to put them in good condition. Some people try to oversell their boats; others tend to undersell. The main point is that you can tell very little about the boat until you actually see it; you could be pleasantly or unpleasantly surprised.

Buying Through Brokers

There are both advantages and disadvantages to buying a boat through a broker. Boat brokers sell boats on a commission basis, usually 10 percent of the selling price of the boat. If you buy a boat, the broker keeps 10 percent of the money and turns the rest over to the seller. Indirectly, the buyer is paying the commission in most cases because most sellers add at least 10 percent to the selling price to cover the broker's commission. This is one of the main disadvantages to purchasing a boat through a broker.

Brokers act as a go-between the buyer and seller. The broker negotiates the terms of the sale and sees that they are carried out. The broker also acts as an escrow agent for deposits and other funds paid by the buyer. These are held until the sale is completed and title is transferred to the buyer. This can be a tremendous advantage for both the buyer and seller and is especially true with higher priced boats. Selling direct works out okay for boats priced at about $5,000 or even $10,000, but more than this point can cause considerable problems in negotiating and carrying out the transfer of funds and other details of the sale. Both buyers and sellers feel more comfortable having a broker handle these details. The broker is (hopefully) a professional who makes his living doing this.

The seller might think the broker's services won't cost him anything. He will simply ask at least 10 percent more for the boat to cover the broker's commission. The buyer, in turn, wants to get the boat for the same price as he would buying direct from an owner. The final price is usually a compromise somewhere in between.

The broker's commission is based on the price the boat actually sells for, not the asking price. Most boats sold through brokers end up selling for less than the asking price. In most cases, the asking price is higher than the broker really expects to sell the boat for. This might be because the owner set the price too high. The broker often goes along with this to get the listing, knowing that most sellers will come down if the boat does not sell in a short period of time. Or the broker might have set the high asking price in consultation with the seller. It is common practice to leave some room to come down on the price to close a deal.

Brokers advertise the boats they have listed at their own expense. They do this by taking out advertisements in newspapers, boating publications, and elsewhere. The brokers have their offices in boating areas, often at marinas or nearby. They post their listings on bulletin boards in the windows of their office. Sometimes photos of the boats are also included. Inside, they have listing books that described all the boats they list. There are often separate books for sailboats, powerboats, and houseboats, assuming that the broker handles all of these. Some brokers specialize, only handling sailboats or powerboats for instance. The listing books are further arranged by boat size and give the make, model, measurements, and a complete equipment list as well as the asking price. There might also be one or more photos of the boat, advertising sheets, accommodation plans, and other materials about the boat if the seller has provided these.

Many brokerage firms are highly specialized. Many only handle boats that are in certain price ranges. A small, local broker at a marina might handle mainly boats selling for under $20,000. Slightly larger firms with several salesmen might concentrate on boats priced from about $15,000 to $40,000. Larger firms with offices in several large boating centers might specialize in handling boats that sell for over $40,000. Some of the largest brokerages might only handle boats that are priced over $100,000. When you start looking for a boat, go to those brokers that sell boats in your price range.

You can go to a broker and look at his listings. If you see something you might be interested in, ask to see the boat. Also look at other boats listed in the general size and price range that you are interested in.

If the broker doesn't have anything you like, tell him what you are looking for and have him contact you if he comes up with anything. Many brokers have cross-listings with other brokers in other areas, so they might locate something for you this way.

Boat brokers try to match a prospective buyer to the right boat, or so they claim. In my opinion, this service is overrated. I've known too many boat brokers who were little more than super salesmen to place much faith in them as boat consultants. You might want to find a broker that you can call "your" broker and let him find the right boat for you. Good luck, but check the reputation of the broker first. As in most businesses, there are honest brokers and dishonest ones. There is no licensing (other than regular business licenses) or qualifying standards for becoming a boat broker. A broker should be bonded and use an escrow account for client funds. There are some professional associations for brokers; membership in these should be a plus factor. Check the office of the broker. It should be properly organized and staffed and make you feel confident about transferring funds into the broker's escrow account.

Especially avoid brokers who are lackadaisical. They, and there are many of them, are too lazy to even get out of their office chair to go show you a boat. They expect you to go down and take a look at the boat and come back if you decide to buy it. Don't bother.

Once you locate a boat you want to buy, make an offer through the broker. While procedures vary, it is typical to pay a deposit, usually 10 percent of the price you are offering. Make an offer that is lower than the asking price. It should not be more than you are willing to or can pay. A sales agreement will be written out by the broker. If the offer is lower than the asking price, it will be pending acceptance by the seller. If the seller does not accept the offer, your deposit will be returned. The seller might make a counteroffer that is lower than the original asking price, but higher than the offer. You can either reject this or accept it and go ahead with the purchase. You might be able to make another offer that is lower than the seller's, but higher than your first offer. The seller might also tell the broker that he has given his lowest offer and will not hear any lower offers. If the boat does not sell for a long period of time, however, the asking price might even be lowered beyond this point, and the seller might wish he had accepted your offer.

Whenever you make an offer, even if it is for the asking price, the sale can be pending certain conditions. Typical conditions include satisfactory survey and a sea trial, and if you are going to finance the purchase, satisfactory financing. These conditions should be written into the sales agreement. They should be based on your own opinion. You should be the one who has the final say as to what is satisfactory, not a professional surveyor or a loan institution or anyone else. It should clearly state in the agreement that the deposit will be refunded if you do not accept the boat for any of these reasons.

How far you can go with conditions varies. It might even be possible to include a condition such as pending sale of present boat. There will usually be a time limit placed on the conditions, however. The owner will not want to tie up the boat with pending conditions for too long a time.

If everything turns out to be satisfactory, the balance of the money is paid to the broker and a signed (by seller) bill of sale or title transfer (this varies in different states) is turned over to you. Part of the money you paid might be used to pay off a lien on the boat, while the remainder stays in the brokers escrow account. This money is not turned over to the seller until you have clear title to the boat, at which time the remainder of the money is taken out of the escrow account. The broker takes his commission and pays the rest to the seller. The sale is thus completed.

Used Boat Prices

It is quite difficult to know what a particular model and year of a certain make should cost. One guide is to study the advertised prices for similar used boats. This is feasible if you are interested in a boat that was manufactured in large numbers. A standard source is *Used Boat Directory*.

Other Considerations

You must be certain the boat meets all safety requirements and has the required safety equipment aboard. In some states you must pay sales tax on used boats. You must also register the boat in the state in which you are a resident or document the boat with the federal government. If the boat is already documented, the procedure is simple. If not, the procedure can be complicated. Check with the Coast Guard district headquarters in your area for details and procedures.

You should get insurance coverage that will be in effect as soon as you buy the boat.

OTHER WAYS TO BUY A BOAT

Another possibility is to have a fiberglass boat custom-built for you by one of the companies that specialize in this type of construction. They will use one of the one-off construction methods detailed in Chapter 14. First you go to a designer and have the plans drawn up. Then you take the plans to a builder and have the boat constructed. The main advantage to this method is that you can get a custom boat constructed to your exact needs and requirements. The main disadvantage is that this is a very expensive way to buy a boat.

You can also build your own fiberglass boat, either from scratch or using a factory-molded hull as a starting point. These methods are detailed in later chapters.

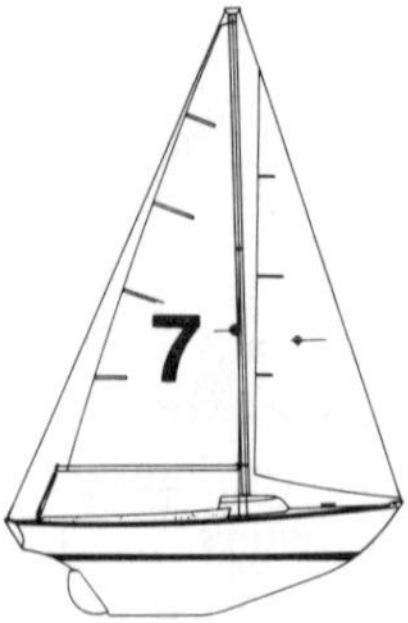

Costs and Responsibilities of Boat Ownership

In addition to the purchase price of a fiberglass boat, there are ongoing costs of boat ownership. There are also responsibilities involved. These costs and responsibilities should be considered before you buy a boat.

A PLACE TO KEEP THE BOAT

Once you own a boat, you need a place to keep it. The cost of this can range from free to quite expensive.

On a Trailer

A boat trailer can reduce or eliminate the cost of a place to keep a boat. There are still costs associated with the boat trailer itself, including registration fees, maintenance costs, and insurance. There is also the cost of fuel and other expenses involved with a vehicle used to tow the boat and trailer.

A boat trailer allows you to store the boat in your yard at home or some other place for free. This is one of the reasons why trailer boats are so popular. Storing your boat at your house makes it convenient for maintaining the boat.

To protect your boat while it is being stored, especially if it is outside in the open, a canvas boat cover is a good idea. These are fairly expensive, but a quality boat cover, especially one made from boat acrylic fabric, will last many years. This can be a sound investment because it helps protect the gel coat finish from sun damage. It also adds to the value of the boat if you ever decide to sell it.

If possible, the boat should be stored inside a garage or other building. If this is not possible, storing it under a roof can be a second choice.

Many people do not have space to keep a boat where they live, or they prefer not to. Some people make arrangements to keep their boats where they work. There are many possibilities here.

There are also storage centers. Monthly rental for outside storage starts at about $10 or so, depending on where you live and other factors. In some parts of the United States it runs much higher. Covered spaces and inside storage is also available and more expensive than outside open storage. Most storage centers are fenced and have security systems, although these vary. Check this over carefully. You will also want to have adequate insurance coverage.

A main disadvantage of this type of storage is the cost. The rent comes due month after month. This is still much less than the rent for a boat slip to keep your boat in the water. Another disadvantage of storage centers is that you can be limited in the amount of work you can do on the boat at the storage center, the rules vary on this point. You might also have limited hours of access to your boat, although some storage centers have 24-hour access.

There are a growing number of special storage yards with launching facilities for trailer boats. In many cases, they tow the boat to the ramp or launching hoist for you and launch the boat. When you return after boating, they haul the boat and return it on the trailer to the storage area. These facilities have become popular in areas where marina slips are scarce. In the future, this concept might expand; it might even be adapted to nontrailer boats.

An important advantage to this method is that you don't have to worry about hauling or towing the boat. It also allows leaving trailerable sailboats rigged. This is an important advantage because it means less time getting ready and more time for boating.

There are many variations to this system. While the fees can be expensive (usually a monthly storage fee and a set charge for each launching and retrieving of the boat), they are less than for renting a boat slip. Security, hours of operation, and services offered vary. Check the particular boat storage and launching business over carefully before signing a rental agreement.

One problem with trailer boats is that going boating can become too much trouble. When you first get a new boat, the trailering to the waterfront, setting up the boat (this is especially a problem with sailboats), launching the boat at a boat ramp, then hauling again after a day of boating, unstepping the mast for sailboats, and preparing the boat for trailering might not seem like much of a problem. This routine can get old fast. Many people soon find that they are using the boat less and less.

It's important that the boat be easy to set up, launch, retrieve, and take down for trailering again. It's also important that the trailer be designed and constructed so that it does not damage the boat.

In some areas, there are free launching ramps; in other locations there are fees. These vary and should be taken into account in determining the costs of boat ownership. Security of tow vehicle and boat trailer while you are out boating can also be a problem. Check this out carefully.

Taking everything into consideration, trailering can be an inexpensive solution to the problem of where to keep your boat. This applies mainly to fairly small boats. After a certain size and weight, it becomes impractical.

In the Water

An increasing number of boats are being kept in the water, either all year or for the boating season. The possibilities for in-the-water mooring vary considerably depending on the area you live in and other factors.

One possibility is to tie the boat up to a bank. Unless it is your own property, you probably won't be able to do this, at least not for long periods of time. Security would also be a problem.

In some places it is possible to anchor free. There are more and more restrictions on this, however. While anchoring for limited periods of time might be tolerated, anchoring more or less permanently isn't. There is often little security when you are not around. If you use a dinghy to get back and forth from shore to the boat, you will need a place to leave the dinghy. This might be at a dock, loaded onto a cartop rack, or taken home with you. Unless the water where you anchor the boat is well protected, you will have the possibility of the boat dragging anchor in storms.

If you live aboard your boat, however, anchoring might be a real budget possibility, especially if you do not stay in any one place too long. If you want to leave the boat for a period, you can probably find space at a marina for the boat until you return.

Another place to keep your boat in the water is at a mooring buoy. These are similar to anchors, except they are permanently set. When you leave the mooring, the mooring line stays. A float is attached, usually with a pennant, so that you can moor again when you return with the boat.

Sometimes you can set your own mooring buoy. A permit might be required before you can do this, or you might not be allowed to do it at all. If you can, you are responsible for maintaining the mooring buoy as well as paying any permit fees.

All this might lead you to ask, "Who owns our waterways?" The answer to this question is complicated. Our boating waters are public property, then again they are not. They are often sold and traded like real estate.

Mooring buoys maintained by someone else, such as the city or county or private business, are sometimes available on a rental basis. You will need a way to get back and forth to your boat from land. A boat taxi service might be provided, or you can use your own dinghy. A secure dock or other place for leaving your dinghy when you are ashore should be provided.

Mooring buoys rent for less than boat slips at marinas, although this varies. Many people have found them to be a satisfactory solution to their boat storage problems.

The most convenient, but also the most expensive, place to keep your boat is at a dock or slip. If you live at the edge of the water, you might have your own boat dock. Most people are not so fortunate, however.

Docks are frequently arranged into marinas. In tidal areas, the docks float so they move up and down with the tidal changes. A *slip* means that the docks extend along both sides of the boat and forward of the boat. A *side-tie* means that you only have a dock on one side of your boat. Full slips rent for more than side-ties in marinas that have both of these arrangements, although policies vary.

In many areas of the United States, space available in marinas lags far behind the demand. There are a number of reasons for this. It is often difficult to get the necessary permits to build new marinas or expand existing ones. Environmental restrictions often preclude construction of marinas. Some people believe that the "shortage" of marina slips has been created deliberately so that the rents can be increased.

Regardless of the reasons, this means that it can be difficult to get a space for your boat in some areas. The problem is most acute in large cities located in popular boating areas and in locations where there are few protected harbor areas. A marina in Long

Beach, California, for example, is reported to have over a 10-year waiting list for slips.

You should investigate the marina situation in your area before you buy a boat. You can make the availability of a marina slip a condition of the sale. If you purchase a boat from a broker who is also the manager of a marina, your name might well move to the top of the waiting list and a slip be made available to you immediately. I'm not at all in favor of this practice, but it is common.

Marinas vary considerably. Some are well managed and maintained, others aren't. Some have modern docks, others are old. Many have at least restrooms and showers, and some are even like country clubs, with swimming pools, saunas, and even golf courses.

In a particular area, slip rentals vary according to the facilities offered. Prices depend on supply and demand. In popular boating centers, slips sometimes rent for $10 or more per foot of boat per month.

Not only do slip rental rates vary, but so do rental agreements. Most marinas have a number of rules and restrictions listed in the rental agreements. Many of these will be for the convenience and enjoyment of the slip renters; others won't. Typical restrictions apply to living aboard boats. This might not be allowed, or there might be a quota on the number of live-aboards and perhaps a waiting list. Or you might be able to live aboard if you want to if you pay a live-aboard fee in addition to the slip rental charges. This is likely in marinas where electricity is not on individual meters. Most marinas allow you to stay aboard your boat overnight on weekends and during vacations, however. The restrictions apply mainly to those who want to make their boats their homes.

There can be restrictions regarding the amount and types of work you can do on your boat at the boat slip. You can usually wash your boat and do routine maintenance work, but when you start setting up workshops on the docks, there might be problems. Many people purchase fiberglass kit boats the finish them to the point where they can be launched. They then finish them at a boat slip. Some marinas allow this, others don't. This can be an advantage or disadvantage, depending on whether you are the one building the boat or the person in a nearby slip who has to put up with the noise and mess.

Some marinas allow painting, others don't. This often depends on the present condition of the docks. If they are modern and well maintained, boat painting that is likely to get paint on the docks probably won't be allowed. If the docks are old and beat up, there probably won't be any restrictions regarding painting.

Some marinas are open grounds for parties; others have restrictions and some degree of noise control. Choose your marina accordingly.

Some marinas have restrictions concerning pets. Check these out to see if any apply to you.

Most slip rentals are paid month to month without a lease agreement. You might be required to pay a deposit or an extra month's rent in advance. The regular rent is paid in advance also. This, in effect, means you have to give a month's notice if you intend to vacate the slip.

Some marinas require leases. The advantage to this is that you cannot ordinarily be given notice to vacate the slip during the period the lease is in effect, at least not without just cause. This advantage is offset by the fact that you are obligated to continue paying the slip rent for the period of the lease even if you move elsewhere or sell the boat. The lease agreement might allow you to sublease the slip, with approval of the management, but this can be a lot of trouble. For this reason, most boaters prefer month-to-month slip rentals rather than long-term leases.

A recent trend is to actually sell the slips, a sort of condominium concept applied to marinas. As with condominiums, there is a monthly maintenance fee for the common facilities. The few marinas in my area that have sold slips on this basis all started out with fairly reasonable maintenance fees. These went up quickly after the slips were all sold, presumably with each slip holder having a vote in the matter, to the point where the monthly maintenance fee alone was as high as the rent for many marina slips in the area. The advantages to purchasing a slip instead of just renting includes ownership and having a vote in the management of the marina.

Before purchasing a slip, investigate the situation thoroughly. There have been many complaints concerning this already. While some purchasers seem satisfied, others aren't. You might want to check with an attorney to find out exactly what you are purchasing and what the legalities are.

Regardless of whether you rent, lease, or buy, you must consider the security of the marina. Is the marina fenced with locked gates? Is there a security guard on duty at night? Are there live-aboarders? Marinas that have live-aboarders have much less problems than those that don't; these people are a deterrent to would-be thieves.

With everything considered, a marina slip can be a convenient solution to the boat storage problem. It offers maximum convenience for using your boat with the least time and effort involved. The main disadvantage is that marina slips can be expensive. With modern fiberglass boats, there is no harmful effect to leaving the boats in the water year round. Since slip rental costs are on-going costs of owning a boat, these should be figured into your boating budget.

Dry Storage

There are times when you might want to put your boat in dry storage. In areas where boating is seasonal, the boats are often hauled, prepared for winter storage, and stored, usually with boat placed on a cradle or stand. At the beginning of the next boating season, the boat is again commissioned and put back in the water. Dry storage is sometimes used when a boater must be away, perhaps out of the country, from the boat for a long period of time.

Dry storage varies. Sometimes the boats are stored outside in the open where it is anything but "dry." A winter cover or other type of shelter over the boat is therefore a good idea. If it snows in the area where the boat is stored, covers and shelters must be quite substantial.

Methods of hauling and launching the boats vary. Different types of hoists, rail systems, and elevator lifts are used. Once out of the water, boats are moved to the area where they will be stored. This is sometimes outside in the open or under a roof structure or even inside a building.

Costs of hauling and storing boats vary. There might be an added cost for preparing the boat for storage or launching if you don't do this work yourself. Before launching, the additional preparation charge might cover the annual painting of the bottom of the boat with antifouling paint.

OTHER COSTS

There are other costs you must consider in addition to the purchase price, payments and interest on a loan, sales tax, and other one-time fees paid at the time of purchase. There is an annual registration fee. In some states, there is a property or use tax that must also be paid annually. This is often based on the assessed value of the boat. Most owners of fiberglass boats carry insurance. Liability insurance is especially important.

You will also have the costs of operating and using the boat, such as fuel, ice, chemicals for the toilet, etc. In addition, consider the cost of any fittings, equipment, or other items added to the boat or inventory. Add to that any costs associated with the maintenance and repair of the vessel.

It is important, especially if you are on a tight budget, to make a realistic total cost estimate of boat ownership. Many people who purchase a boat without first doing this find that boat ownership costs much more than they expected. This often leads to strained budgets, marriages, and bailing out of boat ownership, often at a loss.

RESPONSIBILITIES

In addition to financial responsibilities, there are other responsibilities associated with boat ownership. You are responsible for the safe operation of the vessel. The boat should be kept in a safe operating condition. All required safety equipment and gear should be aboard. This equipment should be inspected frequently to make certain that everything is in good working order and is ready if needed.

You should learn as much about boating safety and the operation of the vessel as possible. Boating courses, such as those offered by the Coast Guard or Power Squadron, are a good starting point. If boating is a family venture, all members of the family who are old enough to benefit from these courses should take them. Swimming, lifesaving, and water safety courses, such as those offered by YMCAs and the Red Cross, can be useful. I believe that being able to swim well is important for boating safety.

Many people purchase sailboats without first learning how to sail. After a first day, usually of horror, these people often seek sailing instruction. This should have been done before purchasing a boat, but it's not too late even if you already own one.

In many areas, low-cost sailing lessons are available from community colleges, universities, recreation departments, and so on. These courses are often a good starting point. You might also want to join a local sailing club that offers sailing instruction and practice. More expensive, but often well worth the cost, are sailing lessons and courses from a private sailing school. These courses often are at various levels of skill (beginning, intermediate, advanced) and are offered on a class or private basis.

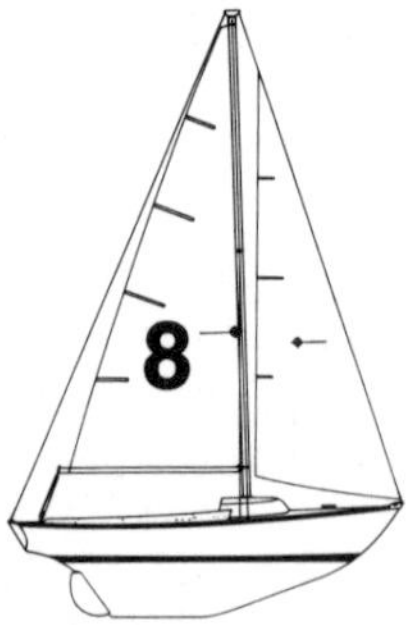

Equipping, Fitting Out, and Commissioning

Most new boats are sold as basic boats, then most buyers purchase optional extras. If you are willing to pay the price, you can have the boat fully equipped when you purchase it. This assumes, however, that you already know exactly how you want the boat equipped and fitted out. After using the boat for a time, most owners want additional equipment or changes in or replacement of existing equipment.

Some new boats are purchased without being fully equipped or fitted out. The buyer then purchases this equipment later, installs it, and does the fitting out himself. The same thing applies to used boats. While you can have equipment installed at boatyards, you can save considerable money by installing this equipment yourself. In most cases, this is quite easy to do. The term *commissioning* means getting the boat ready or setting it up. This is done when the boat is delivered or taken out of winter storage. It can be compared to a "dealer's preparation" when purchasing a new car. With boats, it includes not only clean-up work, but also rigging and setting up tasks and even adding fittings and hardware. There is an overlap between equipping and fitting out and commissioning.

COMMISSIONING

Commissioning requires the least amount of handyman work, provided all necessary holes have been drilled and everything was prefitted. What remains is basically straightforward assembly.

Most dealers try to discourage a buyer from doing his own commissioning. There are reasons for this. For one thing, the dealer charges a hefty commissioning fee. Take painting the bottom of the boat with antifouling paint, for example. While this job is sometimes done at the factory, it is frequently done at the dealer level, especially on larger boats that will be left in the water. These paints must be applied within so many hours before launching if they are to be fully effective. It is not unusual for a dealer to charge several hundred dollars or more for applying $25 worth of antifouling paint. By doing this yourself, the savings can be considerable. If you plan to do your own maintenance work later, including annual painting of the bottom of the boat with antifouling paint, why not start with the first time? (See Chapter 9.) But this is easy money for the dealer, so he is reluctant to give up this work.

A second reason why dealers try to discourage buyers from doing their own commissioning is that the dealers want to make certain that the job is done properly. This does not mean that the dealers can necessarily do the work properly themselves, some of them can't, but they fear that the buyer might completely botch the job. This might, in turn, reflect back on the dealer who sold the boat.

A third reason is that the dealers do not want the word to get out as to how easy this work can be. Do-it-yourselfers take away from the work of their service departments. The service centers are often a big part of the profits of a boat dealer.

Still another reason is that there might not be any assembly instructions provided. The dealer might feel that he will be spending more time explaining how it should be done than if he did the work himself.

You must weigh a number of factors before deciding on whether or not to do your own commissioning. First, how much work is required for the particular boat, and how difficult is it? This varies, depending on the particular boat. On a small trailer boat, it might be little more than routine cleaning. Or an outboard engine and controls might need to be installed on the boat.

Many small boats that take outboards come from the manufacturers without engines. The engines and controls are often installed by the dealer, and the boat and engine is sold as a package. You can expect to pay not only for the installation, but also a top price for the outboard engine and controls. This is the case in the area where I live. The do-it-yourselfer, however, can drive 70 miles and get the same brands of outboards and controls at discount marine outlets for over 40 percent less. The outboard motors are quite easy to install. The controls are sometimes a little more difficult, but well within the skills of the typical do-it-yourselfer. The local dealers will tell you that if you do this, the warranties on the engines will be void. You get the same factory warranty, however, which clearly states that if you live more than a certain distance from the dealer where you purchased the engine, the warranty must be honored by the authorized service center in the area where you do live. By installing the engine and controls yourself, your savings can be considerable.

As the boats get larger and more expensive, the commissioning becomes more expensive and often more difficult—at least you are dealing with heavier weights and larger surface areas. It has been said that it's no more difficult to build a large boat than a small one, there is just more of it. The same idea applies to commissioning boats. See what is involved, then decide if you have the necessary skill, experience, and time to do the job properly yourself.

If you are a newcomer to boating, a new boat is not the place to start do-it-yourself work if it involves such things as drilling holes through fiberglass moldings or fiberglassing. Commissioning work, especially on smaller boats, is another matter.

You should also determine how much money you can save by doing the commissioning work yourself. Sometimes the dealer still charges the same price for the boat whether he does the commissioning or not. Then you would probably have him do it. When there is a difference in the cost, you need to weigh the amount against the time and effort of doing this work yourself.

Let's take a close look at a typical commissioning job—rigging a sailboat. Most sailboats are shipped from the factory with the spars and rigging already made up. No splicing or swaging is required. If this is not the case, leave the rigging to the dealer unless you are an experienced rigger yourself. Trailerable sailboats are often shipped with the spars and rigging mounted to the boat like it is when the boat is carried on the trailer. If you purchase such a boat with the trailer, this is the way the mast and rigging would be mounted for trailering when you tow the boat home after you buy it. There would be no commissioning of the rigging required unless the dealer set it up to show you how it is done.

If you take in-the-water delivery of the boat, the rigging is normally done immediately prior to launching. With trailerable boats, the rigging is essentially the same. For larger sailboats, it's similar, except a hoist might be required for stepping the mast.

I once purchased an imported sailboat on a trailer in the Midwest, which I towed to California. I then painted the bottom of the boat with antifouling paint and had the boat lifted from the trailer and lowered into the water with a boat hoist. With the boat in the water, I stepped the mast and did the rigging. Everything had been set up and marked at the factory so that I really couldn't go wrong, even though there were no rigging instructions with the boat. All the rigging was already attached to the mast. It might not be so in your case, and you will have to do this yourself. The standing rigging wires (forestay, backstay, shrouds, etc.) are marked so that you will know where they go.

To step the mast, first remove the mast hinge bolt, set the mast in place, and reinstall the bolt. Attach the backstay and the two aft lower shrouds to the appropriate chain plates. To make the attachments, remove a cotter key from the jaw of each turnbuckle, remove the pin, place the jaw of the turnbuckle over the chain plate, line up the holes, and install the pin and cotter key. Adjust the turnbuckles to their longest length, making certain they are threaded in far enough so that the threads will not be damaged.

At this point, check all standing and running rigging attached to the mast. This is easy to do with the mast down, but once you step the mast it can be more of a problem.

Next, with some helpers walk the mast up to the upright position. With taller and heavier masts, however, use a crane or hoist. With the mast upright, attach the forestay, the two forward lower shrouds, and the upper shrouds to the appropriate chain plates.

Turn the rigging by adjusting the tension of the stays and shrouds with the turnbuckles. Line up the mast vertically with the centerline of the boat. This is accomplished by first adjusting the forestay, backstay, and upper shrouds with the lower shrouds fairly loose. From the dock, sight the mast from forward or aft the boat to check for vertical alignment. Do this in calm water. If the mast leans to port, loosen the port upper shroud turnbuckle and then tighten the starboard turnbuckle. Check the alignment again. Adjust in reverse if the mast leans to starboard.

Make similar adjustments for fore and aft vertical alignment of the mast. Make necessary adjustments in forestay and backstay turnbuckles.

It takes considerable experience to know how tight the rigging should be. When in doubt, it is better to leave the rigging too loose than too tight.

Next, adjust the lower shrouds. When properly adjusted, the mast will still be perfectly straight. The tension in the lower shrouds must be adjusted in relation to the tension in the upper shrouds and forestay and backstay.

Again, it takes practice and experience to properly tune the rigging of a sailboat. If you have a trailerable sailboat, however, you must do this each time you step the mast. You can leave the backstay and the two aft lower shrouds properly adjusted. Then, the next time you step the mast, you only have to readjust the remaining turnbuckles.

Set the boom in its track or attach it to the mast (various methods are used). Set up the running rigging. You are now ready for the sails.

This might sound like a long and drawn-out process. It is, but with practice, you will be able to set up for sailing fairly rapidly, if only relatively. This is one of the reasons why trailer sailboats are not more popular. It's also a common reason for keeping sailboats in the water. Care must be taken to prevent damage to turnbuckles and rigging when setting up and taking down (stepping and unstepping) the mast.

If you are going to be trailering your sailboat, you must learn to rig the boat yourself. If you are taking in-the-water delivery of the boat, there are both advantages and disadvantages to stepping the mast yourself. By doing it yourself, you can learn a lot in the process, but you might not do it properly. Perhaps a good compromise is to have this done for you, but watch so that you can see how it is done. This way, you will (hopefully) have it done properly. If it ever needs to be done again, you will probably know how to do it yourself.

It is difficult to know when commissioning ends and fitting out and equipping begins. While opinions vary, I think that once you drill holes and do other similar tasks, you have crossed the line into fitting out and equipping.

FITTING OUT AND EQUIPPING

A variety of fittings and equipment are available for boats. The displays in marine stores often look like jewelry shop displays. This chapter discusses two types of fittings and equipment. The first type does not require attachment or installation to the boat. The second type does.

Items Not Requiring Attachment or Installation

This category includes flotation jackets, flare guns, dinghies, and hundreds of other items. They are carried aboard the boat, but do not require attachment or installation, though there may be brackets attached to the boat to hold the flare gun or dinghy. Some items, such as an ice box, can be portable nonattached or installed.

There are also items, such as boat or sail covers, that must fit the particular boat or sail and might even be custom-made and fitted, but do not require any fittings attached to the boat. Some boat covers and similar items might require fasteners attached to the boat.

Anchors are another item that can be nonattached or installed, such as part of an automatic windlass anchoring system. The anchor can also be stowed free or held in place by chocks, which are fastened to the boat. Before purchasing equipment for your boat, it's important to see if any installation is required.

The same items of marine equipment are sold at many different prices. The most expensive places to buy, but often the most convenient, are marine stores. These are found in most boating areas. Even here, the prices can vary. Two marine stores in the same area might have different prices for the same or similar items, yet the store that was higher priced on this item might be the lower priced one on another item. Or one store might offer lower prices than the other. Marine stores could also have sale prices on some items.

You shop directly at a marine store. You go into the store, look at and examine the merchandise, and buy it at the marked price if you decide that you want to. You might have some return privileges. Some stores even special order items that they don't have in stock for you. This could include fast delivery from a central supply warehouse. But these advantages must be balanced against the fact that you will be paying top prices.

An alternative is to shop at discount marine stores, which are often found in large cities in boating areas. They frequently advertise in newspapers and local and regional boating publications. These stores have top quality and brands of merchandise. Some, for example, sell top brands of outboard motors for considerably less than the typical outlets.

Still another good source is mail-order discount stores. For a listing of these, see the Appendix. Most of these have catalogs, for which there could be a charge. These mail-order sources are often part of marine discount stores; others sell only by mail order.

I have had especially good results with Defender Industries, Inc., 255 Main St., P.O. Box 820, New Rochelle, NY 10801. Their catalog sells for $1.

Most mail-order firms ship by parcel post, United Parcel Service (UPS), truck, or air. Both parcel post and UPS have size and weight limitations.

A main disadvantage of mail ordering is that you have to wait for the merchandise. If you order from a dependable firm and have your order shipped by UPS (assuming that it qualifies by size and weight), your order can arrive in a short period of time. Other firms never seem to have whatever it is you order in stock and have to back-order, which can add days to the time when you will receive your merchandise.

There is always the possibility that the merchandise will arrive damaged, defective, or not be what you want, in which case it can be a lot of trouble to return it, then more waiting to get your money back. The mail-order firms often have their prices so much lower than the typical marine retail store, however, that it is still worth the risk of problems. While the cost of shipping must be figured in as part of the cost of the merchandise, the saving can still be considerable.

I also find the catalogs extremely useful. I can compare the prices with those of the same merchandise at local marine stores. If the savings are small, I purchase at the local marine store. If the mail-order firm offers a substantial discount, I mail order unless I need the item right away. I also find the catalogs useful for planing what equipment and fittings I want and seeing what's available and what the possibilities are. The catalogs are good dream books.

You might, at first, think that the marine mail-order firms can sell at lower prices because they offer lower quality merchandise. This is seldom the case. They offer the same brands and quality of merchandise as the typical marine stores. The lower prices are possible because of volume marketing. With the present high cost of shipping, the savings are perhaps less than they once were, but they can still be considerable.

Items Requiring Attachment or Installation

There are hundreds of fittings and items of equipment that require some form of attachment or installation. Sometimes the attachment or installation is simple and straightforward; at other times it can be quite involved and difficult. Sometimes the fitting or item of equipment comes with directions for attaching it to the boat or installing it; at other times it comes without instructions.

The installation boils down to attaching the item to the boat. Some form of mechanical fasteners is used. While "self-adhesive" backings are used for some light-duty attachments, this is very limited. Some equipment installation will require fiberglassing skills and techniques (see Chapter 10) and/or other handyman skills, but most equipment can be installed easily.

Many items do not require drilling holes or making any other modification to the boat itself. An example of this type of equipment is an anchor holder that attaches to a bow-pulpit. Assembly and attachment involves placing plastic pieces over the pulpit tubing, placing the anchor holder brackets over the plastic pieces, and then bolting the anchor holder clamps in position. Complete easy-to-follow directions come with the anchor holder. The only required tools for installation are a couple of wrenches. Installation time is only a few minutes.

This type of attachment is within the range of most anyone who can follow simple directions and use simple hand tools. Perhaps there is someone who could botch the job, but it's difficult to see how this could be done.

Many fittings and equipment installations require drilling holes in some part of the boat for mechanical fasteners. The most suitable fasteners are through bolts or machine screws; wood screws are suitable for making attachments to wood. Self-tapping screws are sometimes used in fiberglass laminates, but they are not recommended. The screws do not have much holding power, and once the fiberglass is slightly damaged around the screw, repair is difficult. While rivets are sometimes used on low-quality fiberglass boats, this is also not recommended. Sooner or later, the rivets are almost sure to work loose. Nails also have only limited use. Special ring boat nails, available in monel, stainless steel, and silicon bronze, can sometimes be used for fastening wood to wood. Their use is not common on fiberglass boats, however, especially those of high-quality construction.

Most marine hardware, fittings, and equipment come with the necessary fasteners for installing them; others don't. And some otherwise good-quality fittings or equipment come with unsuitable fasteners. For example, I once purchased a stainless steel cabin vent. It was of high quality, yet self-tapping screws instead of through bolts came with it for installing it to a deck or cabin top. The only logical course was to purchase small through bolts and do the installation correctly.

Another problem that I've seen, fortunately rarely, is to include fasteners of the correct type, but of an unsuitable metal. In general, marine fasteners should be stainless steel or marine bronze. Those of monel are also excellent but not so readily available. Brass is unsuitable, yet many people seem to think that it is the same as bronze. Unfortunately to confuse the situation, brass fasteners, as well as brass fittings and hardware, are sometimes sold at marine stores. A magnet can be used to separate monel, the nonmagnetic marine stainless steels, and marine bronze from ordinary steel, which is magnetic. Unfortunately, brass is nonmagnetic, so a magnet test cannot be used to separate marine bronze from brass.

Fasteners of regular steel, even if plated, should be avoided, especially if the boat will be used in salt water environments. This includes not only exterior fasteners used below the waterline, but also fasteners used anywhere else on the boat, including the interior.

If the proper fasteners are not included with the fittings or equipment when you buy them, get these before you start the installation. Do not try to make do with a fastener of unsuitable metal with the idea that you will replace it later. They have a habit of remaining until they bleed rust or, worse, fail. A common cause of do-it-yourselfers botching installation jobs is not having the proper fasteners. In the case of bolts, this means not only the proper bolts, but also nuts, washers, lock washers, etc.

When you need fasteners, the quick and easy way is to go to the nearest marine store and purchase them in small packages. Most marine stores have racks of these. This method can be incredibly expensive, however. The same quality fasteners can usually be purchased at a fraction of the price if you go to a store that specializes in marine fasteners and has them in bins. The price seems to jump dramatically when they are put in small plastic packages, often several hundred percent or even more. Or you can mail order fasteners (see Appendix for sources).

There are times when you might want to use the higher priced fasteners in the small packages, such as when you only need a few, or if the nonpackaged ones aren't available in your area, or you have to mail order them. If you need a large number of fasteners, however, it would probably be worth the trouble to travel further or even mail order them. Some of the mail-order firms promise that orders will be filled within 24 hours. If you use UPS delivery, you should receive them in a few days.

In most cases, you must drill holes for the fasteners. In fiberglass, metal drilling bits and cutting blades can be used. In the smaller sizes, twist bits are used. For larger size holes, holesaws that have a variety of blade sizes are useful. While the latter might not give the exact size hole you require, you can cut the size smaller and then file the hole out to the proper size.

While hand-turned drills could be used, a portable electric drill is recommended. Fiberglass typically drills very easily, so even a fairly low-power electric drill will suffice.

There are several problems involved in drilling holes in fiberglass for installing fittings and equipment. First, you must know exactly where you want the hole centered. Second, you must know exactly what size hole you want to make. And third, you must drill or cut the hole without damaging the surrounding fiberglass.

Some fittings and equipment come with templates for the holes for mounting fasteners. Some fittings or piece of equipment themselves can be used as a template. For example, the holes in the base of a cleat can serve as a template for marking where the holes are to be drilled. You still have to decide where you want the cleat mounted. In other cases, you will have to rely on measurements.

Hole sizes depend on the diameter of the fasteners that pass through them and other factors. The hole diameter can be the same as the diameter of the fastener. A 1/4-inch diameter bolt requires a hole that is drilled with a 1/4-inch diameter drill bit. If a tighter fit than this is required, a drill bit 1/64 inch smaller than the fastener diameter can be used. This allows threading the fastener through the hole in a fiberglass laminate. If you drill the hole too much smaller than the diameter of the fastener, however, you will not be able to thread the fastener through without damaging the laminate. If possible, try the hole size on a scrap piece of fiberglass laminate before making the hole in the boat itself.

You might need to measure the diameters of fasteners and drill bits. Metal or plastic templates, such as those that come with drill bit sets, are ideal for this. To use these, insert the bit or fastener in the holes until you find the smallest size hole that it will fit into. With fasteners, it's usually the diameter to the outside of the threads or the diameter of the unthreaded portion if the bolt is not threaded all the way to the head that is measured.

For larger size holes, such as those to be drilled with a holesaw, use calipers to measure the diameter of the fastener or other item that must fit in or pass through the hole. Before drilling a hole in fiberglass that is part of the boat, drill a test hole in a scrap piece of fiberglass laminate or plywood to test the fit. You might need to drill the hole slightly undersize, then file it out for an exact fit.

After you have marked the hole centers and determined the drill bit or holesaw size to use, make the holes. Whenever practical, begin the hole on the gel coat side of the fiberglass laminate. This reduces the possibility of chipping the gel coating when drilling or cutting the hole. Use a center punch to give a pilot indentation for the center of each hole to be drilled. It only requires a light tap with a hammer on the center punch.

In most cases, the holes are made perpendicular to the surface of the fiberglass laminate. To do this accurately by simply hand-holding an electric drill can be difficult, and many beginners botch jobs by trying to do this. When a cleat with four mounting holes in a symmetrical pattern is mounted properly, for example, the fasteners extend through the holes in the fiberglass laminate in the same symmetrical pattern. If they don't, the holes were not made perpendicular to the surface of the laminate. Since tightening down on the fastener tends to move the fastener to a perpendicular position, this can stress the laminate and possibly damage it.

Special guide attachments are available for standard electric drills to help you drill accurate holes perpendicular to the surface being drilled through. These can be extremely useful for boat work.

Sometimes, however, you must drill holes without using a jig attachment. To do this, carefully sight the angle of the bit from two directions 90 degrees apart. If this is done carefully, the holes can be made reasonably close to perpendicular to the surface or at other desired angles.

In some cases, you can drill through the fitting holes. If you are installing a cleat, for example, you can drill the first hole directly through the fiberglass, then bolt the cleat in position with one bolt. To drill the remaining holes, pass the drill bit through the hole in the cleat first. Drill carefully so you do not damage the cleat.

To drill a hole, center the point of the tip of the drill bit in the center punch indentation. Start the drill. Drill through the gel coating and on through the laminate. Allow the drill to do the cutting. Do not force it through. When the bit passes through the opposite side of the laminate, support the electric drill so that the angle is maintained and the drill does not drop downward. This will help prevent chipping the fiberglass laminate as the bit passes through.

When using a holesaw, the procedure is similar. Holesaws have a number of blade sizes attached to a single holder. To cut a hole, remove all cutting blades except the one that is the size for the hole you want to make. Center the point of the tip of the pilot bit in the center punch indentation. Start the drilling. The cutting blade should contact the surface all the way around when it first makes contact, assuming that you are drilling into a flat surface. Otherwise, the blade will cut the hole at an angle to the surface. When drilling through curved fiberglass panels, the blade will start cutting the highest areas first. The electric drill must be maintained at the desired angle for the hole that is being made.

If you can get to both sides of the fiberglass laminate for drilling, cut the hole only halfway through. Then insert the pilot bit in the same hole from the opposite side and drill the rest of the way through. This will help prevent chipping the laminate as the holesaw blade goes through. If you can only drill from one side, continue drilling through while carefully controlling the drill.

There will be situations where you can only drill from the rough side of a laminate through to the gel coat side. Special care must be taken when the drill or holesaw blade goes through to keep from chipping the gel coat, which is especially brittle because it is a resin layer without reinforcing material.

For light-duty attachments, the fittings or equipment are then bolted in place with a standard washer, lock washer, and nut used on each bolt. This applies to single skin laminates and those with plywood cores. If the laminate has a soft core, such as rigid foam plastic, additional work is required to prevent the tightened fastener and/or load on the attachment from crushing the core material. While wood, plastic, or metal inserts are sometimes used, a better method is to hollow out some of the core material around the hole and fiberglass this area in. This requires fiberglassing skills and techniques (Chapter 10). Laminates with soft cores were sometimes molded to single skin or with wood inserts in areas where fittings are commonly attached, however.

When heavy loadings are placed on the fasteners, backing blocks or plates are used. If you are in doubt as to whether or not these are required, it is probably better to use them. Because it is often difficult to get plates shaped from suitable marine metals, do-it-yourselfers frequently shape these from wood, though large fender washers alone might suffice.

Backing blocks are usually made from hardwood. If a softwood is used, the washers tend to dig into the wood, which can result in the fastener loosening and leaking around the fastener. For heavy loadings, the backing blocks should be large so that the loading spreads over a large area of the fiberglass laminate. It is also good practice to shape the backing blocks with a taper (Fig. 8-1). This

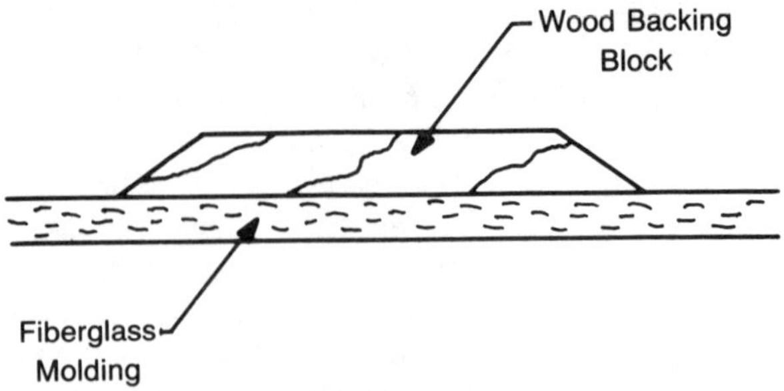

Fig. 8-1. Backing block edges taper to help prevent high stress concentrations.

will help to prevent high stress concentrations with heavy loadings.

After the backing block has been shaped, holes matching those in the fiberglass laminate must be drilled in the backing block. There are various ways of doing this. One way is to position the backing block against the fiberglass laminate and then mark location for holes on the wood by working a sharp pointed object or pencil through the holes in the fiberglass laminate. The block is then removed and the holes are drilled through the wood.

Another method is to hold the backing block in position and then drill one of the holes through the wood by starting the drill bit through one of the holes in the fiberglass laminate. The fitting or other attachment can be held in place with one bolt while the other holes are drilled.

There are a few cases where additional thickening of the fiberglass laminate is required (see Chapter 10). The previous method will suffice for most attachments, however.

Before making final assembly, bedding compound is applied to prevent leakage around the fasteners. To install a cleat, for example, a layer of bedding compound is applied to the contact surface of the cleat, to the contact surface of the fiberglass laminate, to the contact surfaces of the backing block and the back side of the fiberglass laminate, and to the threads of the fasteners. Then using appropriate washers, lock washers, and nuts, finger-tighten each fastener. Using a wrench for tightening the nut and a second wrench or screwdriver for holding the bolt head in a set position, tighten up on the nut but do not overtighten. Excess tightening can damage the fiberglass laminate.

Figure 4-38 in Chapter 4 shows the installation of a typical deck cleat. Stanchions and bow and stern rail plates can be mounted to a fiberglass deck in a similar manner (Fig. 8-2). The mounting of gimbal brackets to a countertop is shown in Fig. 8-3. Hundreds of other standard marine items can be mounted in a similar manner.

Through-hull hittings are frequently installed in fiberglass laminates. These might be below or above the waterline. As a rule, all through-hull fittings for water drains or intakes that are below or near the waterline should be fitted with seacocks. These should be bronze, not brass, like the type of gate valves commonly sold at hardware stores. They come in a variety of sizes in bronze and plastic.

To install through-hull fittings, locate and mark the centerpoint. If practical, start the drilling from the gel coat side of the laminate. Use a center punch to make a small indentation to start the drilling. Use the correct size drilling bit or holesaw blade. If you do not have the exact size, drill or cut one size smaller and then file (use a metal file) the hole out to correct size.

In most cases, a hardwood backing block is used. If the fiberglass laminate is curved in the area, one side of the block should be shaped to fit the curve. Mark and drill the hole for the through-hull fittings through the block.

Apply bedding compound. Install a through-hull connection piece through the hole in the fiberglass laminate and on through the hole in the backing block. Thread the locknut or flange nut in place and tighten down, but do not overtighten. Bedding compound should squeeze out. Remove excess bedding compound.

Deck air vent fittings for fuel, water, and holding tanks; water

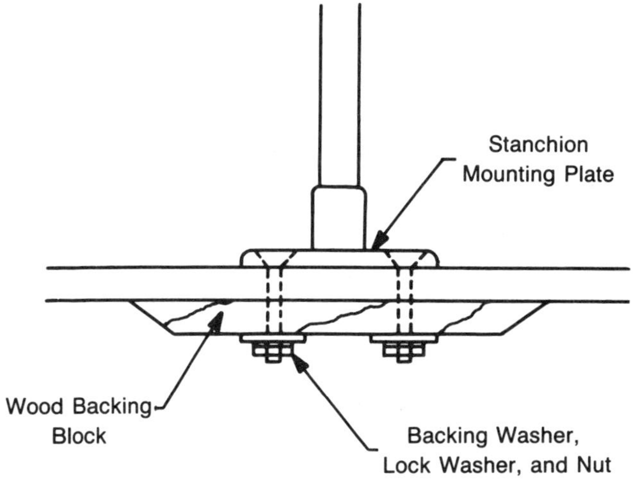

Fig. 8-2. Deck mounting of a stanchion plate.

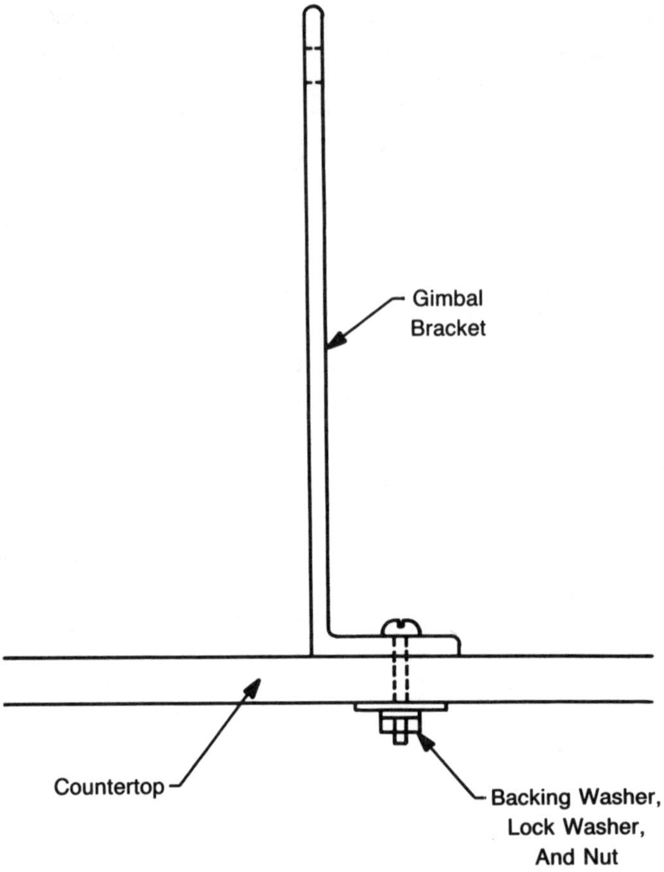

Fig. 8-3. A gimbal bracket mounted to a countertop.

and fuel tank filler deck plates; and holding tank deck pumpout plates are often installed similarly. Another type of deck plate fitting has a mounting flange plate, which is bolted to the deck with three or more fasteners. Whenever you have a choice, however, I recommend the type of fittings that have the flange nuts.

Installation of some fittings and equipment can require holes larger than the largest holesaw you have or cutout shapes other than round, such as for an oval port (window). A saber saw with a fine-tooth, metal-cutting blade can be used to make these cutouts. First, carefully mark the pattern for the desired cutout. When practical, this is done on the gel coat side of the fiberglass laminate. It is sometimes helpful to cover the fiberglass with masking tape.

Then mark the pattern for cutting on the masking tape. Next, drill a pilot hole for the saw blade. Then make the cutout.

The above techniques should allow you to install many items of equipment to fiberglass. These can include holding and water tanks, galley sinks with pumps and drains, bilge pump systems, and hundreds of other pieces of equipment.

Fittings and equipment can be attached to wood in a similar manner. Screws can be used instead of through bolts for making attachments to wood, but only if the loadings will be light. To hide the fasteners, counterbore holes are used to set the fastener below the surface of the wood. The holes are then filled with wood plugs, which are glued in place. After the glue sets, the plugs are trimmed to the level of the surrounding wood and sanded smooth.

A variety of wood items are available, such as magazine and book racks, dish and chart holders, and hand and grab rails. These are available in teak and mahogany, finished or unfinished. They are ideal for the do-it-yourselfer who does not have the time, skill, or desire to construct these items himself. They give a neat finished look, yet the installation is quite easy. Just use the appropriate method of attachment.

It's important to plan carefully. It's much easier to drill a hole in a fiberglass laminate than it is to patch it back in. If you do make a mistake, however, you can repair it (see Chapters 10 and 12). Attaching some fittings and installing some equipment will require that modifications be made to the boat (see Chapter 11).

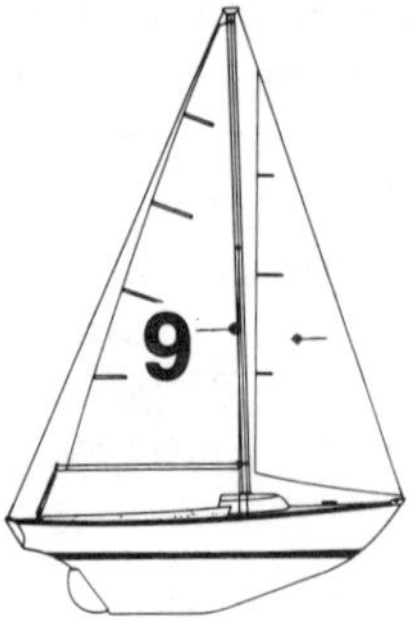

Care and Maintenance of Fiberglass Boats

"Compared to boats made from other common boatbuilding materials, fiberglass boats require less maintenance," is a statement that is often heard. The truth or falsity of this statement depends on what you mean. If a boat is given no maintenance at all and is left in the water, the fiberglass boat would probably still be floating when all the other boats had sunk or broken up, but even this is no certainty.

If a fiberglass boat is to be kept in a sound, functional, and seaworthy condition and the appearance (and resale value) maintained, maintenance is required—and lots of it. The maintenance can be reduced, however, if proper care is taken of the boat. You won't have to remove creosote from the topsides of the fiberglass hull if you don't let the boat rub against the pilings that are coated with it. If you use a boat cover, you can protect the gel coating from the effects of the sun, which in turn can mean less waxing to keep the finish in top condition.

Having spent considerable time around marinas, I've had a good opportunity to make an informal study of the care and maintenance of fiberglass boats and also to compare them with boats of other materials. Some people take good care of their boats, others don't. I'll detail what to do to protect and care for a fiberglass boat later in this chapter. For now, suffice it to say that banging docks without fenders between the dock and boat is an example of not taking care of a boat very well. Careful docking and proper use of fenders is an example of protecting the boat. The latter reduces the need for maintenance; the former means removing marks and scratches or, even worse, making repairs.

Those who take good care of their boats usually do a good job of maintaining their boats. There are exceptions, such as the person who takes poor protective measures and yet does good maintenance work, or vice versa, but these are rare. If the boats are ever put up for sale, the cared for and maintained boats generally fetch much higher prices.

You can hire all or some of the maintenance work, or you can do all or part of it yourself. The more you do yourself, the more money you can save.

PROTECTION AND CARE

Once you own a fiberglass boat, you will want to protect it from abuse and damage and take care of it. This can be thought of as preventing the need for excessive maintenance and repair work.

When you use your boat, there is a fine line between proper use and abuse of the boat. Your first and primary concern should be in the safe operation of the boat. The safety of people comes first. Next you are responsible for the property of others. Finally, you take pride in or are responsible for your own property—your boat. The first two are legal responsibilities that you undertake when you own and operate a boat. The last, beyond keeping the boat in safe operating condition, is more or less up to you.

Fiberglass laminates, including gel coat surfaces, are not very resistant to wear and abrasion. Rub rails are often positioned on fiberglass boats to protect a vulnerable area. A stepping tread is another example. You can't protect all of your boat, but there are many things that you can do to reduce wear and damage.

A first consideration is what is meant by "normal" use. This, of course, will vary. Who will be the crew and passengers? How strict will you be? Normal use with active children aboard will probably be much more intense, to say the least, than if just you and your spouse use the boat. And if you become too strict, you might spoil the fun for everyone else, even to the point where you won't have a crew or passengers to enjoy boating with you anymore.

A compromise must be made between protecting the boat and using it for fun and recreation. How far you go and in which direction depends on your particular situation.

First, proper deck shoes go a long way toward preventing wear on fiberglass walking surfaces, which often have a nonskid pattern woven into the fiberglass laminate. Besides, deck shoes can be thought of as fun shoes. So insist that crew and passengers wear these when aboard the boat, and be sure to set a good example by wearing them as well.

Second, there are places on the boat where you (or crew or passengers) should not sit or stand. The tops of hatches on many boats are one of these areas. While the hatches might support your weight, standing or sitting on them can often be damaging. While it might be argued that the hatches should have been constructed strong enough to stand and sit on them, it will get you nowhere when trying to get the dealer to repair fractured hatch laminate or hatch tracks or other hardware under the new boat warranty.

Most manufactured boats are far from being people proof. A visit to a boat show will quickly convince most anyone of this. After a parade of a few hundred or thousand people pour through the interior of a boat on display, it can be in shambles. Hinges pull loose. The table leg gives way. The curtain rod attachments come loose. And so on. The extent of the damage depends on the quality of the boat, the number of people that go through it, and how freely they are allowed to poke, pull, twist, and whatever else comes to mind. Certain standards of behavior should be required aboard boats—for safety and to prevent damage and wear on the boat.

Proper operation of the boat is extremely important. Improper docking techniques can cause wounds in a fiberglass hull that no amount of polishing or waxing can remove. While some docks are padded with protective fender materials, many aren't, and even those that are often can't be depended on. Hardened rubber bumpers with cracks and sharp areas are common. Nails and other sharp protrusions are other typical hazards.

The solution is docking skill and proper use of your own boat fenders. A little game helps. If you allow the boat to touch a dock directly without a fender between the boat and the dock, you lose the game. This will not only help preserve the boat, but will also help improve your boat handling.

You shouldn't let protecting the boat keep you from enjoying your boat and using it, however. I once knew a snow skier who bragged about never having fallen once on skis. He wasn't a very good skier, and he never seemed to learn anything new. The same thing can apply to boating. You will want to take reasonable care of your boat, but not to the point of not using it or not learning anything new.

Fiberglass gel coating deteriorates from exposure to sunlight.

In time, the gel coating color fades and chalks. There are certain maintenance steps, detailed later in this chapter, that will maintain and restore the color and remove the chalking. There is something you can do to prevent the problem in the first place—that is to use a boat cover.

Over the past three years, I've observed what a difference covering a boat can make. Three years ago two fiberglass runabouts of the same manufacturer, size, and colors arrived on the scene at our marina. One owner purchased a full boat cover with his boat, the other didn't. One of the boats was always covered when it was not in use. The other one was always left exposed. During the rainy season, the owner would merely pump the water out after each rain. The boat with the cover didn't get water inside.

Now, three years after the boats were purchased, the uncovered boat is a mess. Not only have the elements ruined the upholstery, but the sun has also faded and chalked the gel coating to the point where routine maintenance does little to bring the gel coating back to life again.

The boat that was kept covered still looks factory fresh. Not only is the upholstery in good condition, but so is the gel coating.

A boat cover obviously seems like a good idea. This is true for a small open boat that is left out in the open, whether in the water or out on a boat trailer, as well as for larger boats, both power and sail, including those with cabins and self-draining cockpit areas.

In some boating areas, covered slips are available. These are essentially slips with roofs or sheds over, and sometimes around, them. They are only suitable for powerboats. The covers serve not only to protect the boats from rain, but also from the sun. Boats kept in covered slips are better preserved than those kept in open slips and is a possibility to consider. You can expect to pay higher rent for a covered berth than an open one, and this must also be taken into consideration.

You can also preserve fiberglass boats by keeping water from getting inside. But, you say, I bought a fiberglass boat because fiberglass is "waterproof." Water should not have very damaging effects on fiberglass laminates that are protected by gel coatings or paint. There are other materials on most fiberglass boats, however, that are not so resistant to water damage—namely wood, metal, and upholstery fabrics.

With self-bailing boats, the water drains out automatically. Cabin boats have the deck and cabin structures and hatch and window and port arrangements set up so that water cannot get below, that is, unless the hatches or windows or ports are left open so it can. This type of boat has a self-bailing cockpit to automatically drain the water out or off. These boats are intended for being out in all types of weather. They are designed and constructed so water will not get below, at least not in any large quantities.

Most fiberglass boats have a bilge area for any water that does get inside to collect. There is often a bilge pump to pump out any water that collects in the bilge. The pump itself can be hand or battery powered. Some electric pumps are automatic. Any water in the bilge trips the switch, which pumps the water out. When there is no more water, the switch turns off (opening the circuit) and the pump stops. If more water gets in the bilge, the cycle is repeated. Many pumps also sound an alarm when they operate.

It's best not to let water stay in the bilge. The sooner you can get it out, the better. Some bilges on fiberglass boats are essentially fiberglass swimming pools. There are no metal, wood, or other materials that water can damage. Other bilges have keel bolts that can rust and/or wood backing blocks that can dry-rot. There might also be electrical wiring that can be damaged by water. In any case, it is best to keep the water out by not letting it get there in the first place. Pump or bail it out as soon as possible once it does get there.

Without an inboard engine, I've found it possible to have dry bilge fiberglass boats. Water just doesn't get there. To accomplish this, I've had to stop all the deck and cabin leaks and other sources of water. With an inboard engine with a prop shaft passing through a stuffing box, some water in the bilge is almost inevitable. You just have to put up with it, although proper stuffing of the gland can keep the amount of water to a minimum. An automatic bilge pump is a handy way to remove this water from the bilge.

There is still another crucial factor in protecting the interior of fiberglass boats—that is *ventilation*. Lack of ventilation usually means condensation. While this might not be too damaging to fiberglass per se, it can be very hard on wood, some metals, upholstery, and other materials. Good ventilation also makes life below much more comfortable.

You need good ventilation even when the hatches are closed and when no one is aboard or around the boat. You need good ventilation when the sun is shining and when it is raining. Besides opening hatches and ports and windows, this can be supplemented by ventilators, such as the dorade type (Fig. 9-1). The vents are designed to either let air in or draw it out, or both, while at the same

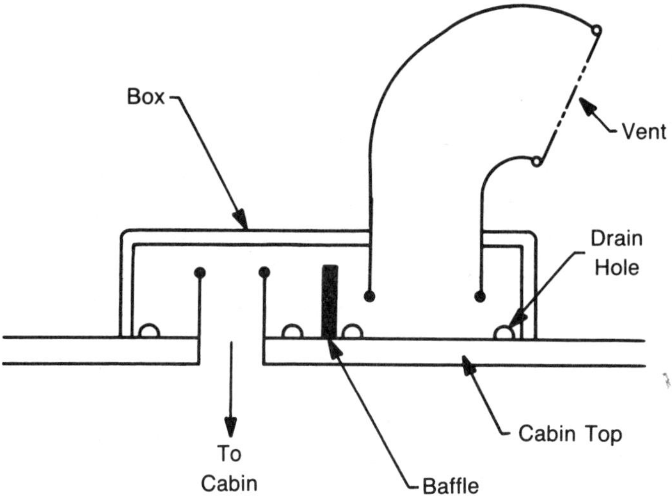

Fig. 9-1. Dorade-type ventilator.

time not letting rain or other water get below. These vents have the advantage over the typical hatches, doors, windows, and ports in that they continue to function when the boat is closed up.

A combination of moisture inside the boat and lack of ventilation can quickly lead to mold and mildew inside. This can also lead to dry rot in plywood bulkheads and other wood parts.

MAINTENANCE

Maintenance is the routine, on-going care a boat receives.

Fiberglass

Fiberglass is a low-maintenance material. It does require regular cleaning and waxing if it is to be kept in top condition.

Washing. Fiberglass boats should be washed frequently to remove dirt and grime. At dockside, there is often a pressure water hose hookup. This, along with a spray nozzle attachment, makes boat washing much easier. You can use the water the boat is floating in, whether fresh or salt water, for cleaning the boat, provided that this water is clean enough.

Regardless, a bucket of water with a biodegradable liquid detergent added can be used for washing. This will remove some types of greasy spots and stains. It can be applied with a sponge, towel or other cloth, soft brush, or mop. If a brush or mop is used, it must be soft with no sharp wood or metal parts that can scratch the fiberglass.

The first step is to wet the entire exterior of the boat down with the spray nozzle on the hose. If you are using the water the boat is floating in, you can dip it out with a bucket or mop or pump it out with a hand or electric pump to a hose with a nozzle on it. Many boat owners rig their bilge pumps so that they can also be used for this purpose. This first washing down removes some of the loose dirt and grime.

Next, wash the boat with the detergent. A sponge is often used for smooth surfaces. A soft brush is handy for nonskid areas of fiberglass.

If you use abrasive cleaners at all, use them with discretion because they can, in effect, sand away gel coating and remove the glossy surface. A sponge with liquid detergent placed on it full strength can remove spots from gel coat surfaces and with less risk than if abrasive cleaners are used.

After applying and scrubbing with the liquid detergent, wash the boat down again with water from the hose or, lacking dockside water supply, with buckets of water or a mop soaked with water.

A final step, sometimes omitted, is to wipe the fiberglass dry with a chamois or cloth.

If you have a trailer boat, the same type of washing can be done with the boat out of the water on the trailer. An added advantage here is that the bottom of the boat can also be washed.

The intervals between washings can vary. Some fiberglass boat owners wash their boats after each time they use them or even more often. Others rarely, if ever, wash their boats. Frequent washings show pride in ownership and also make the boat more enjoyable to use.

Waxing. Another important maintenance job for fiberglass gel coated surfaces is waxing. The gel coating is actually filled with tiny pores. To protect the surface, waxes especially formulated for fiberglass boats should be used, rather than automotive waxes. The wax can be paste or liquid, as desired. The wax should only be applied to a clean boat. If the gel coating is faded or chalked, a special polish or buffing compound might be required before applying the wax.

To apply the wax, follow the manufacturer's directions. Some waxes are applied with a damp cloth or sponge, others are applied dry. Next buff the wax out. By hand, this can be a long job. A power buffer or even a buffer attachment on a portable electric drill can greatly speed the work. To avoid electric shock, do not use these when the boat is in the water, especially anywhere near the waterline. When the boat is in the water, use a cloth and do the job by hand, even if you have to take it small sections at a time. This can be avoided if you give the boat a good wax job once a year at haulout time for bottom cleaning and painting.

If you have a brand new fiberglass boat, it's best to apply the first coat of wax before the boat is launched for the first time. The length of time that a wax application gives good protection and appearance varies, but a quality wax properly applied can last from six months to a year. I suggest at least one thorough waxing with a power buffer or buffer attachment on a portable electric drill each year. This can be supplemented by one or more hand waxings during the year if the boat is kept in the water. Trailer boats can, if desired, be waxed using a power buffer twice a year at six-month intervals. Waxing is especially important for fiberglass boats that won't be stored under cover.

Dulled, faded, and chalked gel coatings can sometimes be brought back to life by using specially formulated fiberglass cleaners, polishing compounds, or buffing compounds. There are two basic types: one works chemically without abrasives, the other is an abrasive polishing or buffing compound. Those called *polishing compounds* are milder than those called *rubbing* or *buffing* compounds. These compounds are applied and buffed out in a manner similar to wax. There are some variations for certain types and brands, however, so follow the manufacturer's directions for the particular product used. If this procedure does not restore the finish, you might want to consider painting, as detailed in Chapter 12.

Painting. A major maintenance task for fiberglass boats is painting the bottoms with antifouling paint. How often this is required varies depending on where the boat is used, how long it is kept in the water, and other factors. As a rule, fiberglass boats kept in salt water require a haulout and bottom painting once a year. In fresh water, this can differ. While once a year is recommended, it might be possible to go longer than this by scrubbing the bottom while the boat is in the water. In the area where I now keep my sailboat, only about 6 inches of the hull by the waterline gets a growth on it. By using a brush to scrub this off at intervals, antifouling paint remains satisfactory for a couple of years. This applies to fresh water, however, and wouldn't work for salt water.

To apply antifouling paint, you must first haul the boat. Sometimes careening is possible, such as with a full-keel sailboat tied against a wall in shallow water at high tide. When the tide goes out, the boat is grounded on the bottom of the keel and held upright by the wall. This might give time for a quick antifouling paint job between tides.

Trailer boats can be hauled out on their trailers for bottom painting. Larger boats are hauled at a boatyard or other area with special hauling equipment. A number of methods are used, including cranes, sling hoists, railways, and elevator lifts. The basic idea is to get the boat safely out of the water to a location where the bottom painting and other work can be done. Often the boats are placed on special cradles or stands.

After the boat has been hauled, it is set up on a cradle or other supports. Trailer boats can sometimes be painted while on the trailers. This can require jacking up sections for painting contact areas where the boat sets on rollers or other supports. The next step is to scrub the bottom with a hose with a nozzle on the end of it and various cleaning compounds. You can also use a stiff scrub brush and/or abrasive cleaning pads. If the boat is in salt water, you also need to use a scraper. The basic idea is to clean the bottom down to the old bottom paint or, if the old bottom paint is chipped or peeled off, to the fiberglass surface. This can be quite easy, though at times it takes considerable work.

Some boatyards have steam cleaning equipment that can make easy work of this. They often come around offering this service for a price. It can be mighty tempting. You can also pay to have the entire job done, for an even larger price.

Thoroughly clean the bottom of the boat up to the level where bottom paint is to be applied. Allow the bottom to dry off.

You must decide what type of antifouling paint to use. If you know what was used previously, and it was satisfactory, you might want to use the same kind again. If you don't know what was used before, or it didn't give satisfactory service, find out what other people in the area use. For each boating area, there are certain kinds that work best.

When you purchase the paint, buy any required special cleaners and/or primers for that particular type and brand of paint. Follow the manufacturer's directions.

The next step is to prepare the bottom of the boat for painting. The procedure here varies depending on factors such as the type of paint that was previously used, its condition, and the type of new paint that is to be applied. Sometimes a chemical treatment is all that is required for preparing the surface for the new paint;

other times light sanding is required. Whenever you sand bottom paint, wear a protective mask and goggles because the dust can be toxic.

The bottom painting can extend to a level just above the waterline to the gel coating or to a painted boot-top stripe. Before painting the bottom with antifouling paint, you might want to repaint the boot-top stripe. This can require sanding. Then, mask the edges and repaint. A boot-top stripe can be added on a boat that did not have one previously in a similar manner.

Next apply masking tape at the top edge of where the bottom paint is to be applied. This is usually the same level used previously, unless you want to change it. You might want to raise or lower the level, depending on whether it was too high or low before.

Apply the antifouling paint by brush or roller, as desired. Again check your directions. Some boats must be launched within a certain number of hours after the paint is applied for the paint to retain its full effectiveness. In other cases, the paint must be allowed to dry for a certain length of time before the boat is launched. Special hard finishes are available for trailer boats that will be taken in and out of the water.

With most types of antifouling paint, only one coat is applied. A second coat will not improve the effects of the paint for keeping marine growth off the bottom of the boat, and it can cause the paint to flake and peel off. Follow the manufacturer's direction carefully regarding thickness of coating and number of coats.

If the boat has a fiberglass rudder, antifouling paint is applied to this up to the waterline. In swing-keel or centerboard sailboats, the inside of the well is also painted with antifouling paint. A sponge paint applicator with a long handle can be used for applying paint inside centerboard trunks and swing-keel wells.

Before returning the boat to the water, a thorough check of all underwater fittings and attachments should be made. While the boat is hauled out, give the topsides a good waxing and perform any other maintenance tasks. It is especially important to take care of all jobs that require a haulout.

Gel Coat. Fiberglass gel coated surfaces on the interior of the boat are maintained like the exterior surfaces: by washing and waxing. Some waxes leave an undesirable odor, however, and might have ingredients that could be harmful to breathe. These should be avoided, especially on fiberglass near berths. Also, avoid waxing fiberglass that is under cushions because the wax can come off onto the upholstery fabric.

The above maintenance is all that is normally required for the fiberglass parts of boats. You might want to paint the nongel coat side of fiberglass laminates. If fiberglass gel coating is scratched or chipped, minor repairs might be called for. (See Chapter 12.)

Other Exterior Maintenance

While maintaining the fiberglass parts of the boat is fairly easy, that of other materials can be more difficult. Exterior wood trim, tiller, hand grab rails, swim platforms, or other similar parts require special maintenance. If the wood is teak, you have a number of choices. First, you can simply let the wood go. Many boat owners follow this path. They are told that this will have little effect on the strength of the teak. The wood turns grayish, which some people think looks okay. It has been my experience, however, that teak cracks more if let go than if finishes are applied.

Teak that has been "let go" can be restored to a light color by using teak cleaner and bleach, which are available from marine stores. These restore the wood to a neat appearance. If this is all that you do, however, the teak will soon start to weather again.

To slow this process, teak oil can be applied to the wood with a brush or cloth. It is allowed to soak into the wood for a period of time, then the excess oil is wiped off with a cloth. This method is somewhat messy, and the oil does not last very long. To keep the teak in top appearance, the oiling has to be repeated regularly. Eventually, the teak becomes darker from repeated oilings, at which time you can repeat the cleaning and bleaching process.

Instead of oiling the teak, a varnish or clear plastic finish can be applied. The problems with traditional marine varnish are that it does not adhere well to teak and the finish is not long lasting. Several coats of varnish are applied, with light sanding between coats. If old varnish has built up on the wood, you must strip to bare wood first. Having gone this route many times, I know how discouraging it can be when you find that the varnish is peeling and yellowing after a month or so, if not sooner.

There are several brands of new plastic finishes especially formulated for teak and other boat woods that are advertised to last a year or more on exterior surfaces. These look promising, though they are very expensive. Unlike urethane plastics, the new finishes are supposed to be a softer plastic that will not crack.

Mahogany and other exterior woods are finished by varnishing or painting with one of the clear plastic coatings or even a color coating. This can be a lot of work, which is one of the reasons why less exterior wood is being used on the exteriors of modern fiberglass boats. Another reason is that boat woods, and especially teak, are being priced out of sight. Thailand teak is presently retailing for over $15 a board foot (1″ × 12″ × 12″).

Rub rails are sometimes made of aluminum with vinyl fender material set in a track. This arrangement requires little maintenance beyond routine washing.

Check fittings periodically to make sure they are in good condition. Check especially for cracking and other signs of fatigue. Replace fittings as required. Also check the fasteners to make certain that they are properly tightened, but do not overtighten because this can damage the fiberglass laminates to which they are attached.

A thorough check should be made periodically of sailboat spars and rigging. Rigging should be tuned as required. Defective rigging should be repaired or replaced.

A frequent problem is leaking around through fasteners that go through the deck or cabin top. This problem can be corrected by removing bolts, applying bedding compound or sealer, and then reinstalling them. When done properly, bedding compound or sealer should ooze out when the fastener is secured. Then wipe away excess bedding compound or sealer before it has a chance to set up.

Other Interior Maintenance

In addition to maintaining interior fiberglass, there are other maintenance tasks that should be done to keep the interior in top condition. Interior woodwork requires a new finish from time to time. Teak can be finished by oiling, varnishing, or applying one of the new plastic finishes formulated for teak. Mahogany and other woods are finished by varnishing or applying a clear plastic finish, such as urethane or one of the new softer plastic finishes that are less prone to cracking.

Interior wood can also be painted, which is more durable than the clear finishes, but gives a less "yachty" appearance. Before switching from a clear finish to a color coating, however, be sure you really want to. It is a devil of a job to switch back again, and a painted finish can lower the value of the boat in some cases. Paint is a good way to hide dry rot, and even if you aren't doing this, other people might think you are. Paint does have an advantage, however, if you want to spend more time using your boat and less time maintaining it. The painted surfaces also make sense for world cruising boats. Why not have something that is practical rather than a floating museum? Then, when you reach those long-dreamed-about ports, you can spend your time sightseeing instead of varnishing.

Keep the interior of the boat clean on a routine basis. A vacuum cleaner is handy when you have shore power. This allows cleaning compartments that are difficult to sweep out.

Carpets present special problems, especially if they are installed in such a way that they cannot be easily removed. It's best to have removable carpets so that they can be taken out and thoroughly dried from time to time. If indoor-outdoor carpeting is used, you can even turn the hose on it and use a mild liquid detergent. This helps remove salt.

Vinyl cushion covers can be cleaned with a damp cloth or vinyl cleaner without removing the foam padding. Fabric covers can be cleaned by removing the padding (there is usually a zipper opening for this) and having them dry-cleaned. If water has gotten to the foam padding, dry this out thoroughly before replacing the padding.

Curtains can also be removed for laundering or dry cleaning, as required. Plastic laminates and other surfaces are easy to clean.

A clean interior no only preserves the appearance and value of the boat, but also makes it more enjoyable to use.

Engines and Other Mechanical Equipment

Outboard or inboard engines require periodic maintenance if they are to be kept functional and in top working order. Oil must be changed, lubrication applied, and the engines tuned. This is a very broad subject, and the procedures depend on the particular type of engine. I suggest that you get the "factory" service and repair manual for the particular engine that are usually available from the engine manufacturers. Carefully follow the recommended maintenance and servicing procedure; that is, unless you intend to have this work done for you.

Other mechanical equipment also requires periodic maintenance. Follow the manufacturer's instructions for the particular piece of equipment.

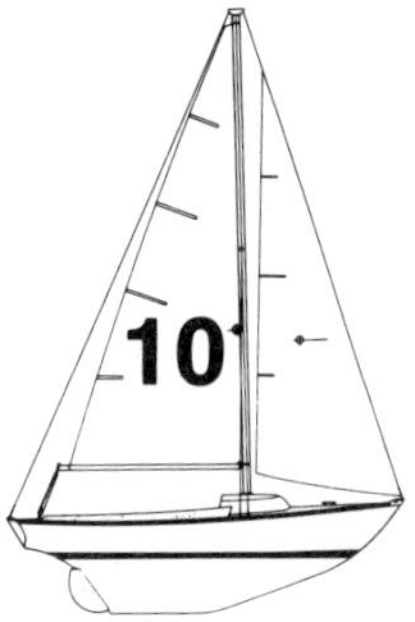

Basic Fiberglassing Skills and Techniques

To do alterations or repairs, finish out a bare hull, or construct a one-off fiberglass boat, you must first learn basic fiberglassing skills and techniques. This is for the do-it-yourselfer who wants to do his own fiberglass work to save money, to get the work done his own way, or for the challenge and satisfaction of doing it himself.

A first requirement for success is that you are a do-it-yourself type person. Even for these people, who perhaps routinely make repairs and constructions with wood and other materials, there is often a reluctance to attempt fiberglassing.

One reason for this is that fiberglassing has a chemical aspect. It is unlike, say, taking a piece of wood and cutting and shaping it. Fiberglassing involves mixing liquid chemicals together, applying them to flexible fiberglass reinforcing materials, and by means of chemical reactions, producing a hard fiberglass laminate.

A second reason for a reluctance to attempt fiberglassing is the lack of how-to information for doing this work. This chapter provides that information.

A third reason is the health and safety precautions you must take to guard your health and reduce or eliminate the risks involved. The chemicals used for fiberglassing are sticky and messy, and fiberglass reinforcing material makes your skin itch. By using protective clothing and learning to properly handle these chemicals and materials, however, it's possible to reduce the magnitude of these problems. Once you learn the basic safety procedures and handling techniques, fiberglassing can become a challenging and enjoyable activity.

The skills and techniques presented in this chapter are intended for the do-it-yourselfer. The basic idea is to achieve professional results with a minimum outlay for tools, equipment, materials, and supplies. To accomplish this, you must invest your time. Whereas the professional fiberglasser almost always considers time as money, the amateur seldom has to. The professional worker probably has better tools and equipment than the typical do-it-yourselfer, and although the latter can still achieve quality results, it will probably take longer.

TOOLS AND EQUIPMENT

You need various tools and equipment for doing the fiberglassing work and for protecting yourself.

Mixing Supplies

You need containers for mixing fiberglassing chemicals and for holding solvents for cleaning brushes and tools, and for other uses. Clean, empty coffee cans serve nicely. Unwaxed paper cups also work, as do most plastic cups other than those made of polystyrene foam plastic. The paper, plastic, and metal buckets sold by paint stores are also satisfactory. Small metal or plastic tubs are convenient for rapid handling of resin, especially for roller applications. To keep spilling to a minimum, short mixing containers with large bases are recommended.

Do not use waxed containers because the wax can contaminate the resin, or at least make finishing resin out of laminating resin. In some cases, the resin will soften the wax and cause the bottoms to fall out of the containers.

Disposable cans, cups, buckets, and tubs are most convenient. After a few uses, these can be discarded. This works out better than using more expensive containers and trying to clean them after each use. It also reduces the amount of acetone that is required for cleaning polyester resin from containers. Sometimes it takes an amount of acetone that costs more than a disposable container to clean a similar, more expensive container. Clean mixing containers are essential in order not to contaminate resins and other chemicals.

It will take some experimenting to discover what types of containers work best for you. Some fiberglass workers prefer buckets without handles; others like them with handles; etc. Try small containers, a pint or less capacity, when you first start out. Later, when you can handle larger volumes of resin at each mixing, you can change to larger mixing containers. Always have an adequate supply of empty mixing containers conveniently at hand before you start fiberglassing. You also need clean mixing sticks. These can be of wood, plastic, or metal, and come in all types and sizes at paint stores.

In order not to contaminate fiberglassing chemicals, two or more clean mixing sticks are required for most jobs. Various lengths of mixing sticks are useful. Use small ones about the size of ice cream sticks for mixing resin in small cups. A longer and bigger stick can stir resin in gallon containers before pouring out the amount to be used into a small mixing container. Once a mixing stick has been in a container of catalyzed resin, do not use it to stir uncatalyzed resin. There is probably enough catalyst present to start a curing reaction, which can take place even if you put the lid back on the container.

Applicators

Brushes. Paintbrushes are used for applying resin to reinforcing materials. The inexpensive, throwaway type brushes are the most economical. While the brushes can be cleaned, the solvents used for this are expensive and only work for uncured resins. With polyester resin, the type most commonly used for boat work, it is very difficult to keep the resin from curing all the time. Once resin hardens in the brush hairs, about all you can do it discard the brush and start again with another one.

Avoid brushes that have painted handles. Resin, acetone, and other chemicals used for fiberglassing often act as a solvent on the paint, which will come off and contaminate your chemicals.

To start, you need mainly small brushes, such as 1/2-, 1-, and 1 1/2-inch widths. Later you might need wider brushes. Larger brushes give less control, but resin can be applied faster with them.

Paint Rollers. Resin can also be applied to reinforcing material with paint rollers. The resin is poured into a plastic or metal tray. After the catalyst is added, the roller is dipped in the tray, then rolled out. The resin is then rolled on the reinforcing material.

These rollers can also be used for smoothing the surface of wet resin. A layer of cellophane or other material that will not stick to the resin is placed over the wet resin. The roller is worked over this, smoothing the surface of the resin. This can sometimes reduce the amount of sanding that is required.

Squeegees. Various types of squeegees with rubber and plastic blades are available for fiberglassing work. They are useful for smoothing out the resin surface and scraping off excess resin from cloth and woven roving reinforcing material when doing lay-up work. Squeegees are also used to rapidly spread the resin and to remove air bubbles by scraping them to the edge of the material so the trapped air can escape.

Squeegee blades have degrees of flexibility. Some are quite stiff; others are quite flexible. It takes some experimenting to find out what works best for you.

Squeegees come in various widths, with or without extension handles. To start, those with blades about 3 inches wide without extension handles are about right. These can be purchased at fiberglassing supply stores. Squeegee strips are also available in long lengths, which you can cut into desired lengths.

Laminating Rollers. Laminating rollers are different than paint rollers. Laminating rollers have a series of metal (usually aluminum) disks or blades (Fig. 10-1). They are useful for laminating layers of reinforcing material and working out air bubbles. Solvent cleans uncured resin from the rollers. Hardened resin can be burned off with a torch. Standard laminating rollers are from about 1 to 2 inches in diameter and from about 3 to 8 inches long. Special rollers are available for use in corners (Fig. 10-2). While laminating rollers can be helpful for lay-up work in a mold, you probably won't need these at first.

Scissors

You need at least one pair of scissors or snips for cutting reinforcing materials. While these don't have to be new or very expensive, it's important that they be sharp and in good working order. If scissors are used, 4- to 6-inch cutting blades are about right to start out with.

Wet resin can be cleaned off scissors with solvent (such as acetone for polyester resin), and hardened resin by burning it off. Cutting fiberglass can quickly dull scissors, so those used for fiberglass should not be the same ones used for general household tasks or sewing. The fiberglass cutting scissors should be sharpened when they become dull. It also helps to do the cutting of reinforcing material away from any wet resin so that you do not get resin on the scissors. If you do get polyester resin on them, clean it off with

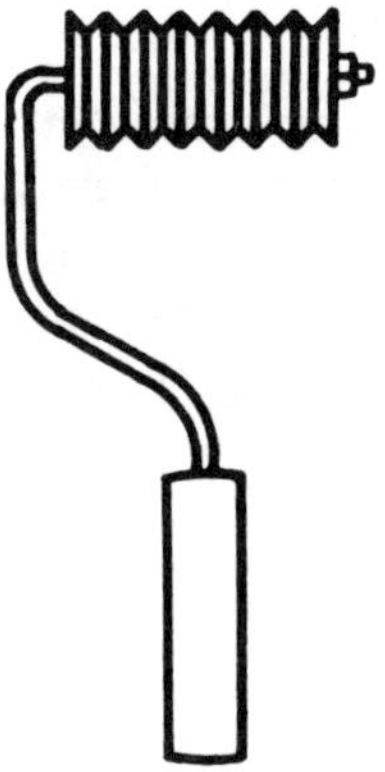

Fig. 10-1. A laminating roller.

acetone before it has a chance to cure. There's also a special epoxy solvent that removes uncured epoxy resin.

Putty Knives

Putty knives have a variety of uses in fiberglassing work including applying fiberglass putty. Putty knives are available in a variety of blade widths. At first, one or two with 1-inch wide blades will probably suffice. You can add other blade widths later if a need develops.

Utility Knife

A sharp utility or razor blade cutting knife also has many uses in fiberglassing work. A razor blade with a single edge is also handy for some jobs.

Fig. 10-2. A laminating roller for use in corners.

Sanding

You need *abrasive paper* in a variety of grits for sanding cured fiberglass and other materials. Aluminum oxide and silicon carbide are the most satisfactory for sanding fiberglass.

Start sanding with coarse grits and work down to finer ones. Dry sanding is used for coarse and medium sanding. Depending on the job, fine sanding is done wet or dry. Thus, it is convenient to purchase wet/dry abrasive paper in fine grits that can be used either wet or dry.

A sanding block can be either a small block of wood that the sandpaper is wrapped around or a special sanding block with a clamp or other means to hold the sandpaper in place. It is useful for many fiberglass sanding jobs.

Surfacing Tools

A variety of shapes and sizes of surfacing tools are available for fiberglassing work. These are very useful, especially if power sanding tools are not available or being used. Surfacing tools do not raise nearly as much dust as power sanders, making the surfacing tools safer to use.

Surfacing tools can't be resharpened when the blades become dull. Replacement blades are readily available, however.

Files

Metal files come in many shapes and sizes for working with cured fiberglass. To start, you will probably want flat, half-round, and round files. Other shapes can be added as needed.

Portable Electric Drill and Attachments

This is probably the most essential power tool. With metal-cutting bits, it can be used for drilling cured fiberglass panels. Spade-type bits and holesaw attachments can be used for making larger size holes. The electric drill can be 1/4-, 3/8-, or 1/2-inch and should be lightweight for easy handling.

Abrasive grinding burr attachments (Fig. 10-3) extend the usefulness of an electric drill. If you don't have a separate disk sander, a disk sanding attachment is useful, along with a selection of sandpaper grits shaped to fit the disk attachment. There are also buffer pads that fit over the disk sanding attachments for fiberglassing

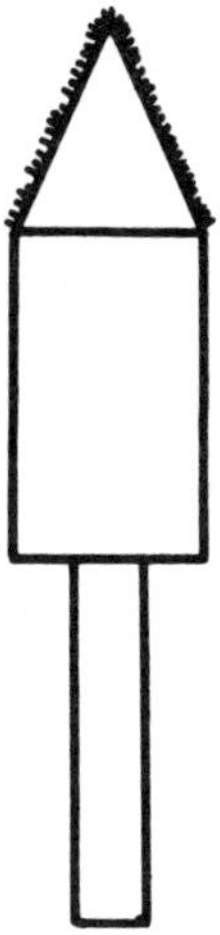

Fig. 10-3. Abrasive grinding burr attachment for a portable electric drill.

work. If you use a variable speed electric drill, use a fairly slow turning speed when using the buffer.

Remember that portable electric drills are designed and intended mainly for drilling holes. They have limited sanding and buffing usefulness. If you are going to do extensive fiberglass sanding and/or buffing, more specialized tools are recommended.

Fiberglass dust is very abrasive and can be hard on power tools. If you purchase power tools for extensive fiberglassing work, select those designed for use in the presence of abrasive dust. An air gun attachment on an air compressor can blow dust out of tools. If done frequently, this should help prolong the life of the tools.

Portable Power Sanders

You can get by without portable power sanders when you first start out and for small jobs, but for large jobs they are almost essential. Basic types include the pad sander or vibrating, disk, and belt sanders.

Pad or vibrating sanders come with orbital, straight line, and combination orbital and straight line actions. The combination works best for sanding fiberglass. These sanders are only used for light-duty and finishing sanding.

Disk sanders are available with disks 5 to 9 inches in diameter. A 7-inch disk is about right for most fiberglassing work. Disk sanders have the disks mounted at right angles to the drive spindles. This makes sanding much easier than with a disk attachment used in an electric drill. A heavy-duty disk sander is recommended for fiberglass sanding.

Some disk sanders feature a low-speed adjustment so that they can also be used as buffers with a buffer attachment. In this way, a single tool can serve two purposes.

Belt sanders use a belt of sandpaper that travels over two drums. They can be adjusted for light, medium, and heavy sanding. This type of sander is sometimes used for sanding fiberglass.

Disk sanders are the most versatile for sanding fiberglass. They are more difficult to use, however, and can leave undesirable swirls if handled improperly. A soft pad between the disk and abrasive paper is helpful. Grinding attachments are also available for many disk sanders.

Anyone planning to do extensive fiberglass work will probably want to invest in a heavy-duty commercial model disk sander and then take the time necessary to learn how to use it properly.

Portable Power Buffers

This can be a combination tool with the portable power sander or a separate tool. The buffer must turn at a slower speed than a sander so the buffing pad does not heat up to the point where it can burn the fiberglass surface.

Small polishing and buffing tasks can be done by hand or with an electric drill buffer attachment. For extensive work, a portable power buffer is a good investment.

Saws

Hacksaws with metal-cutting blades are useful for cutting cured fiberglass. A regular pistol-grip hacksaw will suffice for many jobs. A file-type handle hacksaw is convenient for working in tight places.

Saber saws work well for cutting cured fiberglass laminates. Metal-cutting blades should be used for this. While the same cutting jobs can be done with a hacksaw, the saber saw is much faster and more convenient to use.

External Heat Devices

These are not normally needed for working with polyester resins. If you plan to do lay-up work with epoxy resins, however, methods for applying external heat to speed up the curing process can be helpful. Only flameless devices such as infrared heat lamps, portable electric heaters, hair dryers, and heat guns, should be used. Even then great care should be taken to prevent possible fires and explosions.

Clamps, Wire, and Backing Devices

A variety of clamps, wire, and backing devices are useful for fiberglass repair work and other tasks. These will be detailed in later chapters along with the specific jobs that they are used for.

Compressors

You won't need a compressor to learn the basic skills and techniques of fiberglassing. If available, however, it can blow dust from power tools. An air gun attachment is connected to the compressor for this. Later, you might want to spray resins and other fiberglassing chemicals. The compressor can be used as an air supply for the spray gun. This type of spray work requires very expensive protective equipment if it is to be done safely.

Chopper Gun

This is another device that you won't need unless you plan extensive fiberglassing work. A chopper gun supplies catalyzed resin under pressure to the nozzle for spraying. At the same time, a chopper cuts up fiberglass strands or rovings into short lengths and combines them with the catalyzed resin, which is sprayed into the mold. The use of this device for spraying up, instead of laying up, fiberglass boat moldings is controversial. Laminates sprayed up with the chopper gun are weaker than those hand laid up with reinforcing materials.

The chopper gun is too expensive a piece of equipment for most do-it-yourselfers, so it will not be considered further here.

Other Wood and Metal-Working Tools

Most fiberglassing work also involves the use of wood and/or metal. A variety of wood and metal-working tools are useful for this. These tools can be added as a need develops.

PROTECTIVE CLOTHING AND EQUIPMENT

Protective clothing should always be worn when working with fiberglass. Wearing only swim trunks while you are fiberglassing is an example of what not to do.

While many types of protective clothing can be used, coveralls made from polyolefin fabric, which are available from fiberglassing supply stores and paint stores, work well. They are lightweight, easy to work in, and comfortable. They offer considerable protection from fiberglassing chemicals and fiberglass sanding dust. Reasonable protection is provided for the entire body with the exception of the head, hands, and feet. Although protective clothing is worn, you must still handle the chemicals as carefully as possible. If you get chemicals on the protective clothing, you've goofed. The purpose of protective clothing is not so you can be careless, but rather as a backup in case you accidentally make a mistake when handling the chemicals.

Gloves

You need gloves that are resistant to fiberglassing chemicals. Polyethylene disposable gloves work well and give better fingertip sensitivity than those of most other materials. Polyethylene disposable gloves can be purchased at fiberglassing supply stores and at some paint stores. Protective gloves should be worn whenever fiberglassing chemicals are handled and used to prevent getting the fiberglassing chemicals on your hands.

Boots

Most types of standard work boots can be worn. These can quickly be ruined by resins and other fiberglassing chemicals, however, so it's a good idea to set aside an old pair just for fiberglassing work.

Another possibility is rubber rain boots. These can be worn alone or over shoes or boots.

Disposable polyethylene boots, available from fiberglassing supply stores, are another choice. These are designed to fit over shoes or boots. They provide good protection from resins and other fiberglassing chemicals.

Whatever you use, keep in mind that the primary purpose is to keep fiberglassing chemicals from contacting your skin. Ruining your shoes is a secondary consideration.

Filter Masks and Respirators

Filter or dust masks are available with replaceable filters and in disposable form. These should be used only for nontoxic dusts.

They do not provide protection from fumes from fiberglassing chemicals but can provide protection from fiberglass sanding dust. The filter or dusk mask must fit properly, however, so that the dust cannot get in around the edges. It should be repeated that these filters do not provide protection from vapors and fumes and can even be worse than wearing no mask at all when used for this purpose.

For protection from vapors, fumes, and toxic dusts, you need a respirator that is designed to give protection from the particular chemicals being used. It's extremely important that the respirator is approved for use with the resins and other chemicals you will be using. Be sure you know how to properly wear the respirator and replace cartridges. Purchase extra cartridges and other necessary supplies that go with the respirator so you have them on hand.

Even though many fiberglass workers insist on not using a respirator, it is *essential,* not optional, equipment. Even though wearing a respirator might be inconvenient and uncomfortable, the protection that it provides makes it worthwhile.

Do not use a respirator for protection from particular chemicals unless the respirator and cartridges are approved for use with that particular chemical or material. To do otherwise can, in some cases, be worse than not wearing any respirator at all.

The primary factor is that the respirator provide protection. You should also consider the cost of the respirator and replacement cartridges. The respirator should be comfortable to wear and be as lightweight as possible. Follow the manufacturer's instructions for using the particular respirator.

Some respirators also provide eye protection; others don't. If the type you purchase doesn't provide eye protection, you need additional equipment for this.

Protecting Devices for Eyes, Face, and Head

Safe fiberglassing requires that your eyes, face, and head be protected. Eye protection is provided by some of the better respirators. A variety of goggles are available to provide protection from nontoxic dusts. These can be worn with filter masks and respirators that do not have provisions for eye protection.

You also need a hood or other device to give protection to your head and neck and other parts not protected by the respirator and/or goggles. To find out exactly what you need, go to a large respirator supply company.

Other Protective Equipment

More advanced protective systems, such as those giving complete body protection and a special air supply for breathing, are sometimes used for industrial purposes. These afford the most complete protection. Unfortunately, the cost of this equipment precludes its use by most do-it-yourselfers.

A PLACE TO WORK

Fiberglassing is best done under laboratory conditions with the temperature, humidity, ventilation, and other factors carefully controlled. In most cases this is impractical, however, and you must do the fiberglassing under less than ideal conditions.

From a health and safety standpoint, good ventilation is extremely important. Some fiberglassing work can be done inside garages and other buildings provided there is adequate ventilation. In a garage, keep large doors open while the fiberglassing is done. Large fans drawing air out of the building are also helpful.

For most do-it-yourselfers, it is safer and more practical to work outdoors. This can be in the open, but under a roof or other cover that provides protection from direct sun is better. It's more pleasant to work in the shade, and direct sunlight can have adverse effects on fiberglassing chemical reactions.

Some boat fiberglassing must be done "on location." If the boat is in the water at a marina dock, you might want to do the fiberglassing there. Or perhaps a haulout is required anyway, and you could do the fiberglassing work at this point. If you have a trailerable boat, you can trailer it to your yard and do the fiberglassing there.

Sometimes you can bring the boat to the required tools, equipment, materials, and supplies. Other times you can bring these things to the boat.

MATERIALS AND SUPPLIES

Fiberglassing materials and supplies have been detailed as they apply to manufactured fiberglass boats in Chapter 4. The do-it-yourselfer uses many of the same materials and supplies. You might not need all of these materials at the start. Just make certain that you have everything on hand for the particular work you are attempting. Many jobs are spoiled by not having the necessary items on hand.

Fiberglass Cloth

Fiberglass cloth is a commonly used reinforcing material for fiberglassing. A plain weave is a good one to start with, although you might want to use long shaft satin weaves and unidirectional weaves for special applications.

Fiberglass cloth is available in weights from less than 6 ounces to 20 ounces per square yard. Start with 10-ounce-per-square-yard material. You can purchase other weights later.

Fiberglass cloth comes in widths from 36 to 60 inches with selvaged edges that do not unravel. The 36-inch width is about right for starting out. Cloth is also available in narrow widths that are called *tape.* Tape has selvaged edges and is available in widths from 1 to 12 inches. The 3- to 6-inch widths are about right to start. Cloth comes in plastic packages and by the yard from rolls, which is less expensive.

It is important to select the correct width of cloth for the particular job. The selvaged edges make the cloth much easier to work with. This advantage is lost where cuts are made and at the unselvaged ends because the cloth tends to unravel when you handle the dry cloth or apply resin to it.

Fiberglass cloth should be specially treated for use with resins. The treatment often used is called *chroming*. Be careful about "bargains," which might be unchromed and thus not suitable for fiberglassing work. The treated material has a shiny appearance and the untreated cloth has a dull appearance.

Fiberglass Woven Roving

Fiberglass woven roving, while more difficult to work with than either cloth or mat, gives a good combination of thickness and strength, and thus is an important fiberglass reinforcing material. While many modification and repair jobs can be done without it, it is very useful for some types of work.

Fiberglass woven roving is available in various weights; 24 ounces per square yard is common. On a weight basis, woven roving is more expensive than mat and less expensive than cloth.

Woven roving comes in widths from 36 to 60 inches, in plastic packages or by the yard from rolls, which is less expensive. It doesn't have selvaged edges.

To start out, use 36-inch-wide woven roving in the 24-ounce-per-square-yard weight. Be careful when handling the material so the unselvaged edges do not unravel. Make certain that the fiberglass woven roving is specially treated, usually by chroming, for use with resins.

Fiberglass Mat

Mat is a feltlike material made from chopped strands of glass fibers arranged in a random pattern and held together by a bonding agent. In many ways, mat is the easiest of the reinforcing materials to work with.

Unlike woven roving or cloth, mat is sold in per square foot weights rather than per square yard. It's available in weights from less than 3/4 ounce to 3 ounces or more per square foot. On a weight basis, mat is the least expensive of the reinforcing materials. It is available in plastic packages and by the yard from rolls in widths from 36 to 60 inches.

For starting out, 1 1/2-ounce-per-square-foot weight is about right. Other weights can be purchased later as needed. Make certain that the fiberglass mat is specially treated, usually by chroming, for use with resins.

Milled Fibers

Milled fibers are made from glass strands that are hammer-milled into pieces shorter than chopped strands. Milled fibers look like a fluffy powder. They are available in plastic packages and also in bulk by weight. This material is added to resin to form a fiberglass putty and filler material.

Take care when using milled fibers. They give off a fine dust when handled.

Polyester Resin

The primary resin used for fiberglassing boat work is polyester. Polyester resin is formulated for room temperature curing and already has the necessary accelerator added to the liquid resin. To start the curing process at room temperature, a catalyst—methyl-ethyl-ketone (MEK) peroxide—is added.

Polyester resin is manufactured for specific purposes. Two basic types for boat construction are laminating or lay-up resin and finishing resin. The difference is that the finishing resin has a wax additive. Once the catalyzed resin is added to a laminate, the wax rises to the surface, sealing off the air, which allows the resin to fully cure so that the surface can be sanded. This type of resin is called *nonair-inhibited.* The laminating or lay-up resin is called *air-inhibited.* In the presence of air, the surface remains tacky. This is desirable if additional layers are to be added to a laminate, but undesirable if the surface is to be sanded.

To avoid purchasing two types of polyester resin, I suggest that you purchase laminating or lay-up resin. A special wax additive is available that can be added to this resin to convert it to a finishing resin. I have found this method to simplify fiberglassing, especially if you only plan to do limited work. For large lay-up jobs, using the two types of resin might be more convenient.

Polyester resins are also available in various viscosities. For most work, the regular viscosity will suffice. High viscosity is useful when working on inclined and overhead surfaces. Regular viscosity resin can be converted to a higher viscosity by adding a thixotropic powder that is available from fiberglass suppliers.

Polyester resins cure with various degrees of flexibility. For some applications, the more expensive flexible resins might be worth the extra cost.

Special fire-retardant polyester resins are also available. These are more expensive than regular polyester resins, but are worth the extra cost for some special applications.

Regular polyester resins are formulated for use in a temperature range of 70 to 75 degrees Fahrenheit. By varying the amount of catalyst used, however, satisfactory results can be achieved in a temperature range from 60 to 90 degrees Fahrenheit. Special low-temperature resins can be used in a temperature range of 45 to 60 degrees Fahrenheit.

Another type of polyester resin is gel coat resin. This is often used in repair work for touching up and matching areas with the original gel coating. There are special gel coat kits for color matching. Polyester gel coat resin is catalyzed in the same manner as regular polyester resin.

Polyester resins come in various size containers (pint, quart, gallon, etc.). Because polyester resins only have a shelf life of six months to a year, it's important to purchase fresh resin only in quantities that you will use within a reasonable length of time. Always store polyester resin in a cool place. Special purpose polyester resins often have an even shorter shelf life than regular polyester resins.

In some cases, the necessary catalyst for the resin comes with the resin. In others, it is purchased separately. The catalyst comes in a graded plastic container so you can add the polyester resin in the desired amount. This is often done by drops.

Polyester Putty

A variety of polyester putty is available, or you can mix up your own by adding milled glass fibers to regular polyester resin. Polyester putty requires a catalyst, which comes with the manufactured putty. Some types use a liquid catalyst; other types use a paste form.

Epoxy Resin

Epoxy resin has a number of superior qualities as compared to polyester resin. Epoxy resin is much more expensive, however, over twice as much as polyester resin. Epoxy resins are more difficult to work with than polyester resins, and they present a greater potential health hazard. As a rule, epoxy resins are only used in situations where, for one reason or another, polyester resin will not be satisfactory for the particular job. For most of the modification, repair, and construction work detailed in later chapters of this book, epoxy resin will not be required for lay-up work.

Epoxy Putty

Because of its superior strength and bonding properties, epoxy putty is often used instead of polyester putty. Get an epoxy putty that cures rapidly and is easy to work with.

Solvents and Cleaners

Acetone is a useful solvent for cleaning uncured polyester resin from tools. Acetone should not be used as a thinning agent, however, for polyester resin that is to be used in lay-up work. Acetone is widely used for cleaning hands, a practice that is *not recommended* from a health or safety point of view. Special hand cleaners are available. These should be used to clean hands instead of acetone or other strong solvents.

Phenolic Microballoons

Phenolic microballoons are combined with resin to form a lightweight material that can be trowelled in place. Phenolic microballoons have a density of about 10 pounds per cubic foot. When mixed with resin, the resulting material floats.

Core Materials

Core materials used for fiberglassing work include plywood, balsa, and polyurethane and polyvinyl chloride (PVC) rigid foamed plastic. All of these are available in preformed sheets. Polyurethane also comes in pour- and spray-in-place forms, which can be used to fill compartments and cavities of most any shape or size. Polystyrene, another type of rigid foam plastic, should not be used with polyester resin because it will dissolve the foam.

Mold Release Agent

Special mold release agents are available. These are applied to molds and other surfaces to prevent the resins from sticking to them.

Finishing Supplies

Paint. Many kinds of paint can be used on fiberglass instead of gel coating. Two-part epoxy and two-part polyurethane finishes seem to be the most popular, however.

Rubbing and Polishing Compound. Fiberglass rubbing and polishing compound can restore the appearance of faded and chalked gel coat surfaces and make gel coat repairs. Use the kind that is especially formulated for fiberglass.

Fiberglass Wax. Fiberglass wax is useful for both routine maintenance and fiberglassing repair work. Use the kind that is especially formulated for fiberglass surfaces.

Other Materials and Supplies

Other materials and supplies required are masking tape, construction paper, rags (you need plenty of these), cellophane, sealing compound, and bolts, screws, rivets, and other mechanical fasteners.

WHERE TO PURCHASE SUPPLIES

Fiberglassing supplies are available at many marine stores. The selection is often limited, however, and you can pay top prices here. In some areas there are stores that specialize in fiberglassing materials and supplies, such as TAP Plastics, Inc., which has stores in a number of California cities and also in Portland, Oregon, and Salt Lake City, Utah. For information, write to TAP Plastics, Inc., 3011 Alvarado Street, San Leandro, California 94577. They have a complete line of fiberglassing materials and supplies at very reasonable prices. There are also other fiberglassing material supply stores in various parts of the United States.

Other sources include paint stores, department stores, hardware stores, and auto supply stores. Be careful here, however; I have found many of the supplies and materials from these sources to be of poor quality.

Defender Industries, Inc., 255 Main St., New Rochelle, N.Y. 10801, is an excellent mail-order source for fiberglassing materials and supplies. They stock a complete line of fiberglassing materials, one of the largest inventories anywhere. They offer high-quality name brands at discount prices. I've found that even with the cost of the shipping figured in, they beat the prices of most local sources in the area where I live. Defender Industries, Inc., has a 168-page catalog that sells for $1 and includes not only fiberglassing materials and supplies, but also a complete line of marine products.

Another possible source of discount materials and supplies is through boatbuilding clubs and groups. By volume buying, they can offer discount prices to members. If there is no such club or group presently in the area where you live, you might want to consider forming one.

It is best to stick to quality fiberglassing materials. This is especially important for beginners. Using poor-quality materials, which are often difficult to work with, can be too big a handicap for many beginners who might think that poor results are due to their methods rather than the low-quality materials.

Even with quality materials, there is considerable differences in the way they work. Once you find brands of materials that work well for you, stick with these.

HEALTH AND SAFETY

Protecting your health and safety is an important part of working with fiberglass. There are two main aspects to fiberglassing: chemical and cured fiberglass. The chemical part involves mixing the fiberglassing chemicals and applying them to reinforcing materials and other similar jobs. Working with cured fiberglass involves sanding, grinding, filing, drilling, and so on.

Most people can undertake fiberglassing work with reasonable safety provided that certain health and safety precautions are followed. Anyone who has any reason to believe that he might react badly to the chemicals and materials used in fiberglassing should check with a physician before doing any fiberglassing work.

Follow the instructions under "Protective Clothing and Equipment" in this chapter. Fiberglass reinforcing materials can be irritating to skin, respiratory system, and eyes. Exposure can result in allergic reactions, dermatitis, skin rash, and other problems. Avoid handling fiberglass reinforcing materials with bare hands.

Sensitivity to glass fiber reinforcing materials varies greatly from individual to individual. If you find that you are sensitive to it even when you wear protective clothing and equipment, consult your doctor.

To reduce exposure to glass fibers, store reinforcing materials in plastic bags. This keeps glass fiber strands and particles from getting into the air.

Take special care when cutting reinforcing materials. After cutting, use a vacuum cleaner to pick up loose glass material. With practice, you'll learn to use scissors or shears while wearing thin polyethylene gloves.

If glass fibers do get on your skin, a cold shower followed by hand lotion application may help to relieve itching. If skin rash or other reactions develop, consult a medical doctor.

Protective clothing and equipment should be worn when sanding cured fiberglass because sanding raises a fine dust that can cause skin, respiratory, and eye problems. Use a well-fitted filter mask or respirator and eye goggles or other eye protective equipment. Wear protective clothing to protect your skin, including your hands.

Even hand sanding raises considerable dust. Wear thin polyethylene disposable gloves in addition to other protective clothing and equipment when sanding.

Power sanding raises even more dust. Full body protection is extremely important. It takes practice to learn how to use power sanders while wearing gloves, especially the fairly substantial gloves required here. The thin kind would quickly wear through. Because you will be working with cured fiberglass, chemical resistance of the glove material is not a crucial factor here.

Accumulated sanding dust in the work area can also be a problem because some of it will become air-borne. Clean the work area frequently with a shop-type vacuum cleaner.

If any skin, respiratory, or eye problems develop, consult a physician. If you do get sanding dust on your skin, a cold shower followed by application of hand lotion often helps relieve the itching.

Wearing protective clothing and equipment is often inconvenient and uncomfortable, especially in hot weather. But I believe that protection of health is worth the sacrifice.

Adequate Ventilation

There should be adequate ventilation in the area where you are working. This helps to reduce the concentrations of vapors and fumes from resin and other fiberglassing chemicals. While protective clothing and equipment reduce your exposure to vapors and fumes, they should be in addition to adequate ventilation, not a substitute for it.

When working outdoors, always try to be between the direction the wind is coming and the chemicals being used. This will blow vapors and fumes away from you.

Inside work areas present special problems. There should be at least two large openings on opposite sides of the building or a ventilation system capable of completely changing the room air at least once every five minutes. The expense of the latter is generally too much for most do-it-yourselfers.

Ventilation is poor inside boats. When fiberglassing here, an exhaust fan rigged up to a hatch is helpful. In addition, open as many doors, hatches, windows, and ports to the outside as possible.

Manufacturer's Directions

Always follow manufacturer's directions and recommendations for proper and safe use of the product. Follow all health and safety precautions. Typical warnings include: "Avoid prolonged exposure to vapors and fumes. Avoid skin contact. Use only in well-ventilated areas. May be harmful or fatal if taken internally."

Steps to take might be given in case of accident, such as splattering a certain chemical in the eyes. Read these carefully so that you will know what to do—just in case.

Flammable Chemicals and Materials

Keep resins, catalysts, curing agents, solvents, and other fiberglassing chemicals away from fire and flame. Polyester resins are flammable in both liquid and cured state. Fire-retardant polyester resin is still highly flammable in the liquid state. Some epoxy resins and epoxy hardeners or curing agents are explosive, so even greater care is required in handling them. The catalyst for polyester resins is also explosive. It should be carefully stored and kept away from fire and flame or other high temperatures.

Acetone and epoxy solvents, both highly flammable, give off heavy vapors that travel along close to the ground or floor. Fire, flame, or even a spark can cause an explosion. Use the same care in handling these solvents as you would in handling gasoline.

Remember:

- Do not use open flame heaters in fiberglassing work areas.
- Do not smoke in fiberglassing work areas, especially when fiberglassing chemicals are being used.
- Store fiberglassing chemicals in cool, dry places to reduce the possibility of spontaneous combustion or explosion. It also increases the shelf life of resins and other chemicals.

Avoid Contact with Fiberglassing Chemicals

It is extremely important to avoid contact with resins, catalysts, hardening agents, solvents, and other fiberglassing chemicals. Avoid skin contact.

Skin. Always wear protective clothing when working with these chemicals. Handle, pour, mix, and apply the chemicals carefully. Be especially careful of methyl-ethyl-ketone (MEK) peroxide catalyst for polyester resins and epoxy hardeners. These can cause chemical burns if they come into direct contact with the skin.

If you do get chemicals on your skin, remove them as soon as possible. Use a cloth to wipe them off. Use soap or hand cleaner and water to wash them off as soon as possible.

Eyes. The consequences of getting fiberglass chemicals in your eyes by splattering or other means is extremely serious. Always wear eye protection when using these chemicals. In addition, handle, pour, mix, and apply the chemicals carefully. And just in case, always know the emergency steps to take if you do get any of the chemicals in your eyes.

Avoid Breathing Fumes and Vapors. Do your fiberglassing work in well-ventilated areas. Wear a respirator that is approved for the particular chemicals you are using. Cartridges or elements in respirators should be serviced or replaced as necessary so that they remain effective. When working with chemicals, keep them as far away from your face as possible.

Safe Mixing and Storage of Chemicals

Follow the manufacturer's directions carefully for using resins and other fiberglassing chemicals. Do *not* mix a polyester accelerator like cobalt napthanate directly with a methyl-ethyl-ketone (MEK) peroxide catalyst. An explosion can result. Most polyester resins have the necessary accelerator already added at the factory. If you do add an accelerator, it should be added and mixed with uncatalyzed polyester resin first before adding a catalyst to the mixture.

Do not store methyl-ethyl-ketone (MEK) peroxide catalyst in metal containers. Spontaneous explosions can result from prolonged contact with metal.

Other Safety Rules

Keep working areas clean and organized. Disposable containers, bench covers, and similar items should be disposed of when they are no longer serviceable. Spilled chemicals should be cleaned up as soon as possible.

Keep visitors away from work areas. Keep children especially away from work areas. Likewise pets. Always have one or more fire extinguishers handy. Keep a first aid kit nearby. If you work alone, always have assistance nearby. Avoid working alone when you are remote from assistance in case of an accident.

Always follow safe operating procedures when using portable electric drills, saber saws, sanders, and other tools used in fiberglassing work. Safety is important in the nonchemical part of fiberglassing, too.

You should not only know what the safe working rules and practices are, but you should also follow them in your fiberglassing work. Follow the rules right from the start until they become habit and you no longer have to think about them. You will automatically put on the respirator when it is required, and so on.

The rules and procedures for safe fiberglassing might seem excessive, but in reality many other activities, such as woodworking, have just as many safety rules and procedures. They're just different. If the health and safety rules are carefully followed, fiberglassing can be a safe and rewarding experience.

WORKING WITH CURED FIBERGLASS

Working with cured fiberglass was mentioned in Chapter 8 in connection with equipping and fitting out fiberglass boats. This section goes into greater detail.

I suggest you obtain scrap pieces of cured fiberglass laminates for practice purposes. These can often be obtained from fiberglass molding shops. Try to get pieces that have a color gel coating on one side.

A typical fiberglass laminate is illustrated in Fig. 10-4. The smooth color side is the gel coating, which was applied against the mold first in the molding process. The remainder of the laminate is made up of a combination of cured resin and fiberglass reinforcing material. The back side of the laminate is rough in comparison to the gel coat side. How rough depends on the molding method used, whether or not the back side of the laminate was sanded, and so on.

Common operations used on cured fiberglass laminates include drilling, sawing, filing, and sanding. Practice these tasks on scrap pieces of fiberglass.

Drilling

Fiberglass drills easily. You can use hand drills, but portable electric drills make the work much faster and easier. Use metal twist bits for drilling small holes and spade-type bits to drill slightly larger hole sizes up to about 2 inches in diameter. A separate bit is required for each hole size. A holesaw can make a variety of hole sizes from 3/4 inch up to about 3 inches in diameter. A different blade is required for each desired hole size. Twist bits, spade-type bits, and holesaws can all be used in portable electric drills.

Before drilling, determine and mark the center point for the desired hole. Use a center punch or other sharp-pointed metal object to make a small indentation for centering the point of the bit. This should be done carefully.

Select the proper bit for the desired hole size and install this in the electric drill. You will drill on the gel coat side of the laminate and through to the back side (Fig. 10-5). This method lessens the risk of chipping the gel coat when drilling through.

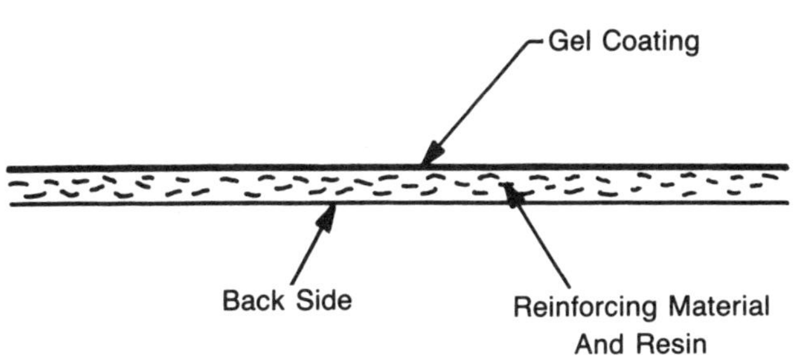

Fig. 10-4. A typical fiberglass laminate.

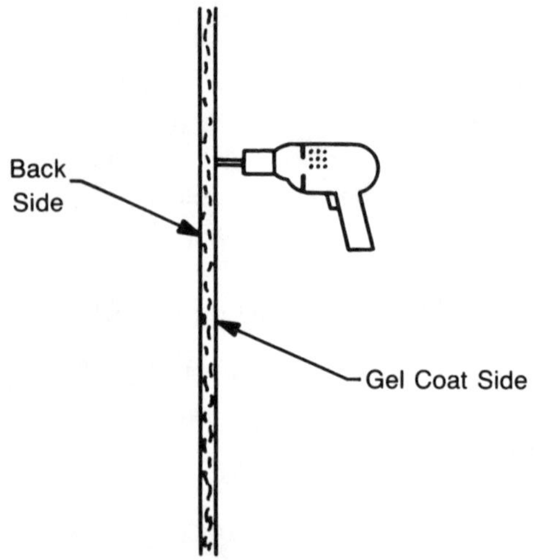

Fig. 10-5. Drilling from gel coat side of laminate.

Center the point of the bit in the center punch indentation. Hold the drill at the desired angle, usually perpendicular to the laminate surface. Start the drill. Drill hole through the laminate. Allow the drill to do the cutting. Do not force the bit through.

Larger hole sizes can be drilled halfway through. Then, using the same center hole, finish the drilling from the opposite side. This reduces the risk of chipping the laminate beyond the edge of the laminate around the hole.

If you do not have a bit or holesaw the exact size of a desired hole, drill one size smaller and then file the hole out to the desired size. Filing is covered later in this chapter.

Practice drilling a variety of hole sizes in scrap pieces of fiberglass laminates. Strive for clean holes without chipping away any of the surrounding laminate.

Sawing

Sawing is a frequently required operation on cured fiberglass laminates. While handsaws can be used, a saber saw makes the work faster and easier. Use a fine-tooth, metal-cutting blade.

The sawing should be done with the saw on the gel coat side of the laminate (Fig. 10-6), whenever possible. This results in the least possibility of chipping the gel coating along the saw cut.

The cutting pattern can be marked directly on the fiberglass, or you can place masking tape on the fiberglass and then mark the pattern on this. For crucial cuts, leave a little extra and then file the laminate down to exact size. It's much easier to take off a little more than it is to add, which requires fiberglassing.

For cutouts, drill a pilot hole for starting the saw cutting. The hole should be large enough for inserting the saber saw blade.

When sawing, allow the saw blade to do the cutting. Do not force the saw blade. Carefully follow the pattern line.

Using scrap pieces of fiberglass, practice making both straight and curved cuts.

Filing

Metal files and surfacing tools are both useful for filing cured fiberglass laminates. Whenever practical, do the filing from the gel coat side of the laminate (Fig. 10-7), when working on the edge of a laminate.

Surfacing tools can also be used on surfaces of fiberglass laminates for fairing and other purposes. A large amount of material can be removed quickly in this manner, though the blades do tend to clog rather quickly and become dull. Because these blades are not ordinarily resharpened, replace the blade with a new one when the old one becomes unuseable.

Hand Sanding

Hand sanding, with or without a sanding block, is an important fiberglassing skill. Suitable abrasive paper includes aluminum oxide and silicon carbide.

Start sanding with the coarsest grit of paper required. Then, work down to finer grits.

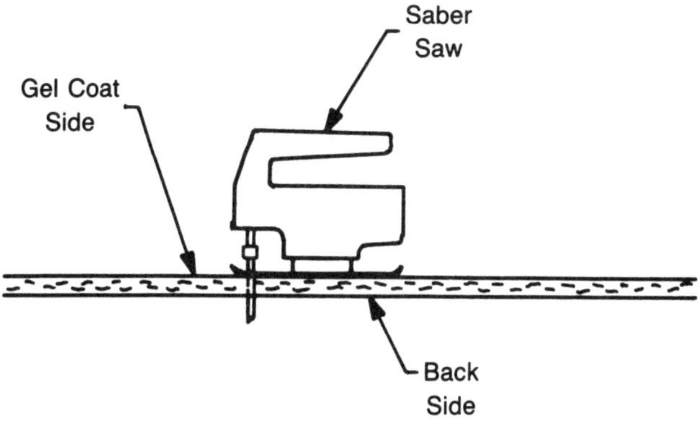

Fig. 10-6. Sawing from gel coat side of laminate.

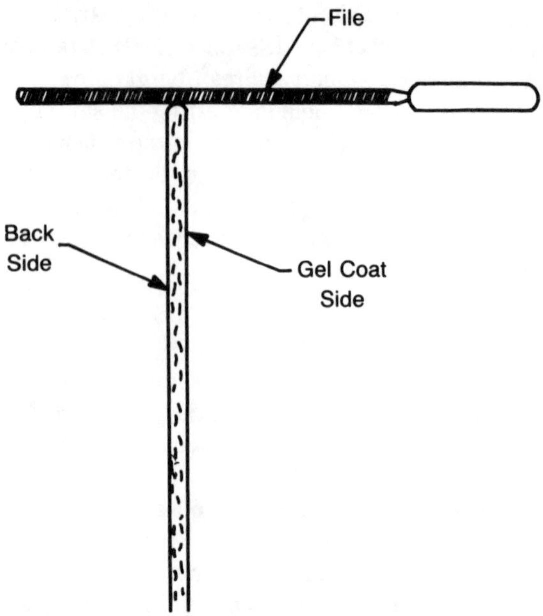

Fig. 10-7. Filing from gel coat side of laminate.

Coarse sanding is usually done dry. Fine sanding can be done wet or dry. For wet sanding, paper with a waterproof adhesive must be used. The water helps keep the grit in the sandpaper from clogging, which in turn reduces scratching of the surface.

The coarser grits that are used first leave the deepest scratches but remove the most material. The medium grits remove these scratches and leave smaller ones, while removing less material than the coarser grits. The smaller scratches can be removed by using finer grits of sandpaper, which in turn leave very tiny scratches. These can be filled in by painting or gel coating or polished out in the case of gel-coated surfaces. It's important to avoid making any scratches below the desired finished surface. Otherwise, these will have to be filled in with fiberglass putty or other surfacing compound if a smooth finish is to be achieved. Deep scratches can be avoided by not using any coarser grit of paper than is absolutely necessary.

The abrasive paper can be folded and held between the thumb and fingers. Care must be taken using this method however, or an uneven and wavy surface can result, especially when coarser grits of paper are used.

A better method is to use a sanding block. This can be a small block of wood with sandpaper folded around it (Fig. 10-8) or a special sanding block with clamps for holding the paper in place. A pad between the block and the sandpaper is also helpful. Block sanding lets you remove high spots without affecting adjacent low areas. This makes fairing possible.

Power Sanding

Although it's practical to do small sanding jobs by hand sanding, power sanding is almost indispensable for large jobs. A disk sander is perhaps the most useful general-purpose sanding tool for fiberglass. It turns at about 5,000 revolutions per minute and removes a large amount of material rapidly. This is both an advantage and disadvantage. It takes considerable skill and practice to operate a disk sander to remove the desired material without damaging the surface or taking away excess material.

To fair uneven surfaces, hold the sanding disk nearly flat. Apply only light pressure and keep the disk moving. To feather edges, hold the sanding disk at a slight angle to the surface. Spend considerable time practicing both operations on scrap materials before using a disk sander on an actual job.

Belt sanders are sometimes used for sanding fiberglass. Belt sanders can be adjusted for coarse, medium, or fine sanding, using the appropriate grit of sandpaper. Again, it takes a lot of practice to learn to use a belt sander properly. Practice on scrap materials before you attempt to use a belt sander on an actual job.

Pad or finishing sanders, also known as vibrator sanders, are

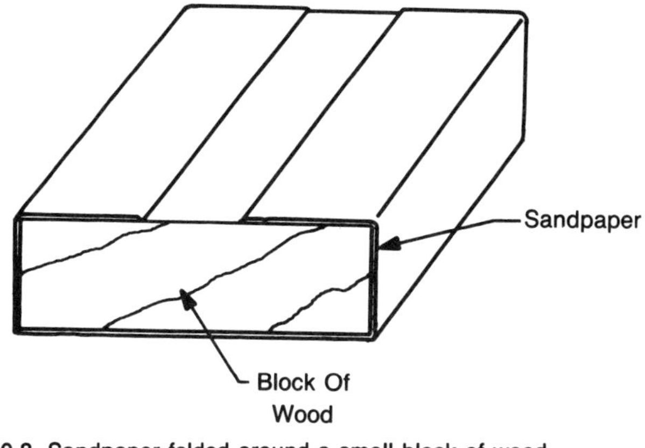

Fig. 10-8. Sandpaper folded around a small block of wood.

suitable only for light or finishing sanding of fiberglass. The main advantage of this type of sander is that it is easy for the beginner to use. Gouging of surfaces is seldom a problem. Apply only light pressure when using pad sanders. Keep the pad moving.

FUNDAMENTALS OF FIBERGLASSING

To learn the fundamentals of fiberglassing, you must actually try fiberglassing. Purchase fiberglassing materials and supplies just for this purpose. This will allow you to make mistakes. It's better to make these on practice exercises than on an actual fiberglassing job on a boat.

Now that you are familiar with the health and safety rules and practices, follow them carefully. Be sure to wear protective clothing and equipment. Follow manufacturer's directions and instructions exactly for each product used.

Catalyzing Polyester Resins

The curing process for polyester resin, called *polymerization,* is fully initiated when a catalyst—methyl ethyl ketone (MEK) peroxide—is added. The amount of catalyst added depends on a number of factors, especially the formulation of the particular resin, the working temperature, the amount of resin to be catalyzed, and the desired working time or pot life.

Polyester resin can be applied from the time when the catalyst is added until it achieves a gelatinous consistency. This time period is the working time or pot life. Any resin that has not been applied by this time should be discarded, because it will result in a lumpy mess if applied to fiberglass reinforcing material. The resin becomes hard soon after this.

Once the catalyst is added, the resin actually cures faster in the container than if spread out into a thin layer when applied to reinforcing material. This is due to a higher heat buildup in the container.

Each brand and type of polyester resin has a different curing rate when the same amount of catalyst is added to the same volume of resin. Follow the manufacturer's directions regarding the amount of catalyst to be used for the particular resin. For these projects, I will use a polyester resin. Keep in mind that this might vary somewhat from the brand or type of resin you use.

In most cases, only a very small amount of catalyst, from about 1/2 percent to 4 percent by volume, is added to a relatively large amount of resin. A primary problem is measuring out such small quantities of catalyst accurately. This is commonly done by drops. The dispenser that the catalyst comes in will probably allow this.

Catalyzing Exercise 1. To start, catalyze 1 ounce of polyester resin at a time. You need a graded measuring device for the polyester resin. Measure out 1 ounce (1 ounce of resin is about 1/16 of a pint) of resin and place this in a clean cup or mixing container. Then, seal the primary container of resin and set it aside. It is extremely important not to allow even a small quantity of catalyst to contaminate the resin in the primary container. This would start the curing, which would take place even if the lid on the container is sealed. Develop clean and efficient working habits.

Let's first consider the amount of catalyst to be added when the working temperature is 75 degrees Fahrenheit, which is considered ideal. If 1/2 percent by volume of catalyst is added to the resin, the working or pot life of the resin is about 60 minutes, at which time the resin starts to gel. Soon after that, it becomes hard. For 1 ounce of resin, 1/2 percent by volume of catalyst would be approximately two drops.

Now add the catalyst to the resin. Lay a piece of wax paper on the work space. Using the plastic dispenser that the catalyst comes in, add two drops of catalyst to the 1 ounce of resin. Then use a small mixing stick to stir the catalyst into the resin. Wait about 30 seconds. Next, pour the catalyzed resin onto the wax paper. Use the mixing stick to get as much out of the mixing container as possible. Bunch the resin up into one area on the wax paper. Set the mixing cup aside. Have a watch or clock handy to time the reaction. In about 60 minutes from the time the catalyst was added, the resin should start to gel. Poke it with the mixing stick to determine when this happens. Soon after that, the resin should become hard. Save the sample of cured resin for experimenting and making comparisons.

Catalyzing Exercise 2. Next, measure out another ounce of resin into a mixing container. Remember not to place the mixing stick used previously for the catalyzed resin into the primary container of resin.

This time add 1 percent by volume of catalyst to the resin. For 1 ounce of resin, add about 4 drops of catalyst. Stir the resin and catalyst together using a small mixing stick. Wait about 30 seconds, then pour the mixture onto the wax paper. This time the pot life of the resin is reduced to about 30 minutes. The resin should become hard soon after it starts to gel. Save the sample of cured resin for experimenting and making comparisons.

Catalyzing Exercise 3. Measure out another ounce of resin into a mixing container. Add 2 percent by volume of catalyst to the resin. For the 1 ounce of resin, add about 8 drops of catalyst. Stir the catalyst into the resin with a small mixing stick. Wait about 30 seconds, then pour the mixture onto the wax paper. The pot life of the resin is now reduced to about 15 minutes with the resin hardening soon after it starts to gel. Again save the sample of cured resin for later.

Catalyzing Exercise 4. Measure out another ounce of resin into a mixing container. Add 3 percent by volume of catalyst to the resin. For the 1 ounce of resin, add about 12 drops of catalyst and stir the catalyst into the resin with a small mixing stick. Wait about 30 seconds, then pour the mixture onto the wax paper. The pot life of the resin is now reduced to about 7 1/2 minutes, with the resin hardening soon after that. Save the sample of cured resin.

Summary. The above practice exercises demonstrate that at a constant temperature of 75 degrees Fahrenheit, the more catalyst added, the shorter the pot life and curing time. The following summarizes this:

Amount of Resin (oz.)	% by Volume of Catalyst	Drops of Catalyst	Pot Life (minutes)
1	1/2	2	60
1	1	4	30
1	2	8	15
1	3	12	7 1/2

Take the four sample pieces of cured resin and place them on a hard surface. Tap each piece with a hammer. Two things should be noted. First, cured resin without fiberglass reinforcing material is very brittle. Second, all the samples, regardless of curing time, should have about equal strength. This works only for a certain range of percentages by volume of catalyst, usually from about 1/2 to 3 percent. This gives you a choice of working times, depending on the particular job you are doing.

Later as you gain experience, you will want to catalyze more than an ounce of resin at a time. To achieve the same percentages by volume of catalyst for 2 ounces of resin, double the number of drops of catalyst from the amounts used previously. In a similar manner, you can determine the amount of catalyst to add to any amount of resin to give the desired pot life at 75 degrees Fahrenheit.

The working temperature will often be something other than 75 degrees Fahrenheit. With regular polyester resin, you can do satisfactory work in a temperature range of 60 degrees Fahrenheit to 90 degrees Fahrenheit. You must use different amounts of catalyst, however, than when the working temperature is 75 degrees Fahrenheit to maintain the same pot life.

For example, if the working temperature is 60 degrees Fahrenheit, and the same percentage by volume of catalyst is added as in the exercises, the pot life would approximately double. This means that if 1/2 percent by volume of catalyst is added, the pot life would be about 2 hours rather than 60 minutes; if 1 percent by volume of catalyst is added, the pot life would be about 60 minutes rather than 30 minutes.

If the working temperature is 90 degrees Fahrenheit, and the same percentage by volume of catalyst is added as used previously at 75 degrees Fahrenheit, the pot life would be approximately cut in half. This means that if 1/2 percent by volume of catalyst is added, the pot life would be 30 minutes rather than 60 minutes; if 1 percent by volume of catalyst is added, the pot life would be 15 minutes rather than 30 minutes.

For temperatures between, the pot life increases or decreases proportionally. Or you can maintain a desired pot life by changing the amount of catalyst added. For most fiberglassing work, a pot life from 15 to 30 minutes is about right. It might take some experimenting to determine what works best for you, however.

To summarize, more catalyst means a faster curing time; less catalyst means a slower curing time. Lower temperatures mean a slower curing time; higher temperatures mean a faster curing time. A desired pot life or curing time can be maintained with regular polyester resin in a temperature range from about 60 to 90 degrees Fahrenheit by varying the amount of catalyst used.

As a rule, best results are obtained at a working temperature of 75 degrees Fahrenheit. Problems increase as the extremes of the temperature range are approached. With practice, you should be able to do satisfactory work in a variety of working temperatures.

Applying Polyester Resin to Reinforcing Material

Although polyester resin alone is weak and brittle, when combined with fiberglass reinforcing material, a material of considerable strength is formed.

Resin to Mat. As a practice exercise, cut a 6-inch square of

1 1/2-ounce-per-square-foot fiberglass mat and place it on wax paper.

The 6-inch square should weigh about 1/4 as much as a 1-foot square, or about 0.38 ounces (1/4 × 1 1/2 ounce). A typical mat laminate is about 25 percent glass fiber material by weight and 75 percent resin by weight. For the 6-inch square of 1 1/2-ounce mat, approximately 1.14 ounces (3 × 0.38 ounce) of resin is required.

Because some resin does not end up as part of the laminate (some remains on the brush and in the mixing cup), measure out about 1.25 ounces of resin and place this in a mixing container. For this practice exercise, you need about 15 minutes of working time. Actually, you won't need this much time, but it's better to plan a little extra working time so you don't waste resin by having it harden in the mixing container. Determine the amount of catalyst to add for your working temperature. If the working temperature is about 75 degrees Fahrenheit, about 10 drops of catalyst are required.

Before adding the catalyst, get a 1/2-inch-wide paintbrush and a piece of cardboard about 1-foot square ready. Place the 6-inch square of 1 1/2-ounce mat on the cardboard. Add the catalyst to the resin. Stir with a small mixing stick. Wait about 30 seconds. Then, with the mat on the cardboard, use the brush to apply a layer of resin to the top side of the mat. Use a dabbing rather than brushing action when applying resin to the mat so that the glass fibers do not bunch up. After applying the resin to the one side of the mat, use the cardboard to flip the mat over wet side down on the wax paper. Apply the remainder of the resin to the other side of the mat, again using a dabbing rather than brushing action.

After applying as much of the resin as possible to the reinforcing material, clean the resin from the brush using acetone. Allow the laminate to harden.

After the laminate has cured, pick it up and examine it (Fig. 10-9). If everything was done correctly, you should have a 6-inch square mat laminate that is approximately 1/20 inch thick. The side of the panel that was directly over the wax paper should be smooth because the wax paper was a molding surface for the flat panel. The same thing could be done with a curved surface.

Set the mat laminate aside. It will be used later.

Resin to Cloth. Cut a 6-inch square of 10-ounce-per-square-yard fiberglass cloth. Cut the cloth so that you have one selvaged edge.

Because a square yard of 10-ounce fiberglass cloth weighs ap-

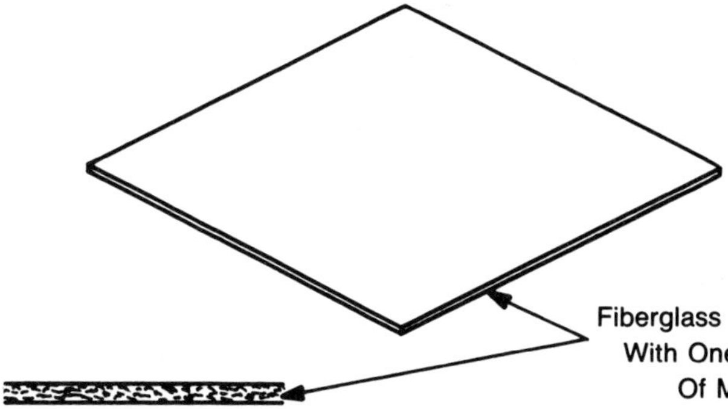

Fig. 10-9. A fiberglass laminate made up of one layer of mat.

proximately 10 ounces, the 6-inch square should weigh about 1/36 as much, or about 0.3 ounce. Cloth laminates are typically about 50 percent reinforcing material and 50 percent resin by weight. Therefore, about 0.3 ounce of resin is required. Because some will be lost on the brush, in the container, and on the cardboard during the application, however, use about 0.5 ounce of resin.

Plan about 15 minutes of working time. Determine the amount of catalyst to add for your working temperature. At 75 degrees Fahrenheit, about 4 drops of catalyst are required for the 1/2 ounce of resin.

Have a 1/2-inch paintbrush and a piece of cardboard about 1 foot square ready. Place the 6-inch square of 10-ounce-per-square-yard fiberglass cloth on the cardboard. Add the catalyst to the resin. Stir with a mixing stick. Wait about 30 seconds. Then, with the cloth on the cardboard, use the brush to apply a layer of resin to the top side of the cloth. Use a brushing action, but take care not to unravel the cloth along the unselvaged edges. After applying the resin to one side of the cloth, use the cardboard to flip the cloth over wet side down on the wax paper. Then apply the remainder of the resin to the other side of the cloth. Spread the resin out into a smooth, even layer.

After applying as much resin as possible to the cloth reinforcing material, clean any remaining resin from the brush using acetone as a solvent. Allow the cloth laminate to harden.

After the laminate has cured, pick it up and examine it (Fig. 10-10). If everything was done correctly, you should have a 6-inch square cloth laminate that is approximately 1/64 inch thick. The side of the panel that was directly over the wax paper should be relatively smooth because the wax paper acted as a flat molding surface.

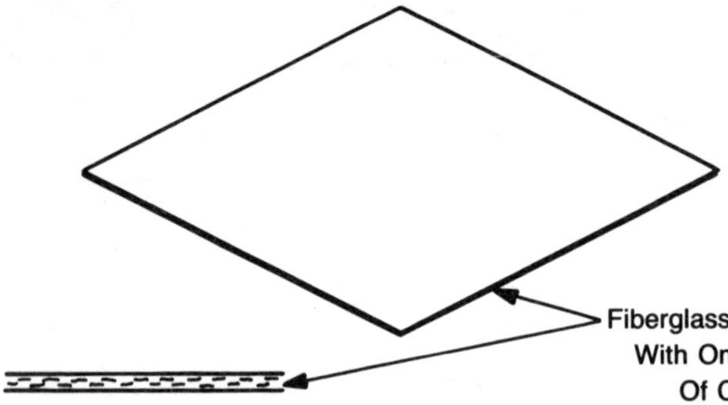

Fig. 10-10. A fiberglass laminate made up of one layer of cloth.

Set the cloth laminate aside. It will be used later.

Resin to Woven Roving. Next, cut a 6-inch square piece of 24-ounce-per-square-yard fiberglass woven roving. The woven roving does not have selvaged edges; be careful when cutting and handling the material so that the roving does not come unraveled at the edges.

Because a square yard of 24-ounce fiberglass woven roving weighs approximately 24 ounces, the 6-inch square should weigh about 1/36 as much, or about 0.68 ounces. Woven roving laminates are typically about 45 percent reinforcing material by weight and 55 percent resin by weight. Therefore, about 0.7 ounce of resin is required. Use 0.8 ounce, however, to account for the resin that will be lost on the brush, in the container, and on the cardboard during the application.

Plan 15 minutes of working time. Determine the amount of catalyst to add for your working temperature. At 75 degrees Fahrenheit, about 7 drops of catalyst are required for the 0.8 ounce of resin.

Have a 1/2-inch paintbrush and a piece of cardboard about 1 foot square ready. Place the 6-inch square piece of 24-ounce-per-square-yard fiberglass woven roving on the cardboard. Add the catalyst to the resin. Stir with a mixing stick. Wait about 30 seconds. Then, with the woven roving on the cardboard, use the brush to apply a layer of resin to the top side of the woven roving. Use a brushing action, taking care not to unravel the edges of the woven roving. After applying the resin to one side of the woven roving, use the cardboard to flip the woven roving over wet side down on the wax paper. Then apply the remainder of the resin to the other side of the woven roving. Spread the resin out into a smooth, even layer.

After applying as much resin as possible to the woven roving reinforcing material, clean any remaining resin from the brush using acetone as a solvent. Allow the woven roving laminate to harden.

After the laminate has cured, pick it up and examine it (Fig. 10-11). You should have a 6-inch square woven roving laminate that is approximately 1/25 inch thick. The side of the panel that was directly over the wax paper should be relatively smooth because the wax paper acted as a flat molding surface. The coarse weave pattern of the woven roving still shows, however.

Set the woven roving laminate aside. It will be used later.

Summary. To this point in the practice exercises, it doesn't really matter whether you used laminating resin or finishing resin. If you used laminating resin, the surfaces of the laminates should have remained tacky. If finishing resin was used, the surfaces should have no tackiness.

As a general rule, use laminating resin whenever you intend to add additional layers to the laminate. The final application of resin is normally finishing resin, which gives a surface without tackiness that can be sanded and painted as desired.

I suggest that you use laminating resin throughout. When you need a finishing resin, use a wax additive to convert the laminating resin into a finishing resin.

If for any reason you apply finishing resin and then decide to add another layer to the laminate, you must first remove the wax from the surface. This can be done by sanding and/or chemically using a solvent, such as acetone, to remove the wax from the surface.

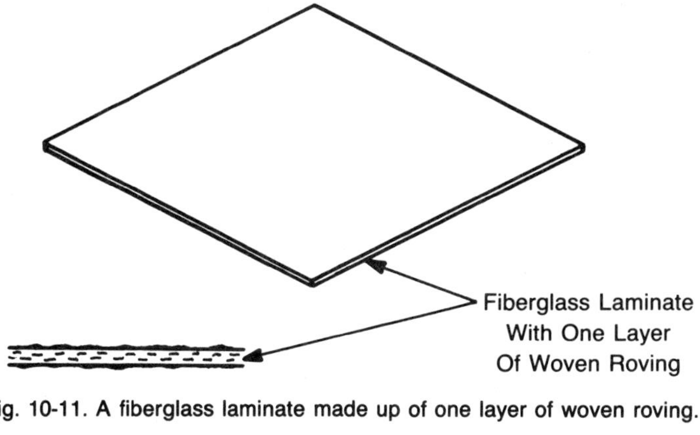

Fig. 10-11. A fiberglass laminate made up of one layer of woven roving.

Laminating Layers of Reinforcing Material Together

Fiberglass laminates are made up of layers of mat, cloth, woven roving, or some combination of these materials, that are laminated together. The question might be raised, "Why not just use a single layer of reinforcing material that has the necessary thickness so that the job could be done in one operation?"

The main reason is the difficulty of handling and properly saturating thick layers of reinforcing material with resin. There have been attempts to make thicker fiberglass reinforcing materials, such as by combining a layer of woven roving and a layer of mat into a single reinforcing material. This, in effect, does in a single operation what would otherwise be done in two, that is, first a layer of woven roving and then a layer of mat. Even this is somewhat difficult to handle and lay up, however, and it isn't recommended for beginners.

The mat, cloth, and woven roving laminates you made will now be used for additional practice exercises. If you used finishing resin, clean the wax from both sides of the panels with acetone.

Adding a Layer of Mat to the Original Mat Laminate. Place the original mat laminate on a piece of wax paper. Cut a 6-inch square piece of 1 1/2-ounce-per-square-foot fiberglass mat. Measure out about 1.25 ounce of resin and place it in a mixing container. For this practice exercise, plan about 15 minutes of working time. Determine the amount of catalyst to add for your working temperature. If the working temperature is about 75 degrees Fahrenheit, about 10 drops of catalyst are required.

Have a 1/2-inch paintbrush and a piece of cardboard about 1 foot square ready. Place the dry piece of fiberglass mat on the cardboard. Add the catalyst to the resin. Stir with a mixing stick. Wait about 30 seconds.

Apply a layer of resin to either the bonding surface of the cured mat panel, the bonding side of the new mat layer, or both. All of these methods give satisfactory results. Experiment to determine which method works best for you.

Position the new mat layer on the cured panel. Use the brush to press the new mat layer down. Dab resin to the other side of the new mat layer. Spread the resin smoothly and evenly, making sure that the mat is thoroughly saturated or wetted out with resin.

After applying as much resin as possible to the reinforcing material, use acetone to clean the brush. Allow the laminate to harden.

After the laminate has cured, pick it up and examine it (Fig. 10-12). If everything was done correctly, you should have a 6-inch

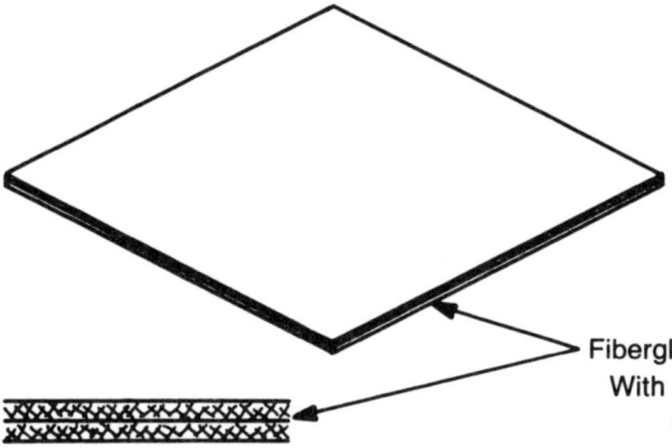

Fig. 10-12. A fiberglass laminate made up of two layers of mat.

square laminate of two layers of mat reinforcing material that is about 1/10 inch thick or twice the thickness of the original one-layer mat laminate. The two-layer laminate should weigh approximately twice as much as the one-layer laminate did. Set this laminate aside.

Adding a Layer of Mat to the Original Cloth Laminate. Place the original cloth laminate on a piece of wax paper. Cut a 6-inch square piece of 1 1/2-ounce-per-square-foot fiberglass mat. Measure out about 1.25 ounce of resin and place it in a mixing container. Plan about 15 minutes of working time. Determine the amount of catalyst to add for your working temperature. At 75 degrees Fahrenheit, about 10 drops of catalyst are required.

Have a 1/2-inch paintbrush and a piece of cardboard about 1 foot square ready. Place the dry piece of fiberglass mat on the cardboard. Add the catalyst to the resin. Stir with a mixing stick. Wait about 30 seconds.

Apply a layer of resin to either the bonding surface of the cured cloth panel, the bonding side of the mat to be added, or both. Position the mat layer on the cured cloth panel. Use the brush to press the mat layer in place. Dab resin to the other side of the mat. Spread it smoothly and evenly over the mat, making sure that the mat is thoroughly saturated or wetted out with resin.

After applying as much resin as possible to the reinforcing material, use acetone to clean the brush. Allow the laminate to harden.

After the laminate has cured, pick it up and examine it (Fig. 10-13). You should have a 6-inch square laminate consisting of one cloth layer and one mat layer of reinforcing material bonded together as a unit. Set this laminate aside.

Adding a Layer of Mat to the Original Woven Roving

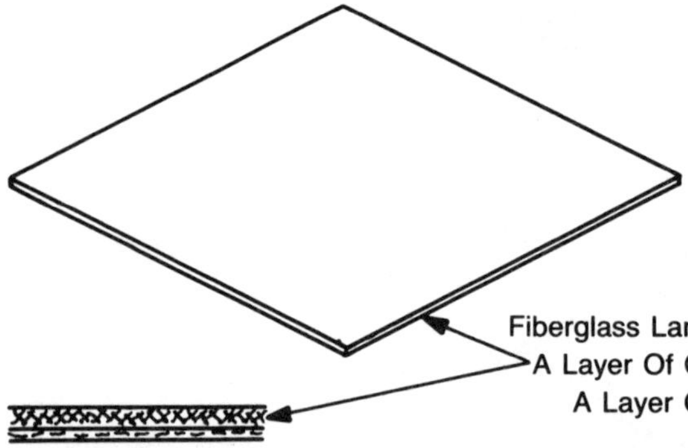

Fig. 10-13. A fiberglass laminate made up of a layer of cloth and a layer of mat.

Laminate. Place the original woven roving laminate on a piece of wax paper. Cut a 6-inch square piece of 1 1/2-ounce-per-square-foot fiberglass mat. Measure out about 1.25 ounces of resin and place this in a mixing container. Plan about 15 minutes of working time. Determine the amount of catalyst to add for your working temperature. At 75 degrees Fahrenheit, add about 10 drops of catalyst.

Have a 1/2-inch paintbrush and a piece of cardboard about 1 foot square ready. Place the dry piece of fiberglass mat on the cardboard. Add the catalyst to the resin. Stir with a mixing stick. Wait about 30 seconds.

Apply a layer of resin to either the bonding surface of the cured woven roving panel, the bonding side of the mat to be added, or both.

Position the mat layer on the cured woven roving panel. Use the brush to press the mat layer in place. Dab resin to the other side of the mat. Spread it smoothly and evenly, making sure that the mat is thoroughly saturated or wetted out with resin.

After applying as much resin as possible to the reinforcing material, use acetone to clean the brush. Allow the laminate to harden.

After the laminate has cured, pick it up and examine it (Fig. 10-14). You should have a 6-inch square laminate consisting of one layer of mat and one layer of woven roving reinforcing material bonded together as a unit. Set this laminate aside.

Adding a Third Layer of Mat to the Two-Layer Mat Laminate. Place this laminate on a piece of wax paper with the desired bonding area upward. Cut a 6-inch square piece of 1 1/2-ounce-per-square-foot fiberglass mat. Measure out about 1.25 ounces of resin and place it in a mixing container. Plan about 15 minutes of working time. Determine the amount of catalyst to add for your working temperature. At 75 degrees Fahrenheit, add about 10 drops of catalyst.

Have a 1/2-inch paintbrush and a piece of cardboard about 1 foot square ready. Place the dry piece of fiberglass mat on the cardboard. Add the catalyst to the resin. Stir with a mixing stick. Wait about 30 seconds.

Apply a layer of resin to either the bonding surface of the cured mat panel, the bonding side of the new mat layer to be added, or both. Position the new mat layer on the cured panel. Use the brush to press the new mat layer in place. Dab resin to the other side of the new mat layer. Spread it evenly over the mat, making sure that the mat is thoroughly saturated or wetted out with resin.

After applying as much resin as possible to the reinforcing material, use acetone to clean the brush. Allow the laminate to harden.

After the laminate has cured, pick it up and examine it (Fig. 10-15). You should have a 6 inch square of laminate with three layers of mat reinforcing material that is about 1/5 inch thick or three times the thickness of the original one-layer mat laminate. The three-layer laminate should weigh approximately three times as much as the one-layer laminate. Set this laminate aside.

Adding a Layer of Cloth to the Mat Side of the Mat and Cloth Laminate. Place the mat and cloth laminate on a piece of wax paper with the mat side upward. Cut a 6-inch square of 10-ounce-per-square-yard fiberglass cloth. Measure out about 1/2 ounce of resin and place it in a mixing container. Plan about 15 minutes of working time. Determine the amount of catalyst to add

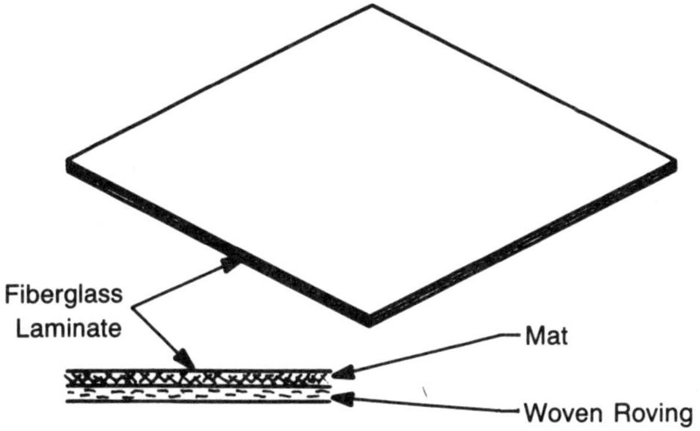

Fig. 10-14. A fiberglass laminate made up of a layer of woven roving and a layer of mat.

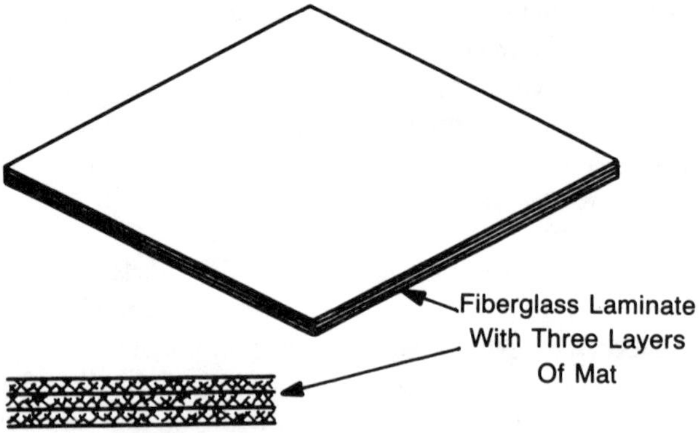

Fig. 10-15. A fiberglass laminate made up of three layers of mat.

for your working temperature. At 75 degrees Fahrenheit, add about 4 drops of catalyst.

Have a 1/2-inch paintbrush and a piece of cardboard about 1 foot square ready. Place the dry piece of fiberglass cloth on the cardboard. Add the catalyst to the resin. Stir with a mixing stick. Wait about 30 seconds.

Apply a layer of resin to either the bonding surface of the cured panel (mat side), the bonding side of the cloth to be added, or both surfaces. Position the cloth layer on the cured panel (mat side). Use the brush to press the cloth in place and smooth it out. Work all air bubbles off to one edge so that the trapped air can escape. Then apply resin to the other side of the cloth. Spread the resin evenly over the cloth, making sure that the cloth is thoroughly saturated or wetted out with resin.

After applying as much resin as possible to the reinforcing material, use acetone to clean the brush. Allow the laminate to harden.

After the laminate has cured, pick it up and examine it (Fig. 10-16). Your 6-inch square laminate should consist of a layer of mat reinforcing material sandwiched between two layers of cloth reinforcing material, with everything bonded together as a unit. Set this laminate aside.

Adding a Layer of Woven Roving to the Mat Side of the Mat and Woven Roving Laminate. Place the mat and woven roving laminate on a piece of wax paper in your work area with the mat side upward. Cut a 6-inch square piece of 24-ounce-per-square-yard fiberglass woven roving. Measure out about 0.8 ounce of resin and place it in a mixing container. Plan about 15 minutes of working time. Determine the amount of catalyst to add for your working temperature. At 75 degrees Fahrenheit, add about 7 drops of catalyst.

Have a 1/2-inch paintbrush and a piece of cardboard about 1 foot square ready. Place a dry piece of fiberglass woven roving on the cardboard. Add the catalyst to the resin. Stir with a mixing stick. Wait about 30 seconds.

Apply a layer of resin to either the bonding surface (mat side) of the cured panel, the bonding side of the woven roving to be added, or both surfaces. Position the woven roving layer on the cured panel (mat side). Use the brush to press the woven roving in place and smooth it out. Then apply resin to the other side of the woven roving. Spread it evenly over the woven roving, making sure that the woven roving is thoroughly saturated or wetted out with resin.

After applying as much resin as possible to the reinforcing material, use acetone to clean the brush. Allow the laminate to harden.

After the laminate has cured, pick it up and examine it (Fig. 10-17). You should have a 6-inch square laminate consisting of a layer of mat reinforcing material sandwiched between two layers of woven roving reinforcing material, with everything bonded together as a unit. Set this laminate aside.

Laminating Fiberglass to Plywood

For the next two practice exercises you will need two 6-inch square pieces of 1/4-inch plywood. You will use these to learn the basic fiberglassing skill of bonding fiberglass to wood.

Bonding Mat to Plywood. To bond a layer of mat to ply-

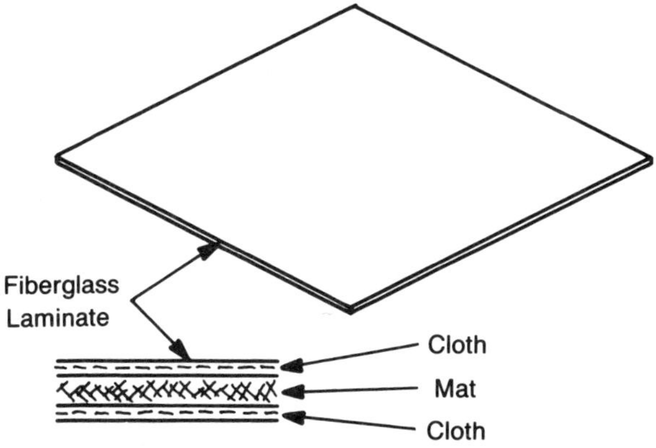

Fig. 10-16. A fiberglass laminate made up of two layers of cloth and one layer of mat.

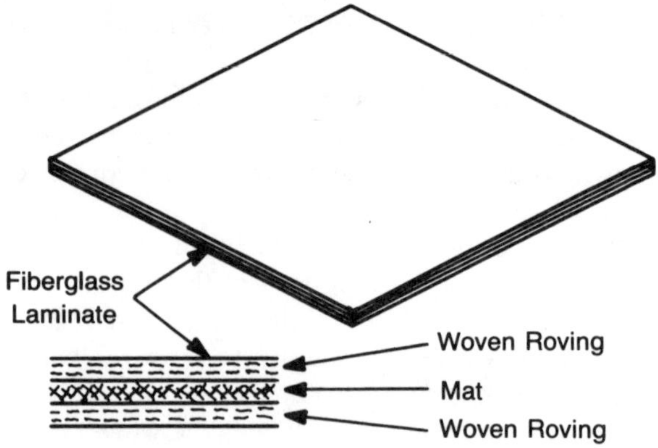

Fig. 10-17. A fiberglass laminate made up of two layers of woven roving and one layer of mat.

wood, place the 6-inch square of plywood on a piece of construction or newspaper. Rough sand one side of the plywood to give a good bonding surface for the fiberglass mat. Clean up all sawdust to keep your area clean for fiberglassing. Place the plywood on a piece of wax paper with the roughened bonding side upward.

Cut a 6-inch square piece of 1 1/2-ounce-per-square-foot fiberglass mat. Measure out about 1 1/2 ounces of resin. You need more this time because some of the resin will be soaked up by the wood. Place the resin in a mixing container.

Plan about 15 minutes of working time. Determine the amount of catalyst to add for your working temperature. At 75 degrees Fahrenheit, add about 12 drops.

Have a 1/2-inch paintbrush and a piece of cardboard about 1-foot square ready. Place the dry piece of fiberglass mat on the cardboard. Add the catalyst to the resin. Stir with a mixing stick. Wait about 30 seconds. Then, apply a thin layer of resin to the bonding surface of the plywood and a layer to the bonding side of the mat. Position the wet side of the mat to the wet side of the plywood. Use the brush to press the mat in place. Use a dabbing rather than brushing motion when working with mat to keep it from bunching up. Apply an even layer of resin over the mat, making sure that the mat is thoroughly saturated or wetted out with resin.

After applying as much resin as possible to the mat reinforcing material, use acetone to clean the brush. Allow the laminate to harden.

After the laminate has cured, pick it up and examine it (Fig. 10-18). You should have a 6-inch square laminate consisting of the plywood with a layer of mat bonded to it. Try to peel the fiberglass layer from the wood. If everything was done properly, there should be a good bond, although bonding fiberglass to wood using polyester resin can be difficult. For crucial jobs, you might want to use the more expensive epoxy resin, which is more difficult to use but gives a much better bond. Set this laminate aside.

Bonding a Layer of Fiberglass Cloth to Plywood. Place a 6-inch square of plywood on a piece of construction or newspaper. Rough sand one side of the plywood to give a good bonding surface for the fiberglass cloth. Clean up all sawdust so that you have a clean working area for the fiberglassing. Place the plywood on a piece of wax paper with the roughened bonding side of the plywood upward.

Cut a 6-inch square piece of 10-ounce-per-square-yard fiberglass cloth. Measure out about 3/4 ounce of resin (you use more this time because some resin soaks into the wood) and place it in a mixing container. Plan about 15 minutes of working time. Determine the amount of catalyst to add for your working temperature. At 75 degrees Fahrenheit, abut 6 drops of catalyst are required for the 3/4 ounce of resin.

Have a 1/2-inch paintbrush and a piece of cardboard about 1 foot square ready. Place the dry piece of fiberglass cloth on the cardboard. Add the catalyst to the resin. Stir with a mixing stick. Wait about 30 seconds. Then, apply a thin layer of resin to the bonding surface of the plywood and a layer to the bonding side of the fiberglass cloth. Position the wet side of the fiberglass cloth to the wet side of the plywood. Use the brush to work the cloth in place

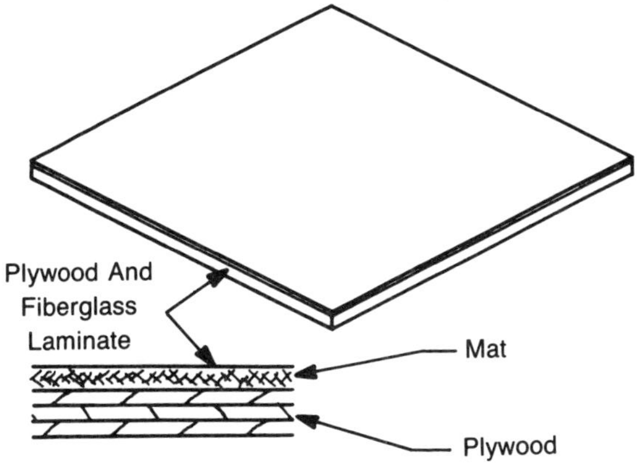

Fig. 10-18. One layer of mat bonded to plywood.

and to work out any air bubbles. Then brush an even layer of resin over the fiberglass cloth, making sure that the cloth is thoroughly wetted out with resin. When properly done, the fiberglass cloth should form a smooth layer over the surface of the plywood.

If everything looks okay, clean the brush with acetone. Allow the laminate to harden.

After the laminate has cured, pick it up and examine it (Fig. 10-19). You should have a 6-inch square laminate consisting of the plywood with a layer of fiberglass cloth bonded to it. Try to peel the fiberglass layer from the wood. If everything was done properly, there should be a good bond. Set this laminate aside.

Bonding a Layer of Cloth to the Previous Plywood and Mat Laminate. Place the plywood and mat laminate on a piece of wax paper with the mat side upward. If you previously used finishing resin, wash the surface with acetone to remove the wax. An alternative method is to sand the surface to remove the wax.

Cut a 6-inch square piece of 10-ounce-per-square-yard fiberglass cloth. Measure out about 1/2 ounce of resin and place this in a mixing container. Plan about 15 minutes of working time. Determine the amount of catalyst to add for your working temperature. At 75 degrees Fahrenheit, add about 4 drops of catalyst for the 1/2 ounce of resin.

Have a 1/2-inch paintbrush and a piece of cardboard about 1-foot square ready. Place the dry piece of fiberglass cloth on the cardboard. Add the catalyst to the resin. Stir with a mixing stick. Wait about 30 seconds. Then, apply a thin layer of resin to the bond-

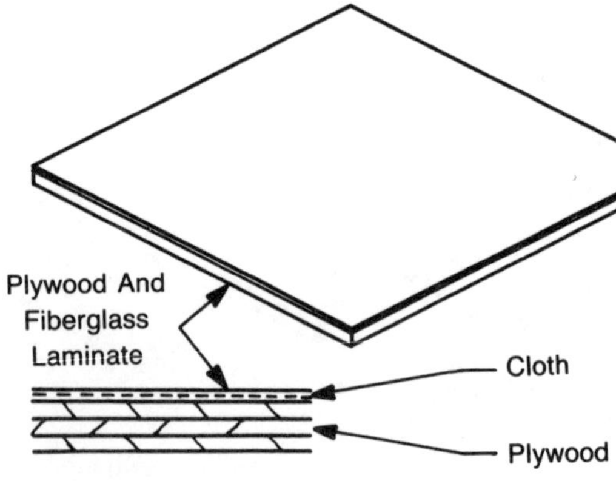

Fig. 10-19. One layer of cloth bonded to plywood.

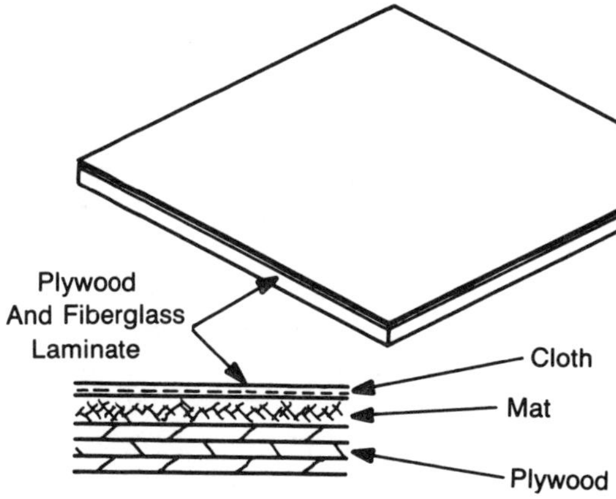

Fig. 10-20. One layer of mat and one layer of cloth bonded to plywood.

ing surface of the plywood and mat panel on the mat side. Next, apply a thin layer of resin to the bonding side of the fiberglass cloth. Position the wet side of the fiberglass cloth to the wet side of the panel. Use a brush to work the cloth in place and to work out any air bubbles. Then brush an even layer of resin over the fiberglass cloth, making sure that the cloth is thoroughly wetted out with resin. When properly done, the fiberglass cloth should form a smooth layer over the surface of the mat layer on the panel.

If everything looks okay, clean the brush with acetone. Allow the laminate to harden.

After the laminate has cured, pick it up and examine it (Fig. 10-20). If everything was done correctly, you should have a 6-inch-square panel consisting of the plywood, a layer of mat, and a layer of cloth, with everything bonded together as a unit. Set this laminate aside.

Bonding a Layer of Mat to the Previous Plywood and Cloth Laminate. Place the plywood and cloth laminate on a piece of wax paper with the cloth side upward. If you previously used finishing resin, wash the surface with acetone to remove the wax from the surface. An alternative method is to sand the surface to remove the wax.

Cut a 6-inch-square piece of 1 1/2-ounce-per-square-foot fiberglass mat. Measure out about 1.25 ounces of resin and place this in a mixing container. Plan 15 minutes of working time. Determine the amount of catalyst to add for your working temperature. At 75 degrees Fahrenheit, add about 10 drops of catalyst.

Have a 1/2-inch paintbrush and a piece of cardboard about 1-foot square ready. Place the dry piece of fiberglass mat on the cardboard. Add the catalyst to the resin. Stir with a mixing stick. Wait about 30 seconds. Then apply a thin layer of resin to the cloth bonding surface of the plywood and cloth laminate and a thin layer of resin to the bonding side of the fiberglass mat. Position the wet side of the fiberglass mat to the wet side of the panel. Use the brush to work the mat in place, using a dabbing rather than brushing action to keep it from bunching up. Then brush an even layer of resin over the fiberglass mat, making sure that is it thoroughly wetted out. When properly done, the fiberglass mat should form a smooth layer over the surface of the plywood.

If everything looks okay, clean the brush with acetone. Allow the laminate to harden.

After the laminate has cured, pick it up and examine it (Fig. 10-21). If everything was done correctly, you should have a 6-inch-square panel consisting of the plywood, a layer of cloth, and a layer of mat, with everything bonded together as a unit.

Summary. If you completed all of the practice exercises, you should now have five fiberglass panels, as follows:

1. A three-layer mat laminate.
2. A three-layer cloth, mat, and cloth laminate.
3. A three-layer woven roving, mat, woven roving laminate.
4. A three-layer plywood, mat, cloth laminate.
5. A three-layer plywood, cloth, mat laminate.

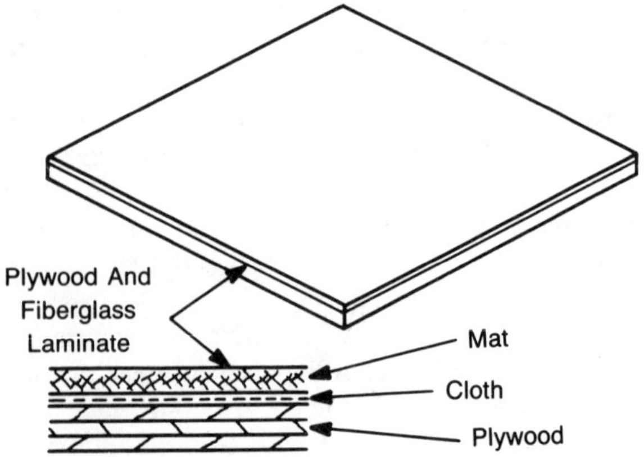

Fig. 10-21. One layer of cloth and one layer of mat bonded to plywood.

If you used laminating resin throughout, catalyze and apply a thin layer of finishing resin or laminating resin with wax added, as detailed previously, to the fiberglass surfaces of each laminate.

Using Polyester and Epoxy Putty and Filler Material

A variety of polyester and epoxy putty and filler compounds are on the market. These are often formulated for special purposes. Use the kind especially formulated for marine use. Some of the compounds intended for auto body repair are unsuitable because they contain metals that will rust in a typical marine atmosphere. A variety of powdered and fibrous additives are used with polyester and epoxy resins to give a putty consistency. Some of these reinforce the resin. Others weaken the resulting cured mixture, sometimes to a brittle plastic like the pure resin formed in the first practice exercises.

You can also mix up your own putty and filler materials by adding milled glass fibers to polyester or epoxy resin. Before use, a catalyst or hardener must also be added.

As a rule, putty and filler materials should only be used to fill in small areas up to about the size of a quarter. Larger areas should be repaired using fiberglass mat or other reinforcing materials, unless the putty area is to be covered over with a fiberglass laminate.

Whenever I fill in surface defects on fiberglass boats, I use epoxy rather than polyester putty. The epoxy putty gives a much better bond than does polyester putty. Modern epoxy putties are available that cure rapidly and are about as easy to use and apply as polyester putties.

As a practice exercise, I suggest that you mix up a small amount of manufactured polyester or epoxy putty. Measure out a small quantity of the resin part of the putty onto a board or a shallow mixing container. Then add the recommended amount of catalyst or hardener for the brand and type of putty used. For polyester putty, the catalyst can be in liquid or paste form. For epoxy putty, the hardener or curing agent is usually in the form of a thick, gel-like liquid. Place the mixture on wax paper and bunch it up, then spread it out into a layer about 1/8 inch thick. Use a putty knife for working the putty.

After the putty cures, place it on concrete or other solid surface and tap it with a hammer. Though the putty will probably break up, it should stand up to a harder blow with a hammer than did the cured pieces of resin without reinforcing material.

As a second practice exercise with putty, mix milled glass fibers with polyester resin. Mix only a small amount. First, place the desired amount of resin in a small cup or other mixing container. Then add milled glass fibers until the desired thickness is achieved. Next, add the catalyst. Use the same amount of catalyst as you would for the resin alone, without milled fibers. Stir with a small mixing stick. Spread the mixture out into a layer about 1/8 inch thick on wax paper. Use a putty knife for working the putty.

After the putty hardens, place it on concrete or other hard surface and tap it with a hammer. Though the putty will break up, it should have much greater strength than cured resin without reinforcing material.

Sanding and Fairing Fiberglass Laminates

The next practice is to sand and fair the fiberglass surfaces of the five practice laminates. Use a sanding block and aluminum oxide or silicon carbide abrasive paper. If there are high spots to be removed, start with a coarse grit sandpaper, but no coarser than is necessary to remove the high spots in a reasonable amount of time (Fig. 10-22). Use the sanding block. Gradually work down to finer grits of abrasive paper.

There may be low areas that require filling with putty (Fig. 10-23). Apply the putty as detailed previously, using a putty knife to scrape off excess putty. If polyester putty is used, leave the area slightly higher than surrounding area, because most polyester putties have some shrinkage. Allow the putty to harden.

After the putty hardens, sand away high spots. Work down to finer grits of abrasive paper. Some manufactured putties sand quite easily, others don't. The polyester putty that you mix yourself using milled glass fibers is quite difficult to sand, about the same as sanding a polyester resin and mat laminate.

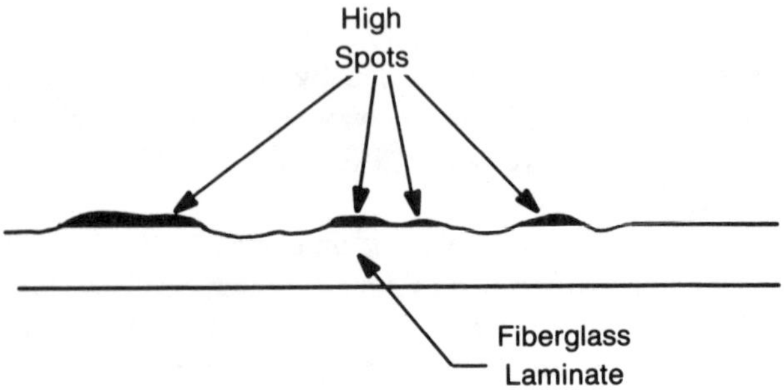

Fig. 10-22. High spots are removed by sanding.

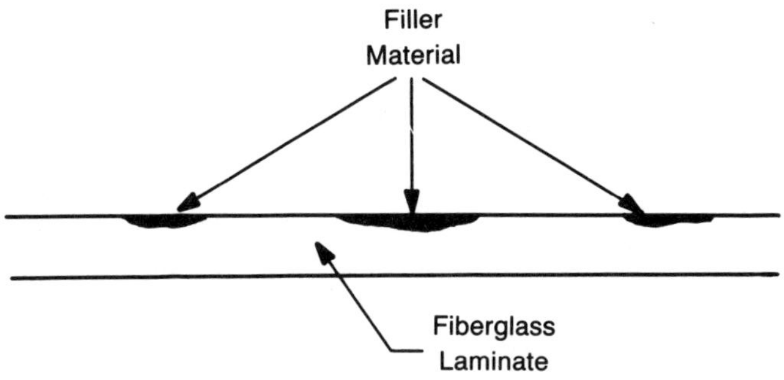

Fig. 10-23. Low areas are filled in with putty.

Finish the sanding using fine grits of abrasive paper. Continue to use a sanding block. The fine sanding can be done wet or dry, as desired.

Sand the fiberglass surfaces on all five practice laminates until they are smooth and fair. This may take considerable time, but is an important practice exercise. Careful sanding achieves professional results in fiberglassing work.

Gel Coating and Painting Fiberglass Laminates

Apply color gel coat resin or two-part epoxy or polyurethane paint to the fiberglass surfaces of the five panels prepared in the practice exercises. Carefully follow the manufacturer's directions for the gel coating or paint used.

After application, allow the gel coating to harden or the paint to dry or cure. If everything was done properly, you should now have five panels, three of which are finished on both sides and two of which are finished on one side only. The finished surfaces should be smooth and fair with a smooth even color coating.

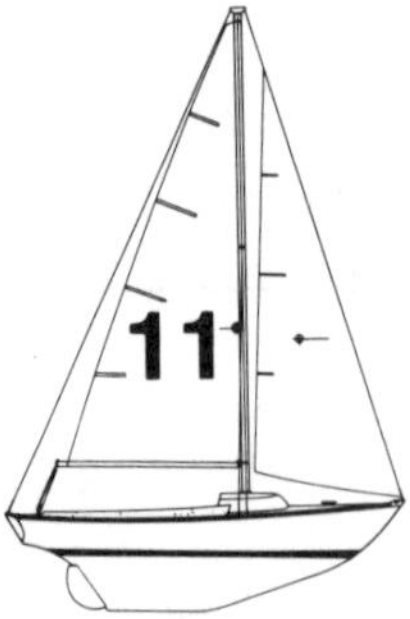

Alterations

By using fiberglassing techniques, you can make alterations on fiberglass boats that would not otherwise be possible. There are many reasons for making alterations. You might want to improve the appearance or performance of the boat or alter it in some way to more closely fit your particular needs and requirements.

Before attempting any alterations on your boat, make sure that you have the necessary skill to do them properly. Any alterations done should be at least the same quality and appearance as the rest of the boat. If not, they will stand out like a sore thumb.

To gain the necessary skill and experience, do the fiberglassing practice exercises in Chapter 10. Then, before doing any alterations on your boat, try them out on scrap materials whenever this is practical. On your first attempts at alterations on your boat, stick to easy jobs that are well within your present skill level. If you plan to go into more extensive fiberglassing work, buy an old, damaged, and/or badly neglected fiberglass boat and recondition and make alterations on it. This is not only a good way to learn a lot about fiberglassing, but also a possible way to earn some extra money. I've purchased damaged fiberglass boats, reconditioned them, and then sold them at a substantial profit.

Only a small part of making alterations on fiberglass boats involves fiberglassing. Much of the work uses standard techniques to work with wood and other materials. This chapter covers the fiberglassing part of making alterations, which is the part that stops most fiberglass boat owners from making certain kinds of alterations.

DESIGN OF ALTERATIONS

A primary problem is the design of alterations that are to be made. Before making any alterations, you should first make certain that they will actually improve the boat. You don't want to do anything that will make the boat unsafe or unseaworthy. And you won't want to decrease the performance of the vessel unless you can accept the compromise involved, such as larger interior accommodations in exchange for slower cruising speed. And you won't want to make the boat look ugly or reduce the value of the vessel should you decide to sell it.

Minor changes, especially on the interiors of the boats, can be made without serious problems. For example, you can add a magazine rack or a shelf or widen a berth. It's important, however, that you don't seriously change the weight distributions of heavy items.

If there are other boats of the same size and design in your area, talk to the owners and see what alterations they have made to their boats. This is a good way to find out what worked and what didn't.

If you intend to do more complicated or extensive modifications, first check them out with a qualified boat designer. There will be a fee for this advice, but it's well worth the cost to keep from doing something that might harm your boat. This applies especially to such modifications as changing the shape of the hull, enlarging cabins and superstructures (I've seen a number of boats ruined by amateur designing and constructing here), and enlarging windows. These types of alterations require not only major boatbuilding techniques, but also an understanding of advanced boat design.

MAKING ATTACHMENTS TO FIBERGLASS MOLDINGS

A major problem in making alterations is in attaching things to fiberglass moldings. In some cases, mechanical fasteners can be used, as detailed in Chapter 8. In other cases, mechanical fasteners cannot be used or are undesirable.

Joining a Block of Wood to a Fiberglass Molding

There are many instances where it is desirable to attach a block of wood to a fiberglass molding without using mechanical fasteners. For example, you might have a curtain rod fitting that is designed for screw attachment to a wall. Obviously, you don't want to drill holes for the screws directly into fiberglass moldings, which often aren't thick enough to hold the screws anyway. A solution would be to first attach a block of wood to the fiberglass molding, then fasten the fitting with screws that extend only into the block, without going through to the molding underneath. You could merely epoxy glue the block of wood to the fiberglass molding, though this would only suffice for a very light load fitting. Curtain rod attachments often support heavy loads, especially when you start to lose your balance and grab the curtain as a handhold.

It is common practice to use fiberglass bonding strips to attach the block of wood, often in addition to the epoxy gluing. When properly applied, fiberglass bonding strips have considerable holding power. The bonding strips form angle bonds that overlap the surrounding fiberglass molding and extend only on the edges of the block of wood (Fig. 11-1). The main problem with this is that the bonding area on the wood is relatively small. In addition, bonding to wood can be a problem anyway, especially if polyester resin is used.

Bonding can be improved considerably by shaping the block as shown in Fig. 11-2. This gives more bonding surface and "traps" the block in position even if part of the bond should fail. There will still be a tendency for the fiberglass to peel back away from the wood at the exposed edges, however. To avoid this, the wood block can be completely embedded in fiberglass (Fig. 11-3). This is done for maximum strength, along with shaping the block.

Using scrap materials, practice bonding a small block of wood to fiberglass laminate. If scrap fiberglass laminate is not available, use a scrap piece of plywood, though remember that a better bond is possible when bonding to fiberglass.

Sharp corners and angles are more difficult to laminate in place then gradual corners and rounded angles. For this reason, shape

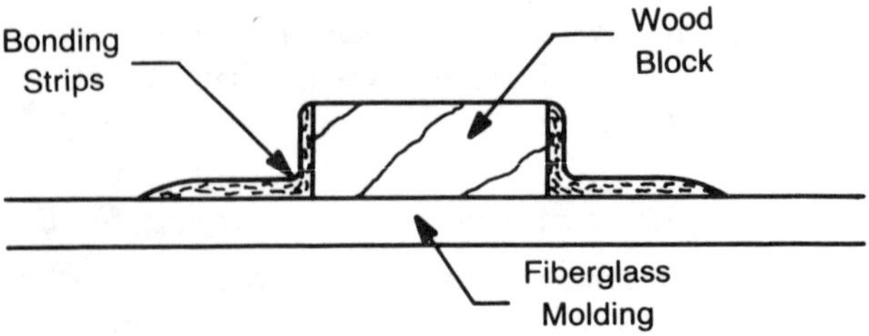

Fig. 11-1. Bonding strips that attach only to edges of block of wood.

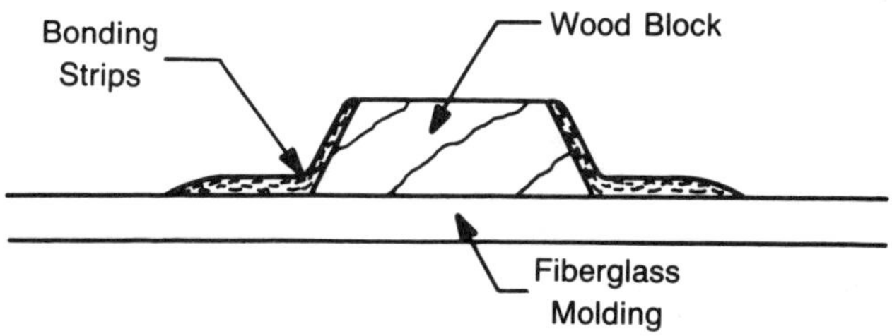

Fig. 11-2. Block shaped for better bonding.

the block of wood (Fig. 11-4). Rough sand all bonding surfaces on the block using a course grit of abrasive paper.

Next, either sand the bonding surface on the fiberglass molding or clean the area chemically with acetone, or both. On an actual job, you might want to mask off areas to keep resin and other chemicals off areas where you don't want them.

With both the block of wood and the bonding area of the fiberglass clean and dry, epoxy glue the block of wood to the fiberglass in the desired position. Use props or other means for holding it in position until the epoxy glue cures. This will vary, depending on the particular situation. After the glue has set, remove the prop or other holding devices.

Various types of fiberglass reinforcing material can be used for bonding the block in place. For a small block of wood, use a 1 1/2-ounce-per-square-foot fiberglass mat. For small blocks of wood, a minimum overlap of 1 1/2 inches onto the fiberglass all the way around the block of wood is recommended. Cut a layer of mat to the required size.

Mat can be shaped over a thin block of wood without making corner cuts. For thicker blocks of wood, corner cuts are used (Fig. 11-5). Corner cuts are also required for cloth. Woven roving, which

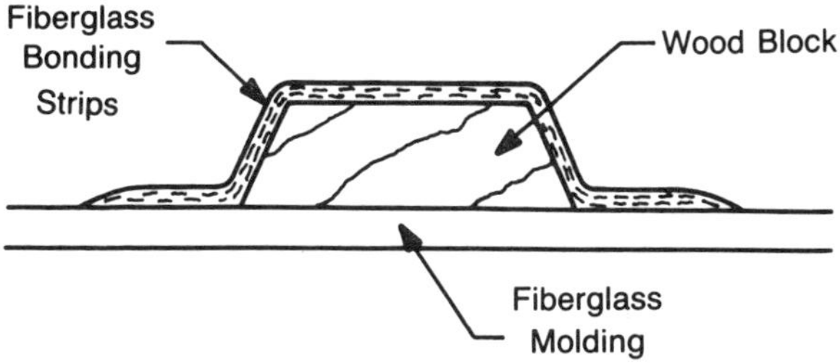

Fig. 11-3. Block completely embedded in fiberglass.

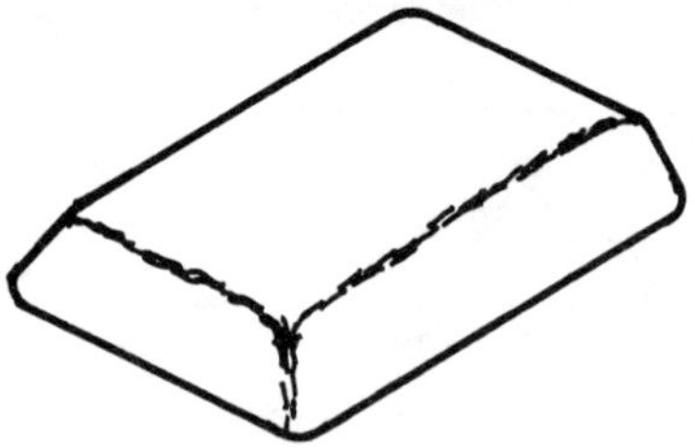

Fig. 11-4. The block is shaped for better bonding.

is used only when very substantial bonding and reinforcing are required, also requires corner cuts.

Next, estimate the amount of resin needed and place this in a mixing cup or other container. Add the required amount of catalyst for the desired working time (about 15 minutes for the present job) and for the particular working temperature (refer to Chapter 10).

Use a 1/2-inch wide paintbrush to apply the resin. Apply a thin layer to the surface of the wood and the bonding area of the fiberglass. Place the fiberglass mat on a piece of cardboard and wet out one side of it with resin. Use a dabbing rather than brushing action with the brush so the mat does not bunch up. Then use the cardboard to transfer the mat to the bonding position. Press the mat into position with the brush, stretching the mat over the corners of the block if corner cuts were not used. After the mat is in the proper position and pressed into place, apply resin to the mat until it is properly saturated with resin. Both too little and too much resin

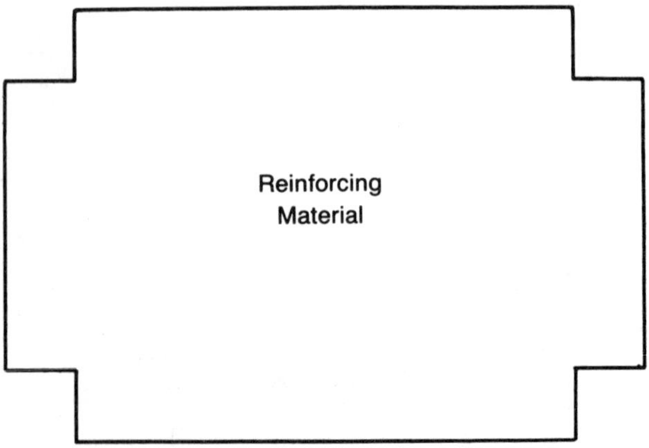

Fig. 11-5. Corner cuts are made in fiberglass reinforcing material for shaping to sharp corners.

is undesirable. If you find that you did not measure out enough resin, add some more to the mixing container, add catalyst, and continue with the resin application. If you have extra resin, do not continue to add it to the mat. Too much resin results in a resin-rich laminate that is quite brittle. When everything looks okay, clean the brush with acetone. Allow the laminate to harden.

Depending on the particular job, you might want to add one or more additional layers to the laminate. Use progressively larger pieces of reinforcing material so that the final layer has the only open edges.

For small blocks of wood, an all-mat laminate is adequate. For larger blocks, cloth and/or woven roving can also be used in the laminate.

Similar attachments are used for wood stringers to attach paneling inside fiberglass cabins. A typical example is shown in Fig. 11-6. The paneling can then be attached to the wood members with screws.

Even large wooden beams like those used for mounting engines are bonded in place with fiberglass in a similar manner. These require thickening the fiberglass laminate in the bonding areas as well as thick fiberglass laminates to bond the wood in place. Through bolts, rather than screws or lag bolts, are used to attach the engines to the wood beams, with the fasteners also passing through the bonding laminates.

Bonding Plywood Edges to Fiberglass Moldings

You can attach plywood edges to fiberglass moldings to install bulkheads, berths, and countertops in a fiberglass shell. In this exercise a major plywood bulkhead is installed in a bare fiberglass hull (see Chapter 13).

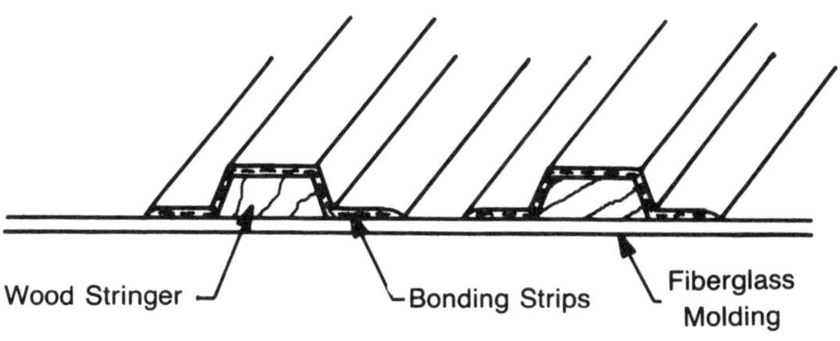

Fig. 11-6. Attachment of wood stringers to fiberglass molding.

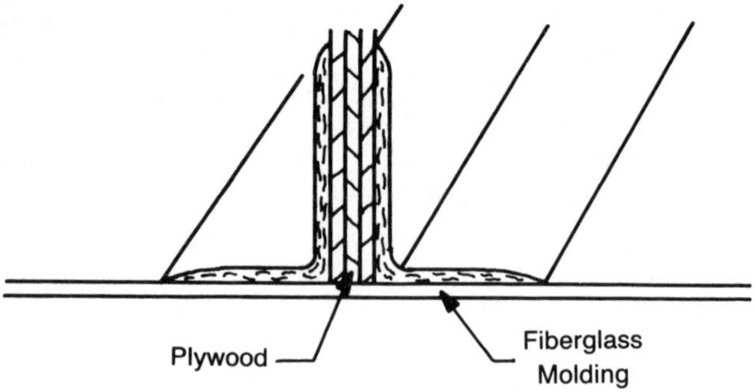

Fig. 11-7. Plywood bonded to fiberglass molding with the edge of the plywood in direct contact.

The joint is made by simply laminating fiberglass angle bonding strips in place on one or both sides of the plywood (Fig. 11-7). With major plywood bulkheads, however, a high-stress area or hard spot can form where the plywood joins the fiberglass molding unless steps are taken to prevent this.

One method is to place a thin strip of rigid plastic foam between the fiberglass molding and the bulkhead. You can also shape it to give a gradual corner between the plywood and the fiberglass molding (Fig. 11-8), which makes bonding strips easier to add and reduces the high-stress concentration on the fiberglass molding at the joint of the plywood. Fit the foam by first using a rectangular strip of foam to fit in the gap between the plywood and the fiberglass molding. If desired, epoxy glue it to both the edge of the plywood and the fiberglass molding. After the glue has cured, shape the foam with a surfacing tool.

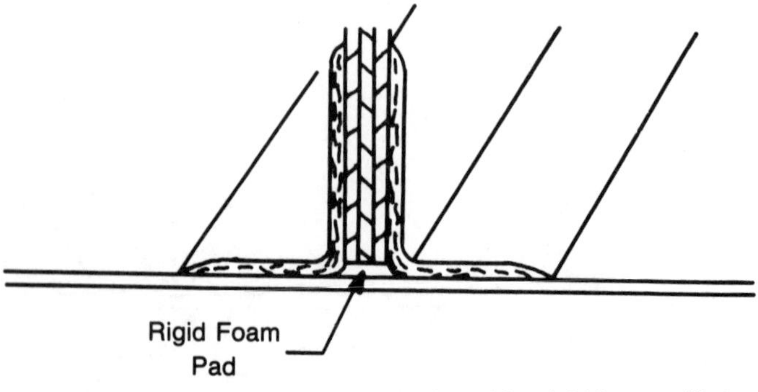

Fig. 11-8. Plywood bonded to fiberglass molding with a rigid foam pad between the edge of plywood and the molding.

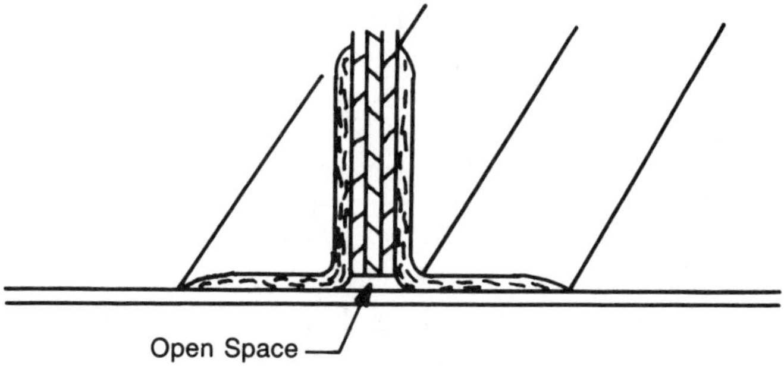

Fig. 11-9. Plywood bonded to fiberglass molding with a narrow space left between the edge of the plywood and the molding.

Another method is to simply leave a narrow space between the plywood and the fiberglass molding (Fig. 11-9). If you use this method, coat the edge of the plywood with epoxy first. The main disadvantage of this method is the possibility of water getting inside the gap and causing dry rot in the plywood.

Still another method is to pad the contact area of the fiberglass molding with three or more layers of fiberglass mat that extend outward 6 or more inches on each side of the plywood bulkhead (Fig. 11-10). Then shape the plywood bulkhead so it fits flush against this padding.

Regardless of the method used, bond the plywood bulkhead in place with progressively wider strips of fiberglassing reinforcing material. For light loadings, use three or more layers of 1 1/2-ounce fiberglass mat. Apply the first layer 6 inches wide (3 inches bonds to the plywood and 3 inches to the fiberglass molding), the second layer 9 inches wide, the third layer 12 inches wide, and so on. For heavier loadings, which are typical on major bulkheads, you might include layers of cloth and/or woven roving in

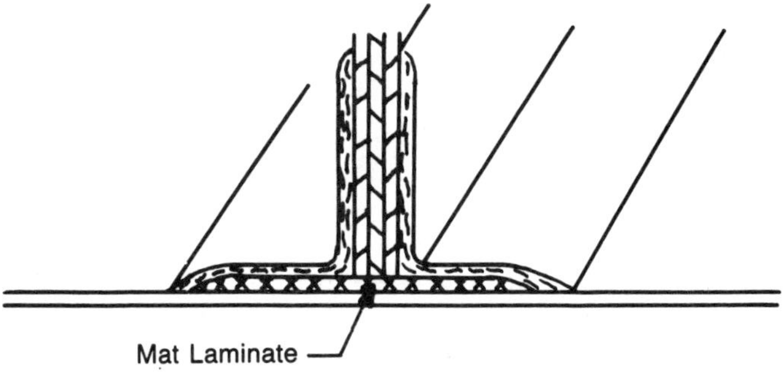

Fig. 11-10. Mat laminate used as pad for plywood bulkhead.

the bonding laminate. Using progressively wider pieces of reinforcing material tapers the bonding laminate gradually to the thickness of the molding and covers the edges of the bonding strips used underneath.

Before applying the bonding strips, rough sand the bonding area on the plywood bulkhead with a course grit of abrasive paper. Prepare the bonding area on the fiberglass molding by sanding and/or cleaning with an acetone-soaked cloth.

Fit and firmly hold the bulkhead in position before applying the bonding strips. Position the narrowest piece of reinforcing material in place first on the angle bond.

Measure out the required amount of resin in a mixing container for the first piece of reinforcing material. If more than a half pint is required, it is better to catalyze and mix it in separate batches, especially until you gain considerable fiberglassing experience. Catalyze the resin for the desired working time at the working temperature. Between 15 and 30 minutes of working time is about right for a 3- or 4-foot-long bonding strip.

Place the bonding strip on a piece of cardboard. Apply resin to the bonding areas on the plywood and the fiberglass molding. Although some fiberglass workers simply place the dry reinforcing material in this wet resin, I also apply a thin layer of resin to the bonding side of the reinforcing material. If mat is used, dab rather than brush the resin so the mat does not bunch up. Then use the cardboard to transfer the reinforcing material to the bonding area. Use the brush and/or glove-covered hands to work the fiberglass reinforcing material into the angle position. Finish wetting out the reinforcing material with an additional layer of resin, making sure that the reinforcing material is thoroughly saturated.

Wait for the resin to harden. Then, in a similar manner, apply the next layer of reinforcing material, which should overlap the first layer on both sides. Allow this layer to cure, then apply the third layer, and so on. As a rule, use laminating resin for all laminating except the final layer of resin, which should be finishing resin or laminating resin with a wax additive. This will allow sanding.

A similar angle bond is usually added to the opposite side of the bulkhead, especially if it is a major reinforcing member. For large bulkheads, the bonding strips can be added in 3- or 4-foot lengths, overlapping the joints a few inches. Do this either at random or in areas where they will not show because they will be covered up. If they are in the open, keep the bonding angles as neat as possible.

Berths, countertops, and other plywood edges can be bonded to fiberglass moldings in a similar manner. Sometimes bonding strips are only necessary on one side of the plywood. Plywood members that also serve as reinforcement might require bonding angles on both sides of the plywood.

These methods for attaching plywood to fiberglass moldings are used extensively for installing interior components and structures to fiberglass hull and other moldings. It is also used extensively for alteration work by do-it-yourselfers. Essentially, it is a strong attachment for connecting plywood edges to fiberglass moldings. From this point onward, it allows the do-it-yourselfer to work with wood.

REINFORCING AND STIFFENING FIBERGLASS MOLDINGS

Many alterations require reinforcing and stiffening fiberglass moldings. For example, a molding might require thickening or other reinforcing in the area where a chain plate or other fitting is to be attached. Three methods used for reinforcing and/or stiffening existing fiberglass moldings on boats are:

- Adding the additional layers of reinforcing material to the laminate.
- Adding backing or core material to the molding.
- Adding reinforcing and/or stiffening members to the fiberglass molding.

Adding Layers to Laminate

One method of strengthening and/or stiffening a fiberglass molding is to add additional layers to the laminate, usually on the nongelcoated side. This is not always easy to do on the fiberglass moldings on an existing boat, however. Stiffening and reinforcing members might be in the way, or there might be molded fiberglass liners that prevent easy access to the back side of hull and other moldings. Bonding to an old fiberglass molding can also be difficult. The longer a fiberglass molding has cured, the more difficult it is to bond fiberglass to it. Also, fiberglass that has been in the water soaks up some water, which can be difficult to dry out and might cause bonding problems.

Because of the possible difficulties, be sure that thickening is really the best approach for the particular alteration you have in mind. For adding chain plates or similar fittings, it might be; or other stiffening methods might work better or be easier to apply. To keep added weight to a minimum, other methods are often better than adding layers to the laminate.

If adding layers to the laminate is the best method for the particular alteration you have in mind, the first step is to remove as many obstacles as possible to get at the area where the layers are to be added. A berth might have to be temporarily removed, or a section of molded fiberglass liner might have to be cut out, for instance.

While extra thickness is usually added to the back side (non-gel coat) of the laminate, sometimes it's desirable to add the thickness to the gel coat side of the laminate. This can be done, provided the gel coating is first sanded away.

If adding to the back side, remove all paint from the laminate. Sand and/or use special paint removers that don't act as a solvent to fiberglass resin. This type of paint remover is available from marine suppliers and fiberglass supply stores. Do *not* use regular paint remover because this will act as a solvent on the fiberglass laminate underneath.

Rough sand the bonding area on the fiberglass molding to give a good bonding surface. Then, use a cloth saturated with acetone to thoroughly clean the area. Remove *all* grease, oil, and wax from the surface. Thorough preparation of the surface is essential to achieve a good bond.

Next, decide on the thickness of the laminate to be added. Determine the reinforcing materials to be used and the number of layers required. The first layer added is often mat. Additional layers can be mat, cloth, or woven roving, or combinations of these materials.

The original fiberglass molding will serve as the form for laying up the laminate to be added. The laminating is much easier if the work can be done on a level or near level plane. In actual boat alterations, however, the laminating is often done on angled, vertical, or even overhead surfaces. In these positions, use special high-viscosity resins or add a thixotropic agent to regular polyester resin.

To give a better bond, use epoxy resin for bonding the first layer of reinforcing material in place. After the epoxy resin has cured, lay up the remainder of the laminate with polyester resin. In most cases, however, using polyester resin alone gives an adequate bond and can be used throughout.

To laminate, add one layer at a time to the laminate. Allow each layer to cure before adding the next layer.

Apply catalyzed resin to the bonding area of the fiberglass molding. Because it is impractical to presaturate large pieces of reinforcing material with resin, set the dry reinforcing material into the wet resin on the bonding surface. Then completely saturate the reinforcing material with resin from the other side. Apply the resin with a brush and use a squeegee to smooth out the resin and work out air bubbles. Apply an even layer of resin. Both too little and too much resin is undesirable.

Allow this first layer to cure, then add the second layer in a similar manner. Let each added layer overlap the layer below by a couple of inches all the way around. This tapers the added laminate to the original fiberglass molding and leaves only the edges of the last layer of laminate exposed.

Use a single piece of reinforcing material for each layer if reasonably small areas are being covered. Larger areas might require more than one section of reinforcing material. Join separate pieces with lap joints by overlapping the edges of the reinforcing material a few inches. A beginner should not attempt to lay up more than about a square yard of reinforcing material at a time. With more experience, larger pieces can be handled.

Roll larger pieces of reinforcing material onto cardboard rolls after the material has been cut to the desired size. After the resin has been applied to the bonding surface, the reinforcing material can then be rolled into place. All types of fiberglass laminates can be reinforced by adding extra thickness. This includes stiffeners and secondary bonding strips and angles.

Adding Backing or Core Material to a Molding

Another method of strengthening and/or stiffening a fiberglass laminate is to add a backing or core material. One possibility is to add a backing material other than fiberglass, such as plywood (Fig. 11-11). The problem with this is bonding the material properly to the fiberglass. Epoxy glue might be adequate for some applications. Another method is to place a layer of mat saturated with wet catalyzed resin on the bonding surface of the fiberglass laminate and press the plywood in place against the wet mat (Fig. 11-12). The plywood is then propped or clamped tightly in position until the resin cures.

Still another way is to use mechanical fasteners to hold the plywood in place, either alone or with one of the bonding methods described. Sometimes the backing plywood can also be used as a backing for fittings and other hardware, which makes drilling ex-

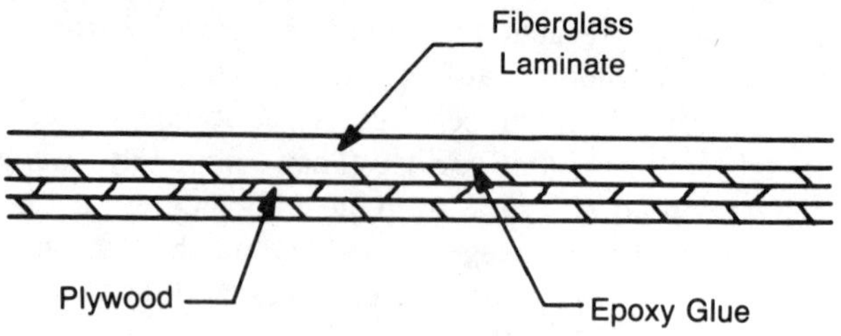

Fig. 11-11. Plywood attached to fiberglass laminate with epoxy glue.

tra holes just for attachment of the backing unnecessary.

Adding a sandwich core material to a single skin laminate is another method for strengthening and stiffening a fiberglass molding. This method can also add insulation to the laminate. First repair the bonding surface by removing any paint, sanding, and cleaning with acetone.

Possible core materials include end grain balsa and closed-cell polyvinyl chloride (PVC) foam. With either, the core should be quite thin, usually from about 1/4 to 1/2 inch.

Epoxy glue the core material to the bonding surface of the fiberglass molding. Allow the epoxy to cure.

The edges of the core material are usually shaped so that they taper back to the fiberglass molding (Fig. 11-13). Laminate a second fiberglass skin in place over the core material. Taper the edges to overlap the main fiberglass molding several inches or more all the way around.

A typical laminate consists of three or more layers of reinforcing material laminated in place, often with progressively larger pieces of reinforcing material being used so that the laminate tapers back further into the main laminate (Fig. 11-14). For some uses, an all-mat laminate suffices. For others, cloth and/or woven roving is also included in the laminate.

To be effective, there must be a good bond between the core

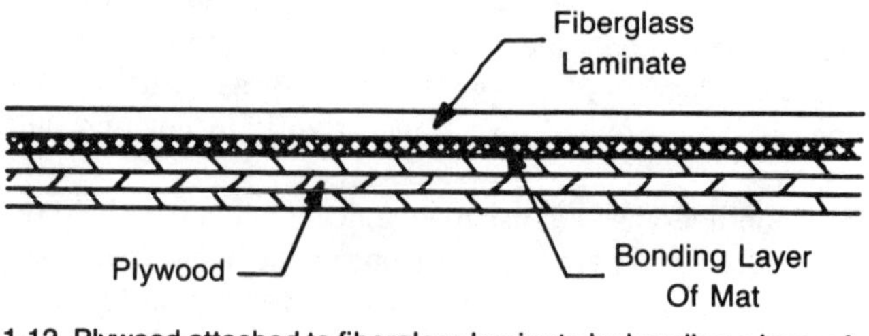

Fig. 11-12. Plywood attached to fiberglass laminate by bonding a layer of mat.

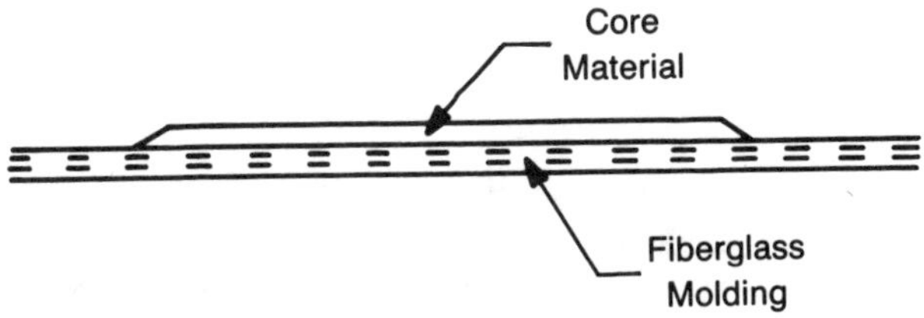

Fig. 11-13. Edges of core material taper back to fiberglass molding.

material and the fiberglass skins on each side. This is the reason for using a fairly thin core material and epoxy gluing it in place. It also helps to keep separate core areas reasonably small so that there is more direct fiberglass-to-fiberglass bonds at the edges around the core material. Plywood can also be used as a sandwich core material in a similar manner, but bonding can be difficult.

Adding Reinforcing and Stiffening Members to Fiberglass Moldings

A variety of stiffening members can be used to strengthen and/or stiffen fiberglass laminates. These are often more effective than thickening a laminate or adding a core material, while adding less weight. This type of reinforcing or stiffening member is attached by fiberglass bonding alone, although mechanical fasteners are also used in some cases.

These members are often laminated in place over a core or forming material. A popular stiffening member is a *hat-section* (Fig. 11-15). The core can be wood, rigid plastic foam, a half section of PVC pipe or tubing, or other material. The core material itself sometimes adds structural strength to the member. At other times it merely serves as a form for laminating a fiberglass stiffener in place.

To install a typical hat-section stiffener with a rigid plastic foam

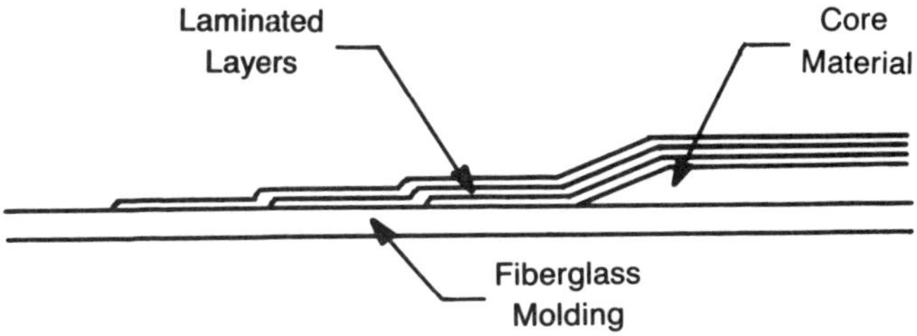

Fig. 11-14. Laminated layers taper back to main fiberglass molding.

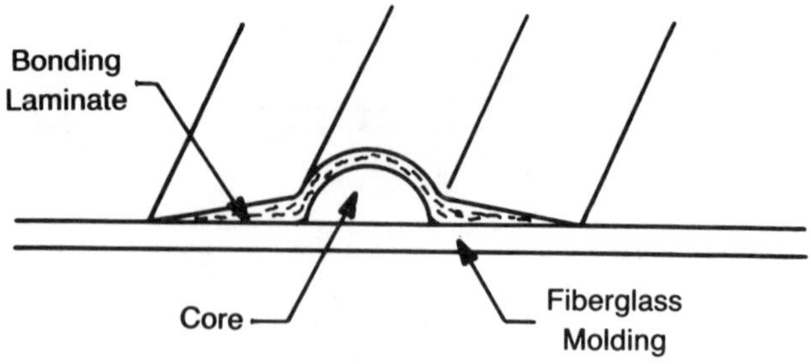

Fig. 11-15. Hat-section stiffening member.

core, prepare the bonding surface of the fiberglass molding by sanding and/or washing with a cloth saturated with acetone.

Next, shape the rigid plastic foam and epoxy glue it in place to the fiberglass molding. Another way is to merely lay the rigid plastic foam in place. It will then be secured by the fiberglass laminate that is laminated over it.

Cut strips of mat and/or other reinforcing material to shape. Use progressively wider pieces for the laminate.

Next, catalyze polyester resin and apply a coat to the bonding area of the fiberglass molding and the rigid plastic foam. Either set the first layer of fiberglass reinforcing material in place dry, or presaturate it with resin on the bonding side by placing it on a piece of cardboard and applying resin with a brush. Then wet out the other side of the reinforcing material. Work any air bubbles off the reinforcing material so that the trapped air can escape. Smooth out the reinforcing material. Both too little and too much resin is undesirable.

Allow the first layer of the laminate to cure, then apply the second layer in the same manner. Extend the edges of this layer outward on both sides an inch or so beyond the edges of the first layer. Allow this layer to cure, then add the third layer, and so on. After applying the final layer of the laminate, use finishing resin or add wax to laminating resin so that the surface will cure completely for sanding. When done properly, the laminate will taper to the thickness of the main molding over a distance of several inches or more.

Wood cores can also be used similarly. With this method, both the wood and the fiberglass laminate over it form part of the structural strength of the stiffener. This is unlike the stiffener with the rigid plastic foam core, which mainly served as a form for laminating the fiberglass to the desired shape and added little structural

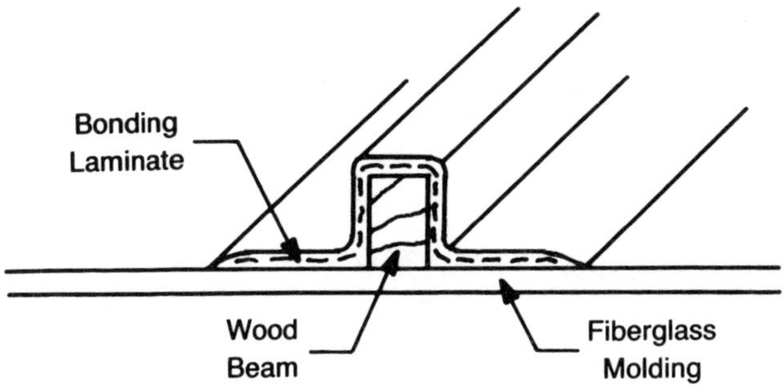

Fig. 11-16. Wood beam bonded to fiberglass molding.

strength over what a similar laminate with a hollow center would have. The rigid plastic foam does keep water from getting inside, however.

A rectangular wood beam can be used as a stiffener member by bonding it in place (Fig. 11-16). You can improve the arrangement by rounding the corner between the wood and the area where the wood joins the fiberglass molding. Before this is done, epoxy glue the wood in place or set it in place in a layer of mat that has been wetted out with catalyzed resin. Allow the epoxy glue or resin to cure. Round the corner by using fiberglass putty and the end of a wood dowel as a drag to shape the putty into a smooth curve (Fig. 11-17). Allow the putty to cure.

The bonding laminate can be angle straps that extend only over the sides of the wood (Fig. 11-18), or the bonding laminate itself can extend over the wood. In this case, round the corners of the wood with a surfacing tool (Fig. 11-19). Next, lay up the bonding laminate using progressively wider strips of fiberglass reinforcing material.

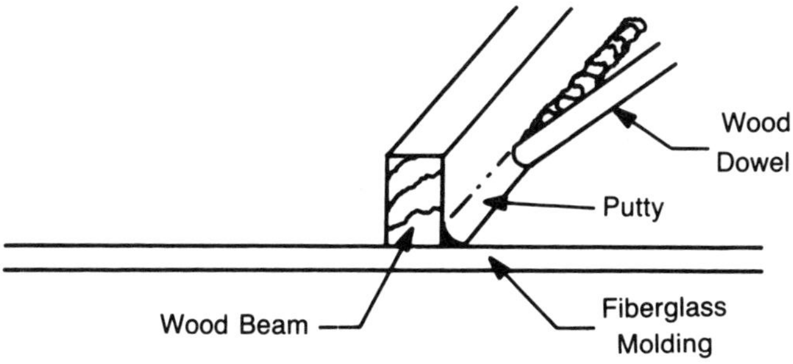

Fig. 11-17. Rounding a corner by shaping putty using a wood dowel as a drag.

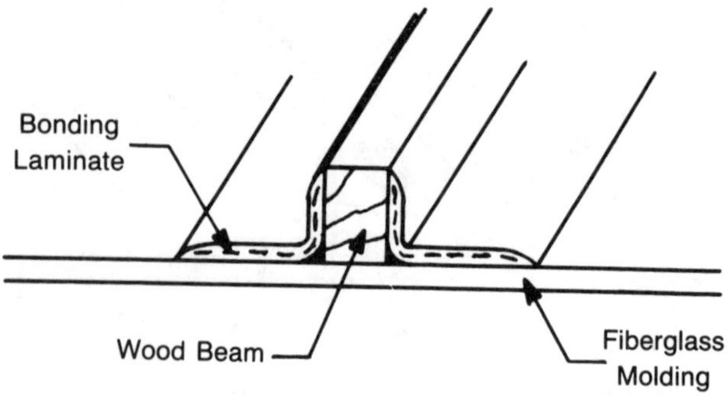

Fig. 11-18. Bonding with angle straps that extend only over the sides of the wood.

Wood beams require hefty fiberglass laminates. When installing heavy wood beams, the fiberglass molding first requires thickening by adding additional layers to the laminate.

USING RIGID PLASTIC FOAM AS A FORM FOR MAKING COMPONENTS

Many alterations require fiberglass laminates of specific shapes. One good method for making these is to first shape rigid plastic foam (polyurethane and closed cell PVC foam are both compatible with polyester resin) to the desired form, minus the thickness of the desired fiberglass laminate, and then to laminate the fiberglass over this. In most cases, the rigid plastic foam will become part of the finished item.

An example is the construction of a fiberglass box. Thin sheets of rigid plastic foam give the desired form (Fig. 11-20). The pieces can be epoxy glued together or even stapled. A fiberglass laminate

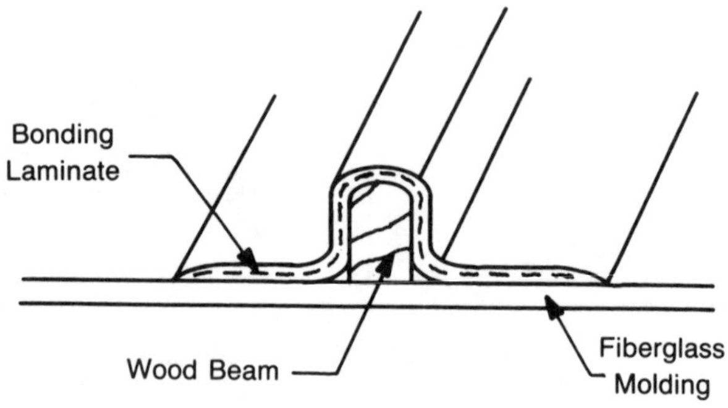

Fig. 11-19. Beam with corners of wood rounded.

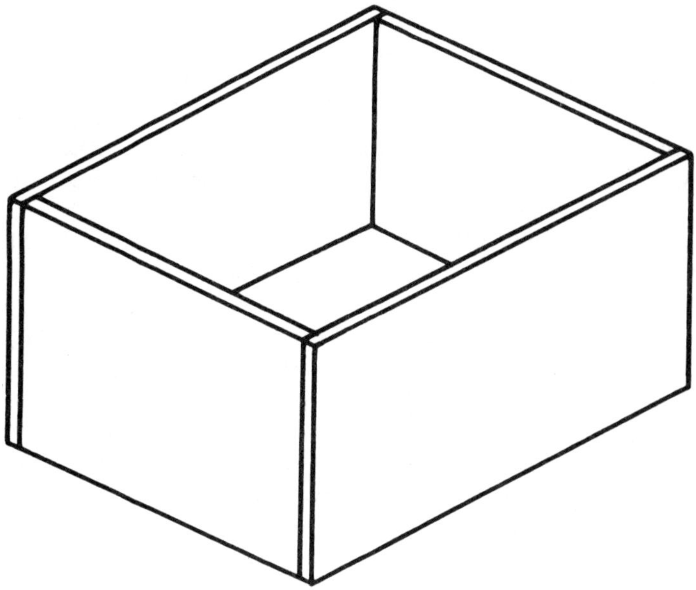

Fig. 11-20. Box constructed from thin sheets of rigid plastic foam.

is then added to the outside and inside of the form. The number of layers used in the laminate, as well as the types and weights of fiberglass reinforcing materials used, depends on the intended use of the finished item. Three or more layers of reinforcing material are typically required. The plastic foam is completely encased in the fiberglass laminate shell.

This has many possibilities for making boat alterations. By using foam that is several inches thick in a manner similar to the box example, an icebox complete with insulation could be formed. Or you might want to shape a storage compartment to fit a particular space. Or make a hatch. There are hundreds of possibilities here. Similar molding methods are often used for one-off boat construction (see Chapter 14).

WORKING WITH WOOD

Working with wood forms an important part of many alteration projects on fiberglass boats. Many people already have considerable skill at using woodworking tools and working with wood, even though this might not include any boat work. Woodworking skills and techniques used around a house or in a garage workshop can be transferred to boat work provided that some basic changes are made. Boats are subject to more severe conditions, or at least different ones, than are typical houses. A boat must be able to withstand severe weather conditions and chemical and physical stresses.

Once you have bonded wood to fiberglass, you often have basically a woodworking project remaining. You have certain skills and tools and materials available. How can you use these to best accomplish a specific job?

The more skills and techniques you learn, the easier it will be to do the job. A class in woodworking allows you to learn under expert supervision. In a few areas, there are even classes offered in boatbuilding. While these are mainly concerned with building wood boats from scratch, the skills and techniques can also apply to making alterations on fiberglass boats.

If your woodworking experience is limited, I suggest you do some practice work on scrap materials before you attempt anything on your boat. You can improve your skills this way and gain confidence before you attempt similar work on your boat. Your first attempts at new woodworking jobs are not likely to be your best, but your skills and techniques will improve as you go along.

Amateurs who consistently achieve professional results divide each job into steps. They then think about how these steps can best be accomplished. They do each job as well as they can, avoiding sloppy work that can accumulate. If each step is done right, the completed job will be done right. The final result will be workmanship that you can be proud of.

Types of Wood

Selecting the proper wood for boat alterations is important. You will want to use wood that is equal to or superior to that used on the same boat by the manufacturer. Not just any wood will do. For a particular job it must have the necessary strength and workability. It might need a finish that matches the surrounding wood. For most boat uses, the wood should be highly resistant to dry rot, which is a fungus disease that affects some species of wood much more than it does others. Teak, for example, is highly immune to dry rot, though it is also very expensive. Most times less expensive wood has to be used.

The wood sold at a lumberyard is usually kiln-dried. This is a fast and inexpensive method. Considerable moisture remains in the wood, however, making it highly susceptible to dry rot. Air-dried wood is superior, but the drying process can take a year or more. Some lumberyards and suppliers handle air-dried wood intended for boatbuilding purposes. For some alteration work, especially on the interiors of boats, kiln-dried wood might be satisfactory, however.

Although many types of wood can be used, here are only a few of the most popular ones.

Douglas fir is a wood of medium hardness that is often used for boat alteration work. Though not exactly ideal for many jobs, it's at least available in most areas. I have used this wood to frame for plywood berths and counters and have had satisfactory results. If the wood is used in areas where it shows, I apply a paint rather than a varnish finish.

Mahogany is a popular wood for rails and trim pieces. Though not as durable as teak, it's much less expensive. It's a viable alternative to teak for interior work, and with a proper finish applied, it can be a long-lasting boat wood for exterior use. African mahogany and Honduras mahogany are both good choices, with the Honduras mahogany considered superior for most boat uses. An even harder variety is Aguano or Peruvian mahogany, but it's also more expensive. Philippine mahogany, which isn't a true mahogany, is lighter in weight than true mahogany and not as strong, but it has good working qualities and is highly resistant to dry rot.

Teak is an imported wood that is considered one of the best for boatbuilding. It's price, however, is fast becoming akin to gold. For this reason, its use for alteration work is kept to a minimum. Whereas production fiberglass boats once made extensive use of teak for both interiors and exteriors, the recent trend is to use teak more sparingly, especially on the interiors. Sometimes less expensive mahogany is substituted for some or all of the teak. For alteration work, preshaped handrails and other items are available in teak and mahogany. The prices are quite reasonable when you consider the difficulty of shaping these yourself.

A variety of other wood, including white and yellow pine, cedar, spruce, ash, and oak, can also be used for making boat modifications. The selection must be based on availability rather than on superiority for the particular job that you are doing.

Plywood is used extensively for making boat alterations. It's ideal for bulkheads, interior components, and reinforcing purposes. Plywood is veneers laminated together. Douglas fir is frequently used. Plywood is also made of various hardwoods and mahogany. Sometimes only the outside veneers on one or both sides are hardwood or mahogany, with the inner ones of Douglas fir or other kinds of wood.

Plywood marked *marine grade*, regardless of wood used in veneers, is usually best for boat alterations. It's also the most expensive. Plywood marked *exterior grade* is made with the same waterproof glue. However, the veneers, especially the inner ones, are a poorer quality than those typically used for marine-grade plywood, which has all voids filled in. For many alteration jobs, the less expensive exterior grade plywood is satisfactory.

Avoid the *interior grades* of plywood that do not have waterproof glue. These tend to delaminate even when painted or sheathed with fiberglass.

Plywood is available in standard 4-by-8-foot sheets and also other sizes, such as 2 by 4 feet and 4 by 16 feet. Available thicknesses include 1/4-, 3/8-, 1/2-, and 3/4-inch thicknesses. These are commonly used for most alteration work.

Shaping Wood

A basic skill required is shaping wood. Many alteration jobs require cutting and shaping a piece of wood to a desired pattern or fit. Patterns can be made from old parts, templates, and from measurements.

Before cutting wood, mark the pattern on the wood with a pencil or other marking device. A straightedge and square are often used for making straight lines. Mark the pattern so that there will be as little waste of wood as possible. For example, if you have a long plank of wood and a particular job requires only a short section of this, cut from one end of the plank rather than taking a section from the middle. An exception to this might be if you had to have a piece of wood without knots, and only the middle section of the plank was free of knots. Keeping waste to a minimum means that more of the wood ends up as part of the boat and less as scraps. You have to look ahead to future work when deciding where to cut a particular pattern from a piece of wood.

Purchase the wood in sizes that will also result in minimum waste. This saves money because lumber is sold by the board foot, which is 144 cubic inches of wood and is equal to a 12-by-12-by-1-inch piece of wood. You pay for the wood based on its rough form before milling, however, so you get less wood than this. This explains why a standard 2 × 4 is actually less than 2 inches by 4 inches. The milling process removes from about 1/8 to 1/4 inch from a board, which ends up as sawdust, though you still pay for it. Take this into account when purchasing wood sizes for making boat alterations.

Plywood is a somewhat different situation. Usually you get the exact thickness, such as 1/2 inch, the plywood is sold as. The same applies to the 4-by-8-foot or other sheet size. You get the full-sheet size.

A lumberyard can often cut a large piece of wood into smaller pieces and do the milling or surfacing work on the rough sawn edges. They charge for this, but it can be worth the extra money, especially if you don't have the shop tools to do this work yourself. One or two simple cuts on a long board or piece of plywood will sometimes be made for free. Some lumberyards will also sell you part of a sheet of plywood.

Special care should be taken when laying out and marking patterns on wood. A sharp pencil or fine scribe should be used for marking. A fine line can reduce error in crucial areas. If you have an old part that can be used as a template for the new one, place it on the new wood and trace around it. Then, when you do the cutting, remember to cut the line away rather than cutting outside the line.

You will often have a board of the desired width and thickness and all that is necessary is to cut it the correct length with square ends. First, select a suitable board. Some pieces might have more checks and cracks than other pieces. Make your selection on the basis of where the board is to be used.

There are frequently checks or cracks near the ends of boards. You might want to remove this section from the end of the board. Use a square to mark the cutting line. Position the blade of the square firmly against the edge of the board with the outside edge of the tongue of the square lined up with the desired cut. Use a sharp pencil to make a line on the board, following the tongue of the square. Make a fine line as close to the edge of the square as possible. This is especially important when making crucial cuts.

Lay off the desired length from the line along the board using a suitable measuring rule. Mark the board at this point. Then use the square to make the second cutting line. With the blade against the edge of the board, line the tongue up with the mark. Then mark the line.

Make the saw cuts either on the inside or outside of the line or along the center of the line. If the length of the board needs to be an exact fit, the system used will be very important. Select one system and stick to it. Then, learn to lay out and mark your work for the system you are using. Once this becomes habit, you will no longer have to think about it.

You might also need to mark the board for lengthwise cutting, which is called *ripping*. Measure and mark two width lines from one edge of the board some distance apart. Then, place the straightedge on the board and line it up with the two marks. Use a sharp pencil for marking the cutting line.

Use a shop protractor to lay out angles or use the protractor to adjust a carpenter's adjusting bevel to the desired angle. Position the handle of the bevel firmly against the edge of the board and mark the cutting line along the blade.

For boat alterations, more complicated patterns are frequently required. If you don't have an old item to use as a pattern, it might be possible to make a template out of cardboard or scrap wood. Even if you have to resort to a trial-and-error method for making the pattern, it's better to do this with cardboard or scrap wood than to take the chance of ruining good wood.

Once you have the pattern marked on the wood, saw it to shape with a handsaw or power saw. Cuts made across the grain of the wood are called *crosscuts*. If done with a handsaw, use a saw with a crosscutting or general-purpose blade. If possible, fasten the board in a vise so that the cutting line is an inch or so beyond the vise. If the board cannot be conveniently clamped in a vise, place it across two or more sawhorses or similar supports.

When a saw cut is made, a narrow section of the wood is actually removed. It ends up as sawdust. Consider this when positioning the saw for cutting.

Use several short strokes to begin the cutting. Use a small square to check that the saw blade is at a right angle to the wood. Then start cutting again, this time using long strokes with the saw. Check the saw angle from time to time with the square. The main idea is to saw through the board without twisting the saw.

Hold the end of the board when you are close to sawing through so that it does not break off from its own weight. Finish the cut with short easy saw strokes.

A miter box and backsaw allows similar cuts with even greater accuracy. A variety of power saws can also be used. In most cases, a crosscutting or general-purpose blade is used. When using power saws, make certain that all safety rules are followed.

Crosscutting can be done at angles other than perpendicular to the edge of the board. While this can be done with a regular crosscutting or general-purpose handsaw, an adjustable miter box gives greater accuracy. Most power saws can also be used for making these cuts accurately.

Cutting with the grain of the wood is called *ripping*. If you use a handsaw, it should have a ripping or general-purpose blade. Whenever it is practical to do so, clamp the board in a vise. Larger boards can be placed across two or more sawhorses.

Start by positioning the saw blade. The cutting edge of the blade should form about a 60-degree angle with the board. Use short easy strokes of the saw. Hold the part of the board you are cutting off or have it positioned over the sawhorse so that it will not break off when you saw through.

Portable power circular saws, stationary table saws, and stationary radial arm saws can make easy work of ripping jobs. Usually, a ripping or general-purpose blade should be used.

You will often need to saw curved patterns. While compass, keyhole, and coping saws can be used for this, a portable electric saber saw makes the work much easier and faster. Power jigsaws and band saws are other possibilities. If you plan extensive alteration work, a band saw is especially useful.

Take special care when sawing plywood. To help prevent chipping and splintering along the edges of the cut, special fine-toothed blades can be used, regardless of whether you are using a handsaw or power saw. Special carbide-tipped blades are even better. It might also help to clamp a board to the underside of the plywood and saw through this too. Applying masking tape over the area where the cut is to be made also helps.

The wood can require additional shaping, planing, and surfacing after the saw cutting has been completed. A common job is to plane the edge of a board in the area where a saw cut has been made using a wood plane. Keep the plane sharp. Adjust it for the particular job at hand. A jointer can also be used. It makes quick and easy work of this type of job.

A variety of hand tools, including drawknifes, files, and surfacing tools, can be used for shaping and dressing curved edges. Whenever possible, completely shape a piece of wood before installing it, because this work is usually more difficult once the wood has been installed.

Drilling Holes in Wood

Alteration work frequently requires making holes in wood for screws, bolts, fittings, and other purposes. A brace and auger bit can be used for drilling by hand.

Begin by marking the position where the hole is to be drilled. Do this carefully. Use an awl or other pointed object to make an indentation for starting the drilling. Select the correct size auger bit. Install the bit in the chuck and hold it securely. Position the feed screw in the starting hole and turn the brace to start the boring. After the hole has been started, use a small square to make certain that the bit is at right angles to the surface of the wood. Then, continue drilling until the tip of the feed screw passes through the other side of the wood. Remove the bit and finish drilling from the opposite side.

A portable electric drill can also be used instead of hand drilling. Ordinary twist drills from about 1/16 inch to 1/2 inch or larger can be used in electric drills for making holes in wood. To drill a hole, select the desired twist drill size. Install it in the chuck of the electric drill, securing it with the chuck key. The drill should always be unplugged when this is done. Remove the chuck key from the chuck, then plug the drill back in. Make a starting indentation for the desired hole using an awl or other sharp-pointed metal object. Place the point of the twist drill in this. Hold the drill by the grip with your right hand while using your left hand to guide the drill. Start the drill and apply light pressure with your right hand. Hold the drill steady to prevent breaking the twist drill, especially when using smaller drill sizes. When the drill goes through the wood, control the drilling so that the chuck does not contact the wood.

For drilling larger size holes—up to about 1 1/2 inches—in wood using a portable electric drill, spade-type bits can be used. When drilling all the way through a piece of wood, reverse the drill when the point comes through, then finish the drilling.

Holesaws can be used for cutting holes from a 1/2-inch diameter to 2 inches or larger. These fit in the chuck of ordinary portable electric drills. Use an awl to make a starting hole. Place the tip of the pilot bit in the hole. Hold the drill at right angles to the wood surface. Start the drill, keeping it at right angles to the wood surface. To prevent splintering when the blade cuts through, clamp a block of wood underneath the board being drilled.

Holesaws limit you to set sizes. If you need a hole of some size in between, drill the next smaller size and then file the hole out to the correct size. Another possibility is to use an adjustable fly-cutter, which can be adjusted for cutting any desired hole size within a certain range. Use the fly-cutter in the same manner as the holesaw.

Combination wood drill and countersink bits are useful attachments for boat alteration work. These make a hole for wood screw threads and screw shank and a countersink for the flathead screw all in a single drilling operation. Each screw size and length requires a different bit. There is also a similar type bit that has a counterbore section, which in addition to the above operations, also makes a counterbore for a wood plug.

You can purchase precut wood plugs or use a plug cutter to cut your own. By making your own, you can cut them from the same stock of wood as you are plugging to give a better match. To cut a plug, install the plug cutter in the chuck of an electric drill. Position the drill at right angles to the wood surface. Cut all the way through the board. Repeat to make additional plugs. Methods for installing these are detailed later in this chapter.

Drill presses allow even greater drilling accuracy. Various jigs and guides are also available that attach to standard portable electric drills to increase drilling precision.

Joining Wood Pieces Together

Many boat alterations require joining separate pieces of wood together. Possible methods include fastening with nails, screws, bolts, and various glues, of some combination of these.

A variety of corner joints are possible. A common *lap joint* is shown in Fig. 11-21. The problem with this joint is that the fasteners go into the end grain of the wood, which is not very secure. This type of joint can be improved by adding a corner post (Fig. 11-22). The fasteners can now go into the corner post. A rabbeted corner

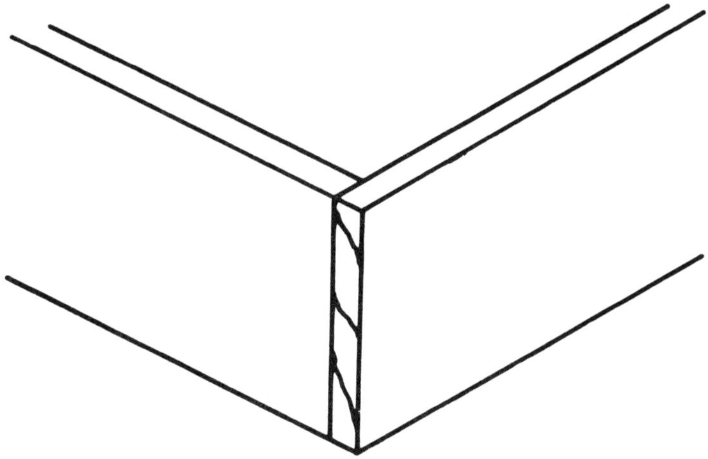

Fig. 11-21. A corner lap joint.

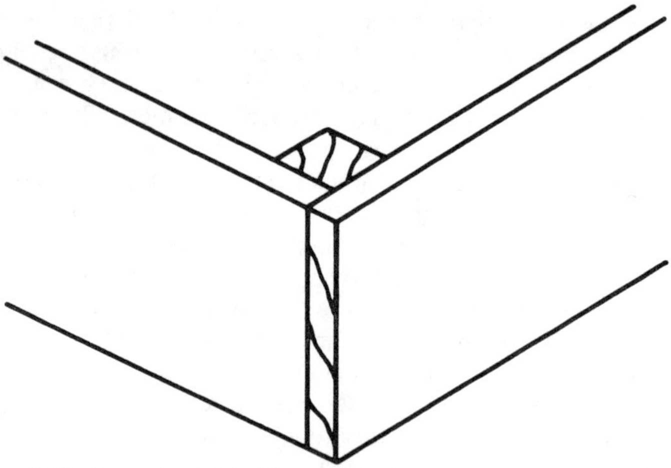

Fig. 11-22. Corner lap joint with corner post.

post (Fig. 11-23) further improves the joint by covering up the end grains of the wood. Another possibility is to use a corner trim piece over a lap joint (Fig. 11-24).

Two basic methods are used for joining boards end to end: a *butt joint with a backing board* (Fig. 11-25) and a *scarf joint* (Fig. 11-26). The scarf joint is frequently used for joining separate pieces of wood to make up the required length for rub rails.

Screws are often used in combination with glue for making these and other wood joints. Flathead, round, oval, and head wood screws are available. For boat work, stainless steel, bronze, or

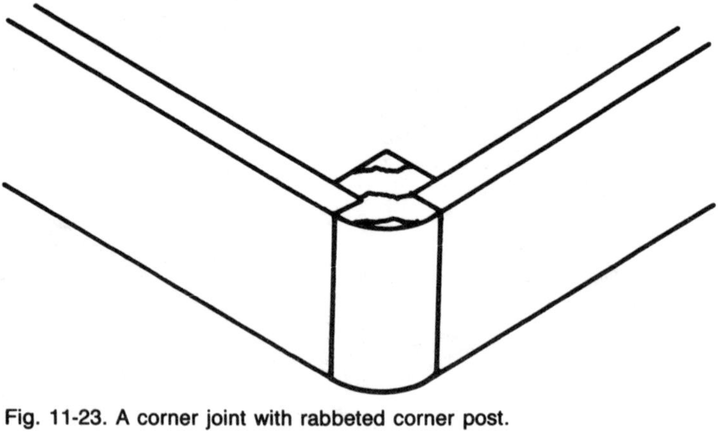

Fig. 11-23. A corner joint with rabbeted corner post.

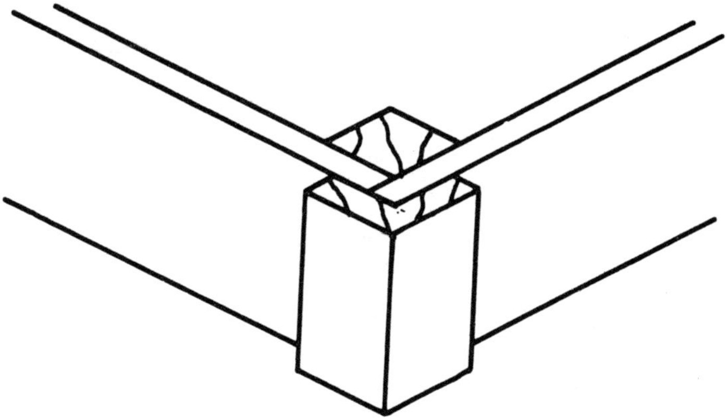

Fig. 11-24. A lap joint with corner trim piece.

monel screws are recommended. Avoid common steel screws. Even when they are hot-dipped galvanized, they can still rust. I don't recommend brass screws either. They are too weak, and in marine environments, tend to dezincify.

Use the correct diameter and length of screw for the particular job. As a rule, the longer the screw, the larger the diameter should be.

Drill pilot holes. While regular twist bits can be used for drilling these, the special drills that make the pilot, shank, and countersink are better. If you want wood plugs to cover the screw heads, use the type of drill that also has the counterbore.

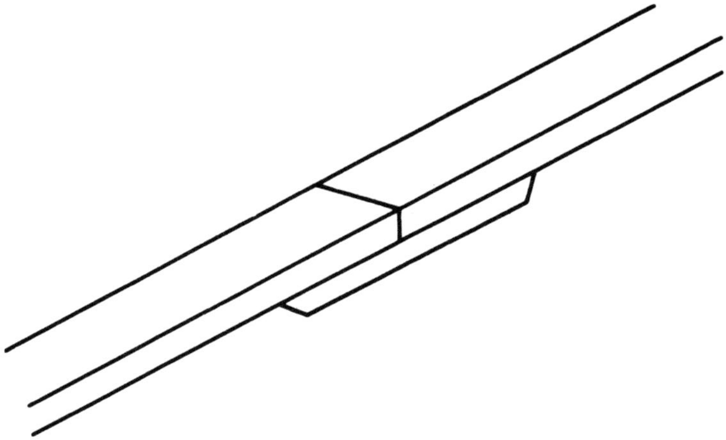

Fig. 11-25. Boards joined with a butt joint and backing block.

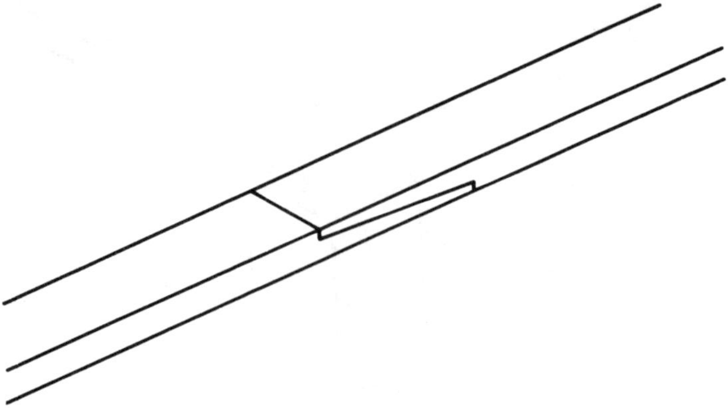

Fig. 11-26. A scarf joint.

To install a screw, first clamp the boards in position. Mark locations for screws. Use an awl to make a starting hole for the bit. Drill the pilot hole. Countersink and counterbore in same operation by using special drills.

If the joint is to be glued, apply the glue before the initial clamping or after the holes have been drilled. Remove the clamps, apply the glue (additional information about gluing is covered later in this chapter), and clamp the boards back together again. For driving screws, use a screwdriver that fits the screw. Hold the screwdriver firmly when turning the screw so that the screwdriver does not slip out of the screw slot.

If wood plugs are to be installed in counterbores, apply glue to each plug. Place the plug over the counterbore, line up the grain, and tap the plug in place. After the glue has set up, use a sharp chisel to remove excess wood. Finish by sanding.

I don't recommend nails for boat alteration work. Bronze or monel ring boat nails are sometimes used for attaching plywood to framing, usually in combination with gluing. Even here I prefer to use screws, however. Do not use ordinary steel nails, even if plated. These are almost certain to rust in a boating environment.

If you do use ring nails for plywood planking, the length of the nails used should be at least three times the thickness of the plywood for adequate holding power. Drill pilot holes for the nails. Stagger the nails instead of placing them in straight lines. As a rule, they must be placed closer together than screws.

Bolts are another possibility. They give maximum holding power. The bolts should be of stainless steel, bronze, or monel.

Avoid regular steel and brass bolts. Washers are required to keep the bolts from digging into the wood at the head or nut ends. Bolts can be countersunk into the wood. A counterbore can be used for installing wood plugs in the same manner as detailed for screws.

Bolts are not only useful for attaching separate pieces of wood together, but also for attaching wood to fiberglass (for example, grab rails to cabin tops) and attaching metal handles and hinges to wood. Whenever it is practical, I try to use bolts rather than screws.

Gluing is an important part of joining wood pieces together. When I first started boatbuilding, I tried urea resin glues and resorcin resin glues, with less than satisfactory results. The wood must be clamped together so that the glue is under pressure for proper setting. This can be a lot of trouble. I have now switched almost entirely to epoxy glue. While the epoxy glue is more expensive, the superior results seem worth the extra cost.

Urea resin glue is a powder that is mixed with water. The glue is said to be water resistant, but not completely waterproof. To be effective, the joints must be clamped together so the glue can set under pressure. The one advantage of this type of glue is the low cost in comparison to waterproof glues.

Resorcin resin glue is a two-part glue: one part is powder, the other liquid. These are mixed together. The glue is cold-setting and waterproof. It is more costly than the urea resin glue, but gives superior joints.

Epoxy glue is also a two-part mixture. The hardener or curing agent is added to the resin part. The wood parts will bond together even if they are not tightly clamped together or perfectly fitted, although it is better if they are.

Regardless of the type of glue used, the first step is to shape the pieces of wood to be joined so there is a tightly fitted joint. When using fasteners, predrill the holes or pilot holes. Use the fasteners to hold the joint together while the glue sets or cures. Otherwise, use clamps, wedges, or other means for holding the pieces tightly together until the glue sets or cures.

Follow manufacturer's directions for mixing and applying the particular glue used. After mixing the glue, apply a thin layer to both surfaces. Use a brush or knife to apply the glue. Position parts together and install fasteners or clamps or wedges. Wipe off excess glue with a rag. Allow glue to set or cure.

Do not use urea resin or resorcin resin glues for filling in areas around poorly fitted wood parts. Though poorly fitted parts should be avoided, thick epoxy glue can be used to fill in any gaps. Don't mix the various types of glue, however. If you are going to fill with epoxy glue, also use epoxy glue for the basic joint.

A good practice exercise is to glue scrap pieces of wood together with the various types of glue. After the glue has set or cured, test the gluing by trying to break the parts loose. I've tried this a number of times, and the epoxy glue has always come out way ahead, usually giving a joint that is stronger than the wood itself. This does not mean that other types of glue cannot also be satisfactory. You might get good results if you use them.

Sanding Wood

Sanding is an extremely important step in preparing wood for varnishing or painting. Use a waterproof wood filler to fill in small holes, checks, and other defects. Another possibility is to mix sawdust from the same kind of wood with clear epoxy resin or glue. Add a curing agent or hardener before applying. If applying a colored finish, use regular epoxy filler compounds. Manufactured epoxy fillers are available for matching mahogany and other woods.

Apply a primer or sealer to Douglas fir plywood before doing any sanding. If this is not done, an uneven surface can quickly result, even if a sanding block is used.

Don't start with any coarser sandpaper than is absolutely necessary for the particular sanding task. Whenever practical, use a sanding block. Gradually work down to finer grits of sandpaper. Sand parallel to the grain of the wood, as cross-grain sanding can scratch and roughen the surface.

Portable power sanders can also be used. A disk sander is suitable only for rough sanding. A belt sander can be used for coarse, medium, and fine sanding with the appropriate sandpaper and adjustment of the sander. Pad sanders are ideal for finishing work.

Laminating Layers of Wood Together

For some alteration jobs, you might want to laminate two or more layers of wood together. Form curved pieces without steaming by clamping the pieces of wood together in a mold or form that holds them in the desired curve until the glue sets. Sailboat tillers are often shaped in this manner.

Veneers for laminating can be of one or more kinds of wood. Alternating layers of two kinds of wood often gives a good effect. While thick pieces of wood can be laminated together, thin veneers are usually used, especially if curves are to be formed. For a curve, construct a clamp mold to hold the wood pieces together in the desired shape. For straight pieces, use regular clamps to hold them together until the glue sets or cures. When everything is ready, lay out the strips of wood. Mix and apply the glue. Clamp the pieces of wood together. Wipe all excess glue off with a rag. Allow the laminate glue to set or cure. Then finish shaping the laminates and sand and finish as desired.

LAMINATING PLASTIC TO WOOD

Boat alteration work sometimes requires adding plastic laminates to plywood for counter and tabletops and for other uses. Select high-quality plastic laminates for boat use. Use waterproof contact cement for bonding the plastic laminate to the plywood.

While strips of plastic laminate can also be applied to the edges of plywood, I don't recommend this for boat work. Use wood, metal, or plastic trim or wood rails that combine as edge trim instead. These should extend over the edge of the plastic laminate (Fig. 11-27).

To install a plastic laminate, fill in all holes and defects on the bonding surface of the plywood. Use epoxy putty for this. Rough sand the bonding surface. Mark the pattern on the plastic laminate, making it slightly larger than the surface to be covered. Then cut the plastic laminate to the pattern with a handsaw or power saw and a fine-tooth blade. Saw carefully to avoid chipping or breaking the plastic laminate.

Another method for cutting plastic laminate is by scoring the plastic. Draw a carbide-tip knife along a metal straightedge to cut through the decorative surface of the laminate. To break the laminate, bend it toward the decorative surface side. This method gives a clean break.

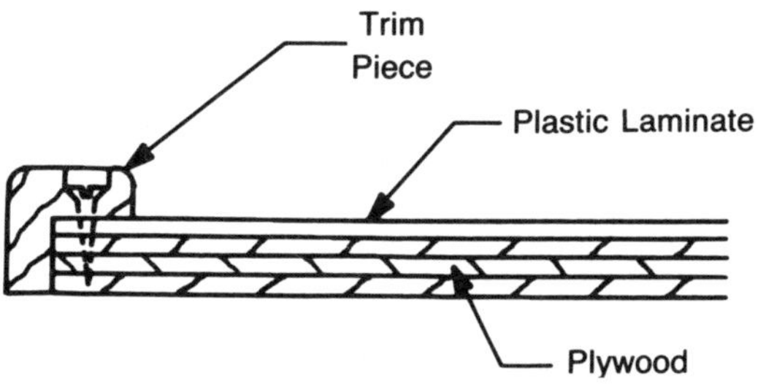

Fig. 11-27. Trim strip extends over the edge of plastic laminate.

Next, apply contact cement to both the bonding surface of the plywood and the bonding side of the plastic laminate. Apply it with a brush or a metal spreader with a serrated edge. Use a thin application. The drying time is usually about 30 minutes, but this varies. Follow the manufacturer's instructions.

After the cement dries, place a sheet of heavy wrapping paper over the cement on the plywood. Position the plastic laminate over the paper. The contact cement shouldn't stick to the paper. Position the laminate exactly because once the two cement surfaces make contact, they stick together immediately, and you will not be able to change the position of the plastic laminate. When everything is ready, pull the paper out so that the plastic laminate and plywood make contact. Place a small block of wood on the laminate and use a hammer to lightly tap the wood, moving to all areas of the laminate. This should firmly secure the plastic laminate in place. Remove excess plastic laminate from the edges with a metal file or a router.

ADDING FIBERGLASS TO WOOD

Adding fiberglass to wood is a technique often used in making boat alterations. The fiberglass can be a thin layer that can protect the wood and/or improve the appearance. Thicker laminates can be added to provide structural strength. In some cases, the wood part is mainly used as a form or male mold for laying up a fiberglass laminate. The wood is left as part of the laminate, however.

Suitable Wood Surfaces

To add an effective fiberglass skin to wood, you need a suitable wood surface. This is especially important if only a relatively thin fiberglass skin is to be applied. The surface must be stable. Plywood usually provides such a surface, although there can be problems at the joints.

An example of an unstable surface is carvel planking (Fig. 11-28). This type of surface expands and contracts with changing environmental conditions. A thin layer of fiberglass applied to this would probably crack and break apart at the plank seams. To effectively cover this type of unstable wood surface with fiberglass would require either some means of holding the wood together as a single unit or a very thick and strong fiberglass laminate capable of performing this function, or some combination of these.

Bonding

Another major consideration is bonding. There must be an effective bond between the wood and the fiberglass so delamination does not occur. This is especially important with relatively thin layers of fiberglass, which would not have the structural strength to hold up on their own.

Even under the best of conditions, it is difficult to achieve a good bond with polyester resin. A better bond can be achieved with polyester resin to new wood than old wood, especially if the old wood has been painted. Even if the paint is removed, oils and other contaminates still remain. Whether new or old, the wood should be as dry as possible. Although polyester bonds reasonably well to relatively soft woods, it is unsuitable for bonding to hard woods.

Epoxy resin gives a much better bond, especially to harder woods. Even though epoxy resin is more expensive and perhaps more difficult to work with, it can be worth the extra expense and difficulties for this type of bonding work. To keep extra costs to a minimum, use epoxy resin only for bonding the initial layer of reinforcing material to the wood. After the epoxy resin has thoroughly cured, finish out the laminate using the less expensive polyester resin.

Applying Fiberglass to Wood

There are two basic methods: wet and dry. For the dry method, place the dry fiberglass reinforcing material (usually an open weave cloth) on the dry wood surface. Sometimes the reinforcing material can be stapled or otherwise mechanically fastened to the wood. Apply the resin to the surface of the reinforcing material.

There are two problems with this method. First, it is difficult to achieve a good bond. Second, it is difficult to thoroughly wet

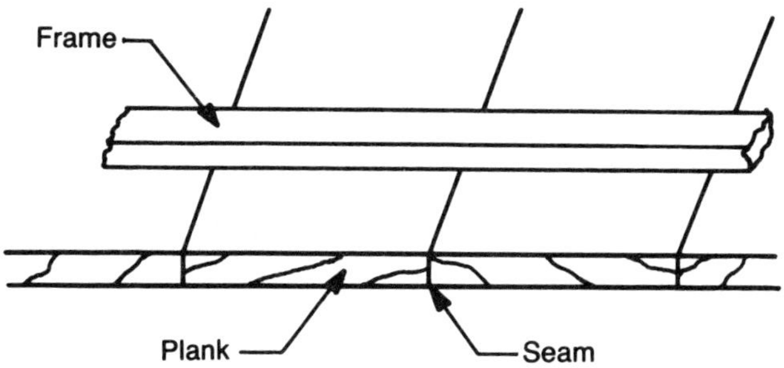

Fig. 11-28. Carvel planking.

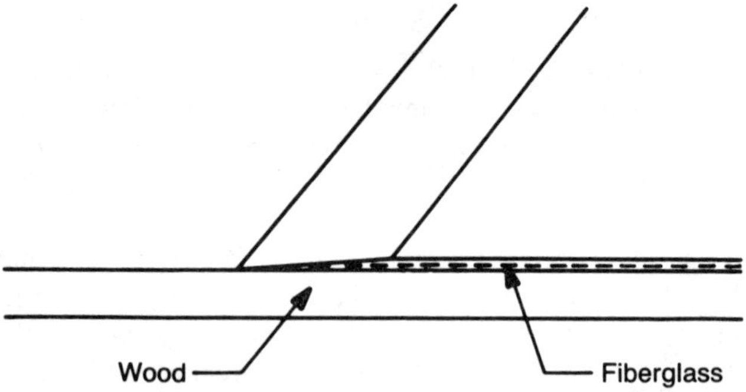

Fig. 11-29. The edge of the fiberglass is feather sanded.

out the reinforcing material. The main advantages are that the reinforcing material can be fitted dry and mechanical fasteners can be used to hold it in place. Additional layers can then be added to the laminate as desired.

For the wet application, first apply a layer of resin to the wood surface. Position the dry reinforcing material in the wet resin and smooth it out. Apply additional resin to the reinforcing material to thoroughly wet it out.

This method gives a better bond than the dry method. It is somewhat more difficult to handle the reinforcing material, however, and using mechanical fasteners is less convenient. Staples can be shot in while the resin is still wet, but resin must be cleaned from the staple gun before it cures to keep it from jamming.

Regardless of the method used, prepare the wood surface carefully before applying the fiberglass. Rough sand the wood across the grain using coarse sandpaper. This will give a good bonding surface.

When adding fiberglass to old wood, remove all paint by sand-

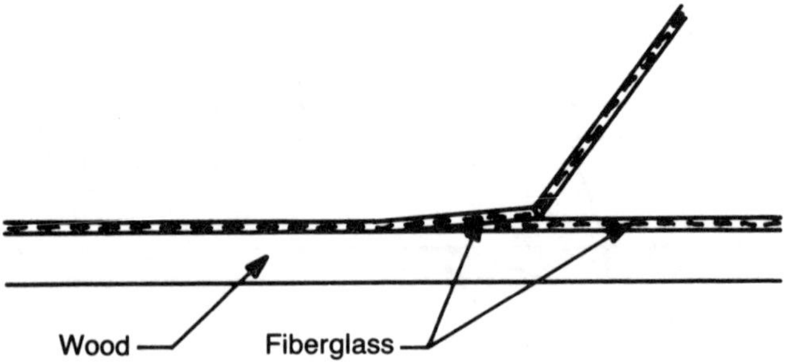

Fig. 11-30. The second section of fiberglass is applied.

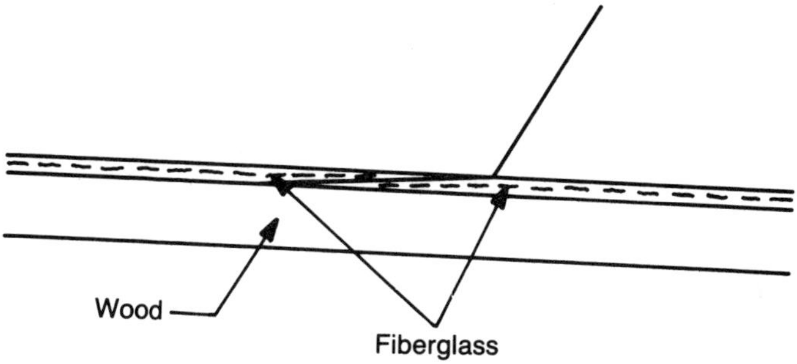

Fig. 11-31. The joint is sanded flush.

ing. If done chemically, the wood surface might be further contaminated.

While small areas can be covered with a single piece of fiberglass reinforcing material, larger surface areas require more than one piece. Usually lap joints are used. If a smooth surface is important, apply one piece of the reinforcing material first. Allow this to cure, then feather sand the edge (Fig. 11-29). Add the next piece of reinforcing material (Fig. 11-30). Allow the resin to cure, then sand the surface flush (Fig. 11-31).

Delaminating is most likely at the edges of the fiberglass. To prevent this, end the laminate under a trim piece, such as a rail.

It is difficult to fiberglass over sharp outside or inside angles. Whenever possible, round off outside angles. Round off inside angles by using a resin putty filler. Use a round dowel as a drag for shaping the putty.

Fiberglass reinforcing materials can sometimes be shaped around corners without making cuts. In other cases, corner cuts will have to be made.

After the complete laminates have been applied and allowed to cure, sand and fair (see Chapter 10). Then apply gel coating or paint.

Repairing Fiberglass Boats

In spite of some claims to the contrary, fiberglass boats can be damaged. Fortunately, damage to fiberglass itself is fairly easy to repair. Not all damage to fiberglass boats is in the fiberglass part of the boats, however. Wood and metal parts can be damaged as well. Repair or replacement of broken or damaged wood and metal usually involves familiar methods.

This chapter describes how to repair fiberglass itself. Many do-it-yourselfers who feel quite comfortable making complicated repairs to wood or metal are often hesitant to attempt repairs to fiberglass. This is often because the methods and techniques for making the fiberglass repairs are less familiar, not because they are any more difficult. Once the techniques are understood, repairs to fiberglass are often much easier to make.

Before undertaking fiberglassing repair work, you should first know the fundamentals of fiberglassing (see Chapter 10). You should also follow the health and safety rules and procedures for working with fiberglassing chemicals and materials.

WORKING CONDITIONS

When you make repairs to fiberglass laminates, the repair should be as strong or stronger than the original. This must be done under working conditions that are not as ideal as those under which the boat was originally constructed at the factory.

Ideally, fiberglass boat repair work should be done under laboratory conditions with factors such as temperature and humidity carefully controlled. For most of your own fiberglassing repair work, you will probably have to work under much less satisfactory conditions. Some repairs can be made with the boat in the water; others require that the boat be hauled out. Regardless, always strive for the best conditions possible, especially for crucial jobs such as fiberglass hull repairs.

A temperature of about 75 degrees Fahrenheit with low humidity works best when laying up laminates with polyester resin. By varying the amounts of catalyst used, however, satisfactory repair work can be done in a temperature range from about 60 degrees to 90 degrees Fahrenheit, though try to avoid the extremes as much as possible. For the most crucial work, the temperature should be as close to the 75-degree Fahrenheit mark as possible. By using special low-temperature polyester resins, repair work is possible at temperatures even below 60 degrees Fahrenheit. Whenever possible, avoid fiberglassing in direct sunlight. Rig up some type of sun shade or awning over the work area if necessary.

While the techniques in the practice fiberglassing exercises in Chapter 10 are basically the same as those used for major repairs, there are some important differences. First, the practice exercises used small, 6-inch square areas of reinforcing material. Fiberglassing repairs often involve much larger areas that might require somewhat different techniques.

Second, the practice exercises were done on a level plane. This often isn't practical when making actual repairs. Fiberglassing is often done on inclined, vertical, and even overhead surfaces. You will have problems with resin dripping, running, and pooling, and with reinforcing material sagging and bunching up. In some cases, high-viscosity resins or regular viscosity polyester resin with a thixotropic agent added can alleviate some of these problems.

And third, actual repair work might have to be done under less sanitary conditions than were the practice exercises. Dust, dirt, and grime can mix in with fiberglassing materials and chemicals and greatly reduce the quality of the resulting laminates. Still, you will want to do your fiberglassing repair work under the cleanest possible conditions. Always clean up the work area as much as possible before starting fiberglassing.

Fiberglass boats can be damaged by wear, abrasion, impact, sun exposure, and other ways. The resulting damage can range from minor to major. Sometimes it is only cosmetic, other times it is structural, and others a combination of cosmetic and structural. While both are important, structural damage should always be repaired to high standards. The appearance of the repair, while extremely important to your pride and maintaining the value of your boat, is secondary. Whenever possible, you will want to make a structurally sound repair that still has a good appearance, or at least doesn't show up readily. If you patch a hole in a fiberglass hull, for example, you probably will want to do it so that no one will know a repair has ever been made. But the number one priority is still to make a structurally sound repair.

REPAIRING SCRATCHES AND MINOR GOUGES

Scratches and minor gouges in the gel coating of a fiberglass boat that cannot be removed by cleaning, polishing, or other routine maintenance can be repaired. If it does not extend below the gel coating, saturate a clean white cloth with acetone. Don't use a colored cloth because the coloring might come off and stain the gel coating. Wipe the area of the scratch or gouge. Use only light pressure so you do not remove the gel coating. The purpose here is to remove dirt and other loose particles from the surface.

The next step is to carefully sand the scratch or gouge until it disappears. Use a sanding block and 220-grit sandpaper. Sand carefully and do not remove any more gel coating than is absolutely necessary. Then thoroughly clean the area using a cloth soaked with water. Follow with wet block sanding using 400-grit abrasive paper. Continue with wet block sanding using 600-grit abrasive paper. Use rubbing compound to polish the surface and remove any remaining scratches.

If in making the repair, you happen to sand all the way through the gel coating, touch up the gel coating using a gel coat touch-up kit. These often allow color matching. Follow the manufacturer's directions for applying the gel coating.

Scratches and minor gouges can go below the gel coating into the laminate itself. To repair them, first clean out the scratch or gouge. A sharp pointed knife or other metal object can be used, though a folded-over piece of 100-grit abrasive paper might work better. It all depends on the particular scratch or gouge. Then clean out the scratch or gouge with acetone on a clean white cloth.

As a rule, use epoxy putty rather than polyester putty. You can color match the putty to the gel coating, or you can touch up the gel coating later.

Apply the putty—following the manufacturer's directions—with a putty knife after the catalyst or hardener has been added. Fill in the scratch or gouge, then use the putty knife as a drag to remove excess putty. Allow putty to cure.

Sand the area using a sanding block. Begin with 100-grit abrasive paper, then use 220 grit. If color pigments were mixed into the putty, finish by wet sanding with 400- and 600-grit abrasive paper. Polish the surface with a rubbing compound, which can be applied by hand using a clean white cloth.

If a separate gel coating is to be applied, finish by wet sanding with 400- and 600-grit abrasive paper, then, touch up the gel coating using a gel coat touch-up kit. Follow the manufacturer's directions. A thin layer, about 10 to 15 mils in thickness, is used. If a thicker layer is applied, it can crack after the resin has cured.

REPAIRING NICKS AND SMALL HOLES

To repair nicks and small holes that do not go all the way through the fiberglass laminate, first prepare the surface by sanding. Use abrasive paper that is coarse enough to remove any loose material or use a sharp pointed knife or other object. An abrasive grinding burr attachment in a portable electric drill can also be used. Then clean out the nick or small hole by wiping with a clean white cloth saturated with acetone.

Small defects can be filled in with epoxy putty. Slightly larger areas can be filled in by laminating with fiberglass mat and polyester or epoxy resin.

Allow the putty or resin to cure. If laminating resin was used, apply a thin layer of finishing resin to the surface so that the resin will have a tack-free surface.

Remove excess material by sanding with a sanding block and 100-grit abrasive paper. The sandpaper should be coarse enough to remove excess material in a reasonable amount of time without sanding scratches beyond the desired finished surface level. When you have sanded too close to the desired surface level, switch to 220-grit abrasive paper. Finish by touching up the gel coating.

REPAIRING GEL COAT CRACKS AND CRAZING

Small cracks and *crazing* (hairline breaks of random patterns) can form in gel coatings for many reasons. Improper application or formulation of the gel coating in the original molding process is one way. Localized stresses on the moldings are another. Improved formulations of gel coatings have made cracking and crazing less likely, though on older fiberglass boats, these conditions are common.

When cracking and crazing is only in the gel coating and does not extend into the laminate, begin by examining the surface to determine the underlying cause. If possible, correct the problem. If fasteners are too tight, you can loosen them. If the laminate flexes or works too much in the area, reinforce the laminate by using one of the methods detailed in Chapter 11. If you do not correct the underlying cause, cracking and crazing is likely to reappear again after the repair has been made.

In most cases, the cracks and crazing extend all the way through the gel coat resin. If they don't, repair as you would a scratch or minor gouge that does not extend all the way through the gel coating.

The cracks in the gel coating are usually too small to fill with putty unless they are first widened out. This is done with a sharp, pointed metal object. Do this until it is possible to get the putty down into the cracks. Then clean the area using a clean white cloth soaked with acetone.

Use epoxy putty, with or without color pigments mixed in to match the gel coating, to fill the cracks. Measure out the required amount of epoxy putty. Add the hardener or curing agent. Mix. Then apply with a putty knife. Use the blade as a drag for leveling the putty even with the top of the surrounding gel coating.

Allow the putty to cure, then sand off excess material. Start with 100-grit or finer (higher grit number) abrasive paper and use a sanding block. Switch to 220-grit abrasive paper. Try not to make scratches in the gel coating that surrounds the repair areas.

If you matched gel coat color by mixing in color pigments, finish by wet sanding with 400-grit and then 600-grit abrasive paper and a sanding block. Then use rubbing compound to remove any remaining tiny scratches. If the gel coat color was not mixed in, finish the job by touching up the gel coating.

FILLING IN SMALL HOLES

There are times when you will want to fill in holes that have previously been drilled through fiberglass laminates. For small holes up to about a 1/2 inch in diameter in unimportant areas, use epoxy putty without additional reinforcement. Important areas require a more substantial repair. Regardless, "V" the hole outward from the back side (Fig. 12-1). A small round file or an abrasive burr attachment in an electric drill can accomplish this.

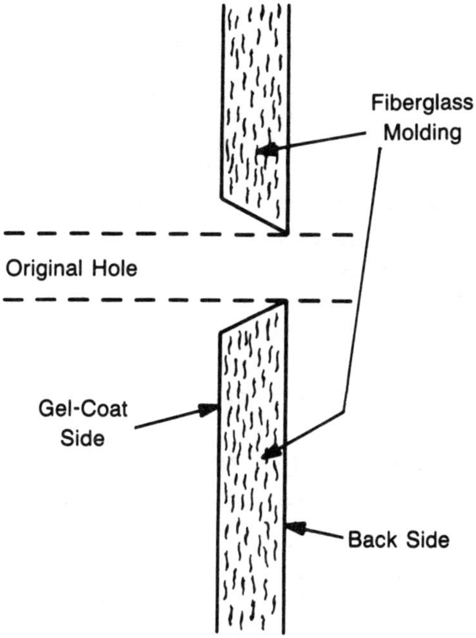

Fig. 12-1. Preparation of small hole in fiberglass for filling.

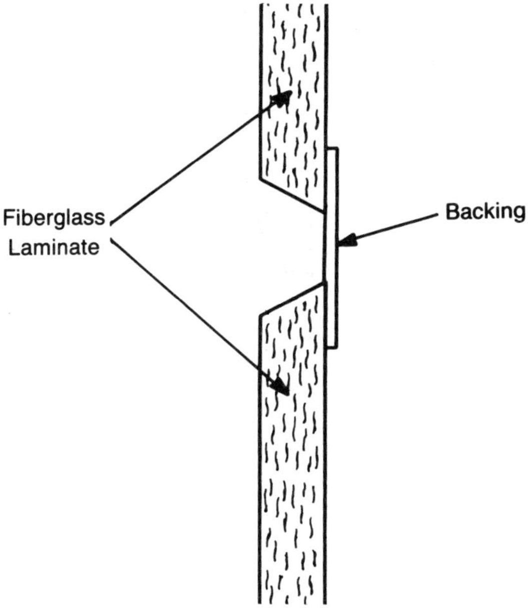

Fig. 12-2. A backing is applied to the hole.

Next, apply a backing behind the hole (Fig. 12-2). Use masking tape or a piece of cardboard propped or held in place. Then, fill in the hole with epoxy putty or by using chopped or milled glass fibers mixed with resin. The backing piece keeps the material from falling out the back side of the hole.

Allow the filler material (Fig. 12-3) to cure, then remove the backing material. Add a backing laminate of one or more layers of mat, extending it well past the hole (Fig. 12-4). If more than one layer of mat is used, use progressively larger pieces.

Allow the backing laminate to cure. Then sand off excess material on the side of the main molding to be finished. Use a sanding block. Gradually work down to finer grits of abrasive paper. Finish job by touching up gel coating.

PATCHING LARGER HOLES AND FRACTURES IN SINGLE-SKIN FIBERGLASS LAMINATES

Larger holes and fractures in fiberglass laminates are repaired by laminating patches in place. Some sort of backing is used behind the damaged area as a molding form.

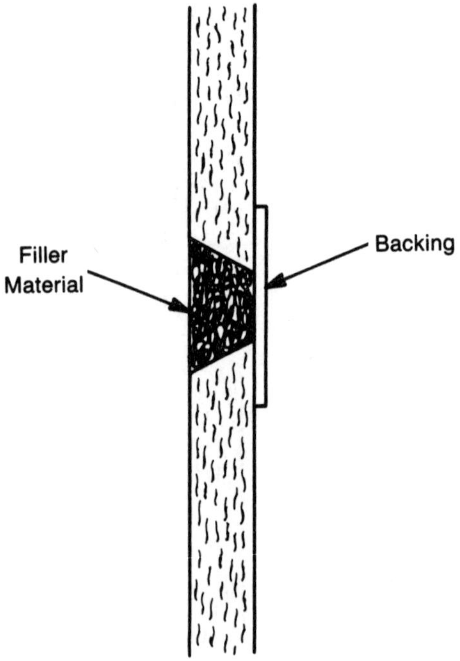

Fig. 12-3. The hole is filled in.

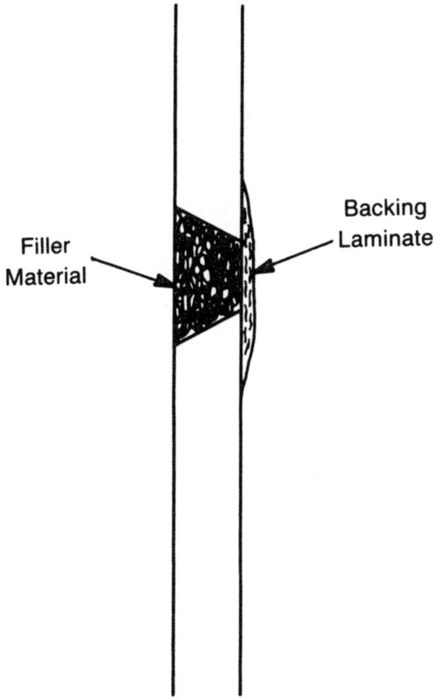

Fig. 12-4. A backing laminate is applied.

First remove loose or weakened fiberglass (Fig. 12-5). Cut it away with a saber saw or grind it away with a disk sander and coarse grit sandpaper. You want to get back to sound fiberglass laminate.

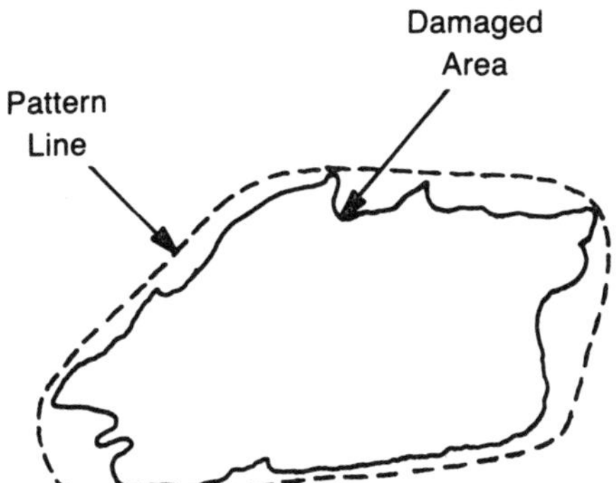

Fig. 12-5. Loose and weakened fiberglass is removed.

Next, taper the hole outward to the desired finished side from the back of the laminate (Fig. 12-6). For reasonably small openings, use a file, surfacing tool, or abrasive burr attachment in an electric drill. For larger jobs, use a disk sander with a coarse grit abrasive paper. The taper gives a larger bonding area for the repair laminate.

The next step is to apply a backing, which can be cardboard, wood, metal, or other materials (Fig. 12-7). Overlap the opening all the way around and position it on the back side of the laminate. Secure it in place with props, clamps, or by other means. Place cellophane over the backing to keep the repair laminate from sticking to it.

Determine the types of reinforcing material to use and the weights and layers required. Try to use the same laminate as was used in the original molding. Precut the pieces of reinforcing material and arrange them in the order that they will be applied. The piece that will be directly over the backing inside the hole goes on first and so on until the repair laminate is built up to the thickness

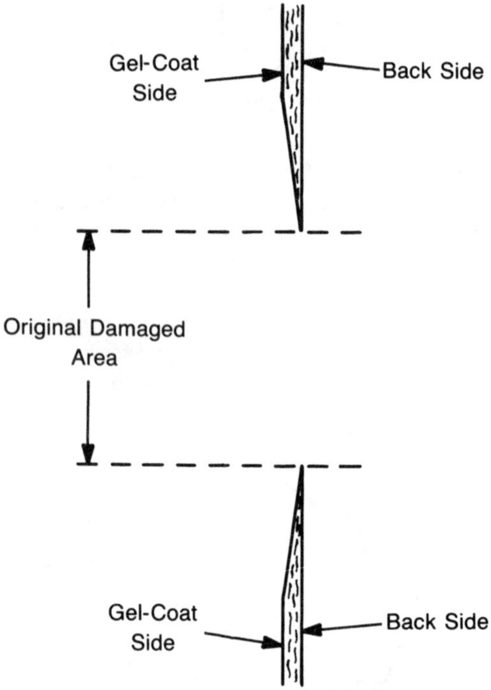

Fig. 12-6. A damaged area is tapered for patching.

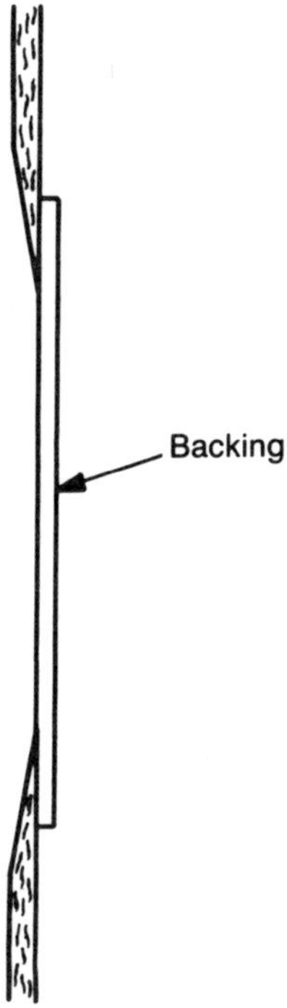

Fig. 12-7. A backing is applied.

of the original laminate. Clean the bonding area on the taper of the original laminate with acetone.

The next step is to lay up the laminate. Lay up the first layer over the backing inside the hole (Fig. 12-8). Allow this layer to cure before adding the second layer. Repeat until the laminate is built up to the desired thickness. Experienced fiberglassers sometimes lay up more than one layer to a laminate without allowing the first layer to cure first.

Use laminating resin for the entire lay-up except for a final coat of finishing resin over the last layer of the laminate. This allows the surface to cure tack-free for sanding (Fig. 12-9).

After the laminate has cured, remove the backing material. The strength of the repair can be reinforced by applying a backing laminate that overlaps the hole that was filled in (Fig. 12-10). To add a backing laminate, first sand the bonding surfaces on the back side of the repair patch and the area of the original laminate where the backing laminate will overlap. Then clean the area with a clean white cloth saturated with acetone.

Determine the types of reinforcing material to use and the

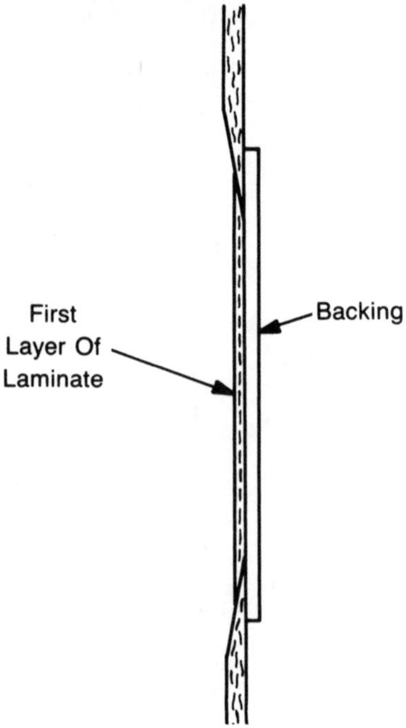

Fig. 12-8. The first layer to laminate is applied directly to the inside of the backing.

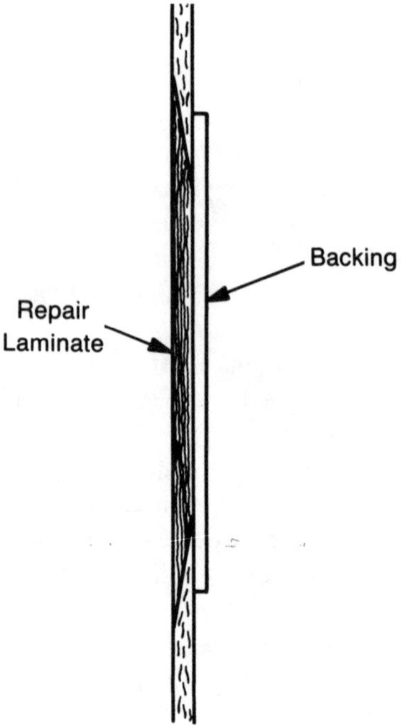

Fig. 12-9. The repair area is filled in with laminate.

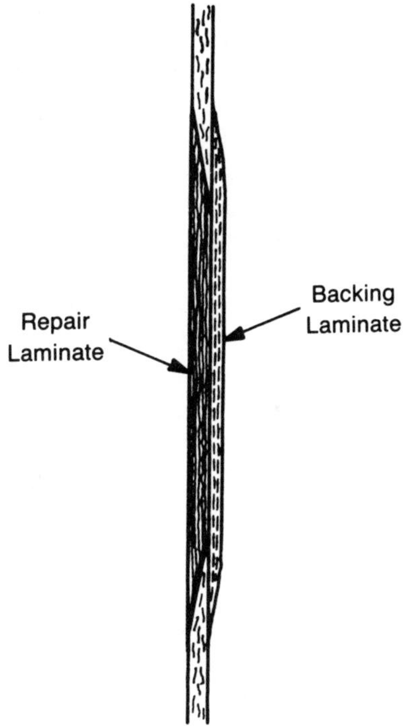

Fig. 12-10. A backing laminate is added.

weights and layers required. Precut the pieces of reinforcing material and arrange them in the order they will be applied.

Lay up the first layer of laminate directly over the back side of the repair patch and the surrounding area of the original laminate. Allow this layer to cure before adding the second layer. Repeat to build up the desired thickness. Although not absolutely necessary, it is good practice to make each added layer progressively larger. This will taper the backing laminate to the original laminate.

Next, go back to the front side of the repair area. Sand off excess material. Small areas can be sanded by hand using a sanding block or surfacing tools. Use a power disk sander for larger jobs. After you have removed most of the excess material, work down to finer grits of abrasive paper. Fill small surface indentations with epoxy putty if desired.

Fair the surface carefully to achieve a professional repair job. Don't hurry. More repair jobs are probably spoiled by hasty sanding and fairing than any other reason.

The final step is to apply matching gel coat resin over the repair area. Blend it in with the original gel coating.

This repair is used when only one side of the laminate needs to be finished. When a finished appearance is important on both sides of the laminate, a somewhat different repair can be made.

Taper the opening on both sides to the center of the opening (Fig. 12-11). Place backing across the opening at the center of the laminate (Fig. 12-12). Use cellophane to keep the lay-up resin from sticking to the backing. Lay up the half of the patch on the side that is most difficult to get, such as the side inside the hull on a hull repair job.

Determine the types of reinforcing material and the weights and layers required. Precut the pieces and arrange them in order. Then lay up the first layer directly over the cellophane on the backing and the taper area of the laminate being repaired. Allow this layer to cure before adding the second layer (Fig. 12-13). Repeat to build up to the thickness that matches the laminate being repaired.

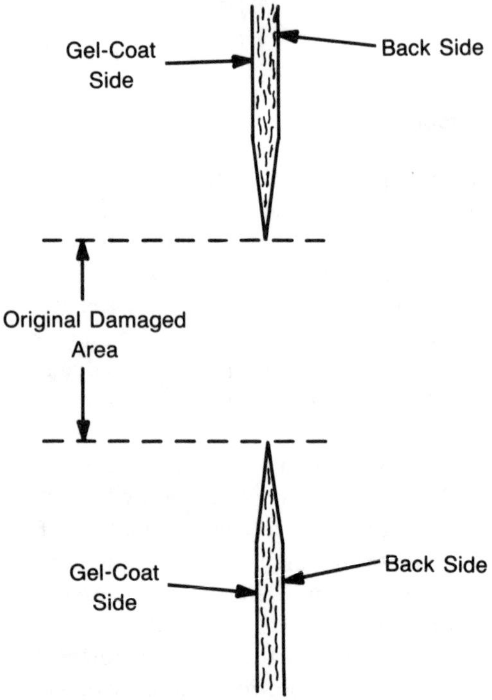

Fig. 12-11. The opening is tapered on both sides.

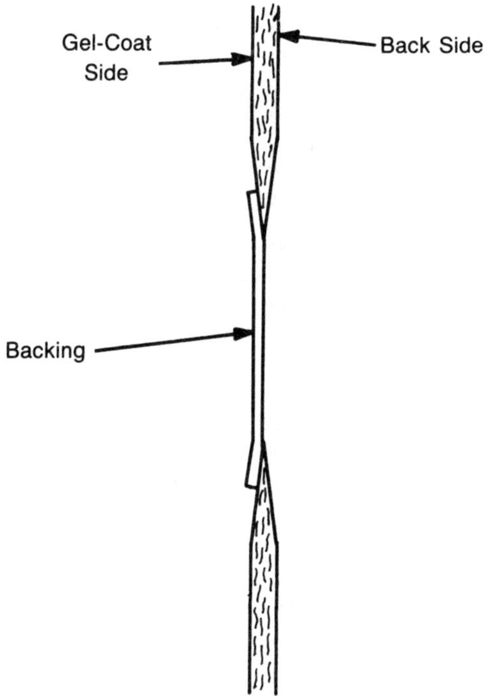

Fig. 12-12. A backing is placed across the center of the opening.

Remove the backing material next. Prepare the surface for laying up the second half of the patch by sanding and cleaning with acetone. Then lay up the second half of the patch in the same manner as the first half, except that this time the first half laminate forms the backing for the second half (Fig. 12-14).

Sand off excess material on both sides. Gradually work down to finer grits of abrasive paper. The final step is to touch up the gel coating on the gel coat side and the paint or otherwise finish the other side.

REPAIRING SANDWICH CORE LAMINATES

Repairing sandwich core moldings is generally more difficult than repairing similar damage on a single-skin laminate. You now have two fiberglass skins and a core to repair instead of a single fiberglass laminate skin. If the damage extends all the way through the sandwich core molding, there will be three repair units: one of the fiberglass skins, the core, and the other fiberglass skin.

Fig. 12-13. The first half of the repair is laminated in place.

Make a careful inspection of the damaged area. Examine the damage from both sides of the laminate whenever possible. Mark off the limits of the damage with a marking pen. Remove weak, broken, and delaminated fiberglass from both fiberglass skins. In some cases, a section of the core will also have to be removed and then replaced. Use gradual curves when marking the outside limits of the damaged area. The patterns for the two skins can be the same or different.

Remove damaged fiberglass to get back to sound fiberglass for bonding in the repair. Use a power disk sander for this job. Try not to do additional damage to the core material. Taper the laminates for bonding in the repair laminates.

Next, repair any damage to the core material. Fill in damaged areas in plywood cores with epoxy putty. It might be necessary to remove a section of the damaged plywood and then fit and glue in a filler piece of plywood. Fill in small damaged areas on rigid plastic foam and balsa cores with epoxy putty. For larger areas, remove a section of the core material and splice in a filler piece of the same material. Epoxy glue it in place to the original core material around the damaged area.

The original or repaired core material will serve as a backing for laminating the two fiberglass skins in place (Fig. 12-15). Determine types of reinforcing material to use and weights and layers required. Use approximately the same laminates as were used in the original moldings. Precut the pieces of reinforcing material and arrange them in the order in which they will be applied. Usually you will laminate one of the skins completely, then move on to the other skin.

Laminate the two skins in place. Allow them to cure. The final layer of resin applied should be finishing resin or laminating resin with a wax additive that will give a tack-free surface cure.

Sand off excess material on one side of the laminate, then move on to the other side. If desired, you can work back and forth, however. When most of the excess material has been taken off, work down to finer abrasive paper.

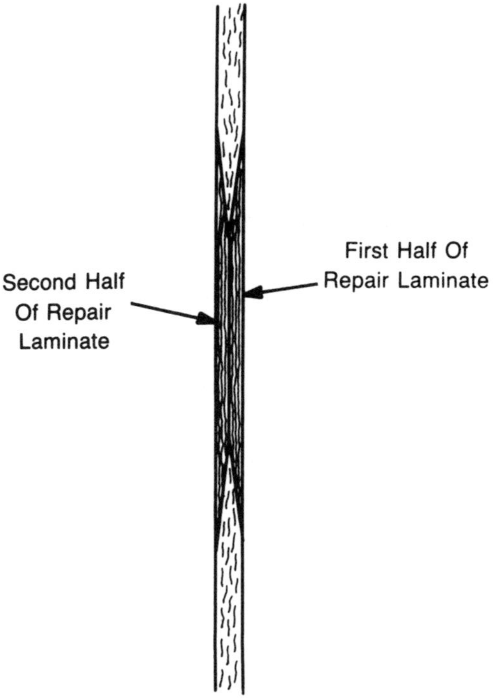

Fig. 12-14. The second half of the repair is laminated in place against the first half.

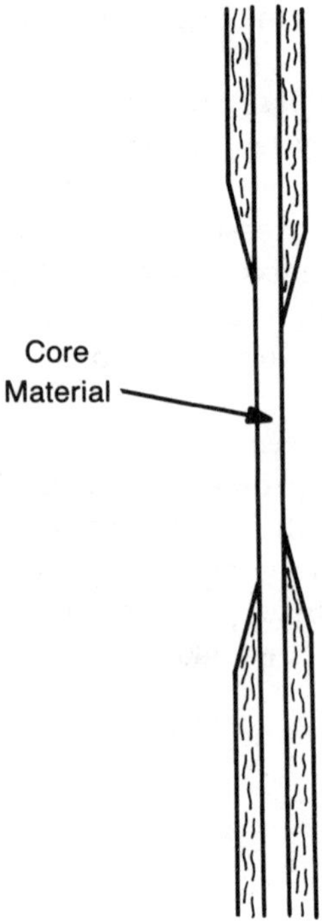

Fig. 12-15. The original or repaired core serves as a backing for repair laminates.

The final step is to touch up the gel coating, which is usually only on one side of the laminate, and then match finish on the other side. If the back side of the laminate does not show, an overlapping reinforcing laminate can be added to reinforce the repair (Fig. 12-16).

REPAIRING MAJOR DAMAGE

Extensive damage to fiberglass moldings can be repaired in a similar manner, except that larger and often more complicated backings and forms are required for laying up patching laminates. For large flat areas or areas with simple gradual curves, plywood makes an excellent backing material. It can be bolted in place using countersunk holes if the fasteners are to be left in place along with the backing plywood. In most cases, however, the backing plywood is removed and the holes used for the fasteners are filled in. If the fasteners are left in place in countersunk holes, they can be covered over with fiberglass filler or epoxy putty.

Rough sand the plywood to give a good bonding surface if it is to be left in place. If it is to be removed, cover with cellophane

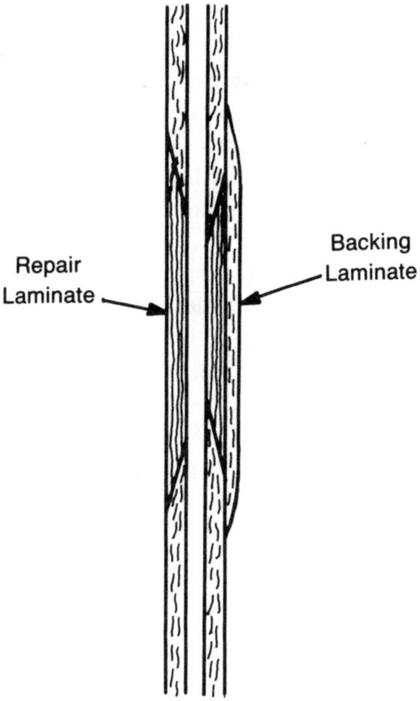

Fig. 12-16. A backing laminate used on the repair of sandwich core laminate.

or apply a release agent so the laminate does not stick to the plywood and the plywood can be easily removed.

Sharp and complex curves often present additional problems. In some cases, a backing can be shaped by using frames or ribs and strip planking. Another method is to use rigid polyurethane foam, which can be shaped with a surfacing tool, or use polyvinyl chloride foam plastic, which can be formed to complex shapes over a form when heated. The plastic foams can either be left as part of the laminates or removed after the repair laminates have been laid up. If the plastic foam is to be removed, use a layer of cellophane between the foam and the first layer of the laminate.

The main idea when repairing major damage to fiberglass moldings is to replace the damaged areas of the moldings with new laminates. Some type of backing, form, or mold is required for laying up the laminate. The purpose is to hold the resin and reinforcing materials in position until the resin cures. Bonding the new laminate to the old one is a major problem. To do this adequately, proper preparation of the bonding surface is essential. Try to make the bonding surface as large as possible. When it is practical to do so, reinforce patches with overlapping backing laminates. Because sanding and fairing can be the most difficult part of many repair jobs, try to keep this to a minimum by making desired finished surfaces of repair laminates as smooth and even as possible. In this way, less sanding and fairing will be required.

To this point, the basic method has been to laminate a repair in place over a male mold or form (the backing). I feel that this is the best approach to use in making repairs to fiberglass laminates. The main disadvantage of this method is that you do not end up with a smooth finished surface like that achieved against a female mold. This, in turn, involves sanding and fairing to achieve a finished surface, and even then it is difficult to achieve an against-a-mold appearance. Even with this in mind, I still think it is the best method to use, especially for beginners.

An alternate method that you might want to use after you gain considerable experience with the previously described methods is to use a female mold backing. This is placed on the desired fin-

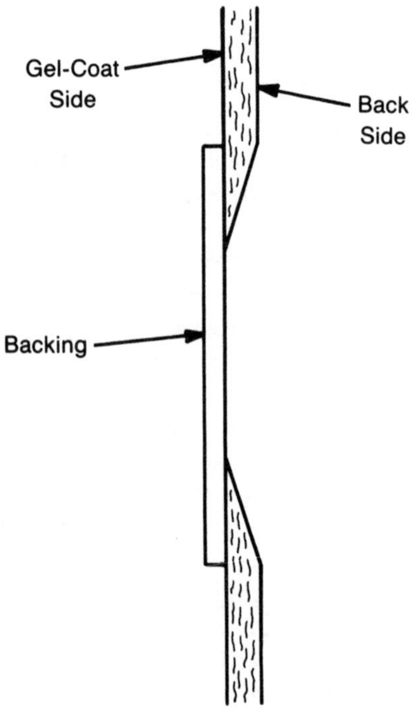

Fig. 12-17. A backing used to provide a female mold for a patch.

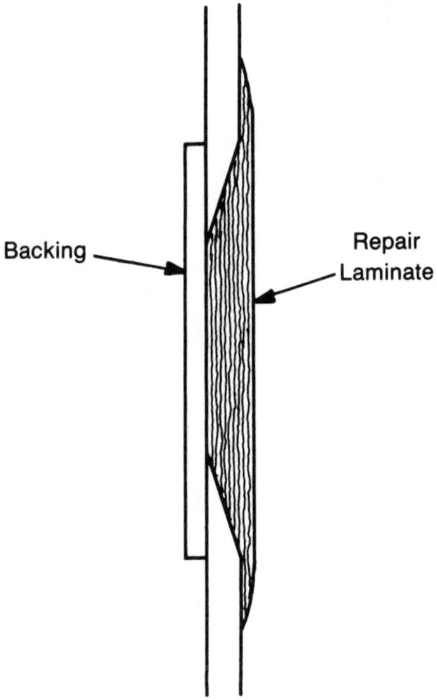

Fig. 12-18. The repair is laminated in place against the female mold.

ished side of the repair. The molding that is being repaired is tapered outward toward the back side (Fig. 12-17). A release agent is used on the mold surface, which will be removed after the lay-up has been completed. Gel coating that matches the original can then be sprayed over the release agent. An alternate method is to omit this and apply the gel coating or other finish later. The repair is then laminated in place against the mold surface, with the laminate overlapping the taper surface on the original laminate (Fig. 12-18).

This method might at first sound like an easy way to eliminate sanding and fairing. There are a number of difficulties associated with this method, however. First, an accurate female mold surface is required. It is difficult to achieve a molded surface without defects under most do-it-yourselfer's working conditions. These defects have to be filled in or otherwise repaired, and much of the reason for using this method will then be lost. Still another problem is that it is almost impossible to achieve a joint that does not show where the patch joins the original laminate, especially if gel coating was applied to the mold surface. The joint line must be widened and filled with epoxy putty, which requires sanding on the finished side of the laminate. This can also weaken the laminate, which can be compensated for by applying an overlapping backing laminate. Thus, while this female molding method for making repairs might sound attractive, it can be difficult to execute.

If you can only get to one side of the laminate for making a repair, you will need to set the backing in place through the opening in the laminate that is to be repaired. The backing can then be held in position by small wires, which can be cut off after a couple of layers have been applied to the repair laminate. If you don't have any access at all to the back side of the laminate, the backing material cannot be removed. This usually will not make any difference, however.

GETTING STARTED

It's important to gain the necessary skill and experience before you try repair work on an expensive boat. You need to feel confident that you can do a particular repair job right.

A starting point is to learn the fundamentals of fiberglassing by doing all of the practice exercises detailed in Chapter 10. Next, I suggest that you go on to alterations, as detailed in Chapter 11. You might also want to do some practice repair work. For example, obtain some scrap panels of fiberglass moldings or part of a fiberglass boat that is damaged beyond practical repair and use these for practice work. Make a hole in a fiberglass laminate, then practice making the repair of filling it back in. Start with small, easy repair jobs and gradually work up to more difficult ones.

REFINISHING FIBERGLASS BOATS

Original gel coatings tend to fade and deteriorate over a period of years to the point where you'll consider refinishing. This is seldom an easy decision. The old gel coating might not look very good, but it might still give adequate protection.

One possible way to refinish is to apply a new gel coating. To do this satisfactorily requires considerable experience and expensive equipment, however. In many ways it's more difficult to apply gel coating to an existing boat than it is during the molding process of a new boat. I've only known a few professionals who could consistently do a good job of applying gel coating to existing fiberglass boats. And the cost of having this work done is high.

An alternate finish is to apply a two-part epoxy paint. One part is the resin, the other is the curing agent or hardener. The two parts are added together just before the paint is applied. This type of epoxy paint gives excellent adhesion, provided that the surface is first properly prepared, and a durable finish. While generally easier to apply than regular gel coating, it can still be difficult. To give a professional appearance, it really must be sprayed on, a job that is usually beyond the scope of most do-it-yourselfers. It requires not only special spraying equipment, as well as the skill and techniques to use it properly, but also expensive health and safety gear.

Perhaps the best bet is to use a brushable two-part polyurethane finish. These give a gel-coatlike finish that is quite durable. A number of brands and a wide choice of colors are now on the market.

If you decide to use a brushable two-part polyurethane finish, select a quality brand and follow the manufacturer's application instructions carefully. In most cases, sanding is required for preparation of the surface. Most of these finishes are formulated so that they can be applied in a temperature range of about 60 to 85 degrees Fahrenheit. If possible, try to avoid the extremes. If done outdoors, the painting should be done in the shade and on windless days. Use natural bristle brushes or short nap rollers for applying the polyurethane. As a rule, 1 gallon covers about 400 to 600 square feet with one coat. For optimum results, two coats are recommended, with about 24 hours between coats.

In any case, refinishing fiberglass boats is a major undertaking. If not done properly, it can actually lower the value of a fiberglass boat. When most people see an amateur-looking paint job on a fiberglass boat, they wonder what is being covered up.

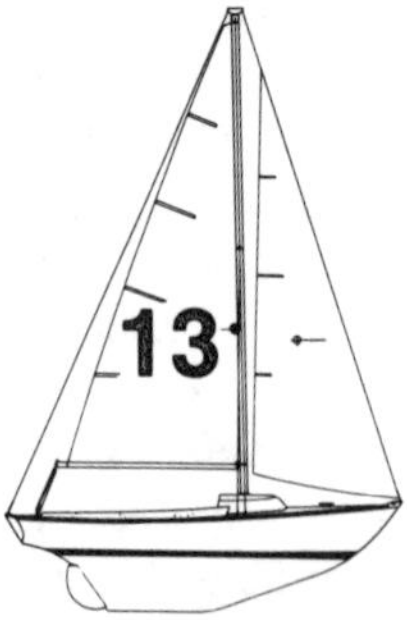

Boatbuilding From Bare Hulls and Kits

You can purchase a manufactured fiberglass boat hull and finish it out yourself by using components and kits from the manufacturer or by supplying your own materials. You can start with the bare minimum—a molded fiberglass hull—and construct your own deck and cabin structures. Or you can use a molded fiberglass deck and cabin structure supplied by the manufacturer. Most builders purchase at least the fiberglass moldings, including not only the hulls and deck and cabin structures, but also hatches, rudders, and other components that are molded from fiberglass for the particular boat.

Some manufacturers offer component kits for finishing the boat. Others offer complete kits with everything you need to finish out a complete boat. The boats can also come in various stages of completion. For example, you can purchase a hull with the ballast already bonded in place, the interior roughed in, and the deck and cabin structure bonded to the hull with the major bulkheads in place. Some are even offered as power-away or sail-away versions, with everything complete except for a bare interior. The buyer then adds his own custom interior.

Today, everything from small dinghies to world cruisers are available in bare hull and kit form, including power, sail, and combination boats. For a list of suppliers, see the Appendix. While some of these manufacturers specialize in kit boats, most offer simply moldings from the line of boats they sell completed.

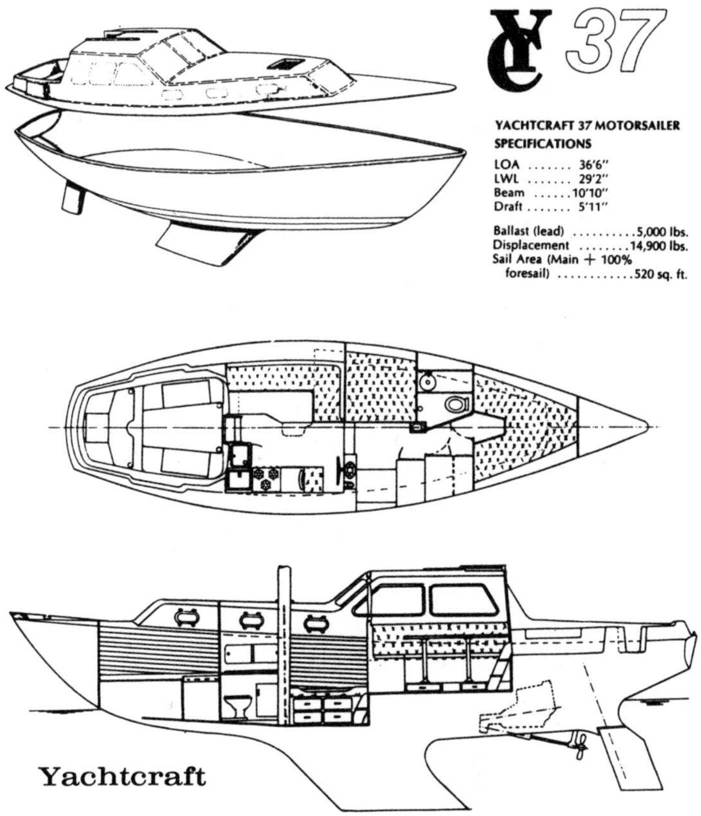

Fig. 13-1. The Yachtcraft 34 is available in kit form. (Courtesy of Yachtcraft)

Do-it-yourself finishing out of bare hulls and fiberglass kit boats is not new. What is new is the complete range of boats that are now available in these forms. I've had several friends who have finished out fiberglass versions of the famed Tahiti ketch, the Dreadnought 32, and actually sailed their boats to Tahiti and beyond. It's no idle dream. It can and has been done many times.

REASONS FOR POPULARITY

Perhaps the primary reason for the popularity of this method for owning a boat is the money saved. The savings over a factory completed equivalent boat can range from about 30 to 60 percent and more. Then there is the possibility of custom-tailoring the boat to your exact needs, especially the interior accommodations. You can design and build it the way you want.

Over the years, I've had considerable opportunity to observe first hand the results of hundreds of amateur boatbuilding efforts. Boatbuilding from a bare fiberglass hull or kit has many advantages over building from scratch (see Chapter 14). The main difference that I have noted is that almost every bare hull and kit boatbuilding effort has resulted in at least a fairly successful boat. With only a few notable exceptions, most of the boats built from scratch were disasters, if they were ever even completed at all, and most weren't. About two thirds of those who went the bare hull or kit route thought that it was well worth the effort. The other third said they wouldn't want to do it over again, but even most of these boats turned out fairly well. A majority of the "from scratch" builders said it just wasn't worth it. The few bare hull and kit builders who sold out before they finished the projects all got good prices for the unfinished boats. The scratch builders who sold out before finishing the boats usually did so at a considerable loss. Some of the boats could not be sold and are still sitting in backyards and boatyards with "For Sale" signs on them. They are monuments of shattered dreams.

Though the bare hull and kit boat method is a major project, you start out with at least a bare hull that has the shape of a boat. The "from scratch" builder might take several years just to get to this point. The bare hull and kit boatbuilders know from the start that they have at least a reasonably good hull, which is the basis for a good boat. And because it looks like a boat right from the start, it's much easier to imagine the completion of the project. For those who start with additional moldings, such as the deck and cabin structures, the beginning can look even closer to the day of launching.

If what I have said so far hasn't discouraged you from wanting to build from scratch, go on to Chapter 14. You just might be the person who has what it takes to successfully build a fiberglass boat from scratch.

Now back to bare hull and kit boatbuilding. How much can you save? This depends on so many factors that there is no way to give a simple answer to this question.

To start with, it depends very much on the person who is undertaking the particular project. The more skills and talents that you have, or the more you can learn, the more money you can save. If you can do your own upholstery work, you save the cost of paying someone else to do it for you. People who hire out almost all the work for completing a boat often end up saving very little. Thus, the more you can do yourself, the more you can save. The more work that you hire out, the less the potential savings.

If you purchase everything you need for finishing the boat from the manufacturer, your savings will probably be less than if you do some of your own shopping. In this way, you can take advantage of discount buying. You can also buy some of the materials, equipment, and supplies secondhand. However, while the manufacturer's component packages might cost slightly more, you get everything you need for a particular part of the construction in a single unit, which is convenient and can save time.

Many times you can start out with just the bare hull, which is usually priced less than the down payment on a similar factory-finished boat. Then you can purchase other components from the factory or elsewhere when you need them and/or can afford them. This can amount to "financing" your purchase without paying any interest. The price of the components might go up in the meantime, but some manufacturers will give you a price guarantee if the additional components are purchased within a stated period of time.

It can cost almost as much to build a fiberglass hull from scratch as it does to purchase one already built from a manufacturer. If you calculated the time that it normally takes a do-it-yourselfer to build a fiberglass hull from scratch—even a lousy one—at fifty cents an hour, the manufactured hull usually turns out to be a bargain. The same thing often applies to deck and cabin structures. Some builders try to save money by constructing their own from wood or other materials. They often end up spending about the same amount for materials as they would have if they had just purchased the factory-molded version, however. Not only that, but they would probably have ended up with a better boat, or at least one that would have more resale value. This is not to say that some do-it-yourselfers haven't built sound deck and cabin structures. They have. But these are the exceptions rather than the rule. Most seem to build unsightly structures that in no way complement the quality of the factory-molded hull.

REQUIRED SKILLS AND DEDICATION

Because building from a bare hull or kit still means a large outlay of money, either all at once or spread out over a period of time, first determine if you have the required skills and dedication before you begin the project. Remember, if you are a do-it-yourself type of person, you can learn additional skills as you go along.

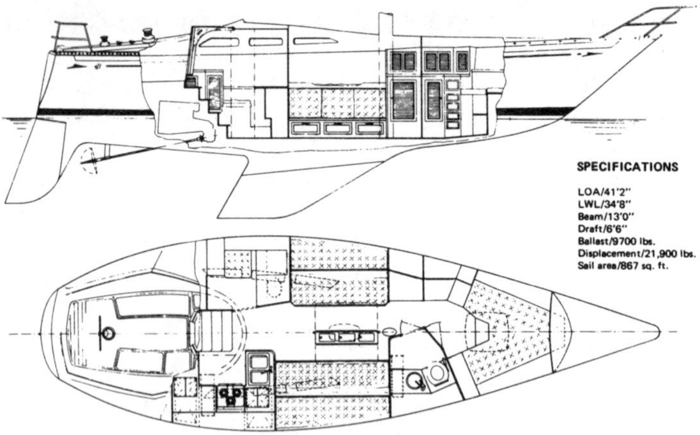

Fig. 13-2. The Yachtcraft 37 motorsailer is available in kit form. (Courtesy of Yachtcraft)

Fortunately, do-it-yourselfers are the only ones who seem to be interested enough to embark on such a project. While it isn't necessary to have much boatbuilding skill per se, if you don't, you had better be the type of person who can catch up on the subject quickly. Most people, once they start considering such a project, read everything they can find on the subject.

Although many manufacturers give estimates on the number of hours it will take to complete their boats, I have found that it usually takes most do-it-yourselfers longer. It is very difficult to be efficient. Much time can be spent dreaming or figuring out what to do next or getting set up to do a job or in a hundred other ways. If you can only work in your spare time, time will be lost getting started each time you arrive at the boat. This type of work schedule probably won't be as efficient as, say, putting in regular eight-hour work days.

Most boats are going to involve a considerable part of your life for a long period of time before you successfully complete them. Are you the type of person who can stick to a long project? All people involved in the project should be dedicated to it, although not necessarily to the same degree. I've seen kit boat projects that have brought couples closer together and others that have led to divorces. It can go either way.

The savings in doing your own construction over buying a completed boat are the result of you providing your own time, labor, and ingenuity. It can make for a challenging and interesting project, but you need to be dedicated to it.

THE RIGHT BOAT AND STARTING POINT FOR YOU

Once you decide that building from a bare hull or kit is the way you want to go, you must decide on a particular boat. You need to select the type, size, and design for the boat that is right for you (see Chapter 2).

Write to manufacturers for information about boats that sound like what you have in mind. Be sure to request their latest price sheets. When you receive this information, you can get an idea of what the possibilities are. You can begin to calculate what it will cost you to start the project and the total price to complete it.

With each boat, you will have a number of possibilities. For example, the minimum is usually a bare hull that is also available in various stages of completion. You can have some of the more important jobs done for you at the factory at a cost—such as having the major bulkheads installed. The hull and deck and cabin structure moldings can be bonded together. Ballast or the engine can be installed. You must decide at what stage of completion you want to start at. At the same time, you must weigh this with how much you can afford to spend.

Will you purchase component kits for finishing out the boat from the manufacturer? If so, will you order them initially or at some later time? There is an advantage to the single order in that the component kits can often be shipped along with the hull at little or no additional cost. The disadvantage is that you have to put out the money all at once.

Be as realistic as possible when selecting a boat. You might have a certain size boat in mind, but the manufacturer's price sheet quickly convinces you that it is out of your price range. Perhaps you can lower your sights to a smaller size boat that costs less.

There are two lines of reasoning here. Some people go the kit boatbuilding route so they can get a bigger or better boat for the same price as purchasing a smaller or lower quality finished boat. Others go this route because they can't afford a finished boat of the size and quality that they desire.

A PLACE TO BUILD

Early in the planning process, before you send in an order for a hull, consider exactly where you will finish out your dream boat. Perhaps the best choice is your yard or, if the boat will fit, garage. You can live close to the boat, making it convenient to use short periods of time for working on it.

Kit boatbuilding is noisy work. Will this disturb your neighbors? If you don't care what they think, you had better find out what they can do about it. Are there any ordinances against boatbuilding in your yard in the area where you live? Neighbors might be fascinated when they see your boat hull arrive, but they could change their minds when the noise continues month after month.

Another possibility is to borrow or rent a building site. There are many possibilities here. Make certain, however, that the security is adequate and that you have a source of electricity, water, and whatever else you need.

Boatyards are another possibility. Especially attractive are do-it-yourself boatyards, which are now found in many parts of the country. These charge a couple of dollars or more per foot of boat length per month. Electricity and water are usually supplied, and sometimes some tools and heavy equipment are on hand for rent also.

It's most convenient to build under cover, especially if you live in a rainy area. Many kit boats can be finished out in the open provided you purchase the deck and cabin structure along with the hull. If you start from just a bare hull, you will need at least some sort of shelter over the boat.

Still another possibility is to purchase a boat at a stage of completion where it can be launched and then finished at dockside. Some people have even lived aboard their boats (something like sleeping on the floor in a bare interior at first) while they completed them. This is also a possibility with the boat on land.

If you do decide to work at dockside with the boat in the water, make certain that this is permitted. Many marinas have rules against doing major boat constructions at the docks. Also, consider the increased difficulties of doing a good job. It is much more difficult to work on a boat with the boat in the water than with it cradled on land.

If at possible, have a convenient workshop close to the boat. You really need one for a major project like this if you are to efficiently do the best possible job. While a workshop away from the boat can be better than nothing, much time can be lost moving back and forth between the boat and the workshop. You shape a board, then take it to the boat. It doesn't quite fit. You need to take off a little more wood on one edge but the special tool you need to do this is back at the workshop. Besides, it's a shop tool that isn't easily moved. So back to the workshop to do this job. And so on.

If at all possible, have a convenient, large storage space close to the boat. You can probably store things aboard the boat, but they will be in your way. You will spend considerable time just moving things about so that you can get to the various work areas. You can also store things somewhere away from the boat, but again you will have the problem of moving things from one place to another.

Make these decisions before you place your order. You should have a place for working on the boat, a workshop area, and storage arrangements ready before your bare hull or kit arrives.

DELIVERY

Getting the bare hull or kit boat from the factory to the building site is another important consideration. There are many possibilities here. If the boat is trailerable, you can purchase a trailer with the hull, pick up the boat at the factory, and tow it behind your own vehicle to the building site. The trailer can then be used as a cradle or stand for the boat while you finish it out.

Some companies specialize in transporting boats. Delivery is made on a low-bed truck or trailer. These companies will help you make the arrangements for having your boat shipped. Sometimes the manufacturer of the boat has delivery equipment. This simplifies arrangements and is often less expensive than a separate delivery firm.

Hulls are shipped on a cradle, which is also used as a building cradle after the boat is delivered to the building site. After the boat is completed, the same cradle can be used when the boat is transported to the launching site. You might have to buy the cradle outright from the manufacturer. Other companies let you pay the cost of the cradle, but refund all or part of this money when you return the cradle to the factory. Make certain that you have any arrangement like this in writing, especially in regards to getting the cradle back to the factory.

Shipping is based not only on the size and weight of the load, but also on the distance. The closer you live to the factory, the less the shipping will be. I'm not suggesting that you buy an unsuitable boat just to get cheaper shipping, but if there are two boats that equally suit your needs, you might want to select the one that is manufactured closest to where you live so you can get lower shipping costs.

Another possibility is to sell out house and home and move to the area where the boat is made. Finish out the boat there, either in an area provided by the manufacturer (some manufacturers make provisions for this) or at a rental site near the manufacturer. You can live aboard the boat while you do so or someplace else. When the boat is finished, launch it and set out on your world cruise.

This might sound remote and hardly worth mentioning, but many bare hull and kit boatbuilders do follow this route. It has the important advantage of allowing you to be close to the factory for advice, components, etc. Also, if the dream is world cruising or building a live-aboard boat home, you have already sold out the old life and can concentrate on the new one.

Still another possibility when you purchase a power-away or sail-away version of a finish-it-yourself boat is to have the boat launched near the factory and power or sail it back to where you live. There must be suitable waterways and conditions for this to be practical, but in some cases it has been done.

OTHER CONSIDERATIONS BEFORE YOU ORDER

Before placing an order, go over everything again to be sure you are purchasing the right boat and that you are not getting in over you head financially. Getting rid of an unsuitable boat can be expensive, although I don't know of any people who have lost very much money here. Some even turned a profit, doing little or no work on the boat and then selling out for more than they had paid.

Before you order the actual hull or kit, order an instruction manual for your tentative choice. You will probably have to pay a rather hefty amount of money for this, at least as a deposit for its return, which is the reason for waiting so long before taking this step. The instruction manual will help you make your final decision, however. If you do order the hull or kit, the price of the instruction manual is then often deducted from the purchase.

Study the manual carefully. If it is a good one, it should clearly show how to perform every step of the assembly.

If at all possible, visit the factory. You will not only get to see the manufacturing process, but also meet some of the people responsible for the production of the boats.

PLACING AN ORDER

When you order a bare hull, a partially completed boat, or a power-away or sail-away version, with or without additional components or kits to complete the boat, you have to pay a certain percentage of the purchase price. The balance is due before delivery is made. Sometimes the arrangement is one-third on order, one-third when the hull is completed, and one-third when the boat is ready for delivery.

The orders are taken by the company before they mold your fiberglass hull or your hull and other fiberglass components. How long it takes before delivery varies—sometimes only a few weeks, sometimes six months or longer. Be sure you get a firm commitment in writing as to when the delivery date will be and what happens if the boat is not ready by that time. Some of the greatest friction between manufacturers and buyers can be about an order that is not ready by a promised delivery date. A few companies already have their hulls and kits ready for shipping. Delivery can be right after the order is received. If you plan to pick up your hull or kit at the factory, you can then just go there, make the payment, and leave with your hull or kit.

GETTING READY

After your order has been placed, you can use the time while you wait for delivery to get everything ready and for planning. You can use some of this time to carefully study the assembly manual. You can also gather up the tools, materials, equipment, and supplies that you will need.

The tools needed vary, depending on the type and size of the boat, its stage of completion, whether or not you use a manufacturer's kit for completing the boat, and how difficult the boat is to assemble.

I don't know of any fiberglass boat kit that can be assembled with just a screwdriver and a couple of wrenches. It just doesn't work that way. Some manufacturers do not even apply the term "kit" to what they are offering, but say that their boats are available as bare hulls and in various stages of completion. Only a few manufacturers offer anything that even approaches a complete kit in the sense that you simply assemble parts that are prefitted.

All but a few of the small open boats require at least some fiberglassing. Most require considerable fiberglassing. While this is usually in the form of secondary bonding rather than primary molding work, it is still fiberglassing that requires fiberglassing skills and tools. In addition, you will often have to cut, drill holes in, file, and otherwise work with cured fiberglass. Interior components, if supplied by the manufacturer, are often preshaped, but you will usually have to do additional shaping, drill holes for fasteners, and other work besides simply fastening parts together with mechanical fasteners. From the assembly manual, you should have a good idea of what work needs to be done and what tools are needed.

At least some power tools are, if not absolutely essential, at least highly desirable. You can probably use a portable electric drill, a saber saw, and a heavy-duty disk sander. The more work you intend to do on your own, the more tools you need. For extensive work, power shop tools make sense.

TYPICAL CONSTRUCTIONS

If you start from just a bare hull and supply all of the materials for finishing the boat, you are in for major boatbuilding work. You will have to cut and shape bulkheads and cabin soles, add shelf clamps to the hull for attaching the deck, and construct deck and cabintop beams. Once the framing is in place, you must install plywood planking and often sheathe the plywood with fiberglass. Obviously, this is more like boatbuilding than assembling a kit.

Purchasing all of the factory moldings for the boat will greatly reduce the construction work required for finishing the boat. It will further reduce the remaining work if you have some of the most crucial and difficult work done for you at the factory. Typical jobs of this type include installing ballast, bonding in major bulkheads, and joining decks to hulls. Installing engines is another job that you might not want to tackle. Usually this can be done for you at the factory, for a price. Of course you must stop somewhere, otherwise you will have a completed boat with nothing left to finish out and probably nothing saved over the cost of simply buying a completed boat in the first place. The more work you do, the more you save. Having some of the work done for you, however, can greatly speed the construction and help to assure the successful completion of the project.

Some of the power-away and sail-away versions of these boats are complete except for bare interiors. Some even have roughed-in interiors. There can still be some savings over factory completed boats here, but perhaps even more important is the possibility of installing a custom interior.

Component kits offered by many manufacturers can be very helpful, or at least make the project more like assembling a kit. For example, a typical interior kit contains all of the required wood components precut to the required shapes, the required glues and fasteners, etc. The rigging kit consists of the spars and all the standing rigging of the correct lengths with the fittings attached.

It's easy to see that this type of boatbuilding can range from quite easy to very difficult, depending on the particular project and how you tackle it. Another important variable is the type of boat that you want. This can range from very plain and simple to custom deluxe. The cost differences between these two extremes can be considerable.

One-Off Fiberglass Boat Construction

A number of methods are used to construct fiberglass boats that do not require the expensive female or cavity molds described in Chapter 4. These methods are often called *one-off* fiberglass construction because they are practical for building a single boat of a new design. A manufacturer can afford to use an expensive female or cavity mold because many boats of the same design can be molded in the same mold. For one-off fiberglass boat construction, a less expensive molding method is required.

One-off boat construction uses a male mold or form. This type of mold is less expensive to construct because a precise molding surface is not required. The finished side of the boat molding is the side away from the mold, the reverse of the female molding method generally used for manufactured boats. There is a price to be paid, however. In exchange for being able to use an inexpensive mold, you end up with an unfinished surface on the desired finished side of the molding. To fair and smooth this surface requires many hours of tedious work if the results are to equal the appearance of a factory-molded laminate with a gel coat surface.

A number of custom boatbuilding firms that specialize in one-off boats use this method. A customer typically goes to a designer and has plans drawn up. The plans are then taken to a custom one-off boatbuilder who constructs the boat. The time from start to finish for building a typical manufactured boat is usually a few weeks in a volume plant. It is also just one of many that came off the assembly line. A single one-off boat might take from six months to a year with a large number of workers on the job to produce one boat.

Custom one-off boatbuilding is obviously expensive. The advantage is that you can have a special design, in some cases the only boat that will be constructed to that particular design. But you have to pay dearly for this advantage. This type of boat construction means big money, the type associated with sailboat racing.

This is perhaps all that needs to be said about one-off boatbuilding—if it weren't for the fact that it is also a popular method for amateur boatbuilding.

After having spent many years observing the amateur boatbuilding scene, I wonder if this type of boat construction isn't overrated. Out of perhaps a hundred one-off fiberglass boats that I've seen started by amateur builders, less than a dozen were finished. Most of these were disasters. Two were masterpieces. On closer examination, however, the builders of these two boats could hardly be considered "amateurs." True, at the time they built their boats they were not making their livings by building boats. But both had years of "amateur" experience building boats behind them. Most custom boatbuilding firms would have bid high to get craftsmen like these. Few professionals could match their skills.

My first word of advice is don't attempt to build a fiberglass boat from scratch unless you have had years of experience with fiberglass and fiberglassing. At least make a careful evaluation of your reasons for wanting to build from scratch. Why not buy a new or used boat that is already completed? If doing it yourself is all that's important to you, why not finish out a bare fiberglass hull or fiberglass kit boat as detailed in Chapter 13?

One answer I sometimes get to this question is that "I want to do all the work." This certainly has merit, though even so-called building from "scratch" uses many preformed and manufactured materials and products, such as resins, fiberglass reinforcing materials, etc. Is it so degrading to start with a manufactured hull?

Another answer is that "I don't have enough money to buy a manufactured hull." In that case, you probably don't have enough money to build one from scratch either. At best, building from scratch can be an awful lot of work for very little savings in money. Sometimes there isn't any savings at all; sometimes it costs more than a manufactured hull of the same type and size. All this can be especially depressing when you end up with a lousy hull to boot. If your reason for wanting to build from scratch is to save money,

I suggest that you examine the economics of the situation carefully.

Perhaps the most disturbing reasons for building from scratch is "I want to build a boat of my own design." Amateur boat designing combined with amateur boatbuilding doesn't seem to be a very realistic combination. Anyone contemplating building from scratch for this reason should first take a realistic look at both their boat designing talent and skill and their boatbuilding abilities.

If what I have said so far hasn't discouraged you from building a fiberglass boat from "scratch," you just might be a candidate for successful completion of such a project.

PLANS

I suggest that you at least start with plans drawn up by a competent boat designer. There are several firms that specialize in plans drawn especially with one-off amateur construction in mind (see Appendix for a listing). These firms not only sell you proven plans, but also give you advice and answer any questions you might have as the construction goes along. These are considerably different from most plans, which assume that the builder knows how to construct the boat.

A PLACE TO BUILD

If you decide to "build from scratch," you need a suitable building site. First, consider your own backyard, assuming that you have one. If this is suitable, it will be much more convenient than having the boat (as soon as "scratch" can be called a boat) some distance from where you live.

Fiberglass boatbuilding from scratch is a long, messy, and sometimes noisy job. Is your yard suitable for this? Will it bother your neighbors? Are there any ordinances against it? If you are building a very small boat, you might be able to do it inside your garage. Be sure there is enough ventilation, though.

Whether you work inside or outside, this type of boatbuilding is messy. Every work area I've seen has been coated with resins, glass fibers, fiberglass sanding dust, and no telling what else. When the work is done outside, these things get scattered about everywhere. When the work is done inside a garage, chemicals and materials—especially the sticky ones—get tracked everywhere, in cluding inside the house.

The main point is to make certain that you are not fiberglassed out of house and home. The advantage of being close to the work area can be quickly lost by living so close to fiberglassing, and the effects thereof.

Another possibility is to borrow or rent a building site. Make certain, however, that security is adequate and that you have electricity and water available. Also, check that there are no zoning codes against the type of work you are intending.

Boatyards are often a better possibility. These are accustomed to fiberglassing work, so you're less likely to get friction here. Do-it-yourself boatyards can be ideal. Be sure, however, that you take the rental cost into consideration. This can add up to a substantial amount of money by the time the boat is completed.

It is almost essential that you build under a cover of some type. Fiberglassing should not be done in direct sunlight. Dry conditions are important. At the same time, you need good ventilation. An open-sided structure with a roof that doesn't leak works well. Many builders rig up something from materials purchased secondhand. It is handy to also have a workshop and storage building at the work site.

TOOLS AND EQUIPMENT

You need at least a basic set of fiberglassing and woodworking tools. You should also have the basic portable power tools, including a drill, disk sander, saber saw, and circular saw. Additional power shop tools make sense. Boatbuilding from scratch can be a long project. You will need all the help in the way of tools that you can get.

TYPICAL CONSTRUCTION METHODS

While some form of male mold is used, there are many variations to this. You will, hopefully, follow building plans for constructing the boat. Construct the hull first. Make a form for laying up the fiberglass hull laminate from wood and/or other materials (Fig. 14-1). In most cases, the form does not become part of the finished hull molding. Sometimes the basic form is little more than a framework for a wire mesh, closed-cell PVC foam, or glass planking that has fiberglass rods bound together in the form of sheets with a dry fiberglass reinforcing material (Fig. 14-2). All of these materials can be shaped to compound curves. They are attached to the basic framework in some manner. Their purpose is to give the basic form for laying up the fiberglass laminate.

Lay up the outside laminate first, with the hull constructed upside down. Follow a laminating schedule. A number of layers of

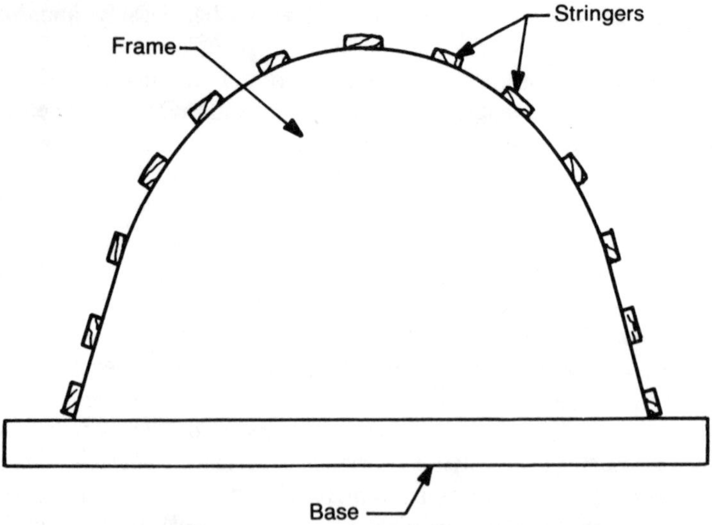

Fig. 14-1. Frames and stringers are used for shaping a male mold.

reinforcing material are required, which should be detailed in the building plans. Follow the plans to the letter. It is extremely important to keep the laminate as smooth and fair as possible. Even then, there will be a lot of fairing and sanding left to do later. Careless fiberglassing only adds to this.

After the laminate has been completed, sand and fair it while the hull is still upside down. The basic technique is to remove high

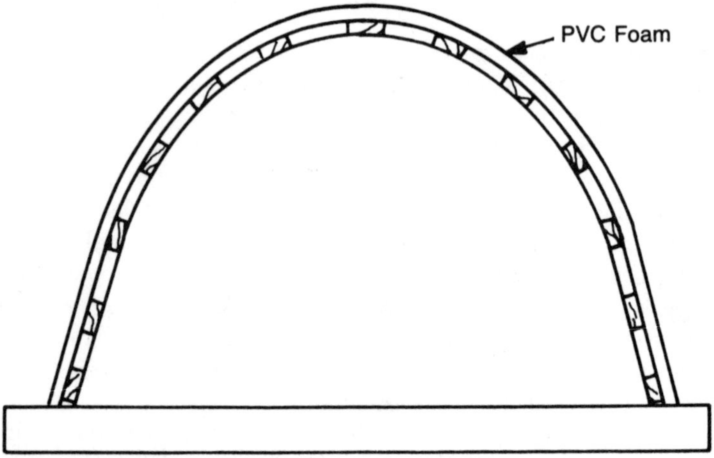

Fig. 14-2. Closed-cell PVC foam is shaped over a male mold.

spots and to fill in low areas. Remove the high spots by sanding. Fill in low areas with a fiberglass putty or glazing compound. This should be done in such a way as not to weaken the laminate. If putty and filler compounds and applied too thick, cracking is likely.

After the hull is sanded and faired, turn it upright and set it on a cradle (Fig. 14-3). Remove the framework for the building form. If wire mesh, closed cell PVC foam, or glass planking was used, these materials usually become part of the hull. Apply a second fiberglass laminate inside the hull over these.

When this is completed, install plywood bulkheads and cabin soles next. Bond these to the hull with secondary fiberglass bonding straps.

The remainder of the construction can take a variety of directions. For example, the deck and cabin structures can be constructed from wood with plywood planking, which can in turn be sheathed with fiberglass. Or the deck and cabin structure can be constructed from fiberglass in the same manner as detailed for the hull.

At some point, the outside of the hull must be gel coated or painted (see Chapter 12). The remainder of the construction is similar to finishing out a manufactured fiberglass hull or kit boat.

All this might sound like it's fast and easy work, but this is far from the truth. A large fiberglass hull alone can take one person working in his spare time months and even years to complete.

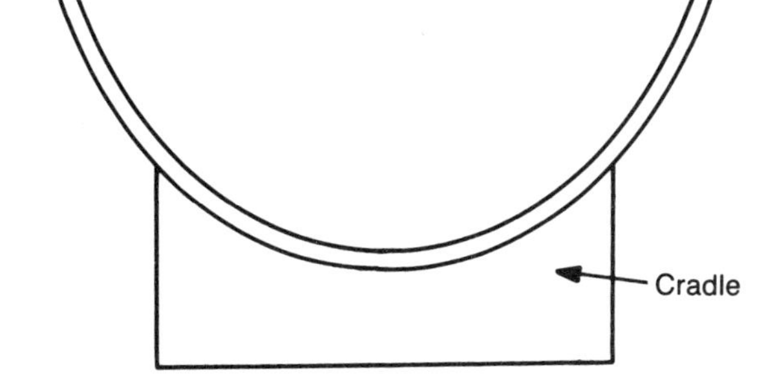

Fig. 14-3. The hull is removed from the mold and turned upright for laminating the inside skin in place.

And the completed hull is only the first step toward a completed boat.

Perhaps the biggest drawback to such a long fiberglassing job is the potential risks to your health. While the risks can certainly be reduced by carefully following safety rules and taking health precautions, you still face a lot of exposure.

In spite of the odds against it, successful one-off fiberglass boats have been constructed by amateur builders.

Appendix: Suppliers

Mail-Order Fiberglassing Materials and Supplies

CLARKCRAFT, 16 Aqualane, Tonawanda, NY 14150.

Polyester and epoxy resins; fiberglass cloth, mat, and woven roving; plastic foams; etc.

DEFENDER INDUSTRIES, INC., 255 Main St., New Rochelle, NY 10801.

Offers complete line of fiberglassing materials and supplies at discount prices. Also has large selection of marine equipment, hardware, and supplies. Their 168 page catalog is $1.

GLEN-L-MARINE, 9152 Rosecrans, Bellflower, CA 90706.

Complete line of fiberglassing materials and supplies.

Retail Fiberglassing Material and Supply Stores

TAP PLASTICS, INC.

Offers a complete line of fiberglassing materials and supplies at the following retail stores: 1401 N. Clovis Ave., #101, Fresno, CA 93727; 1212 The Alameda, San Jose, CA 95126; 4227 Pacific Ave., Stockton, CA 95207; 3011 Alvarado St., San Leandro, CA 94577; 2041 East St., Concord, CA 94520; 4538 Auburn Blvd., Sacramento, CA 95841; 606 South B St., San Mateo, CA 94401; 12404 N.E. Halsey, Portland, OR 97230; and 2945 S.W. Temple, Salt Lake City, UT 84115.

Other Fiberglassing Material and Supply Sources

ALADDIN PRODUCTS, INC., RFD2, Wiscasset, Maine 04578.

STR-R-STCH MESH® and FER-A-LITE® .

AMERICAN KLEGECELL CORPORATION, 204 North Dooley St., Grapevine, Texas 76051.

Klege-Cell® polyvinyl chloride rigid foam core material in four different densities ranging from 2.0 to 15.0 lb./cu. ft.

BALTEK CORPORATION, 10 Fairway Center, Northvale, NJ 07647.

Balsa core material.

DEVCON CORPORATION, Endicott St., Danvers, MA 01923.

Underwater epoxy.

FIBRE GLASS EVERCOAT COMPANY, 6600 Cornell Rd., Cincinnati, OH 45242.

Resin, fiberglass reinforcing materials, filler materials, and repair kits.

LAN-O-SHEEN, 1 W. Water St., St. Paul, MN 55107.

Resin and fiberglass reinforcing materials.

LONZA, INC., 22-10 Rt. 208, Fairlawn, NJ 07410.

Airex® polyvinyl chloride rigid foam core material.

PETTIT PAINT COMPANY, INC., 36 Pine St., Rockaway, NJ 07866.

Complete line of marine paint (including two-part polyurethane) and resins, fiberglass reinforcing materials, and fiberglass repair kits.

PLASTIC SALES AND MANUFACTURING COMPANY, INC., 3030 McGee Trafficway, Kansas City, MO 64108.

Polyester and epoxy resins and fiberglass reinforcing materials.

RAM CHEMICALS, 210 E. Alondra Rd., Gardena, CA 90248.

Gel coat resins and release agents.

RULE INDUSTRIES, INC., Cape Ann Industrial Park, Gloucester, MA 01930.

Resins, fiberglass reinforcing materials, and fiberglass repair kits.

TRAVACO LABORATORIES, INC., 345 Eastern Ave., Chelsea, MA 02150.

Marine-Tex® epoxy repair compound.

Fiberglass Kit Boats

AHG BOAT COMPANY, 31 Water St., Mystic, CT 06355.

23-foot powerboat.

ACAPULCO YACHTS, P.O. Box 7824, San Diego, CA 92107.

40-foot sailboat.

ALAJUELA YACHT CORP., 5181 Argosy Dr., Huntington Beach, CA 92649.

36-foot cruising sailboat.

BELLEVILLE CORP., 4001 Georgine St., Santa Ana, CA 92703.

26-foot sailboat.

BLUE WATER BOATS, P.O. Box 625, Woodinville, WA 98072.

38-foot cruising sailboat.

CRAFT MASTER BOATS, 6440 Flying Cloud Dr., Eden Prairie, MN 55344.

15-foot bass boat.

DECK HANDS MARINE, Hwy. 98E, Ft. Walton Beach, FL 32548.

48-foot houseboat.

DREADNOUGHT BOATWORKS, P.O. Box 221, Carpinteria, CA 93013.

32-foot world cruising type sailboat.

GLANDER BOATS, INC., P.O. Box 1107, Tavernier, FL 33070.

23-foot and 33-foot sailboats.

HERITAGE MARINE, INC., 2919 Gardena, Long Beach, CA 90806.

27-foot cruising sailboat.

HOLDIAY MANSION, 2328 Hein Rd., Salina, KS 67401.

Houseboats.

HOUSEBOATING CORP. OF AMERICA, 365 Maple St., P.O. Box 950, Gallatin, TN 37066.

Houseboats.

IRWIN YACHT & MARINE CORP., 13055-49th St. N., Clearwater, FL 33520.

Sailboats.

KELLS CORPORATION, 1 Shove St., Tiverton, RI 02878.

22-, 23-, and 28-foot sailboats.

LAKEVIEW BOAT COMPANY, P.O. Box 5595, Riverside, CA 92507.

Canoes and kayaks.

LUGER INDUSTRIES, INC., 3800 West Hwy. 13, Burnsville, MN 55337.

Sailboats ranging from 16 to 30 feet in length and powerboats ranging from 21 to 30 feet in length.

PACIFIC SEACRAFT, 3301 South Susan St., Santa Ana, CA 92704.

20-, 25-, and 31-foot cruising sailboats.

ROBERTS & MATTHEWS YACHT CORP., INC., P.O. Box 10324, Bradenton, FL 33507.

25-, 26-, and 40-foot sailboats.

TRAILCRAFT, INC., P.O. Box 606, Concordia, KA 66901.

Kayaks, canoes, and crossbreeds.

YACHT CONSTRUCTORS, INC., 7030 N.E. 42nd Ave., Portland, OR 97218.

Sailboats ranging from 27 to 43 feet in length.

YACHTCRAFT CORP., 551 W. Crowther Ave., Placentia, CA 92670.

Sailboats ranging from 30 to 44 feet in length.

Plans for One-Off Fiberglass Boatbuilding

CLARKCRAFT, 16 Aqualane, Tonawanda, NY 14150.

GLEN-L-MARINE, 9152 Rosecrans, Bellflower, CA 90706.

BRUCE ROBERTS INTERNATIONAL, INC., P.O. Box 1548, Newport Beach, CA 92663.

Glossary

abaft—Further aft or toward rear of boat than something else.

abeam—Off to one side of the boat perpendicular to a fore-and-aft centerline.

accelerator—A highly active oxidizing material, such as cobalt, that is added to polyester resin to produce internal heat so the resin will cure at room temperature.

acetone—A cleaning solvent for removing uncured resin from brushes and tools.

aft—Toward the rear of the boat.

air-inhibited resin—A resin in which the presence of air inhibits the cure of the surface. The surface becomes hard but is tacky.

ambient temperature—Surrounding temperature or "room" temperature.

amidship—Midway between the bow and stern of a boat; toward the middle of the boat.

astern—Behind a boat.

athwartships—Across a boat.

barrier cream—A skin cream used to protect skin from possible contact with resins.

binder—An adhesive that is soluble in resin that is used to loosely bind glass fibers together to form fiberglass mat.

bow—The forward part of a boat hull.

buttocks—Lines that represent vertical cuts in a longitudinal plane.

catalyst—Component added to polyester resin to initiate the curing, usually by oxidizing an accelerator.
cavity—A female mold or the laminating space between matched molds.
chopped strands—Glass fiber strands chopped up into short lengths.
close weave—Reinforcing fabric with the woven strands almost touching.
color pigments—Pigments that are added to resin to change its color.
core—Material used between two fiberglass skins to space them apart and give greater stiffness.
counter—Part of boat extending from the waterline to the bottom of the transom.
crazing—Tiny cracks in the surface of a fiberglass molding.
cure—The process of resin changing from a liquid to a solid state.
curing time—The time from when the catalyst or hardener is added to a resin until the resin reaches a cured state.

deck—A platform extending from one side of a boat to the other, often at or near the level of the rail.
draft—The distance from the waterline to the bottom of keel on a boat.

epoxy resin—A resin that is usually stronger and has better physical properties than polyester resin, but is more difficult to use and considerably more expensive.
exothermic heat—Developed within the resin.

feathered edge—Tapered edge of fiberglass laminate.
fiberglass—Fine fibers of glass. Reinforcing materials made from glass fibers. Laminates of glass fiber reinforcing material and cured resin.
filler—A substance added to resin to form a putty. A resin filler or putty.
finish—Chemicals applied to glass fibers to allow resin to flow around and adhere to the fibers.
foam—A rigid plastic material that is very light in weight.
foam core—Foam used as a core material between two skins of fiberglass.
foredeck—The forward part of the deck on a boat.
forefoot—The part of a boat hull between the bow and the keel.

forward—Toward the front of a boat hull.

gel—A semisolid or jellylike state of resin when partially cured.

gel coat—Surface coat of resin that does not contain glass fibers and is usually colored.

glass fiber—A fine fiber of glass.

hardener—Component added to epoxy resin to initiate the curing.

keel—Applied to powerboats, it's the main structural member running longitudinally from the stem to the stern along the bottom. Applied to sailboats, it's a vertical downward extension on the bottom of the hull.

lamination—Layers of glass reinforcing materials and resin that form a fiberglass panel.

lay-up—Process of applying resin to reinforcing materials placed in a mold or on a form.

length of waterline (LWL)—Length of a boat hull at the waterline.

Length overall (LOA)—A boat's greatest length, not counting rudders, bowsprits, or other protuberances.

mold—The form used for fiberglass lay-up to give desired shape and surface.

mold release—Substance used to prevent the molding from sticking in the mold.

nonair-inhibited resin—A resin that gives a surface cure in the presence of air by excluding air from the surface of the resin.

open weave—Reinforcing fabric with considerable space between woven strands.

plain weave—Common over and under weave used for making fabrics.

plastic—Synthetic materials. Sometimes used to mean *fiberglass.*

polyester resin—Resin commonly combined with reinforcing materials to form fiberglass boat moldings. Because of its lower cost, it is often used instead of the more expensive epoxy resin.

port—The left side of the boat when looking forward.

pot life—The length of time that a resin remains useable in a con-

tainer after a catalyst or hardening agent has been added.
putty—A resin filler material.

release agent—A coating applied to mold to prevent the molding from sticking to the mold.
resin—A liquid plastic substance that cures to a solid state when a catalyst or hardener is added. It is combined with reinforcing material to form fiberglass.
roving—Continuous strands of glass fibers used to form untwisted yarn that can be woven into woven roving reinforcing material.
rudder—A flat vertical member that extends from the hull and is used for steering the boat.

sandwich construction—A core material with fiberglass skins.
shelf life—The length of time uncatalyzed resin remains useable when stored in sealed container. Also applies to paints, glues, and other substances.
starboard—The right side of the boat when looking forward.
stations—Athwartship vertical slices or vertical cuts in a transverse plane.
stem—The forwardmost part of the bow of a boat.
stern—The after or rear part of a boat.
styrene—Liquid plastic used to thin polyester resin.
surfacing agent—Oil or wax material that goes to the surface of polyester resin during curing to inhibit air.

tack-free—A surface that is not sticky.
tacky—Sticky.
tensile strength—Resistance of a material to a force tending to pull it apart.
thixotropic—A liquid that has a high viscosity so that it will not flow easily.
thixotropic paste or powder—Added to resin to increase viscosity.
topsides—The sides of a boat from the waterline to the rail.
transom—Aftermost part of the stern of a boat.

undercut—Reverse draft in a mold.
unidirectional—Strength is greater in one direction than another.

vacuum bag molding—A method of molding that uses a flexible bag and a vacuum.

viscosity—Degree to which a liquid resists flow.

warp—Fibers woven across a fabric.
waterline—The level of water on a floating hull.
waterlines—Horizontal cuts in a longitudinal plane.
woven roving—Reinforcing fabric woven from strands of rovings, which are untwisted groups of glass fibers.

yarn—Twisted strands of glass fibers that are woven to form cloth.

Index